Why Do You Need This New Edition?

If you're wondering why you need this new edition of *One World, Many Cultures*, here are five good reasons!

1. **Thirty-three new readings**—more than a third of the book—represent an expanded range of countries (including Vietnam, Iran, Iraq and Somalia), ethnicities (including Kurdish), and voices and introduce you to good writing from multiple contexts and perspectives.

2. **An excerpt from *Persepolis*,** Marjane Satrapi's influential graphic novel, encourages you to develop critical skills for reading images as well as texts and reflects the expanding need for visual literacy in our image-laden world.

3. **A new chapter, The Role of Food in Different Cultures,** offers compelling new selections about what and how we eat, and the cultural significance attached to this basic act.

4. **New annotated lists of recommended films** support each thematic chapter and expand your resources for exploring different kinds of "texts" about compelling themes.

5. **Two new "Debates"—sets of pro-con readings**—model persuasive writing from both sides of important contemporary topics including global warming (Chapter 6) and genetically engineered food (Chapter 7).

PEARSON
Longman

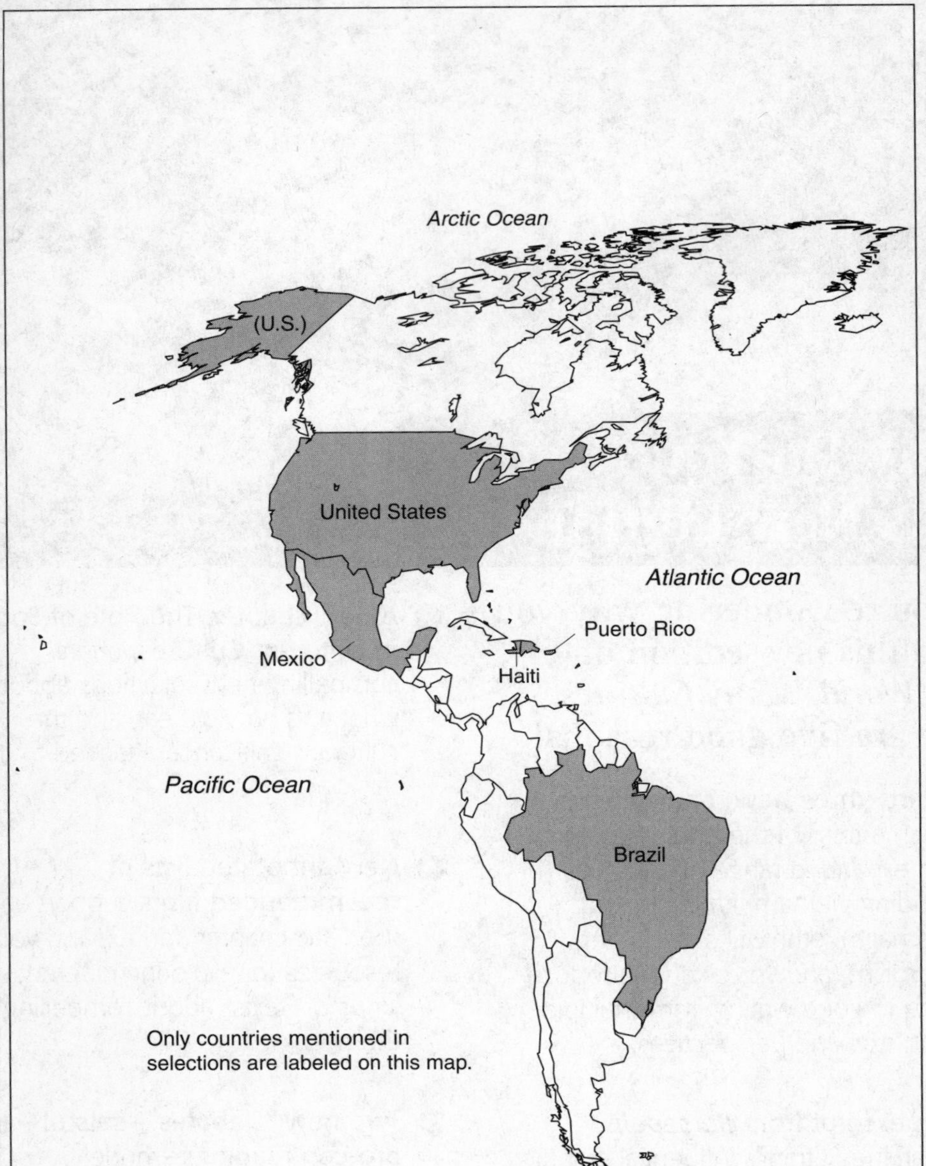

Arctic Ocean
(U.S.)
United States
Atlantic Ocean
Puerto Rico
Mexico
Haiti
Pacific Ocean
Brazil
Only countries mentioned in
selections are labeled on this map.

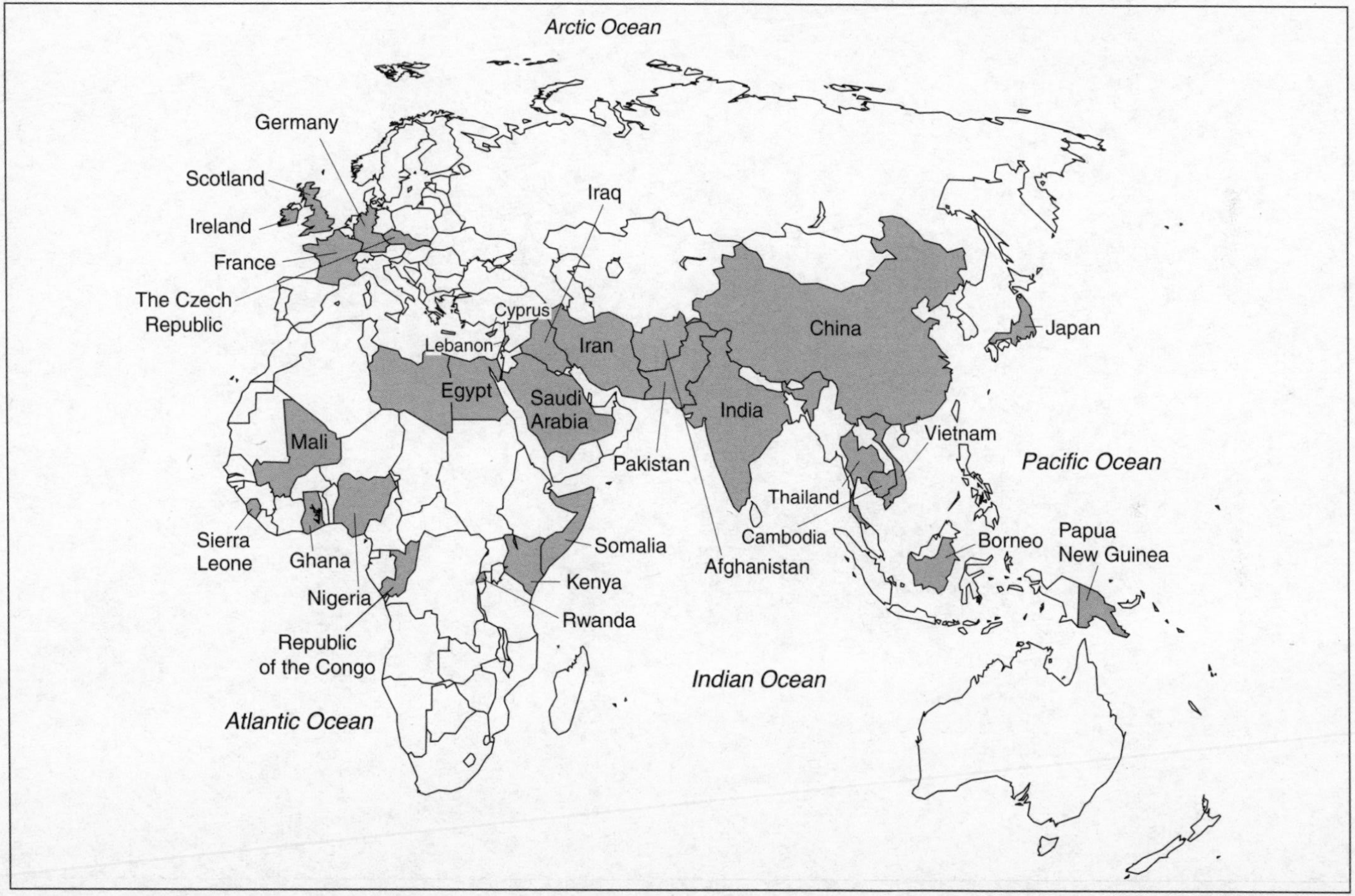
Arctic Ocean
Germany
Scotland
Ireland
France
The Czech Republic
Iraq
Cyprus
Lebanon
Iran
China
Japan
Egypt
Saudi Arabia
India
Mali
Vietnam
Pakistan
Pacific Ocean
Thailand
Cambodia
Sierra Leone
Ghana
Nigeria
Somalia
Afghanistan
Borneo
Papua New Guinea
Kenya
Rwanda
Republic of the Congo
Indian Ocean
Atlantic Ocean

One World, Many Cultures

Eighth Edition

STUART HIRSCHBERG
Rutgers: The State University of New Jersey, Newark

TERRY HIRSCHBERG

PEARSON

Boston • Columbus • Indianapolis • New York • San Francisco • Upper Saddle River
Amsterdam • Cape Town • Dubai • London • Madrid • Milan • Munich • Paris
Montreal • Toronto • Delhi • Mexico City • Sao Paulo • Sydney • Hong Kong
Seou • Singapore • Taipei • Tokyo

Senior Sponsoring Editor: Virginia L. Blanford
Senior Marketing Manager: Sandra McGuire
Production Manager: Stacey Kulig
Project Coordination, Text Design, and Electronic
Page Makeup: TexTech International
Cover Designer: John Callahan
Cover Images (from top to bottom): Nolte Lourens/Shutterstock, Lucian Coman/Shutterstock, © Free Agents Limited/CORBIS, Michelle D. Milliman/Shutterstock
Photo Researcher: Chrissy McIntyre
Senior Manufacturing Buyer: Roy Pickering
Printer and Binder: R.R. Donnelley and Sons
Cover Printer: R.R. Donnelley and Sons

For permission to use copyrighted material, grateful acknowledgment is made to the copyright holders on pp. 436-438, which are hereby made part of this copyright page.

Library of Congress Cataloging-in-Publication Data
One world, many cultures / [compiled by] Stuart Hirschberg, Terry Hirschberg. —8th ed.
p. cm.
Includes bibliographical references and index.
ISBN-13: 978-0-205-80110-7 (alk. paper)
ISBN-10: 0-205-80110-2 (alk. paper)
1. College readers. 2. Cultural pluralism—Problems, exercises, etc. 3. Ethnic groups—Problems, exercises, etc. 4. English language—Rhetoric. 5. Readers—Social sciences. I. Hirschberg, Stuart. II. Hirschberg, Terry.
PE1417.o57 2010
808'.0427—dc22

2010037234

3 4 5 6 7 8 9 10—DOH—15 14 13 12

Longman
is an imprint of

PEARSON

www.pearsonhighered.com

ISBN-13: 978-0-205-80110-7
ISBN-10: 0-205-80110-2

Contents

Rhetorical Contents

DEFINITION

CLASSIFICATION AND DIVISION

COMPARISON AND CONTRAST

CAUSE AND EFFECT

ARGUMENTATION AND PERSUASION

Arguments That Define and Draw Distinctions

Arguments That Establish Causes and Draw Consequences

Preface

This eighth edition of *One World, Many Cultures* is a global, contemporary reader whose international and multicultural selections offer a new direction for freshman composition courses.

In eight thematic chapters consisting of fifty-eight readings by internationally recognized writers from twenty-three countries, we explore cultural differences and displacement in relation to race, class, gender, region, and nation. *One World, Many Cultures* also reflects the emphasis on cultural studies and argumentation that has become an integral part of many college programs.

The selections challenge readers to see similarities between their own experiences and the experiences of others in radically different cultural circumstances. Compelling and provocative writings by authors from the Caribbean, Africa, Asia, Europe, and Latin America reflect the cultural and ethnic heritage of many students. The fifty-six nonfiction selections include essays and autobiographies. These and the two short stories encourage readers to perceive the relationship between a wide range of experiences in different cultures and corresponding experiences of writers within the United States. The eighth edition of *One World, Many Cultures* continues to provide a rich sampling of accounts by writers who are native to the cultures that they describe, allowing the reader to hear authentic voices.

New to This Edition

We have included thirty-three readings that are new to this edition, representing a wide range of countries, ethnicities, and voices. In addition, you will find:

- A new chapter (Chapter 7, "The Role of Food in Different Cultures"), which looks at an important cultural element in today's world.
- Lists of recommended films for each thematic chapter that enhance the reading experience.
- Sets of pro–con readings in two chapters: Chapter 6, "Experiencing a Different Culture," and Chapter 7, "The Role of Food in Different Cultures."
- In Chapter 6, an essay by Cameron M. Smith and an editorial from the Melbourne *Herald Sun* offer contrasting arguments about placing the polar bear on the endangered species list.
- In Chapter 7, paired essays by Mark I. Schwartz and Jeffrey M. Smith, respectively, present arguments about genetically modified food.

Chapter Descriptions

The eight chapters move from the most personal sphere of family life through various turning points, questions of sexual identity, the relationship of work in various environments, and conflicts of class and race to the more encompassing dimensions of citizenship, immigration, and social customs.

Chapter 1, "The Family in Different Cultures," introduces families in France, China, the United States, Iran, the Czech Republic, India, Mexico, and Vietnam. These selections illustrate that the family, however defined (as a single-parent household, a nuclear family, or the extended family of an entire community), passes on the mores and values of a particular culture to the next generation.

Chapter 2, "Turning Points," provides insights into both formal and informal rituals of passage, initiation ceremonies, and moments of discovery in the lives of a Chinese American girl, a young boy in Ireland, an adventurer in Borneo, an art historian, a Japanese American school girl, a Lebanese immigrant, and a blind traveler on a train trip in India.

Chapter 3, "How Culture Shapes Gender Roles," explores the role of culture in shaping sexual identity. Readers gain insight into how gender roles are culturally conditioned rather than biologically determined. The extent to which sex role expectations, both heterosexual and homosexual, differ from culture to culture can be seen in societies as diverse as those in Puerto Rico, Cambodia, Brazil, Iraq and Kurdistan, Kenya, Somalia, and the United States.

Chapter 4, "Working Lives," explores work as a universal human experience through which we define ourselves and others. The role of culture and the importance of the environment in shaping attitudes toward work can be seen in the different experiences of a Peace Corp volunteer working with a midwife in Mali and an FBI agent in Alabama. We can share the work experiences of a disillusioned Japanese corporation employee, a Swedish activist in the Himalayas, a chronicler of lost luggage in a small town in Alabama, the Mexican custodian of a synagogue, and the many immigrant workers who remit wages to support their families back home.

Chapter 5, "Race, Class, and Caste," takes up the crucial and often unrecognized relationships among race, identity, and social class through readings that explore positions of power and powerlessness. Selections include Immaculée Ilibagiza's tale of survival during the civil war in Rwanda. The voices heard are those of men and women of many races in several nations, including Viramma's account of her life as an "untouchable" in south India. Unusual perspectives on class issues are provided by Mary Crow Dog's account (written with Richard Erdoes) of her experiences in a government-run school for Native Americans, Jo Goodwin Parker's poignant narrative on being poor, Gordon Parks's account of a young boy living in the favelas outside Rio, and Kate Chopin's classic story of race and class in turn-of-the-century Louisiana.

Chapter 6, "Experiencing a Different Culture," explores the condition of all those who are estranged politically, linguistically, or culturally. The need of those who are caught between two cultures (whether actually or psychologically) and are at home in neither is the theme explored by Poranee Natadecha-Sponsel from Thailand, Gino Del Guercio in Haiti, David R. Counts in New Guinea, and Napoleon A. Chagnon in Brazil. Ralph Linton also explores international cultural contributions to American life. Cameron M. Smith and an editorial from the Melbourne *Herald Sun* offer contrasting arguments about placing the polar bear on the endangered species list. Finally, Fareed Zakaria discusses China's rising world supremacy.

Chapter 7, "The Role of Food in Different Cultures," looks at questions arising from the increasing use of genetically modified foods, in essays by Mark I. Schwartz and Jeffrey M. Smith. The historic role food played in the South is explored by Frederick Douglass. The cultural importance of food is portrayed in cultures as diverse as Scotland by Ethel G. Hofman, Vietnam by Andrew X. Pham, China by Amy Tan, and Afganistan by Saira Shah. Trends in meal making are identified by the founder of McDonald's, Ray Kroc, and a pragmatic approach to cooking while traveling is described by Chris Maynard and Bill Scheller.

Chapter 8, "Customs, Rituals, and Values," focuses on the role that ritual, religion, and popular culture (East and West) play in shaping social behavior. The influence of cultural values is explored through an analysis of foot-binding practices in ancient China, patterns of addiction in the United States, and the daily rituals of an unusual tribe in North America. Chapter 8 looks at the culturally variable concepts of being on time around the world (in Brazil, Japan, and other countries), at how the games of the Mbuti pygmies in the Republic of the Congo eliminate conflict, and the practice of arranged marriages in India.

Editorial Apparatus

The introduction covers the important aspects of critical reading, keeping a journal, and responding to the text, and includes a sample selection by Edward T. Hall ("Hidden Culture") for students to annotate. Chapter introductions discuss the theme of each chapter as related to the individual selections. Biographical sketches preceding each reading give background information on the writer's life and identify the cultural, historical, and personal context in which the selection was written. Prompts ("Before You Read") that precede each selection alert students to an important cultural idea expressed in the selection. Relevant background information is provided for unfamiliar ethnic groups before the selections.

The questions that follow each selection are designed to encourage readers to discover relationships between personal experiences and ideas in the text, to explore points of agreement and areas of conflict sparked by the viewpoints of the authors, and to provide ideas for further research and inquiry.

The first set of questions, "Evaluating the Text," asks readers to think critically about the content, meaning, and purpose of the selections and to evaluate the author's rhetorical strategy, voice projected in relationship to his or her audience, evidence cited, and underlying assumptions.

The questions in "Exploring Different Perspectives" focus on relationships between readings within each chapter that illuminate differences and similarities between cultures. These questions encourage readers to make connections between diverse cultures, to understand the writer's values and beliefs, to enter into the viewpoints of others, and to understand how culture shapes perception and a sense of self.

The questions in "Extending Viewpoints through Writing and Research" invite readers to extend their thinking by seeing wider relationships between themselves and others through writing of many different kinds, including personal or expressive as well as expository and persuasive writing and more formal research papers.

At the end of each chapter, "Connecting Cultures" challenges readers to make connections and comparisons among selections within the chapter and throughout the book. These questions provide opportunities to consider additional cross-cultural perspectives on a single issue or to explore a particular topic in depth.

A rhetorical table of contents, a pronunciation key to authors' names, a geographical index, an index of authors and titles, and a map of the world identifying countries mentioned in the selections are included to allow the text to accommodate a variety of teaching approaches.

Instructor's Manual

An *Instructor's Manual* provides guidelines for using the text, including teaching short works of fiction, supplemental bibliographies of books and periodicals, suggested answers to discussion questions in the text, relevant background information on countries from which the selections are drawn, a filmography, as well as optional discussion questions and classroom activities.

Acknowledgments

We are grateful to the following reviewers, whose comments helped us prepare this eighth edition: Donna Gessell, North Georgia College and State University; Eric Hyman, Fayetteville State University; Rachida Jackson, Shaw University; Helen Hadley Porter, Montana State University; Harvey Rubinstein, Hudson County Community College; and Julie Stenberg, Inver Hills Community College.

Introduction

Critical Reading for Ideas and Organization

One of the most important skills to have in your repertoire is the ability to survey unfamiliar articles, essays, or excerpts and to come away with an accurate understanding of what the author wanted to communicate and how the material is organized. On the first and in subsequent readings of any of the selections in this text, especially the longer ones, pay particular attention to the title, look for introductory and concluding paragraphs (with special emphasis on the author's statement or restatement of central ideas), identify the headings and subheadings (and determine the relationship between these and the title), and identify any unusual terms necessary to fully understand the author's concepts.

As you work your way through an essay, you might look for cues to enable you to recognize the main parts of the argument or help you perceive the overall organization of the article. Once you find the main thesis or claim, underline it. Then work your way through fairly rapidly, identifying the main ideas and the sequence in which they are presented. As you identify an important idea, ask yourself how this idea relates to the thesis statement you underlined or to the idea expressed in the title.

Finding a Thesis

Finding a thesis involves discovering the idea that serves as the focus of the essay. The thesis is often stated in the form of a single sentence that asserts the author's response to an issue that others might respond to in different ways. For example, the opening paragraph of "Body Art as Visual Language" presents Enid Schildkrout's assessment of an important aspect of body art, including tatooing, piercing, and scarification:

> Body art is not just the latest fashion. In fact, if the impulse to create art is one of the defining signs of humanity, the body may well have been the first canvas. Alongside paintings on cave walls created by early humans over 30,000 years ago, we find handprints and ochre deposits suggesting body painting.

This thesis represents the writer's view of a subject or topic from a certain perspective. Here, Schildkrout states a view of body art that will serve as a focus for her essay.

Writers often place the thesis in the first paragraph or group of paragraphs so that the readers will be able to perceive the relationship between the supporting evidence and this main idea. As you read, you might wish to underline the topic sentence or main idea of each paragraph or section (because key ideas are often developed over the course of several paragraphs). Jot it down in your own words in the margins, identify supporting statements and evidence (such as examples, statistics, and the testimony of authorities), and try to discover how the author organizes the material to support the development of important ideas. To identify supporting material, look for any ideas more specific than the main idea that is used to support it. Also look for instances where the author uses examples, descriptions, statistics, quotations from authorities, comparisons, or graphs to make the main idea clearer or prove it to be true.

Pay particular attention to important transitional words, phrases, or paragraphs to better see the relationships among major sections of the selection. Noticing how certain words or phrases act as transitions to link paragraphs or sections together will dramatically improve your reading comprehension. Also look for section summaries, where the author draws together several preceding ideas.

Writers use certain words to signal the starting point of an argument. If you detect any of the following terms, look for the main idea they introduce:

> since, because, for, as, follows from, as shown by, inasmuch as, otherwise, as indicated by, the reason is that, for the reason that, may be inferred from, may be derived from, may be deduced from, in view of the fact that

An especially important category of words is that which includes signals that the author will be stating a conclusion. Words to look for are these:

> therefore, hence, thus, so, accordingly, in consequence, it follows that, we may infer, I conclude that, in conclusion, in summary, which shows that, which means that, and which entails, consequently, proves that, as a result, which implies that, which allows us to infer, points to the conclusion that

You may find it helpful to create a running dialogue with the author in the margins, posing and then trying to answer the basic questions *who, what, where, when,* and *why,* and to note observations on how the main idea of the article is related to the title. These notes can later be used to evaluate how effectively any specific section contributes to the overall line of thought.

Responding to What You Read

When reading an essay that seems to embody a certain value system, try to examine any assumptions or beliefs the writer expects the audience to share. How is this assumption related to the author's purpose? If you do not agree with these assumptions, has the writer provided sound reasons and evidence to persuade you to change your mind?

You might describe the author's tone or voice and try to assess how much it contributed to the essay. How effectively does the writer use authorities, statistics, or examples to support the claim? Does the author identify the assumptions or values on which his or her views are based? Are they ones with which you would agree or disagree? To what extent does the author use the emotional connotations of language to try to persuade his or her reader? Do you see anything unworkable or disadvantageous about the solutions offered as an answer to the problem the essay addresses? All these and many other ways of analyzing someone else's essay can be used to create your own. Here are some specific guidelines to help you.

When evaluating an essay, consider what the author's purpose was in writing it. Was it to inform, explain, solve a problem, make a recommendation, amuse, enlighten, or achieve some combination of these goals? How is the tone or voice the author projects toward the reader related to his or her purpose in writing the essay?

You may find it helpful to write short summaries after each major section to determine whether you understand what the writer is trying to communicate. These summaries can then serve as a basis for an analysis of how successfully the author employs reasons, examples, statistics, and expert testimony to support and develop his or her main points.

For example, if the essay you are analyzing cites authorities to support a claim, assess whether the authorities bring the most timely opinions to bear on the subject or display any obvious biases, and determine whether they are experts in that particular field. Watch for experts described as "often quoted" or "highly placed reliable sources" without accompanying names, credentials, or appropriate documentation. If the experts cited offer what purports to be a reliable interpretation of facts, consider whether the writer also quotes equally trustworthy experts who hold opposing views.

If statistics are cited to support a point, judge whether they derive from verifiable and trustworthy sources. Also, evaluate whether the author has interpreted them in ways that are beneficial to his or her case, especially if someone who held an opposing view could interpret them quite differently. If real-life examples are presented to support the author's opinions, determine whether they are representative or whether they are too atypical to be used as evidence. If the author relies on hypothetical examples or analogies to dramatize ideas that otherwise would be hard to grasp, judge whether these examples are too far-fetched to back up the claims being made. If the essay depends on the stipulated definition of a term that might be defined in different ways, check whether the author provides clear reasons to indicate why one definition rather than another is preferable.

As you list observations about the various elements of the article you are analyzing, take a closer look at the underlying assumptions and see whether you can locate and distinguish between those assumptions that are explicitly stated and those that are implicit. Once the author's assumptions are identified, you can compare them with your own beliefs about the subject, determine whether these assumptions are commonly held, and make a judgment as to their validity. Would you readily agree with these assumptions? If not, has the author provided sound reasons and supporting evidence to persuade you to change your mind?

Marking as You Read

The most effective way to think about what you read is to make notes as you read. Making notes as you read forces you to go slowly and think carefully about each sentence. This process is sometimes called annotating the text, and all you need is a pen or a pencil. There are as many styles of annotating as there are readers, and you will discover your own favorite technique once you have done it a few times. Some readers prefer to underline major points or statements and jot down their reactions to them in the margin. Others prefer to summarize each paragraph or section to help them follow the author's line of thinking. Other readers circle key words or phrases necessary to understand the main ideas. Feel free to use your notes as a kind of conversation with the text. Ask questions. Express doubts. Mark unfamiliar words or phrases to look up later. If the paragraphs are not already numbered, you might wish to number them as you go to help you keep track of your responses. Try to distinguish the main ideas from supporting points and examples. Most important, go slowly and think about what you are reading. Try to discover whether the author makes a credible case for the conclusions he or she reaches. One last point: Take a close look at the idea expressed in the title before and after you read the essay to see how it relates to the main idea.

Distinguishing between Fact and Opinion

As you read, distinguish between statements of fact and statements of opinion. Statements of fact relate information that is widely accepted and objectively verifiable; facts are used as evidence to support the claim made by the thesis. By contrast, an opinion is a personal interpretation of data or a belief or feeling that however strongly presented should not be mistaken by the reader for objective evidence. For example, consider the following claim by Edward T. Hall in "Hidden Culture," an essay we include below to encourage you to try your hand at critical reading and annotation.

> Each culture and each country has its own language of space, which is just as unique as the spoken language, frequently more so. In England, for example, there are no offices for the members of Parliament. In the United States, our congressmen and senators proliferate their offices and their office buildings and simply would not tolerate a no-office situation.

The only statement that could be verified or refuted on the basis of objective data is "In England . . . there are no offices for the members of Parliament." All the other statements, *however persuasive they may seem,* are Hall's interpretations of a situation (multiple offices and office buildings for U.S. government officials) that might be interpreted quite differently by another observer. These statements should not be mistaken for statements of fact.

A reader who could not distinguish between facts and interpretations would be at a severe disadvantage in understanding Hall's essay. Part of the difficulty in separating fact from opinion stems from the difficulty of remaining objective about statements that match our own personal beliefs.

Take a few minutes to read and annotate the following essay. Feel free to "talk back" to the author. You can underline or circle key passages or key terms. You can make observations, raise questions, and express your reactions to what you read.

A SAMPLE ESSAY FOR STUDENT ANNOTATION

Edward T. Hall

Hidden Culture

1 A few years ago, I became involved in a sequence of events in Japan that completely mystified me, and only later did I learn how an overt act seen from the vantage point of one's own culture can have an entirely different meaning when looked at in the context of the foreign culture. I had been staying at a hotel in downtown Tokyo that had European as well as Japanese-type rooms. The clientele included a few Europeans but was predominantly Japanese. I had been a guest for about ten days and was returning to my room in the middle of an afternoon. Asking for my key at the desk, I took the elevator to my floor. Entering the room, I immediately sensed that something was wrong. Out of place. Different. I was in the wrong room! Someone else's things were distributed around the head of the bed and the table. Somebody else's toilet articles (those of a Japanese male) were in the bathroom. My first thoughts were, "What if I am discovered here? How do I explain my presence to a Japanese who may not even speak English?"

2 I was close to panic as I realized how incredibly territorial we in the West are. I checked my key again. Yes, it really was mine. Clearly they had moved somebody else into my room. But where was my room now? And where were my belongings? Baffled and mystified, I took the elevator to the lobby. Why hadn't they told me at the desk, instead of letting me risk embarrassment and loss of face by being caught in somebody else's room? Why had they moved me in the first place? It was a nice room and, being sensitive to spaces and how they work, I was loath to give it up. After all, I had told them I would be in the hotel for almost a month. Why this business of moving me around like someone who has been squeezed in without a reservation? Nothing made sense.

3 At the desk I was told by the clerk, as he sucked in his breath in deference (and embarrassment?) that indeed they had moved me. My particular room had been reserved in advance by somebody else. I was given the key to my new room and discovered that all my personal effects were distributed around the new room almost as though I had

done it myself. This produced a fleeting and strange feeling that maybe I wasn't myself. How could somebody else do all those hundred and one little things just the way I did?

4 Three days later, I was moved again, but this time I was prepared. There was no shock, just the simple realization that I had been moved and that it would now be doubly difficult for friends who had my old room number to reach me. *Tant pis,* I was in Japan. One thing did puzzle me. Earlier, when I had stayed at Frank Lloyd Wright's Imperial Hotel for several weeks, nothing like this had ever happened. What was different? What had changed? Eventually I got used to being moved and would even ask on my return each day whether I was still in the same room.

5 Later, at Hakone, a seaside resort where I was visiting with friends, the first thing that happened was that we were asked to disrobe. We were given *okatas,* and our clothes were taken from us by the maid. (For those who have not visited Japan, the okata is a cotton print kimono.) We later learned, when we ventured out in the streets, that it was possible to recognize other guests from our hotel because we had all been equipped with identical okatas. (Each hotel had its own characteristic, clearly recognizable pattern.) Also, I noted that it was polite to wave or nod to these strangers from the same hotel.

6 Following Hakone, we visited Kyoto, site of many famous temples and palaces, and the ancient capital of Japan.

7 There we were fortunate enough to stay in a wonderful little country inn on the side of a hill overlooking the town. Kyoto is much more traditional and less industrialized than Tokyo. After we had been there about a week and had thoroughly settled into our new Japanese surroundings, we returned one night to be met at the door by an apologetic manager who was stammering something. I knew immediately that we had been moved, so I said, "You had to move us. Please don't let this bother you, because we understand. Just show us to our new rooms and it will be all right." Our interpreter explained as we started to go through the door that we weren't in that hotel any longer but had been moved to *another* hotel. What a blow! Again, without warning. We wondered what the new hotel would be like, and with our descent into the town our hearts sank further. Finally, when we could descend no more, the taxi took off into a part of the city we hadn't seen before. No Europeans here! The streets got narrower and narrower until we turned into a side street that could barely accommodate the tiny Japanese taxi into which we were squeezed. Clearly this was a hotel of another class. I found that, by then, I was getting a little paranoid, which is easy enough to do in a foreign land, and said to myself, "They must think we are very low-status people indeed to treat us this way."

8 As it turned out, the neighborhood, in fact the whole district, showed us an entirely different side of life from what we had seen

before, much more interesting and authentic. True, we did have some communication problems, because no one was used to dealing with foreigners, but few of them were serious.

9 Yet, the whole matter of being moved like a piece of derelict luggage puzzled me. In the United States, the person who gets moved is often the lowest-ranking individual. This principle applies to all organizations, including the Army. Whether you can be moved or not is a function of your status, your performance, and your value to the organization. To move someone without telling him is almost worse than an insult, because it means he is below the point at which feelings matter. In these circumstances, moves can be unsettling and damaging to the ego. In addition, moves themselves are often accompanied by great anxiety, whether an entire organization or a small part of an organization moves. What makes people anxious is that the move usually presages organizational changes that have been coordinated with the move. Naturally, everyone wants to see how he comes out vis-à-vis everyone else. I have seen important men refuse to move into an office that was six inches smaller than someone else's of the same rank. While I have heard some American executives say they wouldn't employ such a person, the fact is that in actual practice, unless there is some compensating feature, the significance of space as a communication is so powerful that no employee in his right mind would allow his boss to give him a spatial demotion—unless of course he had already reached his crest and was on the way down.

10 These spatial messages are not simply conventions in the United States—unless you consider the size of your salary check a mere convention, or where your name appears on the masthead of a journal. Ranking is seldom a matter that people take lightly, particularly in a highly mobile society like that in the United States. Each culture and each country has its own language of space, which is just as unique as the spoken language, frequently more so. In England, for example, there are no offices for the members of Parliament. In the United States, our congressmen and senators proliferate their offices and their office buildings and simply would not tolerate a no-office situation. Constituents, associates, colleagues, and lobbyists would not respond properly. In England, status is internalized; it has its manifestations and markers—the upper-class received English accent, for example. We in the United States, a relatively new country, externalize status. The American in England has some trouble placing people in the social system, while the English can place each other quite accurately by reading ranking cues, but in general tend to look down on the importance that Americans attach to space. It is very easy and very natural to look at things from one's own point of view and to read an event as though it were the same all over the world.

11 I knew that my emotions on being moved out of my room in Tokyo were of the gut type and quite strong. There was nothing intellectual about my initial response. Although I am a professional observer of cultural patterns, I had no notion of the meaning attached to being moved from hotel to hotel in Kyoto. I was well aware of the strong significance of moving in my own culture, going back to the time when the new baby displaces older children, right up to the world of business, where a complex dance is performed every time the organization moves to new quarters.

12 What was happening to me in Japan as I rode up and down elevators with various keys gripped in my hand was that I was reacting with the cultural part of my brain—the old, mammalian brain. Although my new brain, my symbolic brain—the neocortex—was saying something else, my mammalian brain kept repeating, "You are being treated shabbily." My neocortex was trying to fathom what was happening. Needless to say, neither part of the brain had been programmed to provide me with the answer in Japanese culture. I did have to put up a strong fight with myself to keep from interpreting what was going on as though the Japanese were the same as I. This is the conventional and most common response and one that is often found even among anthropologists. Any time you hear someone say, "Why *they* are no different than the folks back home—they are just like I am," even though you may understand the reasons behind these remarks you also know that the speaker is living in a single-context world (his own) and is incapable of describing either his world or the foreign one.

13 The "they are just like the folks back home" syndrome is one of the most persistent and widely held misconceptions of the Western world, if not the whole world. There is very little any outsider can do about this, because it expresses views that are very close to the core of the personality. Simply talking about "cultural differences" and how we must respect them is a hollow cliché. And in fact, intellectualizing isn't much more helpful either, at least at first. The logic of the man who won't move into an office that is six inches smaller than his rival's is *cultural* logic; it works at a lower, more basic level in the brain, a part of the brain that synthesizes but does not verbalize. The response is a total response that is difficult to explain to someone who doesn't already understand, because it is so dependent on context for correct interpretation. To do so, one must explain the entire system; otherwise, the man's behavior makes little sense. He may even appear to be acting childishly—which he most definitely is not.

14 It was my preoccupation with my own cultural mold that explained why I was puzzled for years about the significance of being moved around in Japanese hotels. The answer finally came after further experiences in Japan and many discussions with Japanese friends.

In Japan, one has to "belong" or he has no identity. When a man joins a company, he does just that—joins himself to the corporate body—and there is even a ceremony marking the occasion. Normally, he is hired for life, and the company plays a much more paternalistic role than in the United States. There are company songs, and the whole company meets frequently (usually at least once a week) for purposes of maintaining corporate identity and morale.

15 As a tourist (either European or Japanese) when you go on a tour, you *join* that tour and follow your guide everywhere as a group. She leads you with a little flag that she holds up for all to see. Such behavior strikes Americans as sheeplike; not so the Japanese. The reader may say that this pattern holds in Europe, because there people join Cook's tours and the American Express tours, which is true. Yet there is a big difference. I remember a very attractive young American woman who was traveling with the same group I was with in Japan. At first she was charmed and captivated, until she had spent several days visiting shrines and monuments. At this point, she observed that she could not take the regimentation of Japanese life. Clearly, she was picking up clues, such as the fact that our Japanese group, when it moved, marched in a phalanx rather than moving as a motley mob with stragglers. There was much more discipline in these sightseeing groups than the average Westerner is either used to or willing to accept.

16 It was my lack of understanding of the full impact of what it means to belong to a high-context culture that caused me to misread hotel behavior at Hakone. I should have known that I was in the grip of a pattern difference and that the significance of all guests being garbed in the same okata meant more than that an opportunistic management used the guests to advertise the hotel. The answer to my puzzle was revealed when a Japanese friend explained what it means to be a guest in a hotel. As soon as you register at the desk, you are no longer an outsider; instead, for the duration of your stay you are a member of a large, mobile family. *You belong.* The fact that I was moved was tangible evidence that I was being treated as a family member—a relationship in which one can afford to be "relaxed and informal and not stand on ceremony." This is a very highly prized state in Japan, which offsets the official properness that is so common in public. Instead of putting me down, they were treating me as a member of the family. Needless to say, the large, luxury hotels that cater to Americans, like Wright's Imperial Hotel, have discovered that Americans do tenaciously stand on ceremony and want to be treated as they are at home in the States. Americans don't like to be moved around; it makes them anxious. Therefore, the Japanese in these establishments have learned not to treat them as family members.

Keeping a Reading Journal

The most effective way to keep track of your thoughts and impressions and to review what you have learned is to start a reading journal. The comments you record in your journal may express your reflections, observations, questions, and reactions to the essays you read. Normally, your journal would not contain lecture notes from class. A reading journal will allow you to keep a record of your progress during the term and can also reflect insights you gain during class discussions and questions you may want to ask, as well as unfamiliar words you intend to look up. Keeping a reading journal becomes a necessity if your composition course will require you to write a research paper that will be due at the end of the semester. Keep in mind that your journal is not something that will be corrected or graded, although some instructors may wish you to share your entries with the class.

TURNING ANNOTATIONS INTO JOURNAL ENTRIES

Although there is no set form for what a journal should look like, reading journals are most useful for converting your brief annotations into more complete entries that explore in depth your reactions to what you have read. Interestingly, the process of turning your annotations into journal entries will often produce surprising insights that will give you a new perspective. For example, a student who annotated Edward T. Hall's "Hidden Culture" converted them into the following journal entries:

- Hall's personal experiences in Japan made him realize that interpreting an action depends on what culture you're from.
- Hall assumes hotels should treat long-term guests with more respect than overnight guests. "Like someone who had been squeezed in without a reservation" shows Hall's feelings.
- What does having your clothes replaced with an okata—cotton robe—have to do with being moved from room to room in a hotel? The plot thickens!
- The hotel in Hakone encourages guests—all wearing the same robes—to greet each other outside the hotel in a friendly, not formal, manner.
- Hall says that in America, size of office = personal value and salary. Hall compared how space works in the United States in order to understand Japanese attitudes toward space.
- Thesis—"culturally defined attitudes toward space are different for each culture." Proves this by showing how unimportant space is to members of Parliament in England when compared

with the great importance office size has for U.S. congresspersons and senators.

- Hall is an anthropologist. He realizes his reactions are instinctual. Hall wants to refute the idea that people are the same all over the world. Says that which culture you are from determines your attitudes and behavior.
- He learns from Japanese friends that workers are hired for life and view their companies as family. Would this be for me? In Japan, group identity is all-important.
- Hall describes two tour groups, one Japanese and one American, as an example of Japanese acceptance of regimentation, whereas Americans go off on their own.
- The answer to the mystery of why he was being moved: moving him meant he was accepted as a member of the hotel family. They were treating him informally, as if he were Japanese: a compliment, not an insult. Informality is highly valued because the entire culture is based on the opposite—regimentation and conformity.

SUMMARIZING

Reading journals may also be used to record summaries of the essays you read. The value of summarizing is that it requires you to pay close attention to the reading in order to distinguish the main points from the supporting details. Summarizing tests your understanding of the material by requiring you to restate, concisely, the author's main ideas in your own words. First, create a list composed of sentences that express in your own words the essential idea of each paragraph, or each group of related paragraphs. Your previous underlining of topic sentences, main ideas, and key terms (as part of the process of critical reading) will help you follow the author's line of thought. Next, whittle down this list still further by eliminating repetitive ideas. Then formulate a thesis statement that expresses the main idea behind the article. Start your summary with this thesis statement, and combine your notes so that the summary flows together and reads easily.

Remember that summaries should be much shorter than the original text (whether the original is one page or twenty pages long) and should accurately reflect the central ideas of the article in as few words as possible. Try not to intrude your own opinions or critical evaluations into the summary. Besides requiring you to read the original piece more closely, summaries are necessary first steps in developing papers that synthesize materials from different sources. The test for a good summary, of course, is whether a person reading it without having read the original article would get an accurate, balanced, and complete account of the original material.

Writing an effective summary is easier if you first compose a rough summary, using no more than two complete sentences to summarize each of the paragraphs or group of paragraphs in the original article. A student's rough summary of Hall's essay might appear as follows. Numbers show which paragraphs are summarized from the article.

1–3 Hall describes how a seemingly inexplicable event that occurred while he was staying in a Tokyo hotel, frequented mostly by Japanese, led him to understand that the same action can have a completely different significance from another culture's perspective. Without telling him, the hotel management had moved his personal belongings to a new room and had given his room to another guest.

4 Three days later when Hall is again moved without warning, he is less startled but begins to wonder why this had never happened during his stay at Frank Lloyd Wright's Imperial Hotel in Tokyo.

5 At another hotel in Hakone, Hall is given an *okata,* a kind of cotton robe, to wear instead of his clothes and is encouraged to greet other guests wearing the same *okata* when he sees them outside the hotel.

6–7 At a third hotel, a country inn near Kyoto, Hall discovers that he has been moved again, this time to an entirely different hotel in what he initially perceives to be a less desirable section of town. Hall interprets this as an insult and becomes angry that the Japanese see him as someone who can be moved around without asking his permission.

8 The neighborhood he had initially seen as less desirable turns out to be much more interesting and authentic than the environs of hotels where tourists usually stay.

9 Hall relates his feelings of being treated shabbily ("like a piece of derelict luggage") to the principle that in the United States, the degree of one's power and status is shown by how much control one has over personal space, whether in the Army or in corporations, where being moved to a smaller office means one is considered less valuable to the company.

10–11 Hall speculates that the equation of control over space with power may pertain only to the United States because in England, members of Parliament have no formal offices, while their counterparts in the United States—congressmen and senators—attach great importance to the size of their offices. Hall begins to realize that he has been unconsciously applying an American cultural perspective to actions that can be explained only in the context of Japanese culture.

12 Hall postulates the existence of an instinctive "cultural logic" that varies from culture to culture, and he concludes that it is necessary to understand the cultural context in which an action takes place in order to interpret it as people would in that culture.

13–14 Once Hall suspends his own culturally based assumption that one's self-esteem depends on control over personal space, he learns from conversations with Japanese friends that in Japan one has an identity only as part of a group. Japanese workers are considered as family by the companies that hire them for life.

15 The emphasis Japanese society places on conforming to a group is evident in the behavior of Japanese tourists, who move as a coordinated group and closely follow their guide, while American tourists refuse to accept such discipline.

16 Hall realizes that wearing an *okata* and being moved to different rooms and to another, more authentic, hotel means that he is being treated in an informal manner reserved for family members. What Hall had misperceived as an insult—being moved without notice—was really intended as an honor signifying he had been accepted and was not being treated as a stranger.

Based on this list, a student's formulation of a thesis statement expressing the essential idea of Hall's essay appears this way:

> Every society has a hidden culture that governs behavior that might seem inexplicable to an outsider.

The final summary should contain both this thesis and your restatement of the author's main ideas without adding any comments that express personal feelings or responses to the ideas presented. Keep in mind that the purpose of a summary or concise restatement of the author's ideas in your own words is to test your understanding of the material. The summary would normally be introduced by mentioning the author as well as the title of the article:

> Edward T. Hall, writing in "Hidden Culture," believes every society has a hidden culture that governs behavior that might seem inexplicable to an outsider. In Japan, Hall's initial reactions of anger to being moved to another room in a hotel in Tokyo, having his clothes replaced by a cotton kimono or *okata* in Hakone, and being relocated to a different hotel in Kyoto led him to search for the reasons behind such seemingly bizarre events. Although control over space in America is related to status, Hall realizes that in other cultures, like England, where members of Parliament have no offices, this is not the case. Hall discovers that, rather than being an insult, being treated informally meant he was considered to be a member of the hotel "family."

Although some features of the original essay might have been mentioned, such as the significance of office size in corporations in the United States, the student's summary of Hall's essay is still an effective one. The summary accurately and fairly expresses the main ideas in the original.

USING YOUR READING JOURNAL TO GENERATE IDEAS FOR WRITING

You can use all the material in your reading journal (annotations converted to journal entries, reflections, observations, questions, rough and final summaries) to relate your own ideas to the ideas of the person who wrote the essay you are reading. Here are several different kinds of strategies you can use as you analyze an essay in order to generate material for your own:

1. What is missing in the essay? Information that is not mentioned is often just as significant as information the writer chose to include. First, you must have already summarized the main points in the article. Then, make up another list of points that are not discussed, that is, missing information that you would have expected an article of this kind to have covered or touched on. Write down the possible reasons why this missing material has been omitted, censored, or downplayed. What possible purpose could the author have had? Look for vested interests or biases that could explain why information of a certain kind is missing.

2. You might analyze an essay in terms of what you already know and what you didn't know about the issue. To do this, simply make a list of what concepts were already familiar to you and a second list of information or concepts that were new to you. Then write down three to five questions you would like answered about this new information and make a list of possible sources you might consult.

3. You might consider whether the author presents a solution to a problem. List the short-term and long-term effects or consequences of the action the writer recommends. You might wish to evaluate the solution to see whether positive short-term benefits are offset by possible negative long-term consequences not mentioned by the author. This might provide you with a starting point for your own essay.

4. After clearly stating what the author's position on an issue is, try to imagine other people in that society or culture who would view the same issue from a different perspective. How would the concerns of these people be different from those of the writer? Try to think of as many different people, representing as many different perspectives, as you can. Now, try to think of a solution that would satisfy both the author and at least one other person who holds a different viewpoint. Try to imagine that you are an arbitrator negotiating an agreement. How would your recommendation require both parties to compromise and reach an agreement?

Writing Your Essay

One of the basic writing forms you are expected to master in college is the analytical essay (often of approximately five pages) in which you argue for an interpretation. In it, you build on previously developed critical thinking and reading skills. When you write an analytical essay, you move beyond your personal reactions to what you have read and evaluate some aspect of the article—the author's claims, use of evidence, chain of reasoning, organization, or style. You also need to recognize the author's values, beliefs, and purpose before writing your essay.

PREWRITING TECHNIQUES

Discovering how best to approach your topic is easier if you try one or several of the prewriting, or invention, strategies many writers have found helpful. Prewriting techniques allow you to explore ideas in an informal way before putting time and effort into writing a rough draft. The basic strategies we will discuss include freewriting, the five W's, and mapping (or clustering).

FREEWRITING

Freewriting is a technique for setting down whatever occurs to you on the topic within a few minutes. You will find you are more creative when you simply free-associate without stopping to censor, evaluate, or edit your ideas. Your goal is to get a clear perception of key aspects of the issue in order to discover how to focus your argument. At this point, you need not worry about spelling, punctuation, or grammar.

THE FIVE W'S

In this technique you write down your topic, and then ask yourself the questions that journalists often use to find out about a subject.

1. *Who* is involved?
2. *What* is at stake?
3. *Where* did it happen?
4. *When* did it happen?
5. *Why* is what happened important?

By answering some or all of these questions, you can get a clearer picture of the different aspects of the whole situation. You can then decide which of these elements to focus on to produce an effective essay.

MAPPING

This technique allows you to graphically plot the relationship between important ideas. Begin by writing down the word that contains a key idea or represents a starting point and draw a circle around it; when you think of related ideas, topics, or details that are connected to it, jot them down nearby and draw lines as a way of representing the connections between related ideas. When you group ideas in this way, you discover a map, or cluster, of ideas and patterns that will help you decide which ideas are central and which are subordinate. This strategy can help you narrow your topic and see details and examples that you can use to support your thesis. See page 18 for an example of mapping.

IDENTIFYING YOUR THESIS

As you explore and narrow your topic using the invention strategies mentioned above, try to identify an idea that expresses your opinion and contains a specific claim that your essay will explore and defend. Your thesis is a sentence or two that identifies the paper's topic and your opinion or the approach that you plan to take. The thesis or claim is an assertion that must be genuinely debatable; that is, there should be some alternative, or opposing, opinion. Because others might disagree with your assessment or interpretation, you must present evidence (most often, in the form of relevant quotations drawn from sources you use) and a chain of reasoning that explains your interpretation in a way that will persuade your readers. The thesis is a type of contract or promise; it tells readers what to expect.

For example, consider the following thesis that a student formulated based on her critical reading and annotation of Judith Ortiz Cofer's essay "The Myth of the Latin Woman" (reprinted in Chapter 3):

> In "The Myth of the Latin Woman," Judith Ortiz Cofer refutes the "Maria" stereotype by creating an impression of herself as an articulate, educated and accomplished Latina.

This example of a trial thesis (which may be revised as the paper takes shape) contains the title of the original essay, the author's name, and the student's primary assertion, stated as a single sentence. Considered as a contract, this thesis obligates the student to

1. Define the "Maria" stereotype and demonstrate that Cofer finds it demeaning
2. Show specifically how and where Cofer creates "an impression of herself as an articulate, educated and accomplished Latina"
3. Analyze Cofer's use of rhetorical techniques to win her audience's sympathy

Each of these three ideas can then be developed in separate sections of the paper. You can also create an informal outline to explore the ideas and relationships in the thesis and test the kind of evidence that will best support these ideas. Remember your essay doesn't have to analyze every single aspect of the original. Discuss only those elements that support your thesis.

After formulating a thesis that expresses a claim, you need to start assembling evidence. You do this by summarizing (see pages 12–14), paraphrasing, and quoting particular passages that will illustrate and support your assertion.

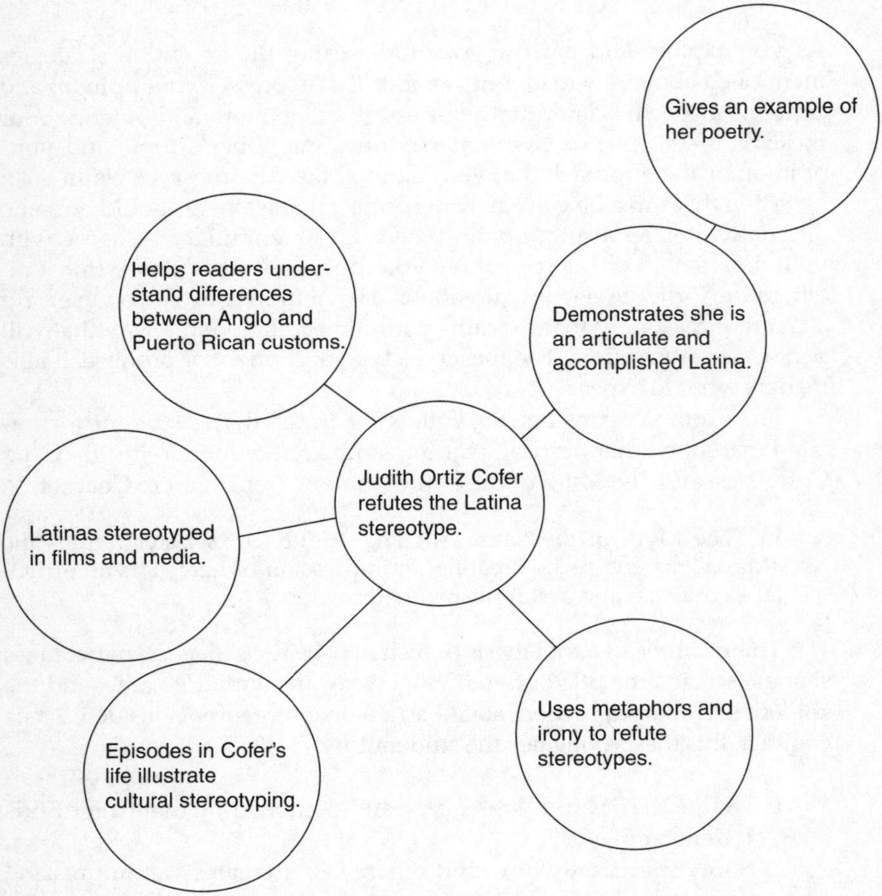

An example of mapping based on Judith Ortiz Cofer's "The Myth of the Latin Woman" (Chapter 3).

CREATING A ROUGH DRAFT

Creating a rough draft offers the best way in which to explore the ideas you developed during the prewriting stage and serves as a precursor to your final paper. A rough draft helps you see the relationships implicit in the materials you generated during your prewriting activities, and in your reading journal (see page 11), annotations (see page 11), and an informal outline, if you used one. Plan to write one section of the paper at a time.

WRITING THE INTRODUCTION

Some writers find it helpful to compose the introduction first, informing readers in a straightforward way of the issue, topic, or idea the essay will cover. At other times, the introduction is not sufficiently focused, so it is better to proceed to subsequent paragraphs and return to the introduction later when you have a clearer idea of the focus of the paper. Introductions should capture the readers' attention and can include one or more of the following:

- A provocative question that challenges readers to reexamine their beliefs on the subject
- A dramatic or amusing story or anecdote, or an attention-getting quotation
- A brief overview of the issue in its historical context
- A striking statistic
- A brief description of both sides of a debate
- A description of a central person, place, or event

Whichever of these you choose, be sure your introductory paragraph includes the idea your paper will develop and/or suggests the kind of analysis you intend to pursue in developing your thesis.

WRITING THE MIDDLE OF THE ESSAY

The choices open to you when you write the middle portion, or body, of your essay depend on the best way to support your thesis. Each strategy or method of development is suited to a particular purpose. These organizational patterns (traditionally referred to as rhetorical modes) include:

illustration (or exemplification)
description
definition

classification/division
comparison and contrast
causal analysis
narration

To clarify and support a thesis, writers also use a wide variety of evidence—including examples drawn from personal experience, the testimony of experts, statistical data, and case histories (where the experiences of one person typify the experiences of many people in the same situation).

When you use *illustration* (or *exemplification*), you provide one or more examples that document or substantiate the idea you wish to clarify. In "Social Time: The Heartbeat of Culture" (Chapter 8), Robert Levine and Ellen Wolff use the fact that "Unlike their North American counterparts, the Brazilian students believe that a person who is consistently late is probably more successful than one who is consistently on time" as an illustration to support their claim that "Formal 'clock time' may be a standard on which the world agrees, but 'social time,' the heartbeat of society, is something else again."

Descriptions are powerful because they can evoke an image in readers' minds and create an emotional response. Effective descriptions use specific language, carefully chosen details, and an orderly sequence. For example, Douchan Gersi in "Initiated into an Iban Tribe of Headhunters" (Chapter 2) creates a vivid picture of the place where women having their period go that is off limits to men: "Each women has her own refuge. Some have shelters made of branches, others deep covered holes hidden behind bushes with enough space to eat and sleep and wait until their time is past."

Definition is a useful method for specifying the basic nature of any phenomenon, idea, or condition. A definition can be a sentence that gives the exact meaning of a word or key term (to eliminate ambiguity), or it might extend several paragraphs or even become a complete essay. For example, the definition of the term *individualism* is central to Poranee Natadecha-Sponsel's investigation in "Individualism as an American Cultural Value" (Chapter 6) of contrasting Thai and American values.

Writers use *classification* or *division* to sort or group ideas, issues, and topics into categories based on one or more criteria. Enid Schildkrout in "Body Art as Visual Language" (Chapter 2) uses this pattern to categorize the different body art techniques, including body painting, makeup, hair, body shaping, scarification, tatooing, and piercing.

Comparison and *contrast* are useful techniques for helping audiences understand basic differences and for pointing out unsuspected similarities between two or more subjects. In "Learning from Ladakh" (Chapter 4), Helena Norberg-Hodge compares and contrasts how agrarian life changed in a northern Indian community when commerce replaced cooperation: "Previously, with cooperative labor between people, farmers had no need for money. Now, unable to pay larger and larger wages for farm hands, some are forced to abandon the villages to earn money in the city." Comparisons may be arranged either subject by subject (in which the writer discusses all the relevant features of one and then retraces the same points for the other) or point by point (which alternates between relevant features of the two subjects).

Causal analysis is a technique often used in persuasive essays. Its purpose is to determine whether a cause-and-effect relationship exists. For example, Philip Slater in "Want-Creation Fuels Americans' Addictiveness" (Chapter 8) works backward from an effect to seek the cause(s) that could have produced the observed effect: "But in our society we spend billions each year creating want. Covetousness, discontent and greed are taught to our children, drummed into them—they are bombarded with it." Writers can also explore potential effects from a known cause, as Anwar F. Accawi does in "The Telephone" (Chapter 2) when he describes the dire social consequences of the installation of a telephone in a rural Lebanese village ("And the telephone, as it turned out, was bad news. With its coming, the face of the village began to change"). Causal analysis can go off track when a writer confuses sequence with causation (called the *post-hoc fallacy*) and assumes that because one event happens after another the early event must have caused the later one.

Narration is a recounting of events to entertain and to persuade. For example, Judith Ortiz Cofer relates various anecdotes in "The Myth of the Latin Woman" (Chapter 3) to illustrate the pervasiveness of the "Maria" stereotype. An entire essay can take the form of a narrative. In "Why I Quit the Company" (Chapter 4) Tomoyuki Iwashita recounts the history of his employment with a prestigious corporation as a framework for his readers to understand why he decided to quit.

WRITING THE CONCLUSION

The conclusion brings together the lines of reasoning developed in the body of the essay. Your readers should feel that you fulfilled the promise you made when you presented your thesis. You can achieve a sense of closure in several ways, including:

- Summarizing the points made in the paper as they relate to the thesis
- Referring to points presented in the opening paragraph or introduction
- Challenging the reader to think further about the issue

REVISING YOUR ESSAY

You will probably revise several times, and you may wish to read your paper aloud to discover errors in grammar, syntax, or style. Many campuses have writing centers or tutoring services that can help you.

First, examine your essay's overall structure. Is the introduction effective? Then, evaluate whether the sections follow each other in a logical manner. Are the issues raised in the best possible order? Let your thesis guide you as to the best sequence to follow. Do transitions help readers to perceive relationships between different sections of your paper? Check to see whether some of your assumptions need to be supported with more evidence.

Next, consider whether each paragraph has enough supporting evidence and is clearly related to your thesis. You can improve your style by recasting passive sentences into the active voice. You can also express your ideas more clearly by substituting single words for roundabout phrases (such as *because* for *due to the fact that*). Consider how you might improve your choice of words by eliminating confusing metaphors, jargon, and clichés. Last, rework your title to more accurately reflect your claim.

PROOFREADING AND FORMATTING

Proofreading means focusing on spelling, punctuation, repeated words, spacing, margins, and anything else that would mar the look of the final paper. Make a list of words that you consistently misspell and check it when you proofread.

If you use a computer, do not rely on your computer's spell-check program because it cannot tell you when you have typed the wrong word—for example, *too* for *two, piece* for *peace*, and *there* for *their.* Most English and Humanities instructors require papers to be formatted in Modern Language Association (MLA) style. Guidelines are available at http://www.mla.org. The latest edition of the published guidelines is *MLA Handbook for Writers of Research Papers*, seventh ed., by Joseph Gibaldi (New York: MLA, 2009). Unless your instructor specifies otherwise, the following format is standard in MLA style:

- 1-inch margins on the top, bottom, and sides of each page
- Your last name and page number on each page, upper right corner
- ½-inch indentation of the first line of each paragraph
- Double-spaced text in the standard 12-point font
- Works Cited (or References) on a separate page at the end of the paper (following MLA citation guidelines)

- Your name, the name of the course, your professor, and the date in the upper left corner of the first page of the essay

PROVIDING EVIDENCE FROM SOURCES

After formulating a thesis, you must support it with reasons, arguments, and analyses, based on relevant passages in the text. For some papers, you may do additional research, using books and journals from your library, or information found on the Internet (we have provided Web sites for half the readings in the questions following the selections). Whatever sources you use, whether print or electronic, you must evaluate the quality of the information and select material that genuinely illuminates your argument.

Paraphrases

A good portion of your analysis will rely on paraphrasing information from your sources. Paraphrasing is a restatement of an author's ideas in your own words. Unlike summaries (which compress entire articles down to several paragraphs), paraphrases aim to convey the complexity and richness of the original passage—the ideas, the tone, and the pattern of reasoning. Your paraphrase must be different enough from the original so that you do not commit plagiarism (using someone else's words as if they were your own).

Quotations

Quotations are an indispensable form of evidence to use to illustrate or support your assertions. Direct quotation requires you to copy the author's words exactly as they appear in the original. Direct quotations are preferable to paraphrases when the original passage is important or memorable. On the other hand, be sure that your paper is not a patchwork of stitched-together quotations.

Brief quotations (of fewer than four lines) are normally run into the text and enclosed in double quotation marks (""). Include the author's name with the quotation either in the text or in a parenthetical reference and be sure to reproduce all punctuation and capitalization as it appears in the original. (See the MLA guidelines.)

Longer quotations (of more than four lines) are separated from the text, indented 1 inch from the left margin, double-spaced like the rest of the manuscript, and reproduced without quotation marks. These block quotations are introduced with a colon (:) if they follow a grammatically complete introductory clause. Parenthetical citation of page numbers follows the quotation's final punctuation. If you need to omit a part of the quotation in order to more easily integrate it into your own text, you must place ellipses or three spaced periods (. . .) where the omitted phrase occurred.

AVOIDING PLAGIARISM

Any paper you write in which you draw on the words and ideas of others, whether in the form of quotations, paraphrases, summaries, or factual references, must accurately document these sources. This is important even if you are not using the exact language used by the author. You must specify the author, title of the work, and location within the work where the reference can be found. For this reason it is important to take accurate notes including specific page numbers. Not to do this may later lead you to believe that these were your own ideas, and you may fail to acknowledge that this information derives from an external source. Be especially careful in making sure you have included quotation marks so that you do not, however unintentionally, mistake someone else's words for your own and not give proper credit.

You must also do this whether you are drawing on print sources or on sources available on the Internet. That is, you must carefully document the words and ideas of others that you have downloaded and incorporated from Internet sources. The sole exception to this rule is for information that might be considered common knowledge and would include facts, phrases, and concepts that most educated people would already know (for example, the concept of a "matrilineal society" used in anthropology).

When you summarize or paraphrase material, you must take care not to reproduce the exact words, sentence structure, or phrasing of the original. For example, here is an original passage from Edward T. Hall's *Beyond Culture* (Garden City, New York: Anchor Books/Doubleday, 1981, p. 61):

> As it turned out, the neighborhood, in fact the whole district, showed us an entirely different side of life from what we had seen before, much more interesting, and authentic. True, we did have some communication problems, because no one was used to dealing with foreigners, but few of them were serious.

The following paraphrase is *unacceptable* because it is too close to the sentence structure of the original and merely offers synonyms. Moreover, it does not introduce the paraphrased material with a signal phrase that identifies the author or the source. Nor does it conclude with a parenthetical in-text page citation required by MLA guidelines:

> The neighborhood and, in fact, the whole region, displayed a quite different aspect from what we had previously seen, although it was

> more interesting. While we did encounter some difficulties in communicating because they were unused to visitors from other countries, none of these were a big problem.

By contrast, the following is an *acceptable* paraphrase that restates the author's words in different words and style, and includes the introductory signal phrase and page citation:

> Edward T. Hall observes that this new section of the city that he had initially seen as less desirable proved to be more exciting. Despite minor difficulties in being understood, Hall felt he had a glimpse of the real Japan that visitors hardly ever get to see (*Beyond Culture* 61).

Keep in mind that plagiarism is a serious offense and can result in harsh consequences ranging from failing a course to being suspended or expelled from school. It denies you the opportunity to display your understanding of the original material and keeps you from receiving the benefits of doing your own research and drawing your own conclusions.

ELECTRONIC SOURCES

If you use sources from the Internet, you must be especially careful to assess their validity because anyone can create a Web page and post information. Ideally, information found on the Internet should be able to be corroborated by print sources such as books and journals.

When you begin the process of locating and evaluating information on the Internet, it is important that you focus the topic of your research as exactly as possible. Conduct your search using a sequence or string of search terms that will narrow the list of Web pages to those that most closely match your inquiry. For example, if you want information about Serena Nanda's article on arranged marriages in India ("Arranging a Marriage in India" in Chapter 8) the use of the key words "arranged marriages" and "India" will turn up only those sources that are appropriate to your research.

When you find a Web site that you wish to quote, make a careful note of the specific address because you will need to acknowledge it within your paper and in the list of Works Cited (for information on documenting electronic sources, see the MLA Web site at http://www.mla.org or consult the seventh edition of their handbook). Web pages should be evaluated as to their timeliness, relevance, authoritativeness, and lack of bias. The most reliable Web pages have links that provide information about the creator or at least give the e-mail address of the creator or Web master.

WHAT KIND OF ARGUMENT ARE YOU MAKING?

The purpose of any argument is to persuade an audience to accept the validity (or at least the likelihood) of an idea, proposition, or claim. The claim is an assertion that would raise doubt if it were not supported with sound evidence and persuasive reasoning. Different kinds of arguments seek to accomplish different objectives or goals. Generally speaking, four kinds of goals can be identified (we have classified selections that are arguments according to type in the rhetorical table of contents).

1. People can disagree about the essential nature of the subject under discussion, what it is similar to or different from, or how it should be defined. These are called *arguments of fact.*
2. Even if people agree about the essential nature of X, they may disagree about what caused it or what effects it would cause, in turn. These are *arguments of causation.*
3. Even if all sides agree on what X is, what caused it, and what its effects may be, they may disagree over whether it is good or bad, or whether its effects are harmful or beneficial. These are *arguments about value.*
4. The most complex kind of argument—those that require not merely agreement, but action on the part of the audience—are known as *policy arguments.*

For convenience, we will discuss each of these four types separately, but it should be realized that real-world arguments frequently rely on more than just one type of claim.

- *Arguments of fact* define a key term or concept in a way that clearly distinguishes it from all other things with which it might be confused. An entire argument can often hinge on the definition of a key term or concept. For example, Judith Ortiz Cofer's essay "The Myth of the Latin Woman" (Chapter 3) turns on the question of how the Latina stereotype ought to be defined. She not only identifies its key features; she explains how it operates to allow people to rationalize their discrimination against Hispanic women.
- *Arguments of causation* try to answer the question, What caused X to be the way it is? or What will happen as a result of X? Causal arguments also offer plausible explanations as to the cause(s) of a series of events, or a trend. For example, in "Want-Creation Fuels Americans' Addictiveness" (Chapter 8) Philip Slater argues that the "quick fix" mentality, or an "intolerance of

any constraint or obstacle," is the cause of pervasive drug use (of heroin, cocaine, alcohol, speed, tranquilizers, and barbiturates) in American culture. This kind of claim obligates the writer to demonstrate the means by which the effect was produced.

- *Arguments about value* make claims about value that do not merely express personal likes or dislikes, but offer reasoned judgments based on identifiable standards (ethical, moral, aesthetic, or utilitarian). They must demonstrate that the criterion applied is an appropriate one, and also consider the beliefs and attitudes the audience holds about the issue. Writers frequently use the rhetorical pattern of comparison and contrast to organize this kind of argument, as Andrew Sullivan does in "My Big Fat Straight Wedding" (Chapter 3). Sullivan evaluates how the right to marry someone of your own choosing, gay or straight, should operate as a civil right for everyone ("No other institution has an equivalent power to include people in their own familial narrative or civic history as deeply or as powerfully as civil marriage does").
- *Policy arguments* try to answer the question, What ought, should, or must we do about X? This type of argument first establishes that a serious problem exists, investigates the circumstances that created it, describes who suffers because of it, and weighs different solutions before selecting one that will be feasible, effective, and attractive to the audience to whom it is proposed. Mark I. Schwartz in "Genetically Modified Food Is Safe" (Chapter 7) uses argumentation (and persuasion) to support his claim that genetically modified crops are safer than conventional ones. The effectiveness of his argument depends in large part on the audience's sense of Schwartz as a principled advocate who deploys both intellectual and emotional appeals.

A Final Word

The readings in this anthology present innovative ideas and require close and careful reading. Being a critical reader means taking an active role rather than passively absorbing information. Maintain an active, questioning perspective by carefully looking at the assumptions on which the author's argument rests. Evaluate the quality of the evidence presented and assess how it serves to support the author's case. Compare what one writer says with the observations and claims of other writers. Create a dialogue with the text as if you were talking to another person.

1

The Family in Different Cultures

As the family goes, so goes the nation and so goes the whole world in which we live.

—John Paul II [Karol Wojtyla] (1920–2005), Polish Ecclesiastic, Pope. Quoted in *Observer* (London, 7 December 1986)

The family has been the most enduring basis of culture throughout the world and has provided a stabilizing force in all societies. The complex network of dependencies, relationships, and obligations may extend outward from parents and children to include grandparents, cousins, aunts and uncles, and more distantly related relatives. In other cultures, the entire community or tribe is seen as an extended family. The unique relationships developed among members of a family provide a universal basis for common experiences, emotions, perceptions, and expectations. At the same time, each family is different, with its own uniquely characteristic relationships and bonds. Family relationships continue to exert a profound influence on one's life long after childhood. In the context of the family we first learn what it means to experience the emotions of love, hope, fear, anger, and contentment. The works in this chapter focus on parent-child relationships, explore the connections between grandparents and grandchildren, and depict the impact of cultural values on these relationships.

The structure of the family is subject to a wide range of economic and social influences in different cultures. For example, child-rearing in China is a different enterprise from what it is in America because of the differences in economic circumstances and political systems. The variety of family structures depicted by writers of many different nationalities offers insight into how the concept of the family is modified according to the constraints, beliefs, and needs of particular societies.

For many, the family history is inseparable from the stories told about particular members that define the character of the family and its relationship to the surrounding society. These stories can be told for entertainment or education and often explain old loyalties and antagonisms. Some are written and some are part of an oral history related by one generation to the next. The complex portraits of family life offered in this chapter allow us to share, sympathize, and identify with writers from diverse cultures and more completely understand our own family experiences in the light of theirs.

Joe Bageant in "Valley of the Gun" describes the unusual role that guns played in providing a way for his family to pass on traditions. Fritz Peters in "Boyhood with Gurdjieff"recalls an experience from his childhood in France when he learned an important life lesson from his eccentric mentor. The editors of *Psychology Today* in "Plight of the Little Emperors" report on the extremes parents go to in order to give their only children a competitive edge in modern China. The Iranian-born writer Firoozeh Dumas in "Save Me, Mickey" recalls the trauma of being separated from her parents while visiting Disneyland. Patricia Hampl in "Grandmother's Sunday Dinner" tells of the pleasures of a home-cooked Czechoslovakian family meal. Meeta Kaur writes a compelling account in "Journey by Inner Light" of how, as a young Sikh woman, she risked alienating her family by having her hair cut short. "American Dream Boat" by K. Oanh Ha expresses the author's problems with her family when she decided to marry a non-Vietnamese. Marjane Satrapi in "The Convocation" uses the unconventional form of the graphic novel to describe what it was like being a female student at the university in Iran where women had to wear traditional dress.

To help you understand how the works in this chapter relate to each other, you might use one or several of the following guidelines before writing about family:

1. What motivates the author in telling his or her story?
2. Which conflicts or issues raised by the writer are purely personal and which address important social themes?
3. How would you characterize the author's tone and attitude toward the relationship he or she describes?
4. To what extent is the writer's experience similar to yours?
5. Is the writer especially interested in the social interactions that result from the use of language?
6. What is the writer's purpose—to inform readers, to change their attitudes, or to offer a solution to a problem?

Recommended Films on This Theme

- *Ordinary People* (United States, 1980) The story of a wealthy family devastated by the death of their oldest son;
- *Fanny and Alexander* (Sweden, 1983) an engaging tale of a Swedish family as seen through the eyes of their two young children;
- *The Joy Luck Club* (United States/China, 1993) a film based on Amy Tan's novel that explores the relationships of four Chinese mothers and their American-born daughters;
- *Kolya* (Czech Republic, 1996) the story of a womanizing cellist who marries for money and is left to raise his wife's five-year-old son.

Joe Bageant

Valley of the Gun

Joe Bageant was born in 1946 in Virginia, served in the Navy during the Vietnam War, and has developed a unique voice as an iconoclastic curmudgeon speaking out on many social issues. He has written for many newspapers and magazines and has been a senior editor for Primedia Magazine Corporation and for the Weider History Group. He currently spends half the year in Belize where he sponsors a development project with the Black Carib families of Hopkins Village. In this essay originally published in Deer Hunting with Jesus: Dispatches from America's Class War *(2007), he reveals the important role that the gun culture played in forging enduring family connections when he was growing up in Winchester, Virginia, near the West Virginia border.*

Before You Read

How might growing up in a gun culture provide important life lessons that might seem strange to outsiders?

1 "Take 'em, Joe!" cried Grandpap as the three deer, a buck and two does, stretched out at a lope across the ridgeline above us, swift dark silhouettes against the tan buckwheat stubble of what we called the ridgefield. My father, "Big Joe," leaned into the frost-tinged air. KA-KRAK, KA-KRAK, KA-KRAK, KA-KRAK—the sound of each shot was followed by that rattling echo through the chilled gray woods that every meat hunter knows and can hear in his sleep. The first deer, the buck, was thrown sideways by the impact and went down at a running roll. The two does did approximately the same thing; the second one would later be found after an hour of tracking the blood on fences and grass. We had just witnessed an amazing feat still talked about in the Bageant family all these years after my father's death.

2 That was in the late fall of 1957. I had been allowed to go with the deer hunters for the first time, and already I had seen family history made. Dad had stepped into family folklore, become one of those to be talked about for generations in a family of hunters, mentioned in the same breath with old Jim Bageant, who shot a whole washtub full of squirrels one November morning just before World War II.

3 These men—Daddy, Grandpap, and two of my uncles, Uncle Toad and Uncle Nelson—were meat hunters who trudged the fields and woods together right up until the day they got too crippled up to do it

or died. And it was because they were meat hunters that they let my dad take the three deer, one each on their tags, on the last legal day of hunting season. Everyone knew that my dad, the best shot in the family, had the most likelihood of getting more than one of the deer.

4 Later in the day, after dressing the deer and hanging them on the back porch to chill, we sat around the living-room woodstove, cleaned the guns, and talked about the day's hunt. To an eleven-year-old boy, the smell of gun oil and the stove's searing raw heat on the face, the polishing of blued steel and walnut, the clean raspy feel of the checked gun grips, the warm laughter of the men, well . . . that's primal after-the-hunt stuff so deep you can feel the sparks from Celtic yew log fires and the brush of bearskin leggings on your knees. It has been going on in this place and on this land for 250 years.

5 I quit hunting years ago, yet this remembered room and the long-dead men who inhabited it that day in the fall of '57 remain for me one of the truest and finest places and events on this earth. Guns can have a place inside a man, even remembered guns in the soul of an arthritic sixty-year-old old socialist writer. The crack of a distant rifle or the wild meat smell of a deer hanging under a porch lightbulb on a snowy night still bewitches me with the same mountain-folk animism it did when I was a boy. And though I have not hunted since 1986, the sight of a fine old shotgun still rouses my heart.

6 In families like mine, men are born smelling of gun oil amid a forest of firearms. The family home, a huge old clapboard farmhouse, was stuffed with guns, maybe thirty in all. There were 10-, 12-, 14-, and 20-gauge shotguns, pump guns, over-and-unders, and deer rifles of every imaginable sort from classic Winchester 94 models to 30-ought-sixes, an old cap and ball "horse pistol" dating back to the mid-1800s, and even a set of dueling pistols that had been in my family since the 1700s. No hillbilly ever threw a gun away, even when it could no longer be repaired. And until they stopped working completely, guns were endlessly cared for and patched back together. Otherwise they weren't to be parted with except under the direst circumstances, either on your deathbed or because you were so broke your cash bounced. For example, there is one ancestral family gun that my brother Mike did not inherit—my father's prized old Ivers and Johnson double-barrel shotgun, which had been in the family since the turn of the twentieth century. An out-of-work trucker at Christmastime, Daddy sold it to buy us kids the standard assortment of Christmas junk so we would not feel disappointed. I remember a Robert the Robot for me, a tin stove for my sister, a little red wheelbarrow for my brother, and, of course, toy guns and holsters. That was in 1952. We still have the photographs, and we still lament the loss of that fine old Ivers and Johnson.

7 Through our early years we boys could not hunt, but we were allowed to beat rabbits out of the bush for the dogs to chase back

around to the hunters. With clothes torn in the blackberry thickets and feet frozen in the winter creeks, faces pricked and bleeding, we rustled the brush piles. This would be considered child abuse today, but so would a lot of things we once did. Besides, there are far fewer boys hunting nowadays, thanks to computer games and television. Anyway, surviving the brush torture test of manhood earned us the right to sit around with the men-folk when they told hunting stories—so long as we kept our mouths shut unless spoken to. It was then we learned the family lore, who did what back when and with which gun. This imbued each gun with a sense of ancestry, made us feel part of a long and unbroken chain of men, a history we would contemplate over decades of seasons during that long patient waiting game that makes up most of successful hunting—or getting skunked.

8 After a couple more years came a day when they let us help clean the guns, running oil-soaked patches down the barrels and polishing the stocks and metalwork self-consciously under the eyes of grandfathers, fathers, and uncles, our mouths set serious and every move as careful as if each gun were made of dynamite, trying to demonstrate that we respected their destructive capability enough to be trusted with one. Then the mighty time came when Pap would pull the small 22-caliber "cat rifle" down from the bedroom wall to begin real target practice, along with what would today be called gun-safety training, though it was more instinct and common sense for farm boys back then. We had observed gun-carrying practices for years, absorbing such lessons as these: Never crawl through a fence with a loaded gun. Never point a gun at anyone, even accidentally while walking together. Never kill anything you are not going to eat, unless it is a varmint like a groundhog or a pest such as a copperhead snake under the front porch. Never shoot in the known direction of a house, no matter how distant. In 251 years of hunting these hills, no one in the Bageant clan was ever accidentally shot while hunting, which testifies to the practical responsibility native to the three-century-old gun culture of the southern uplands.

9 Half a dozen years after the Christmas Daddy sold the Ivers and Johnson, I turned thirteen, grown up enough to start hunting with an old family 12-gauge, the entire barrel and forestock of which was held together with black fabric "tar tape," as electrical tape was then called. And when I looked down at that 12-gauge shotgun cradled in my arm under a bright cold October sky, I knew that my grandfather had walked the same fields with it when it was brand-new from the Sears catalog, and had delivered mountains of meat to the smoky old farmhouse kitchen with it. I knew that my father had contemplated all this too under the same kind of sky, carrying the same gun, and that my younger brother would too. Ritual and clan. My family has hog-butchering knives that have been passed along for generations. I've

heard that Norwegian carpenters do the same with tools. And perhaps there is the same ritual passing of male family heritage and custom when upper-class sons of, say, the Bush family go off to the alma mater prep school and are handed the keys to the Lincoln. I wouldn't know. My symbol of passage was an old shotgun with black tape along the barrel.

10 For millions of families in my class, the first question asked after the death of a father is "Who gets Daddy's guns?" That sounds strange only if you did not grow up in a deeply rooted hunting culture. My brother Mike uses the same guns our daddy used. If there is a hunting gene, he's got it, so he inherited the family guns. True to form, Mike is a meat hunter who puts a couple of bucks and a doe in the freezer every year and probably could bring them home given only a bag of rocks with which to hunt.

11 If you were raised up hunting, you know that it is a ritual of death and plenitude, an animistic rite wherein a man blows the living heart out of one of God's creatures and then, if he deserves to be called a hunter, feels deep, honest gratitude for the creator's bounty. The meat on our tables links us to the days of black powder and buckskin. I can see why millions of urban citizens whose families came from teeming European cities through Ellis Island don't understand the links between Celtic and Germanic settler roots, guns, survival, and patriotism. Gunpowder is scarcely a part of their lives. Unfortunately, utter lack of knowledge and experience doesn't keep nonhunting urban liberals from believing they know what's best for everybody else—or simply laughing at what they do not understand.

12 To nonhunters, the image conjured by the title of this book [*Deer Hunting with Jesus*] might seem absurd, rather like a NUKE THE WHALES bumper sticker. But the title also captures something that moves me about the people I grew up with—the intersection between hunting and religion in their lives. The link between protestant fundamentalism and deer hunting goes back to colonial times, when the restless Presbyterian Scots, along with English and German Protestant reformers, pushed across America, developing the unique hunting and farming-based frontier cultures that sustained them over most of America's history. Two hundred years later, they have settled down, but they have not quit hunting and they have not quit praying. Consequently, today we find organizations such as the Christian Deer Hunters Association (christiandeerhunters.org), which offers convenient pocket-size books of meditations, such as *Devotions for Deer Hunters,* to help occupy the time during those long waits for game. Like their ancestors, deer hunters today understand how standing quietly and alone in the natural world leads to contemplation of God's gifts to man. And so, when a book like *Meditations for the Deer Stand* is seen in historical context, it is no joke. For those fortunate enough to spend whole days quietly

standing in the November woods just watching the Creator's world, there is no irony at all in the notion that his son might be watching too, and maybe even willing to summon a couple of nice fat does within shooting range.

✧ *Evaluating the Text*

1. What role did the gun culture play in Bageant's family and how did it provide him with important values?
2. Why is the question, "Who gets Daddy's guns?" not considered strange in the environment in which Bageant grew up?
3. How would you characterize the tone of Bageant's essay and his attitude toward the events he describes?

✧ *Exploring Different Perspectives*

1. How does the theme of self-reliance play an important role in the accounts by Bageant and Firoozeh Dumas?
2. Compare the lessons that both Bageant and Fritz Peters learned in unusual circumstances.

✧ *Extending Viewpoints through Writing and Research*

1. Would the experience of hunting as described by Bageant be appealing to you? Why or why not?
2. How important are hunting seasons to different regions in America, especially where you live?
3. To what extent has the gun control controversy impinged on the everyday activities that Bageant describes? What are your views on this issue?

How does this picture of a family on a hunting excursion communicate values that were important to Bageant as described in his essay?

Fritz Peters

Boyhood with Gurdjieff

Fritz Peters's (1916–1979) association with the philosopher and mystic George Gurdjieff began when Peters attended a school founded by Gurdjieff in Fontainebleau, France, where he spent four and a half years between 1924 and 1929. Peters's experiences with Gurdjieff were always unpredictable and often enigmatic and rewarding. Peters wrote two books about his experiences, Boyhood with Gurdjieff *(1964) and* Gurdjieff Remembered *(1965). In the following essay, Peters reveals the highly unconventional methods Gurdjieff used to compel his protégé to develop compassion.*

Before You Read

Who in your life, other than a relative, has taught you great life lessons?

1 The Saturday evening after Gurdjieff's return from America, which had been in the middle of the week, was the first general "assembly" of everyone at the Prieuré,[1] in the study-house. The study-house was a separate building, originally an airplane hangar. There was a linoleum-covered raised stage at one end. Directly in front of the stage there was a small, hexagonal fountain, equipped electrically so that various coloured lights played on the water. The fountain was generally used only during the playing of music on the piano which was to the left of the stage as one faced it.

2 The main part of the building, from the stage to the entrance at the opposite end, was carpeted with oriental rugs of various sizes, surrounded by a small fence which made a large, rectangular open space. Cushions, covered by fur rugs, surrounded the sides of this rectangle in front of the fence, and it was here that most of the students would normally sit. Behind the fence, at a higher level, were built-up benches, also covered with Oriental rugs, for spectators. Near the entrance of the building there was a small cubicle, raised a few feet from the floor, in which Gurdjieff habitually sat, and above this there was a balcony which was rarely used and then only for "important" guests. The cross-wise beams of the ceiling had painted material nailed to them,

[1]*Prieuré:* a priory; a large chateau in Fountainebleau, France, where G. I. Gurdjieff conducted his school.

and the material hung down in billows, creating a cloud-like effect. It was an impressive interior—with a church-like feeling about it. One had the impression that it would be improper, even when it was empty, to speak above a whisper inside the building.

3 On that particular Saturday evening, Gurdjieff sat in his accustomed cubicle, Miss Madison sat near him on the floor with her little black book on her lap, and most of the students sat around, inside the fence, on the fur rugs. New arrivals and "spectators" or guests were on the higher benches behind the fence. Mr. Gurdjieff announced that Miss Madison would go over all the "offences" of all the students and that proper "punishments" would be meted out to the offenders. All of the children, and perhaps I, especially, waited with baited breath as Miss Madison read from her book, which seemed to have been arranged, not alphabetically, but according to the number of offences committed. As Miss Madison had warned me, I led the list, and the recitation of my crimes and offences was a lengthy one.

4 Gurdjieff listened impassively, occasionally glancing at one or another of the offenders, sometimes smiling at the recital of a particular misdemeanour, and interrupting Miss Madison only to take down, personally, the actual number of individual black marks. When she had completed her reading, there was a solemn, breathless silence in the room and Gurdjieff said, with a heavy sigh, that we had all created a great burden for him. He said then that he would give out punishments according to the number of offences committed. Naturally, I was the first one to be called. He motioned to me to sit on the floor before him and then had Miss Madison re-read my offences in detail. When she had finished, he asked me if I admitted all of them. I was tempted to refute some of them, at least in part, and to argue extenuating circumstances, but the solemnity of the proceedings and the silence in the room prevented me from doing so. Every word that had been uttered had dropped on the assemblage with the clarity of a bell. I did not have the courage to voice any weak defence that might have come to my mind, and I admitted that the list was accurate.

5 With another sigh, and shaking his head at me as if he was very much put upon, he reached into his pocket and pulled out an enormous roll of bills. Once again, he enumerated the number of my crimes, and then laboriously peeled off an equal number of notes. I do not remember exactly how much he gave me—I think it was ten francs for each offence—but when he had finished counting, he handed me a sizeable roll of francs. During this process, the entire room practically screamed with silence. There was not a murmur from anyone in the entire group, and I did not even dare to glance in Miss Madison's direction.

6 When my money had been handed to me, he dismissed me and called up the next offender and went through the same process. As

there were a great many of us, and there was not one individual who had not done something, violated some rule during his absence, the process took a long time. When he had gone through the list, he turned to Miss Madison and handed her some small sum—perhaps ten francs, or the equivalent of one "crime" payment—for her, as he put it, "conscientious fulfilment of her obligations as director of the Prieuré."

7 We were all aghast; we had been taken completely by surprise, of course. But the main thing we all felt was a tremendous compassion for Miss Madison. It seemed to me a senselessly cruel, heartless act against her. I have never known Miss Madison's feelings about this performance; except for blushing furiously when I was paid, she showed no obvious reaction to anything at all, and even thanked him for the pittance he had given her.

8 The money that I had received amazed me. It was, literally, more money than I had ever had at one time in my life. But it also repelled me. I could not bring myself to do anything with it. It was not until a few days later, one evening when I had been summoned to bring coffee to Gurdjieff's room, that the subject came up again. I had had no private, personal contact with him—in the sense of actually talking to him, for instance—since his return. That evening—he was alone—when I had served him his coffee, he asked me how I was getting along; how I felt. I blurted out my feelings about Miss Madison and about the money that I felt unable to spend.

9 He laughed at me and said cheerfully that there was no reason why I should not spend the money any way I chose. It was my money, and it was a reward for my activity of the past winter. I said I could not understand why I should have been rewarded for having been dilatory about my jobs and having created only trouble.

10 Gurdjieff laughed again and told me that I had much to learn.

11 "What you not understand," he said, "is that not everyone can be trouble-maker, like you. This important in life—is ingredient, like yeast for making bread. Without trouble, conflict, life become dead. People live in status-quo, live only by habit, automatically, and without conscience. You good for Miss Madison. You irritate Miss Madison all time—more than anyone else, which is why you get most reward. Without you, possibility for Miss Madison's conscience fall asleep. This money should really be reward from Miss Madison, not from me. You help keep Miss Madison alive."

12 I understood the actual, serious sense in which he meant what he was saying, but I said that I felt sorry for Miss Madison, that it must have been a terrible experience for her when she saw us all receiving those rewards.

13 He shook his head at me, still laughing. "You not see or understand important thing that happen to Miss Madison when give money.

How you feel at time? You feel pity for Miss Madison, no? All other people also feel pity for Miss Madison, too."

14 I agreed that this was so.

15 "People not understand about learning," he went on. "Think necessary talk all time, that learn through mind, through words. Not so. Many things can only learn with feeling, even from sensation. But because man talk all time—use only formulatory centre—people not understand this. What you not see other night in study-house is that Miss Madison have new experience for her. Is poor woman, people not like, people think she funny—they laugh at. But other night, people not laugh. True, Miss Madison feel uncomfortable, feel embarrassed when I give money, feel shame perhaps. But when many people also feel for her sympathy, pity, compassion, even love, she understand this but not right away with mind. She feel, for first time in life, sympathy from many people. She not even know then that she feel this, but her life change; with you, I use you like example, last summer you hate Miss Madison. Now you not hate, you not think funny, you feel sorry. You even like Miss Madison. This good for her even if she not know right away—you will show; you cannot hide this from her, even if wish, cannot hide. So she now have friend, when used to be enemy. This good thing which I do for Miss Madison. I not concerned she understand this now—someday she understand and make her feel warm in heart. This unusual experience—this warm feeling—for such personality as Miss Madison who not have charm, who not friendly in self. Someday, perhaps even soon, she have good feeling because many people feel sorry, feel compassion for her. Someday she even understand what I do and even like me for this. But this kind learning take long time."

16 I understood him completely and was very moved by his words. But he had not finished.

17 "Also good thing for you in this," he said. "You young, only boy still, you not care about other people, care for self. I do this to Miss Madison and you think I do bad thing. You feel sorry, you not forget, you think I do bad thing to her. But now you understand not so. Also, good for you, because you feel about other person—you identify with Miss Madison, put self in her place, also regret what you do. Is necessary put self in place of other person if wish understand and help. This good for your conscience, this way is possibility for you learn not hate Miss Madison. All people same—stupid, blind, human. If I do bad thing, this make you learn love other people, not just self."

✧ *Evaluating the Text*

1. How did Gurdjieff's seemingly arbitrary allotment of rewards violate conventional expectations?

2. What consequences did this have in changing Peters's view of Miss Madison?

3. How does Peters's description of the elaborate ritual Gurdjieff follows in doling out rewards and punishments add to the suspense of the narrative?

✧ *Exploring Different Perspectives*

1. How do both Gurdjieff in Peters's essay and Patricia Hampl's grandmother (see "Grandmother's Sunday Dinner") help the narrators learn something important about themselves?

2. What role do mentors and lessons learned play in Peters's account and in Joe Bageant's memoir?

✧ *Extending Viewpoints through Writing and Research*

1. What personal experiences have you had that forced you to completely reevaluate your attitude toward another person or group?

2. For more information about G. I. Gurdjieff, you might read *Meetings with Remarkable Men* (1963) and compare the way Gurdjieff presents himself in that book with the way Fritz Peters describes him.

Psychology Today

Plight of the Little Emperors

The July 2008 issue of Psychology Today *addresses the consequences of China's population management program that encourages couples to marry late and have only one child. Faced with a staggering doubling of the population during Mao Tse-tung's rule, China, the world's most populous country, has, for the most part, adhered to this one-child policy for urban dwellers while allowing rural couples two children.*

Before You Read

How has the stress and competition of having to succeed in college influenced you?

1 When Dawei Liu was growing up in the coastal city of Tai'an during the 1990s, all of his classmates—95 percent of whom were only children—received plenty of doting parental support. One student, however, truly stood out from the rest. Every day, this boy went from class to class with an entourage of one: his mother, who had given up the income of her day job to monitor his studies full-time, sitting beside him constantly in order to ensure perfect attention. "The teacher was OK with it," Liu shrugs. "He might not focus as much on class if his parent wasn't there."

2 Across China, stories of parents going to incredible lengths to give their only children a competitive edge have become commonplace. Throughout Jing Zhang's youth in Beijing, her parents took her to weekly résumé-boosting painting classes, waiting outside the school building for two hours each time, even in winter. Yanming Lin enjoyed perfect silence in her family's one-room Shanghai apartment throughout her five-plus hours of nightly homework; besides nixing the television, her mother kept perpetual watch over her to make sure she stayed on task. "By high school, my parents knew I could control myself and only do homework," Lin says. "Because I knew the situation."

3 The situation for urban young people in today's China, from preschoolers on up, is this: Your entire future hinges on one test, the national college entrance exam—China's magnified version of the SAT. The Chinese call it *gao kao,* or "tall test," because it looms so large. If students do well, they win spots at China's top universities and an easy route to a middle-class lifestyle. If not, they must confront the

kind of tough, blue-collar lives their parents faced. With such high stakes, families dedicate themselves to their child's test prep virtually from infancy. "Many people come home to have dinner and then study until bed," says Liu. "You have to do it to go to the best university and get a good job. You must do this to live."

4 When China began limiting couples to one child 30 years ago, the policy's most obvious goal was to contain a mushrooming population. For the Chinese people, however, the policy's greater purpose was to turn out a group of young elites who would each enjoy the undivided resources of their whole family—the so-called *xiao huangdi,* or "little emperors." The plan was to "produce a generation of high-quality children to facilitate China's introduction as a global power," explains Susan Greenhalgh, an expert on the policy. But while these well-educated, driven achievers are fueling the nation's economic boom, their generation has become too modern too quickly, glutted as it is with televisions, access to computers, cash to buy name brands, and the same expectations of middle-class success as Western kids.

5 The shift in temperament has happened too fast for society to handle. China is still a developing nation with limited opportunity, leaving millions of ambitious little emperors out in the cold; the country now churns out more than 4 million university graduates yearly, but only 1.6 million new college-level jobs. Even the strivers end up as security guards. China may be the world's next great superpower, but it's facing a looming crisis as millions of overpressurized, hyper-educated only children come of age in a nation that can't fulfill their expectations.

6 This culture of pressure and frustration has sparked a mental-health crisis for young Chinese. Many simmer in depression or unemployment, unwilling to take jobs they consider beneath them. Millions, afraid to face the real world, escape into video games, which the government considers a national epidemic. And a disturbing number decide to end it all; suicide is now China's leading cause of death for those aged 20 to 35. "People in China—especially parents and college students—are suddenly becoming aware of huge depression and anxiety problems in young people," says Yu Zeng, a 23-year-old from Sichuan province. "The media report on new campus suicides all the time."

7 "In this generation, every child is raised to be at the top," says Vanessa Fong, a Harvard education professor and author of *Only Hope: Coming of Age under China's One-Child Policy*. "They've worked hard for it, and it's what their parents have focused their lives on. But the problem is that the country can't provide the lifestyle they feel they deserve. Only a few will get it." China's accomplished young elites are celebrated on billboards as the vanguard of the nation, yet they're quickly becoming victims of their own lofty expectations.

8 Bringing up a high-achieving child in a crowded and impoverished city like Hohhot, parents sometimes have to get creative. Since the government issued minuscule rations of milk, for instance, Yu Wang's parents scraped together the money to buy a sheep and kept it with relatives outside the city. Every day, Wang's father cycled 40 minutes to fetch fresh milk for his son. Out of his parents' meager monthly salary of 45 RMB (about $6), 35 RMB went to Wang's education—including a packed slate of piano, painting, guitar, and even dancing classes.

9 The pressure to succeed was all the greater given that his parents' own dreams had been dashed during China's Cultural Revolution, when Mao Zedong closed schools and sent difficult-to-control intellectuals to be "reeducated" by working the fields. Wang's father spent eight years herding goats. His own dreams destroyed, he poured all his hopes and ambitions into his son. "Because of the Cultural Revolution, my parents literally wasted 10 years," explains Wang, 29, who was among the first Chinese only kids born under the one-child policy. "I was explicitly told that they had lost a lot in their lives, so they wanted me to get it back for them."

10 In recent years, however, Chinese parents have sometimes blurred the line between sacrifice and slavery in aiding their child's success: Mothers carry their child's backpack around; couples forgo lunch so their kid can have plentiful snacks or new Nikes. Vanessa Fong recalls meeting one mother who resisted hospitalization for her heart and kidney troubles because she feared it might interfere with her daughter's *gao kao* preparation; when Fong gave the mother money for medication, it mostly went to expensive food for her daughter.

11 Parents go to such lengths in part because Chinese culture has always emphasized success, but also for a more pressing reason: Traditionally, children support their parents in old age. With only one child to carry the load, parents' fortunes are tied to their child's, and they push (and pamper) the little ones accordingly. "In China, the term for a one-child family is a 'risky family,'" says Baochang Gu, a demography professor at Beijing's Renmin University who advises the Chinese government on the one-child policy. "If something happened to that child, it would be a disaster. So from the parents' point of view, the spoiling is all necessary to protect them."

12 Since the policy's inception, the Chinese have worried that the extreme combination of discipline and indulgence would result in maladjusted kids, self-centered brats who can't take criticism and don't understand sharing. Asked if he wished he'd had siblings, one 22-year-old from Sichuan province replied, "Does this mean everything I have would have to be cut in half or shared? No, I don't want that."

13 Yet despite the stereotype, the research has revealed no evidence that only kids have more negative traits than their peers with siblings—in

China or anywhere else. "The only way only children are reliably different from others is they score slightly higher in academic achievement," explains Toni Falbo, a University of Texas psychology professor who has gathered data on more than 4,000 Chinese only kids. Sure, some little emperors are bratty, but no more than children with siblings.

14 This isn't to say Chinese only kids are pictures of mental health—it's just that their psychological issues stem not from a lack of siblings but from the harsh academic competition and parental prodding that pervade their lives. Susan Newman, a New Jersey psychologist and only-child expert, says the notion that little emperors are bossy, self-obsessed little brats is simply part of the greater myth of only kids as damaged goods. "Pinning their problems on having no siblings is really making them a scapegoat," she says. Being an only child is not the problem.

15 Chinese parents bemoan their only child's desire for instant gratification, excessive consumption, and a life free of hardship, but such complaints are just proof that the policy worked: The children are like little Americans. "These kids have the same dreams as all middle-class kids: to go to college, to get white-collar jobs, to own their own home, to have Nikes and name brands," says Fong. "They expect things that are normal in developed countries, but by China's standards, are unheard of."

16 Yu Zeng remembers hearing of the first suicide at his school in 2005, when he was a junior at Sichuan University. By the next year, three more of his classmates had leapt to their deaths from campus buildings, and Zeng noticed a wave of news stories about suicides—all of them for a similar, perplexing reason. "It was after they got a bad grade on a test," Zeng says. "They think to die is better than to have that bad mark."

17 In the pressurized world of Chinese academics, any setback can seem fatal. Last January, for example, one 17-year-old Beijing girl tried to kill herself after learning that a paperwork snafu might prevent her from registering for the *gao kao*. Suicide has become China's fifth most common cause of death overall, with young urban intellectuals at highest risk. A study by the Society Survey Institute of China concluded that over 25 percent of university students have had suicidal thoughts, compared to 6 percent in the United States.

18 The number of Chinese college graduates per year has nearly tripled in the last half-decade—from 1.5 million in 2002 to 4.1 million in 2007—which means more than 2 million grads a year end up with expensive diplomas, but no job. With so few top positions available and so many seekers, urban only children must study constantly just to have a shot. Out of Yanming Lin's five hours of schoolwork per night, four hours went to "voluntary" homework designed to boost test scores. "That one grade becomes the only standard to justify you as a

person," says Zeng. "If you have a good personality or maybe you're good in math but not Chinese, all of that is your downfall, because it's all about your grade."

19 The extra homework is not required by the teacher, explains Lin. "But all the other students do the extra homework, so if you do not do it you will lag behind." At one top Beijing kindergarten, students must know pi to 100 digits by age 3.

20 Many young only children opt for escape from reality through online gaming worlds. Every day, the nation's 113,000 Internet cafes teem with twitchy, solitary players—high school and university students, dropouts, and unemployed graduates—an alarming number of whom remain in place for days without food or sleep. Official estimates put the number of Chinese Internet addicts at over 2 million, and the government considers it such a serious threat that it deploys volunteer groups to prowl the streets and prevent teens from entering Internet cafes.

21 The mostly male youth who turn to virtual realms find there a place to realize ambitions that are frustrated in real life, says Kimberly Young, a psychologist and Internet addiction expert who has advised Chinese therapists. "With the click of a button, they go from a 19-year-old with no social life to a great warrior in World of Warcraft," Young says. "Why bother doing things in the real world when they can be in this game and be fulfilled?" Burnt-out and overtaxed, even kids who did well on the *gao kao* turn into virtual dropouts, choosing the respite of computer games over the university spots they worked so hard to win. Without a parent to push them, many stop going to class. "In Chinese universities, so many just give up," says Howe, a college student from Chengdu.

22 Faced with bleak prospects, elite only children often don't know how to cope; they've been brought up to do only one thing: succeed. Indeed, in a 2007 survey on stress in young people by the Chinese Internet portal Sina.com, most respondents—56 percent—blamed their misery on the gap between China's developing-world reality and their own high expectations. "They have trouble adjusting to the idea that they're going to be working-class," says Fong.

23 For the frustrated, depressed, and anxious Chinese kids buckling under the constant pressure—the news agency Xinhua estimates there are 30 million Chinese under 17 with significant mental-health problems—finding someone to talk to can be tough. Taught to strive and achieve from an early age, they've never had the time for heart-to-heart chats. "It's not like American universities where you have many friends," says Yu Zeng. "At Chinese universities, you compete for limited resources and everyone is concerned about themselves. And if you wanted to talk to your parents, they wouldn't understand. When they were your age, they were reading Mao's little red book."

Plus, the conversation would be strained even if you did find a sympathetic ear. "In the 20th century, the term 'depression' didn't even exist in China," Toni Falbo says. "It couldn't be talked about because there was no vocabulary for it yet."

24 Nor is professional help readily available. When Mao cracked down on intellectuals during the Cultural Revolution, he decimated the nation's already thin psychological establishment. "Back then, every mental problem was seen as anti-socialist," says Kaiping Peng, a University of California Berkeley professor who was among the first generation of Chinese psychologists to receive formal clinical training, in the late 1970s. "If you were depressed, they thought you were politically impure and sent you to a labor camp." For decades, Chinese psychiatrists dealt exclusively in pills and electroshock, and until recently, China had just a handful of university psychology programs—which is why Peng believes there are only about 2,000 qualified therapists at work there today for a population of 1.3 billion.

25 But as universities work to churn out qualified psychologists and as teens and twentysomethings realize they need more help with their unrealistic expectations than with their grades, Peng grows optimistic. "People in China have more knowledge about mental health today," he says. "Now there are books and popular magazines about it, and the training infrastructure gets better all the time." Cities are also experimenting with crisis hotlines. China's inaugural suicide-prevention line debuted in 2003; it received more than 220,000 calls over its first two years.

26 Meanwhile, Chinese officials are taking steps to ease the pressure on young students. Schools no longer publicly announce each student's exam scores and class rank, for one, and the government is also asking parents to let their precious little emperors actually *play* every once in a while.

27 Besides, all of that studying can only take you so far. "On your resume, you can't put. '1988 to 2001: studied 10 hours every day,'" laughs Howe, the Chengdu student. "You have to actually do stuff."

✧ *Evaluating the Text*

1. How has China's one-child policy resulted in a whole range of pressures for the only child and his or her parents?
2. What measures have some Chinese parents taken in order to increase the chances for their only child's success?
3. In the authors' view, why have some children turned to online gaming and virtual realities as a release from the pressures and stress of their lives?

✧ *Exploring Different Perspectives*

1. How do both the accounts by the editors and K. Oanh Ha emphasize how American-type aspirations have permeated Chinese and Vietnamese cultures?

2. Contrast the different rites of passage that define success in Joe Bageant's world and that of the little emperors in China.

✧ *Extending Viewpoints through Writing and Research*

1. How has the expectation of being successful in school and having a prestigious white-collar job led to the fear of not doing well and having to be working class?

2. In what ways has your experience as a college student reflected some of the same pressures as those experienced by the little emperors?

Firoozeh Dumas

Save Me, Mickey

Firoozeh Dumas was born in 1966 in Iran and came to the United States when her family immigrated to southern California, when she was seven years old. In the following account drawn from Funny in Farsi: A Memoir of Growing Up Iranian in America *(2004), she brings humor to her attempts to assimiliate into American life and transcend stereotypes about the Middle East. In 2008, she wrote* Laughing Without an Accent: Adventures of an Iranian American, At Home and Abroad.

Before You Read

What firsthand experiences of stereotyping have you had or witnessed that reveal the challenges facing immigrants?

1 When we first came to America in 1972, we knew we would be staying only for about two years. This gave us approximately 104 weekends to see everything there was to see in California. From Knott's Berry Farm to Marine World, from the Date Festival to the Garlic Festival, we saw it all. Along the way, we tasted garlic ice cream, date shakes, and cherry slushies, and other foods that we no longer remember, although we do recall the ensuing scrambles to the drugstore for Rolaids.

2 Because we were new to this country, we were impressed not just by the big attractions but also by the little things—smiling employees, clean bathrooms, and clear signage. Our ability to be impressed by the large selection of key chains at the souvenir shops guaranteed that every place we saw delighted us.

3 There was, however, one attraction that stood apart, one whose sweatshirts we wore with pride, one that generated near religious devotion: Disneyland. My father believed that Walt Disney was a genius, a man whose vision allowed everyone, regardless of age, to relive the wonderment of childhood. Ask my father what he considers to be man's greatest creation in the twentieth century and he won't say computers, the Concorde, or knee replacement surgery. For him, "Pirates of the Caribbean" represents the pinnacle of man's creative achievement. No matter how many times my father goes on that ride, he remains as impressed as a Disneyland virgin. "Did you see that pirate leg hanging over the bridge? Could somebody remind me that it wasn't real? And

the battle between the ships, geez, was I the only one ready to duck and cover? What kind of a man would think of creating something like this? A genius, that's who." I doubt that even Walt Disney's mother felt as much pride in her son as my father did.

4 According to my father, any activity that is enjoyed by our family will be exponentially more enjoyable if shared with others. A crowded dinner at his sister's house where only half the guests have chairs is preferred to a meal with four people and ample seating. His tribal nature may result from having grown up with eight siblings, but whatever the root cause, my father decided that if Disneyland was fun for our family, just think how much more fun it would be with twenty other people. That is how one weekend we found ourselves at Disneyland's main entrance with six of my father's Iranian colleagues and their families.

5 I had already been to Disneyland fifteen times and was, frankly, getting a little sick of the place. I knew every turn in every ride and all the punch lines to all the shows. But nonetheless, on yet another Saturday morning, I stood in front of Mr. Toad's Wild Ride with a large group of people, all oohing and aahing, as my father, the self-appointed ambassador to the Magic Kingdom, pointed out fascinating tidbits: "See how people just wait patiently in these long lines? In other countries, you'd have a fight! But not here, this is America."

6 We roamed through Disneyland like a herd of buffalo, stopping only at the rides deemed worthy by my father. At one point, we found ourselves near the telephones where one could talk to Mickey Mouse. As my father was busy explaining the wonders of the nearby Monsanto ride with the big eyeball that looks positively real, I decided to experiment with the phones, which I had somehow never tried before. I picked up the receiver and discovered that there was no conversation with Mickey Mouse on these so-called phones, just a taped message. Disgruntled, I hung up and looked around to find the rest of the herd. They were gone.

7 One of my father's biggest fears in moving to America was child kidnappings. Our hometown, Abadan, was about as safe a place as one could hope for. We knew all the neighbors, everyone looked out for everyone else's kids, and there was basically no crime other than petty theft. Whenever my relatives came to visit us in America, they would watch the evening news a few times, and then refuse to leave the house. "It's too dangerous here," they always said. "Why are there so many shootings?" In Iran, citizens do not have access to guns, so we do not have the types of crimes that so often lead to murders in America. My father was acutely aware of the dangers inherent in our new surroundings and lectured me regularly on the perils of strangers and how I should always go to the police if I ever needed help.

8 There were no police officers in Disneyland, so instead I opted for the young man in the powder blue jumpsuit wearing the hat that resembled an inverted origami boat. "I'm lost," I told him. "Okay," he said in a kind voice. "Can you tell me what your parents look like?" I told him. "Now can you tell me what your parents are wearing?" he asked. No seven-year-old, except maybe a young Giorgio Armani, could tell you what his parents were wearing on a given day.

9 After my failure to answer the clothing question, Mr. Polyester escorted me to a small building near the main entrance. This was the Lost and Found, a place that, not surprisingly, I had never noticed during my previous visits. Once I entered the room, I started to cry. Several women surrounded me and asked me my name, which I, in the midst of my mucus-choked sobs, had to repeat several times. "What kind of a name is that?" one of them asked. It was as if I was doomed to answer the same questions over and over again, for the rest of my life.

10 "I'm from Iran," I sniffled.

11 "How nice," she said. From the look on her face, I could tell she had no idea where that was. Another one complimented me on my English. Then they told me not to worry. I could just sit down here and color while I waited for my parents to come and get me. I continued to cry. The three women tried to comfort me, but by then I had decided to cry the whole time.

12 A few minutes later, the door opened and in came a screaming boy who looked to be a few years younger than I. As Team Comfort rushed to his side, it became apparent that this boy spoke no English. No matter what the women said to him, he just screamed. When asked his name, he shook his head and cried louder. In desperation, one of the employees turned around and started walking toward me with a big I-have-a-great-idea smile on her face. I knew what was coming. "Is that boy from your country?" she asked me. "Why, yes," I wanted to tell her. "In my country, which I own, this is National Lose Your Child at Disneyland Day."

13 "No," I told her. "He's not from my country." I had no idea where the screamer was from, but I knew he wasn't Iranian. A gerbil would never mistake a hamster for a gerbil, and I would never mistake a non-Iranian for an Iranian. Despite the belief of most Westerners that all Middle Easterners look alike, we can pick each other out of a crowd as easily as my Japanese friends pick out their own from a crowd of Asians. It's like we have a certain radio frequency that only other Iranian radars pick up.

14 After a few futile attempts to communicate with the boy, another one of the women came to me and asked me if I could please, in my language, ask that boy his name. I told her that I spoke Persian and I was certain that the boy did not. The woman then knelt down and got real

close to my face, skills picked up during Coercion 101. Speaking very slowly, she told me that she needed me to do her a favor. I could tell she was trying to remember my name. She was thinking hard. "Sweetie," she finally said, choosing to sidestep the name like a soldier avoiding a land mine, "could you just *try* to talk to him? Will you do it for Mickey?"

15 I wanted to tell her that Mickey was the reason I was lost in the first place. Had I not been trying to talk to him on those so-called phones, I wouldn't be sitting here. I didn't owe that rodent anything.

16 I once again told her that I spoke Persian and I could just tell that the boy did not. "Could you just try?" she pleaded.

17 Just to get rid of her, I walked up to the boy, who, breaking all stamina records, was still crying, and said in Persian, "Are you Iranian?" The boy stopped crying for a moment, then let out the loudest scream heard since biblical times. Not only was he separated from his loved ones, he was now trapped in the Tower of Babel.

18 Although I was sorry for the little boy, I also felt vindicated. I went back to my coloring book, no longer feeling the urge to cry. I colored a few pages; then, lo and behold, in walked my father, looking completely panicked and breathless. He ran and hugged me and asked me whether I had cried. "Of course not," I answered. He told me that I had gotten lost just when the group split in two, so an hour went by before anyone noticed I was missing. "I thought you had been kidnapped," he told me, still out of breath. Timing is key, and I knew this was my moment. "Could we go to the gift shop?" I asked. "Anything you want," he said, "anything at all."

19 We had to leave Disneyland early that day because my father was too weak in the knees to continue. Even the thought of "Pirates of the Caribbean" could not revive him.

20 We spent the usual half hour looking for our car in the parking lot. I clutched closely two helium balloons, items my father prior to this visit had always called a waste of money and never bought for me, a two-foot-long pencil with scenes from Disneyland, a complete set of miniature plastic Seven Dwarves with their own carrying case, and a Winnie-the-Pooh pencil holder. In the midst of my father's newfound appreciation for me, I also asked him if he would take me to the Movieland Wax Museum the following week. "Sure," he said. "Anything you want."

21 My father spent the drive home re-creating my actions in his absence.

22 "So how did you know for sure you were lost?" he asked.

23 "I couldn't see you guys," I answered.

24 "How did you know whom to go to?" he continued.

25 "I looked for someone who worked there."

26 "How did you know he worked there and he wasn't just standing around looking for lost kids?"

27 "He had the same outfit as the other six people around him and he had a name tag."

28 "A name tag, huh? Very clever."

29 I knew what he was thinking. Thanks to Mickey, I had been elevated from child-who-can't-learn-to-swim to child genius.

30 The following weekend, standing in the Movieland Wax Museum gift shop, I was having a hard time deciding among the visor, the inflatable mini pool with the museum logo, and the deck of cards emblazoned with four different movie stars. Then I heard my father utter the magic phrase "Why don't we just get all of them?" "Good idea," I said, hoping his newly generous view of useless purchases was more than a passing phase.

31 We left the gift shop with my father holding firmly on to my hand, just as he had done the entire day. Clutching my purchases with my other hand, I basked in my new status as favorite child. Perhaps I did owe that rodent something.

✧ *Evaluating the Text*

1. How did Dumas's father's fondest hopes and worst fears come to pass when he and his family went to Disneyland?
2. How did Dumas's experience at the lost and found reveal the way Americans look at all Middle Easterners?
3. What rewards does Dumas ensure for herself from her father?

✧ *Exploring Different Perspectives*

1. Compare the different pictures Dumas and K. Oanh Ha (see Chapter 4) present of their respective fathers.
2. Contrast Dumas's experience as a child from Iran living in the United States with those of the only children in China, as discussed in "Plight of the Little Emperors."

✧ *Extending Viewpoints through Writing and Research*

1. If you or anyone you know has had the experience of getting lost, compare it with Dumas's.
2. What particular place or activity symbolizes success to you, your parents, or friends in the way that Disneyland did for Dumas's father?

Patricia Hampl

Grandmother's Sunday Dinner

Patricia Hampl was born in 1946 in St. Paul, Minnesota. She graduated from the University of Minnesota and studied at the Iowa Writer's Workshop. Hampl has often written about her Czech heritage, a theme that emerges in the following autobiographical essay from her book A Romantic Education *(1981). A recent work is* The Florist's Daughter *(2007).*

Before You Read

What vivid memory do you have of a family gathering in which food played an important role?

1 Food was the potent center of my grandmother's life. Maybe the immense amount of time it took to prepare meals during most of her life accounted for her passion. Or it may have been her years of work in various kitchens on the hill and later, in the house of Justice Butler: after all, she was a professional. Much later, when she was dead and I went to Prague, I came to feel the motto I knew her by best—*Come eat*—was not, after all, a personal statement, but a racial one, the *cri de coeur* of Middle Europe.

2 Often, on Sundays, the entire family gathered for dinner at her house. Dinner was 1 P.M. My grandmother would have preferred the meal to be at the old time of noon, but her children had moved their own Sunday dinner hour to the more fashionable (it was felt) 4 o'clock, so she compromised. Sunday breakfast was something my mother liked to do in a big way, so we arrived at my grandmother's hardly out of the reverie of waffles and orange rolls, before we were propped like rag dolls in front of a pork roast and sauerkraut, dumplings, hot buttered carrots, rye bread and rollikey, pickles and olives, apple pie and ice cream. And coffee.

3 Coffee was a food in that house, not a drink. I always begged for some because the magical man on the Hills Brothers can with his turban and long robe scattered with stars and his gold slippers with pointed toes, looked deeply happy as he drank from his bowl. The bowl itself reminded me of soup, Campbell's chicken noodle soup, my favorite food. The distinct adultness of coffee and the robed man with

his deep-drinking pleasure made it clear why the grownups lingered so long at the table. The uncles smoked cigars then, and the aunts said, "Oh, those cigars."

4 My grandmother, when she served dinner, was a virtuoso hanging on the edge of her own ecstatic performance. She seemed dissatisfied, almost querulous until she had corralled everybody into their chairs around the table, which she tried to do the minute they got into the house. No cocktails, no hors d'oeuvres (pronounced, by some of the family, "horse's ovaries"), just business. She was a little power crazed: she had us and, by God, we were going to eat. She went about it like a goose breeder forcing pellets down the gullets of those dumb birds.

5 She flew between her chair and the kitchen, always finding more this, extra that. She'd given you the *wrong* chicken breast the first time around; now she'd found the *right* one: eat it too, eat it fast, because after the chicken comes the rhubarb pie. Rhubarb pie with a thick slice of cheddar cheese that it was imperative every single person eat.

6 We had to eat fast because something was always out there in the kitchen panting and charging the gate, champing at the bit, some mound of rice or a Jell-O fruit salad or vegetable casserole or pie was out there, waiting to be let loose into the dining room.

7 She had the usual trite routines: the wheedlings, the silent pout ("What! You don't like my brussels sprouts? I thought you liked *my* brussels sprouts," versus your wife's/sister's/mother's. "I made that pie just for you," etc., etc.). But it was the way she tossed around the old clichés and the overused routines, mixing them up and dealing them out shamelessly, without irony, that made her a pro. She tended to peck at her own dinner. Her plate, piled with food, was a kind of stage prop, a mere bending to convention. She liked to eat, she was even a greedy little stuffer, but not on these occasions. She was a woman possessed by an idea, given over wholly to some phantasmagoria of food, a mirage of stuffing, a world where the endless chicken and the infinite lemon pie were united at last at the shore of the oceanic soup plate that her children and her children's children alone could drain . . . if only they would try.

8 She was there to bolster morale, to lead the troops, to give the sharp command should we falter on the way. The futility of saying no was supreme, and no one ever tried it. How could a son-in-law, already weakened near the point of imbecility by the once, twice, thrice charge to the barricades of pork and mashed potato, be expected to gather his feeble wit long enough to ignore the final call of his old commander when she sounded the alarm: "Pie, Fred?"

9 Just when it seemed as if the food-crazed world she had created was going to burst, that she had whipped and frothed us like a sack of boiled potatoes under her masher, just then she pulled it all together in one easeful stroke like the pro she was.

10 She stood in the kitchen doorway, her little round Napoleonic self sheathed in a cotton flowered pinafore apron, the table draped in its white lace cloth but spotted now with gravy and beet juice, the troops mumbling indistinctly as they waited at their posts for they knew not what. We looked up at her stupidly, weakly. She said nonchalantly, "Anyone want another piece of pie?" No, no more pie, somebody said. The rest of the rabble grunted along with him. She stood there with the coffeepot and laughed and said, "Good! Because there *isn't* any more pie."

11 No more pie. We'd eaten it all, we'd put away everything in that kitchen. We were exhausted and she, gambler hostess that she was (but it was her house she was playing), knew she could offer what didn't exist, knew us, knew what she'd wrought. There was a sense of her having won, won something. There were no divisions among us now, no adults, no children. Power left the second and third generations and returned to the source, the grandmother who reduced us to mutters by her art.

12 That wasn't the end of it. At 5 P.M. there was "lunch"—sandwiches and beer; the sandwiches were made from the left-overs (mysteriously renewable resources, those roasts). And at about 8 P.M. we were at the table again for coffee cake and coffee, the little man in his turban and his coffee ecstasy and his pointed shoes set on the kitchen table as my grandmother scooped out the coffee and dumped it into a big enamel pot with a crushed eggshell. By then everyone was alive and laughing again, the torpor gone. My grandfather had been inviting the men, one by one, into the kitchen during the afternoon where he silently (the austere version of memory—but he must have talked, must have said *something*) handed them jiggers of whiskey, and watched them put the shot down in one swallow. Then he handed them a beer, which they took out in the living room. I gathered that the *little* drink in the tiny glass shaped like a beer mug was some sort of antidote for the *big* drink of beer. He sat on the chair in the kitchen with a bottle of beer on the floor next to him and played his concertina, allowing society to form itself around him—while he lived he was the center—but not seeking it, not going into the living room. And not talking. He held to his music and the kindly, medicinal administration of whiskey.

13 By evening, it seemed we could eat endlessly, as if we'd had some successful inoculation at dinner and could handle anything. I stayed in the kitchen after they all reformed in the dining room at the table for coffee cake. I could hear them, but the little man in his starry yellow robe was on the table in the kitchen and I put my head down on the oil cloth very near the curled and delighted tips of his pointed shoes, and I slept. Whatever laughter there was, there was. But something sweet and starry was in the kitchen and I lay down beside it, my stomach

full, warm, so safe I'll live the rest of my life off the fat of that vast family security.

✧ *Evaluating the Text*

1. What picture emerges of Hampl's grandmother in the way she prepared and served dinner?
2. What metaphors or similes does Hampl use to communicate aspects of her grandmother's personality?
3. How does the grandmother use guilt to make sure that all the food she made would get eaten?

✧ *Exploring Different Perspectives*

1. Compare Hampl's grandmother's use of food to manipulate her family with the methods used by Gurdjieff to teach Peters an important life lesson.
2. How do both Hampl and Dumas use humor and irony to enhance their narratives?

✧ *Extending Viewpoints through Writing and Research*

1. Describe a memorable family dinner you attended and use vivid images to evoke the sounds, smells, tastes, sights, and feelings connected with this meal.
2. Research and report on the kinds of foods customarily prepared for holiday celebrations in various cultures.

Meeta Kaur

Journey by Inner Light

Meeta Kaur earned an M.F.A. from Mills College in Creative Writing and was awarded a 2006 Hedgebrook Writing Residency. In the following essay, first published in Homelands: Women's Journeys Across Race, Place, and Time *(2006), Kaur tells us about her decision to have her hair cut and the upheaval that resulted in her traditional Sikh family.*

Before You Read

Have you ever rebelled against a traditional religious custom? If so, what were the results?

1 It's naptime and my mother's hair becomes a world of my own. Mama unpins her bun and lets her hair fall, rushing down her back. She combs through any tangles with her fingers. Her long, shampooed tresses are thick pieces of rose-smelling silk. Her shiny hair is black pashmina, an endless journey toward the heart of a dark sky. I lie perpendicular to the length of the bed, on top of tangerine and gold embroidered pillows, flexing my feet and wiggling my toes. Mama lies down next to me. I proceed to thread her locks from the crown of her head through my big and second toes. Her hair fans out like a thousand silk threads suspended in air. Nestling both of my feet into the nape of her neck, I doze off warm, happy, and safe. I wake up to my mother combing out the knots. My father is coming home soon. I am only five years old, but somehow I know I will live my life joyfully. Mama is my light. She is home.

2 Mama teaches me how to take care of my hair during hair-bath days on Saturday mornings. I sit in our white ceramic tub waiting for my shampoo to commence. When the water reaches my waist, I crouch forward and push myself off the front of the tub. I sink under, and under is where I stay. The waves ripple over me as I hold my breath—*one Mississippi, two Mississippi, three Mississippi, four Mississippi.* I release tiny air bubbles with two seconds in between rounds and watch them float to the surface, then hover and pop.

3 "Meeta, *beti,* please get up so I can wash your hair." My mother places a plastic cream-colored stool next to the tub and squats down with her knees bumping up against the tub's side.

4 I surface, a humpback whale disrupted from its southern migration. Mama's fingers sink into my scalp as she begins a relaxed massage.

5 "Close your eyes, *urrahhh,* close your eyes so it will not sting you." Mama piles the strands of hair atop my head and squeezes out more shampoo. She beams as she sculpts my hair into a temple. I tilt my head back for the rinse. The weight of the shampoo washes away, leaving me light as a feather. She towel-dries my hair and draws a line down the middle of my head with a comb. She combs each section of my hair the way she combs her own—carefully, patiently. Mama's slow hands tell me how much respect she gives my body and me. At school, I romp with fluffy, tangle-free hair through recess.

6 As a child, I never question why all of my family members have long thick hair—we just do. It is a natural extension of who we are. I do not realize until later that hair-bath days only exist in our family household, and that the brothers and fathers in other American families do not have long hair.

7 My mother silently declares an allegiance to a homeland that is rooted from our heads and connected to our hearts. As a Sikh woman who migrated from India to America, she carries the strength and solace of spirituality in her hair. It is a light that provides a sense of place and home between any borders, on any soil, whether she is in India, America, or any other country. Although I didn't realize it then, my mother has been stoking the same guiding light in me since my childhood—a light that shows me the illuminating life that extends through my thoughts, out of my head, into my hair, and into the world, a light that shows me the path to who I am becoming, a light that sparks with subconscious knowledge and holds a steady glow.

8 When I am older, in middle school, Mom sends me on solo trips to India during summer breaks. My first trip alone leaves me jet-lagged and anxiously awake in the deep Indian nights. After riding the Shatabdi train from the Bombay airport to Poona, Jeeti Masi and Uncle Ji greet and escort me to their home. Their daughter and my cousin, Baby, is married and has moved away to live with her husband and in-laws in Hyderabad. In her dusty pink-and-bronze room, the night's cool breeze chases the day's humidity out of the room through the half-opened windows. I sit up on the bed not knowing what to do. I slink downstairs and head for the front door and quietly unlock the steel bolt to step outside. I step toward the custard apple tree in the lawn and pick one off. It looks like it has been glazed with green bottle glass. I carry it back upstairs, set it on the wooden nightstand, and wait for sleep to arrive.

9 The next day, jet lag leaves me drowsy on the velvet maroon sitting room sofa with a set of my cousin's old comic books. They are bent at

the corners and have broken spines. They tell the spiritual stories of the ten Sikh Gurus, divine mortals sent as teachers to deliver the wisdom of a new faith, Sikhism. As I read, I travel back in time to the 16th-century Indian subcontinent. Mogul soldiers threaten Hindus to convert to Islam or suffer death. The ninth Sikh Guru, Tegh Bahadur, dons a navy blue turban and a golden robe and has a long silky beard. He states, "All people have a right to practice their own religion."

10 The Mogul leader sarcastically responds, "If you are so interested in defending these people, are you willing to die for them?"

11 In the next scene, Guru Tegh Bahadur is beheaded by a Mogul soldier. Another comic book illustrates the story of Mai Bhago, a great Sikh woman warrior who challenged forty deserters of the Sikh army to return to their posts and fight on behalf of Guru Gobind Singh Ji, the tenth Guru, against the Muslims and the hill chiefs to protect the principles of the faith.

12 As I read the comics, I realize that if there are no people standing at the end of these battles, there will be no principles, because they live within the people. The need to live with dignity and freedom becomes greater than the need to just live. To me, the sacrifices these Gurus made for future generations seem fantastical and out of this world, but in reality the Gurus had compiled scriptures that captured their direct conversations with God, the enlightenment that centered on equality while also drawing from the most progressive Hindu and Muslim tenets to create a just society. On the comic page, the Gurus wear regal turbans that protect their hair. Their long black beards flow freely. They look different from everyone else. I am familiar with the way they look because they remind me of my family, but I also see that they are different. *We* are different.

13 I spend the next two days reading through all one hundred comic books. I learn that my hair is referred to as *kesh*. My *kesh* represents an outward identity I can choose to preserve as a Sikh woman.

14 The comic books fill me with information and history. I learn, in preserving this natural uniform, that I commit to the equality between men and women, rich and poor, black and white, Muslim and Christian. *Kesh* is a commitment to a loving state of mind, to self-control, to faith in humanity, and to the protection of individual and communal rights. Through daily meditations; a commitment to just thought, speech, and action; and a faith in the supreme force, a Sikh can reach a state of rapture here on earth. A Sikh can live in utter bliss while serving humanity. What amazes me is the capacity to care enough to protect the rights of people who I disagree with or who are intolerant of me.

15 I have a hard time developing the discipline it takes to fulfill the destiny that is laid out for me. To me, these spiritual prophets are political ideologues. I dismiss their faith as jargon. I do not see it, cannot

feel it, and have no evidence of it existing around me, so I follow my pleasures and passions as a young adolescent American girl who has bought into the illusions of this world: standardized beauty, romantic love, and the power of money. I want the attention of friends. I want the attention of boys. I want to be picture-perfect stepping out of the swimming pool with styled hair. I want to swoon with my classmates over our class pictures, squealing in delight about how cute we look. I want to date Rick Springfield. But all of this is not going to happen with all of this long, frizzy hair. I think to myself, *Maybe if I imitate my classmates' hairstyles—Stephanie's bangs, or Laura's bouncy blond bob, or Mindy's perm—I'll have a chance.*

16 In my freshman dorm at the University of California at Davis, I am surrounded by young women fawning over their tresses all day and night. Deep conditioners, natural dying, wave relaxers, and mousse are must-have products. Fraternity parties, house parties, and international parties call for one- to two-hour sessions in front of the mirror. But my choices are limited: a ponytail or pigtails, wearing it down with a part in the middle or to the side, a tight or loose bun. Okay, there are choices, but something about my hair feels stale, like old bread. It is ancient, musty, and tired.

17 In my hair, my mother, aunt, and grandmother nest with their stories, their histories, and their spirits. They sit on my head waiting for me to hatch into a woman who makes a difference in the world, who makes a habit of acting fearless in moments that demand it. The women in my family believe that my hair will purify my thoughts. They believe I can expand my thinking with my hair; all the positive energy in the world will be transmitted to me through my hair. Midnight tresses are rolled up into buns at the napes of my mother's, aunts', and cousins' necks. My grandmother wraps her salt-and-pepper hair into an acorn of a bun, nesting her love for God and her ancestors' heritage into her hair.

18 But I am convinced that this is not for me. I am convinced that I belong to the world and the world is a better source of authority for me. The distance between my parents and me grows with fewer conversations and an ocean of misunderstanding. I am in America and I want to be American. I decide it is time to push forward with something new—defined by me—something I can call my own.

19 I step into Select Cut Salons on Fourth and C Streets in downtown Davis. I am convinced that this decision will alter who I am and carve out an entry into my real life, a life waiting to be defined. Inside the salon, peroxide mingles with the receptionist's cigarette smoke.

20 "Who are you here to see?" The receptionist smashes her cigarette into the ashtray and scans the appointment book. Her sandy blond hair is cut like that of a choirboy who does not own a comb.

21 "I'm here to see Tiffany for a hairstyle, umm, a haircut," I tell her. *It is no big deal,* I try to convince myself. *Everyone gets haircuts. Relax.*

22 "Tiffany, your four o'clock is here!"

23 Tiffany greets and ushers me over to a hot-pink leather chair that competes with the black-and-white checkered floor. Cotton-candy-colored vanity lights line the individual station mirrors. The spritzers, mousse, hair relaxing serums, and alcohol-free finishing-hold sprays confirm that hair care is a commitment that cannot be taken lightly.

24 Tiffany lifts my thick braid of hair over my head and lets it drop. Her hands are careless, unlike Mama's.

25 "Wow, what thick and curly hair you have." For Tiffany, my long rope of a braid is just hair, humdrum strands hanging out of my head. "Okay, so do you have any ideas?" she asks.

26 Her clumsiness makes my heart pound faster. I feel my hands quivering, so I sit on top of them and attempt to look genuinely interested. I scan the top of the mirrors for all the European cuts: pageboys, what looks like a Cleopatra cut, and simple unassuming bobs. It's exciting to think about how I might change, but something keeps grabbing at me, telling me to leave this place, to just get out of here. But I won't. My head pounds, weighing heavier and heavier as I take in all the pictures. I survey Tiffany's red, curly, turn-up-the-volume hair. It hangs an inch off of her shoulders. I have to answer her, but I don't want my hair to look like hers. "Umm . . . a bob looks nice, or maybe a Cleopatra cut, or . . . I don't know. What's the difference? Just cut it."

27 Tiffany's eyes widen and her eyebrows bob up and down looking like she is going to skip the *Are you sure?* or *Wanna think about it?*

28 My heart is thumping, and I see the entire Sikh army falling off their horses as they ride into battle—sliding off cliff edges, pierced by arrows, and losing control of their purpose, their direction. *Just shake it off,* I tell myself, *It is just a head of hair, and everyone gets a haircut.* Well, everyone except for Sikhs, Rastafarians, some Native American tribes—and my *entire* living family. Maybe I'm not a Sikh, or don't have what it takes to be one. I am the weakest link. I'm the soldier falling behind, barely able to carry my backpack, late for daily prayers. I'm the one who cannot get my act together, so what does it matter?

29 Tiffany's steel blades skim my neck. She struggles to cut off a lifetime of hair in one snip; it will have to be severed off, decapitated. Half of my braid is disembodied from the back of my skull. I close my eyes and wait for it to be over.

30 "There you go, hon," Tiffany says, holding my thick braid in her hand like a dead animal, "I'll put it in a bag for you so you have a souvenir to remember it by." When Tiffany hands me the bag with my braid, I gingerly set it on the floor. I hear her mumbling something about styling my new hairdo, but my mind is somewhere else.

31 *I really did it. What did I do?*

32 Tiffany uses smaller scissors to "style" my hair. Her glossy lips smack together as she talks, but I can't make out a single word of what she's saying until she's finished with the scissors.

33 "Okay! A quick blow dry and we are finitzio."

34 She blow-dries my hair and asks me to do a quick flip of my head. I see myself in the mirror with tussled hair surrounding my face. I had expected something different. I thought it would be different.

35 Later, I get together with my roommate, Martha. She holds her hands to her mouth when she sees me. She looks like she is going to puke.

36 "Oh my God! You look so cuuuuuute!" *Cute?* I am empty, cold. I run my fingers across the shaved patch on the back of my neck and wonder about this cycle of growing out my hair, cutting it again, growing it out again. What purpose does this serve? Fashion?

37 Three weeks after my haircut, I go home to Yuba City to visit my mother. On my way to the house, I pull on my hair at the back of my head trying to tug it to its original length. I ring the doorbell and wait. The lock clicks open and I throw my arms around her. "Mom! Hey!" She throws her hands around me and they search for my head, for my hair. I freeze.

38 "Meeta!" She whips me back where she can see my face; my hair jostles around near my neck, settling down two inches above my shoulders. Her face crumples and turns red. Her eyes well up. I see the pain denting her face, contorting it into something she is not. She runs toward the kitchen, pleading with my grandmother to enter the prayer room. My mother wipes her face with her *dupatta* and starts her prayers before she even enters the prayer room. She whispers into God's ear. She does not speak to me for four months.

39 I call my mother on the phone and try to explain to her that it is just hair. My mother swallows her tongue in her attempts to explain that it is *not* just hair. "It is identity. It is your commitment to an honest life, to a compassionate life. It is your character, your credibility. Why would you give up your own credibility?" she asks. I want to cry, swallowing the sobs stuck in my throat. The smell of flowers in my shampooed hair makes me nauseous. I reach for my childhood memories, but they slip away quickly, almost running away from me.

40 The next few months, I enter into the ritual of growing my hair out, trimming it, cutting it, and growing it out again. I become indecisive about my school major, and my grades falter. I find studying too overwhelming to deal with. I grow silent. I do not know who I am anymore. I drift and float through my sophomore year of college. I develop an identity through a guy I date and transform myself into an accessory for someone else's life.

41 There is a constant gnawing at my insides for something concrete, something that grounds me. I have no center, so I drift out to sea

without direction or guidance. I lose my connection to myself and to the world. I lose my connection to a deeper sense of who I am. I do not realize that I had put that much faith into my *kesh,* into my long wavy hair, the hair I blame for my problems.

42 Mama accepts me into her house again, but she cannot hide her disappointment. She dismisses me during family conversations. She questions my pride at the dinner table. She tells my younger cousins to follow the example of my cousins in India: "The girls in India know who they are and where they come from." I know my mother doesn't mean India when she says this to my cousins. She doesn't pledge an allegiance to the geography of India or even America, for that matter, but to the spiritual homeland of Sikhism. She stamps my passport: DEPORTED. I am exiled from my family's homeland. I am a foreigner in my family's home. The border between my mother and me expands. She sets up a front line to protect the sanctity of her life against the impiety of mine. I hold on to my illusions, declare my mother narrow in her thinking. We never talk about it—the hair, the *kesh,* the identity I abandoned.

43 A few years after graduation, I join Narika, a South Asian women's hotline that supports survivors of domestic violence. The hotline serves women from India, Bangladesh, Sri Lanka, and Pakistan. There are quite a few counselors who know Hindi, Urdu, and Punjabi and communicate with the women on the hotline in their native languages. I stick with English because it is essentially the language I understand best.

44 I attend two counseling training sessions in the summer and prepare to wo-man the hotline. We receive a directory of domestic violence resources ranging from legal help to emergency room phone numbers. Shoba, our counselor, suggests we prepare a hot cup of tea to keep at our side during our shift. She tells us that we will receive a range of calls from women who may hang up, content with having heard a soothing voice on the other end of the line, to professionals asking for the names of good divorce attorneys.

45 It's a Tuesday night, and I'm naively excited about my first hotline shift. I dial into the hotline and pick up one voice mail. I call the woman back. I listen to her pauses and hesitations when she speaks. I let her know it is okay to talk about what's happened to her, that it is okay to speak her truth. She tells me he has hit her. We rest in the silence between us after she speaks. In this moment, I am humbled by my own history of Sikh women charging into battle, leading communities to fight oppression, and try desperately to pass on this historic courage, this timeless fearlessness through my lips into this woman's ears—down to her heart.

46 Eleven voice mails, three cases, and some court appearances later, the world has turned inside out for me and the distortion of it all hurts

my eyes; these women's stories leak onto my pillow night after night. The counselor-training sessions ring true. Violence transcends class, education, and race. Even though these same realities exist within Sikh communities in America and abroad, the scriptures state that mothers, wives, sisters, and daughters deserve the highest respect from their families and the society around them. Anyone who dares to harm them is violating sacred law. I begin to question the world I am living in. I recall how quiet most of the Sikh girls were at school, how much they held in. I remember my mother demanding that my father respect her as an equal partner in those moments he lost sight of her right to make decisions in our household. I remember my own ability to dismiss myself because I had the ability to shrink, become invisible, smothering my own light because I am scared of where it could take me.

47 I walk down streets imagining that any man passing by is preparing to go home and beat up his wife. I lose two to three nights of sleep during any given week. On weekends, I'm in a deep slumber coma, not waking up for the sunlight, lunch, or even early-evening tea. The sleep pushes the days full of hotline calls into a semidistant past, but the women's voices continue to scream in my head. I help one woman secure a restraining order against her husband who consistently molests his youngest daughter. On the morning of her court date on the way to the courtroom, she shields me with her hands when she sees her husband. She turns to me and says, "I will not leave you alone with him." She sees her daughter in me. I put my arm around her shoulder and let her know that I will not leave her alone with him either.

48 Colleagues and friends see me absorbing these women's lives and making their pain my own. The daily hotline calls push me into daily meditation and prayer. I practice rising early in the morning with the sun: I brush my teeth, bathe, and then have a cup of tea. I recall my mother's and grandmother's practice of sitting down to pray, to clear their minds of any disturbances, to reach a solution or relief from a situation. I return to my bedroom, sit cross-legged on my bed, and cover my head with a *dupatta*. I reach for my Nïtnem bound in red velvet. The small book holds Sikh prayers in Gurmukhi on the right side of the page and gives English translations on the left side. In the concentration of these prayers, I ask for peace of mind and strength, a calming of my nerves that will sketch a decent mind-size portrait of a sane world. I ask for guidance—grounded, firm guidance.

49 The meditation becomes a daily practice I cannot live without. Little by little, I chase fear out of my body to make room for more light. Three months of heavy meditation help me create a healthy detachment from the women without sacrificing my compassion for them. The prayers center me. I realize that all the little hells created on this earth are what the Sikh Gurus fought against. I realize there can be no peace or rest if members in a society suffer or are denied their basic rights.

50 My hair has grown three inches longer. The meditation increases and with it my hair expands in length. I focus on the strength of my mother's hair and the strength and safety she gave me as a child, the comfort I find in my spiritual homeland.

51 I feel a crack in the older self that I mummified when I cut my hair into that Cleopatra bob three years ago in college. The new growth of my hair is the outgrowth of my new mind. I see the world for what it is and realize that faith and my contributions toward realizing the vision of a socially just society are what I have to hold on to. I protect my mind's thoughts with my long wavy hair, warding off the severity of the world, nurturing my ideas and visions for my bright future. I realize all will not be resolved overnight, but I see a spark of light flicker from the steady glow of childhood. The thick plaster of the bandages breaks off, and I return to the original homeland of myself, with the gift of *kesh*.

52 My hair becomes witness to all the love and atrocities in the world. My hair holds the strength, pain, and love of these women on the hotline who I will never forget, cannot forget. I realize that I, too, am on a battlefield similar to the ones I saw in the comic books, even though the landscape is different, and I'm not holding a sword. The guiding light I inherit from the women in my family finds a way to penetrate me at my core and transform me from the inside out. I am duty-bound to the world around me according to the *kesh* I reclaim. I rise daily to my original locks, which are now younger than me. My hair has grown back out to its former length, and I no longer question preserving it until I die. I am on the path to becoming the woman my mother and grandmother prayed I would be.

✧ *Evaluating the Text*

1. What aspects of Kaur's account communicate the importance of having long hair in Sikh culture?
2. How was Kaur's decision to have her hair cut an attempt to assimilate into American culture?
3. What repercussions ensued after she had her hair cut and why did she decide to regrow it?

✧ *Exploring Different Perspectives*

1. Discuss the symbolic meaning of Kaur, as a member of a traditional Sikh family, having her hair cut with Bageant being given his first gun as part of his rite of passage in his family.
2. How does the theme of clash of cultures play an important role in the accounts by Kaur and K. Oanh Ha in "American Dream Boat"?

✧ *Extending Viewpoints through Writing and Research*

1. Have you undertaken some major alteration to change your personal appearance in ways that you came to regret? Tell what happened.
2. What part does hair play in American culture in terms of the way women are supposed to appear, according to popular ads?
3. Research the meaning of long hair for both men and women in the Sikh community.

K. Oanh Ha

American Dream Boat

K. Oanh Ha was born in 1973 in Vietnam and came to the United States when she was six. She grew up in California and worked as a journalist for the San Jose Mercury News. *The following account, which explores the conflict with her family and her American fiancé, first appeared in* Modern Maturity *(2002).*

Before you Read

Have you or anyone you know dated someone from another culture, religion, race, or ethnic group where the differences posed a challenge?

1 The wedding day was only two weeks away when my parents called with yet another request. In accordance with Vietnamese custom, they fully expected Scott Harris, my fiancé, and his family to visit our family on the morning of the wedding, bearing dowry gifts of fruit, candies, jewelry, and a pig, in an elaborate procession.

2 "But it's not going to mean anything to Scott or his family. They're not Vietnamese!" I protested. My parents were adamant: "Scott is marrying a Vietnamese. If he wants to marry you, he'll honor our traditions."

3 Maybe there's no such thing as a stress-free wedding. Small or large, there's bound to be pressure. But our February 12 wedding was a large do-it-yourselfer that required a fusion of Vietnamese and American traditions—a wedding that forced me and my parents to wrestle with questions about our identities, culture, and place in America. After nearly 20 years here, my family, and my parents in particular, were determined to have a traditional Vietnamese wedding of sorts, even if their son-in-law and Vietnam-born, California-raised daughter are as American as they can be.

4 And so I grudgingly called Scott that night to describe the wedding procession and explain the significance of the ritual. It's a good thing that he is a patient, easygoing man. "I'll bring the pig," he said, "but I'm worried it'll make a mess in the car."

5 "Oh! It's a *roasted* pig," I told him, laughing.

6 I was six years old when my family fled Vietnam in July 1979, just one family among the thousands who collectively became known as the "boat people," families who decided it was better to risk the very real possibility of death at sea than to live under Communist rule. But,

of course, I never understood the politics then. I was just a child following my parents.

7 My memories are sketchy. There was the time that Thai pirates wielding saber-like machetes raided our boat. Two years ago, I told my mother, Kim Hanh Nguyen, how I remembered a woman dropping a handful of jewelry into my rice porridge during the raid with the instructions to keep eating. "That was no woman," my mother said. "That was me!" When we reached the refugee camp in Kuala Lumpur, my mother used the wedding ring and necklace to buy our shelter.

8 In September 1980, we arrived in Santa Ana, California, in Orange County, now home to the largest Vietnamese community outside of Vietnam. Those who had left in 1975, right after the end of the war and the American withdrawal, had been well-educated, wealthy, and connected with the military. My family was part of the wave of boat people—mostly middle-class and with little education—who sought refuge in America.

9 For nearly a year after we arrived, we crowded into the same three-bedroom apartment, all 13 of us: brothers, sisters, cousins, uncles, aunts, sisters-in-law, and my father's mother. There were only four of us children in my immediate family then, three born in Vietnam and one born shortly after our resettlement in the U.S.

10 We started school and watched Mr. Rogers on PBS in the afternoons, grew to love hamburgers and ketchup and longed to lose our accents. We older kids did lose our accents—and those who came later never had accents to begin with because they were born here. When we first came, I was the oldest of three children, all born in Vietnam. Now I have seven siblings, 22 years separating me from my youngest brother, who will start kindergarten in the fall.

11 In some ways, I was the stereotypical Asian nerd. I took honors classes, received good grades, played the violin and cello. But there was a part of me that also yearned to be as American as my blond-haired neighbors across the street. I joined the school's swim and tennis teams, participated in speech competitions (which were attended by mostly white students) and worshipped Esprit and Guess. My first serious boyfriend was white but most of my friends were Asians who were either born in the U.S. or immigrated when they were very young. None of us had accents and we rarely spoke our native languages around one another. The last thing we wanted to be mistaken for was FOBs—fresh off the boat. I even changed my name to Kyrstin, unaware of its Nordic roots.

12 I wanted so badly to be a full-fledged American, whatever that meant. At home though, my parents pushed traditional Vietnamese values. I spent most of my teenage years baby-sitting and had to plead with my then overly strict parents to let me out of the house. "Please, please. I just want to be like any other American kid."

13 My parents didn't understand. "You'll always be Vietnamese. No one's going to look at you and say you're an American," was my mother's often-heard refrain.

14 I saw college as my escape, the beginning of the trip I would undertake on my own. We had come to America as a family but it was time I navigated alone. College was my flight from the house that always smelled of fish sauce and jasmine tea.

15 At UCLA, I dated the man who would become my husband. Though he's 17 years older than I am, my parents seemed to be more concerned with the cultural barriers than our age difference. "White Americans are fickle. They don't understand commitment and family responsibility like we Asians do," I was told.

16 Soon after I announced my engagement, my father, Minh Phu Ha, and I had a rare and intimate conversation. "I'm just worried for you," he said. "All the Vietnamese women I know who have married whites are divorced from them. Our cultures are too far apart."

17 My father, I think, is worried that none of his kids will marry Vietnamese. My sisters are dating non-Vietnamese Asians while my brother is dating a white American. "It's just that with a Vietnamese son-in-law, I can talk to him," my father explained to me one day. "A Vietnamese son-in-law would call me '*Ba*' and not by my first name."

18 Although my parents have come to terms with having Scott as their son-in-law and to the prospect of grandchildren who will be racially mixed, there are still times when Scott comes to visit that there are awkward silences. There are still many cultural barriers.

19 I still think of what it all means to marry a white American. I worry that my children won't be able to speak Vietnamese and won't appreciate that part of their heritage. I also wonder if somehow this is the ultimate fulfillment of a latent desire to be "American."

20 Vietnamese-Americans, like Chinese-Americans, Indian-Americans, and other assimilated immigrants, often speak of leading hyphenated lives, of feet that straddle both cultures. I've always been proud of being Vietnamese. As my family and I discussed and heatedly debated what the wedding event was going to look like, I began to realize just how "American" I had become.

21 And yet there was no denying the pull of my Vietnamese roots. Four months before the wedding, I traveled back to Vietnam for the second time since our family's escape. It was a trip I had planned for more than a year. I was in Saigon, the city of my birth, to research and write a novel that loosely mirrors the story of my own family and our journey from Vietnam. The novel is my tribute to my family and our past. I'm writing it for myself as much as for my younger siblings, so they'll know what our family's been through.

22 I returned to Vietnam to connect with something I can't really name but know I lost when we left 20 years ago. I was about to start a

new journey with the marriage ahead, but I needed to come back to the place where my family's journey began.

23 Scott came along for the first two weeks and met my extended family. They all seemed to approve, especially when he showed he could eat pungent fish and shrimp sauce like any other Vietnamese.

24 During my time there I visited often with family members and talked about the past. I saw the hospital where I was born, took a walk through our old house, chatted with my father's old friends. The gaps in the circle of my hyphenated life came closer together with every new Vietnamese word that I learned, with every Vietnamese friend that I made.

25 I also chose the fabric for the tailoring of the *ao dai,* the traditional Vietnamese dress of a long tunic over flowing pants, which I would change into at the reception. I had my sisters' bridesmaid gowns made. And I had a velvet ao dai made for my 88-year-old maternal grandmother, Bā Ngoai, to wear to the wedding of her oldest grandchild. "My dream is to see you on your wedding day and eat at your wedding feast," she had told me several times.

26 Bā Ngoai came to the U.S. in 1983, three years after my family landed in Orange County as war refugees. As soon as we got to the United States, my mother filed immigration papers for her. Bā Ngoai made that journey at age 73, leaving the only home she had known to be with my mother, her only child. Bā Ngoai nurtured and helped raise us grandchildren.

27 I had extended my stay in Vietnam. Several days after my original departure date, I received a phone call. Bā Ngoai had died. I flew home carrying her ao dai. We buried her in it.

28 In Vietnamese tradition, one is in mourning for three years after the loss of a parent or grandparent. Out of respect and love for the deceased, or *hieu,* decorum dictates that close family members can't get married until after the mourning period is over. But my wedding was only a month and a half away.

29 On the day we buried my grandmother, my family advised me to burn the white cloth headband that symbolized my grief. By burning it, I ended my official mourning.

30 Through my tears I watched the white cloth become wispy ashes. My family was supportive. "It's your duty to remember and honor her," my father told me. "But you also need to move forward with your life."

31 On the morning of our wedding, Scott's family stood outside our house in a line bearing dowry gifts. Inside the house, Scott and I lighted incense in front of the family altar. Holding the incense between our palms, we bowed to my ancestors and asked for their blessings. I looked at the photo of Bā Ngoai and knew she had to be smiling.

✧ *Evaluating the Text*

1. How does the narrator present herself? What kind of person does she seem to be?
2. How did Ha's choice of whom to marry create a conflict with her family?
3. What unique Vietnamese customs did her family want honored by her fiancé and his family?

✧ *Exploring Different Perspectives*

1. How do the accounts by Ha and Meeta Kaur project the conflict between their traditional cultural roots and what it means to be an American?
2. Compare the experiences of Ha with those of Dumas in terms of solving cultural conflicts.

✧ *Extending Viewpoints through Writing and Research*

1. Based on what Ha tells you about herself and her family, would you predict that she and Scott would have a happy marriage. Why or why not?
2. Ha changes her name to Kyrstin. Would you ever consider changing your name? If so, what would you change it to and why?

Marjane Satrapi

The Convocation

Marjane Satrapi was born in 1969 in Iran where she spent her childhood. When she was fourteen, she was sent to Vienna by her parents to escape the oppressive regime of Ayatollah Khomeini. She is best known for her series of graphic novels Persepolis. *In the following illustrated excerpt "The Convocation" from* Persepolis 2: The Story of a Return *(2004), we come to understand how a spirited girl reacts to the restrictions placed on women in the school she attended. In this we see how the graphic novel, which emerged in the 1980s from comic strips, has become a major vehicle for social and political protest.* Persepolis *became a film in 2007. It was directed by Vincent Paronnaud and starred Catherine Deneuve and Chiara Mastroianni as the young Marjane. Satrapi currently lives in Paris.*

Before You Read

How can the memoir-in-comic-strip form be used to explore sophisticated and complex personal and social issues?

THE CONVOCATION

MANY OF THE STUDENTS KNEW ONE ANOTHER ALREADY. IN LISTENING TO THEM, I UNDERSTOOD THAT THEY'D TAKEN THE PREPARATORY CLASSES TOGETHER. OUR FIRST LESSON WAS "ART HISTORY."
WHAT IS GENERALLY KNOWN AS ARAB ART AND ARCHITECTURE SHOULD IN FACT BE CALLED THE ART OF THE ISLAMIC EMPIRE, WHICH STRETCHED FROM CHINA TO SPAIN. THIS ART IS A CROSS BETWEEN INDIAN, PERSIAN, AND MESOPOTAMIAN ART. THOSE WHOM WE CONSIDER, LIKE AVICENNA, TO BE "ARAB SCHOLARS" ARE FOR THE MOST PART ANYTHING BUT ARABS. EVEN THE FIRST BOOK OF ARABIC GRAMMAR WAS WRITTEN BY AN IRANIAN.
IT WAS FUNNY TO SEE TO WHAT EXTENT THE ISLAMIC REPUBLIC WAS NOT ABLE TO PUT AN END TO OUR CHAUVINISM. TO THE CONTRARY! PEOPLE OFTEN COMPARED THE OBSCURANTISM OF THE NEW REGIME TO THE ARAB INVASION. ACCORDING TO THIS LOGIC, "BEING PERSIAN" MEANT "NOT BEING A FANATIC." BUT THIS PARALLEL WENT ONLY SO FAR CONSIDERING THE FACT THAT OUR GOVERNMENT WASN'T COMPOSED OF ARAB INVADERS BUT PERSIAN FUNDAMENTALISTS.
AT LUNCH TIME.
THE PROFESSOR IS VERY INTERESTING, BUT OH MY! DOES HIS MOUTH SMELL. EVEN THIRTY FEET AWAY YOU CAN SMELL HIS JACKAL'S BREATH!
HA! HA! HA!
AMONG THE GUYS, A FEW EVEN HAVE HAIR CUTS!!! MY GOD!
DESPITE THEIR UPTIGHT APPEARANCE, THE GIRLS IN MY CLASS SEEMED TO BE QUITE THE COMEDIANS.
HEY! LOOK, THE GUY IN THE BLUE SHIRT... HE'S REALLY NOT BAD!
THEY WERE TALKING ABOUT REZA. I SUDDENLY FOUND THEM A LOT LESS FUNNY.
HI, I'M SHOUKA.
AND I'M NIYOOSHA.
NICE TO MEET YOU. I'M MARJANE.
NIYOOSHA HAD VERY GREEN EYES WHICH MADE HER THE MOST SOUGHT AFTER GIRL AT THE COLLEGE. (THE MAJORITY OF IRANIANS HAVE BLACK EYES.)
YOU'VE LIVED ABROAD?
YES, HOW DID YOU KNOW?
BECAUSE OF YOUR MAGHNAEH.* YOU WEAR IT LIKE A BEGINNER.
SHOUKA WAS VERY FUNNY. UNFORTUNATELY, WHEN SHE GOT MARRIED TWO YEARS LATER, HER HUSBAND FORBADE HER FROM ASSOCIATING WITH ME. TO HIM, I WAS AN AMORAL PERSON.
IT'S TRUE THAT WEARING THE VEIL WAS A REAL SCIENCE. YOU HAD TO MAKE A SPECIAL FOLD, LIKE THIS:
NOT A HAIR SHOWS IN PROFILE.
BUT YOU SEE TUFTS FROM THE FRONT.
NEVERTHELESS, THINGS WERE EVOLVING... YEAR BY YEAR, WOMEN WERE WINNING AN EIGHTH OF AN INCH OF HAIR AND LOSING AN EIGHTH OF AN INCH OF VEIL.
*HOODED HEAD-SCARF

WITH PRACTICE, EVEN THOUGH THEY WERE COVERED FROM HEAD TO FOOT, YOU GOT TO THE POINT WHERE YOU COULD GUESS THEIR SHAPE, THE WAY THEY WORE THEIR HAIR AND EVEN THEIR POLITICAL OPINIONS. OBVIOUSLY, THE MORE A WOMAN SHOWED, THE MORE PROGRESSIVE AND MODERN SHE WAS.
COMING HOME THAT EVENING.
HI EVERYONE!
HI.
SO, HOW WAS YOUR FIRST DAY?
LOOK WHAT GRANDMA BROUGHT FOR YOU.
GRANDMA?
EVER SINCE MY COWARDLY ACT MY GRANDMA HADN'T BEEN SPEAKING TO ME.
WHAT'S THIS?
IT'S A COTTON HEAD-SCARF!
THIS WAY YOUR HEAD CAN BREATHE. OTHERWISE YOU'LL BE BALD IN NO TIME.
SHE HAD GIVEN ME A GIFT, SHE HAD THOUGHT OF MY HAIR, SHE WAS TALKING TO ME ...
... WHEW! SHE HAD FORGIVEN ME.
OH, GRANDMA! THANK YOU!!
FINE, FINE, IT'S OKAY!
I HAD FORGOTTEN HER EXTREME INTRANSIGENCE.

ONE WEEK LATER.
THE CLEAN-SHAVEN GUY, RIGHT OVER THERE, WHAT'S HIS NAME...? REZA, YES, REZA, DO YOU KNOW HIM?
NO, WHY?
WELL, HE CAN'T STOP OGLING YOU, HEE! HEE! HEE! HEE!
NO, NO, I HADN'T EVEN NOTICED HIM!
YOU'RE RIGHT, HE'S NOT THAT GREAT.
OH, HE'S NOT SO BAD.
SEE, YOU DO KNOW HIM!
FACED WITH THE PERSPICACITY OF MY GIRLFRIENDS, I HAD NO CHOICE BUT TO ADMIT THE TRUTH.
STUDENTS, STUDENTS.
SUCH DISCERNMENT!
I CONFESS! I SAW HIM LAST NIGHT IN YOUR CAR.
DIRTY LIAR! YOU REALLY GOT ME!
SHHH! LISTEN TO WHAT THE DIRECTOR IS SAYING!
YOUR PRESENCE IS REQUIRED AT 3 O'CLOCK AT THE MAIN CAMPUS! ALL THOSE WHO ARE ABSENT WILL BE BARRED FROM ATTENDING CLASSES FOR TWO WEEKS!
IT WAS AT THE MAIN CAMPUS THAT THE SUBJECTS COMMON TO ALL THE COLLEGES WERE TAUGHT. IT WAS MUCH MORE REPRESSIVE THAN OUR COLLEGE. AS ARTISTS, WE BENEFITED FROM A LITTLE MORE LIBERTY. FOR EXAMPLE, THERE GIRLS AND BOYS HAD TO TAKE DIFFERENT STAIRCASES, WHILE WHERE WE WERE, EVERYONE USED THE SAME STAIRCASE.
I DIDN'T GET THE STAIRCASE THING, BECAUSE IN ANY CASE, WE FOUND OURSELVES TOGETHER UPSTAIRS. BUT SHOUKA SAID THAT IT WAS TO KEEP THE BOYS FROM WATCHING OUR BUTTS WHILE WE CLIMBED.
I THINK SHE WAS RIGHT.

ONCE IN THE AMPHITHEATER, WE DISCOVERED THE REASON FOR OUR CONVOCATION: THE ADMINISTRATION HAD ORGANIZED A LECTURE WITH THE THEME OF "MORAL AND RELIGIOUS CONDUCT," TO SHOW US THE RIGHT PATH.
WE CAN'T ALLOW OURSELVES TO BEHAVE LOOSELY! IT'S THE BLOOD OF OUR MARTYRS WHICH HAS NOURISHED THE FLOWERS OF OUR REPUBLIC. TO ALLOW ONESELF TO BEHAVE INDECENTLY IS TO TRAMPLE ON THE BLOOD OF THOSE WHO GAVE THEIR LIVES FOR OUR FREEDOM. ALSO, I AM ASKING THE YOUNG LADIES PRESENT HERE TO WEAR LESS-WIDE TROUSERS AND LONGER HEAD-SCARVES. YOU SHOULD COVER YOUR HAIR WELL, YOU SHOULD NOT WEAR MAKEUP, YOU SHOULD...

DOES ANYONE HAVE ANY QUESTIONS? IF NOT, THIS MEETING IS OVER.
SIR, I HAVE A QUESTION!
YOU SAY THAT OUR HEAD-SCARVES ARE SHORT, THAT OUR PANTS ARE INDECENT, THAT WE MAKE OURSELVES UP, ETC., . . .
BUT AS A STUDENT OF ART, A GOOD PORTION OF MY TIME IS SPENT IN THE STUDIO. I NEED TO BE ABLE TO MOVE FREELY TO BE ABLE TO DRAW. A LONGER HEAD-SCARF WILL MAKE THE TASK EVEN MORE DIFFICULT.
AS FOR OUR TROUSERS, YOU CRITICIZE THEM FOR BEING TOO WIDE EVEN THOUGH THEY EFFECTIVELY HIDE OUR SHAPE. KNOWING THAT THESE TROUSERS ARE IN VOGUE RIGHT NOW, I ASK THE QUESTION: IS RELIGION DEFENDING OUR PHYSICAL INTEGRITY OR IS IT JUST OPPOSED TO FASHION?
YOU DON'T HESITATE TO COMMENT ON US, BUT OUR BROTHERS PRESENT HERE HAVE ALL SHAPES AND SIZES OF HAIRCUTS AND CLOTHES. SOMETIMES, THEY WEAR CLOTHES SO TIGHT THAT WE CAN SEE EVERYTHING.
WHY IS IT THAT I, AS A WOMAN, AM EXPECTED TO FEEL NOTHING WHEN WATCHING THESE MEN WITH THEIR CLOTHES SCULPTED ON BUT THEY, AS MEN, CAN GET EXCITED BY TWO INCHES LESS OF MY HEAD-SCARF?
OHHHH!!

AFTER THE LECTURE.
YOU'RE REALLY COURAGEOUS.
BRAVO! WHAT FRANK SPEAKING!
THANKS.
SATRAPI!
YOU'VE BEEN SUMMONED BY THE ISLAMIC COMMISSION... GOOD LUCK!
IS IT SERIOUS?
I REALLY DON'T KNOW.
THE DIRECTOR OF OUR COLLEGE HAD STUDIED IN THE UNITED STATES AND REMAINED QUITE SECULAR.
WHAT IS IT?
I'VE BEEN SUMMONED BY THE ISLAMIC COMMISSION!
OH SHIT!
WISH ME LUCK!
IT WAS AS IF I WERE GOING TO MEET MY EXECUTIONER.
... BUT TO MY PLEASANT SURPRISE, MY EXECUTIONER PROVED TO BE THE "TRUE RELIGIOUS" MAN, THE ONE WHO HAD PASSED ME ON THE IDEOLOGICAL TEST.
SO MISS SATRAPI... ALWAYS SAYING WHAT YOU THINK ... IT'S GOOD! YOU'RE HONEST, BUT YOU ARE LOST.
YES.
READ THE SACRED TEXT. YOU'LL SEE THAT WEARING THE VEIL IS SYNONYMOUS WITH EMANCIPATION.
IF YOU SAY SO.
IT IS NOT I WHO SAYS IT, IT'S GOD... I'M GOING TO GIVE YOU A SECOND CHANCE. THIS TIME, YOU'RE NOT EXPELLED. IN EXCHANGE, I AM ASKING YOU TO IMAGINE THE UNIFORM ADAPTED TO THE NEEDS OF THE STUDENTS IN YOUR COLLEGE. NOTHING EXTRAVAGANT, YOU UNDERSTAND.
OF COURSE.
I APPLIED MYSELF. DESIGNING THE "MODEL" THAT WOULD PLEASE BOTH THE ADMINISTRATION AND THE INTERESTED PARTIES WASN'T EASY. I MADE DOZENS OF SKETCHES.
THIS WAS THE RESULT OF MY RESEARCH.
SHORT HEAD-SCARF
WIDE TROUSERS
THOUGH SUBTLE, THESE DIFFERENCES MEANT A LOT TO US.
THIS LITTLE REBELLION RECONCILED MY GRANDMOTHER AND ME.
IT'S FEAR THAT MAKES US LOSE OUR CONSCIENCE. IT'S ALSO WHAT TRANSFORMS US INTO COWARDS. YOU HAD GUTS! I'M PROUD OF YOU!
AND THIS IS HOW I RECOVERED MY SELF-ESTEEM AND MY DIGNITY. FOR THE FIRST TIME IN A LONG TIME, I WAS HAPPY WITH MYSELF.

Evaluating the Text

1. What problems related to how women should dress did Satrapi confront when she went to the state university as an art student?
2. How did women seek to adapt a uniformly prescribed outfit to express subtle but important differences in their personalities?
3. Why did Satrapi's comment during a convocation lead to a meeting with a senior religious adviser at the school? How did this result in her being reconciled with her grandmother?

Exploring Different Perspectives

1. How do both Meeta Kaur and Satrapi explore the social messages, intended and unintended, of different kinds of dress and hairstyles in different cultures?
2. Contrast the very different expectations of being Iranian and female in Iran and in the United States as seen by Satrapi and Dumas, respectively.

Extending Viewpoints through Writing and Research

1. Although the cultural contrasts are obvious, in what respects are the relationships between male and female students like those in the United States?
2. Research the point that the professor in the art history class is making about the origins and forms of expression of Islamic art. What singular architectual monuments embody these ideas? Examples might be the Taj Mahal in India or the new Sheikh Zayed mosque, in Abu Dhabi, United Arab Emirates, the third largest in the world and one of the few to permit non-Muslims to enter.
3. What is your favorite graphic novel and or film or game? Describe why it appeals to you.

Connecting Cultures

Joe Bageant, "Valley of the Gun"

What rituals provide a sense of belonging for Bageant and Tepilit Ole Saitoti as described in "The Initiation of a Maasai Warrior" in Chapter 3?

Fritz Peters, "Boyhood with Gurdjieff"

What insights that involve money does Peters's essay and Helena Norberg-Hodge's "Learning from Ladakh" in Chapter 4 offer?

Psychology Today, *"Plight of the Little Emperors"*

Compare the importance of education to parents for their children in Lydia Minatoya's "Transformation" in Chapter 2 and in this essay.

Firoozeh Dumas, "Save Me, Mickey"

Compare the sense of culture shock Dumas felt with that of Napoleon A. Chagnon in "Doing Fieldwork among the Yąnomamö" in Chapter 6.

Patricia Hampl, "Grandmother's Sunday Dinner"

Compare the experiences of Hampl with that of Amy Tan in "Fish Cheeks" in Chapter 7.

Meeta Kaur "Journey by Inner Light"

Discuss the symbolic meaning of Kaur having her hair cut with the meaning of Tepilit Ole Saitoti's having his head shaved as he describes it in "The Initiation of a Maasai Warrior" in Chapter 3.

K. Oanh Ha "American Dream Boat"

Compare the kinds of problems described by Ha with Serena Nanda's discussion in "Arranging a Marriage in India" in Chapter 8.

Marjane Satrapi "The Convocation"

Discuss the symbolism of Satrapi redesigning her outfits with the significance of design as discussed by Enid Schildkrout in "Body Art as Visual Language" in Chapter 2.

2

Turning Points

The old believe everything. The middle-aged suspect everything. The young know everything.

—Oscar Wilde (1854–1900),
The Picture of Dorian Gray (1891)

In almost every society, certain rites or ceremonies are used to signal adulthood. Although many of these occasions are informal, some are quite elaborate and dramatic. This chapter offers a range of perspectives that illustrate how such turning points are marked by informal and formal rituals across a broad spectrum of cultures. These moments of insight may be private psychological turning points or ceremonies that initiate the individual into adulthood within a community. These crucial moments in which individuals move from childhood innocence to adult awareness often involve learning a particular society's rules governing what should or should not be done under different circumstances, values, knowledge, and expectations as to how one should present oneself in a wide variety of situations.

These turning points often occur during adolescence, when we explore the limits of what society will and will not allow us to do. This is the time in which rebellion and defiance against society's rules take place. We acquire societal norms through imitation, identification, and instruction into what behavior patterns our society deems acceptable or unacceptable. From internalizing these values we get a sense of personal and social identity. This is often the time when we form our first voluntary associations or friendships and discover our capacity to trust and develop relationships, whether strong or fragile, that can lead to reward or disappointment.

In some cases, belonging to a group, association, fraternity, or sorority involves passing some initiation or test to gain acceptance. Because this chapter is rich in a wide variety of perspectives, it invites you to make discoveries about the turning points in your own life.

The essays and short work of fiction in this chapter focus on the psychological and cultural forces that shape the identity of those who are about to be initiated into their respective communities. The Chinese-American writer Sucheng Chan describes with honesty and humor her struggle to confront her disabilities in "You're Short, Besides!" From Ireland, we read the moving narrative of Christy Brown, who, in "The Letter 'A'," describes his struggle to communicate signs of intelligence by drawing the letter "A" with his left foot after having been diagnosed as hopelessly retarded by cerebral palsy. The international explorer Douchan Gersi offers a hair-raising account appropriately titled "Initiated into an Iban Tribe of Headhunters," a first-hand narrative based on his experiences in modern-day Borneo. Enid Schildkrout in "Body Art as Visual Language" addresses the issue of extreme body decorations in cultures around the world. As a daughter of Japanese American immigrants, Lydia Minatoya in "Transformation" describes her parents' elaborate search for a suitable name for her. In "The Telephone," Anwar F. Accawi tells of the irreversible effects that the installation of a telephone brought to his remote village in Lebanon. Ruskin Bond, in his short work of fiction "The Eyes Are Not Here," evokes the surprising consequences of a train journey in India taken by a blind man.

To help you understand how the works in this chapter relate to each other, you might use one or several of the following guidelines before writing about turning points.

1. What problem or issue does the author address?
2. Is the author's approach subjective or objective?
3. Does the writer's tone communicate a positive or negative view of the event and its aftermath?
4. What assumptions or values underlie the author's view of the subject?
5. In what way has the author's analysis of the subject changed your opinion?
6. What specific ethical or moral set of choices does the author address?

Recommended Films on This Theme

- *The Razor's Edge* (United States, 1946) The tale adapted from Somerset Maugham's novel about a young man on a spiritual quest who discovers a mystical kingdom in Tibet;
- *Duel* (United States, 1971) The encounter of an everyman traveling alone through the desert with a malevolent trucker pursuing him;

- *Central Station* (Brazil; 1998) The story of a woman in Rio de Janeiro's railway station who adopts a young boy and seeks to locate his father;
- *American East* (Egypt/United States, 2008) The story of an Egyptian immigrant living in Los Angeles who tries to pursue the American dream.

Sucheng Chan

You're Short, Besides!

Sucheng Chan (b. 1941) graduated from Swarthmore College in 1963 and received an M.A. from the University of Hawaii in 1965. In 1973 she earned a Ph.D. from the University of California at Berkeley, where she subsequently taught for a decade. She is currently Professor Emeritus of Asian American studies at the *University of California at Santa Barbara. Her works include* Quiet Odyssey: A Pioneer Korean Woman in America *(1990) and the award-winning* The Asian Americans: An Interpretive History *(1991). "You're Short, Besides!" first appeared in* Making Waves: An Anthology of Writing by and about Asian-American Women *(1989). In recent years, she has served as the editor of numerous collections, including* Remapping Asian American History *(2001). She is the author of* In Defense of Asian American Studies *(2005). In 2008, Chan, along with Madeline Y. Hsu, edited* Chinese Americans and the Politics of Race and Culture.

Before You Read

Consider to what extent culture shapes concepts of normalcy and disability and the ways in which Asian cultures, in Chan's view, differ from Western ones.

1 When asked to write about being a physically handicapped Asian American woman, I considered it an insult. After all, my accomplishments are many, yet I was not asked to write about any of them. Is being handicapped the most salient feature about me? The fact that it might be in the eyes of others made me decide to write the essay as requested. I realized that the way I think about myself may differ considerably from the way others perceive me. And maybe that's what being physically handicapped is all about.

2 I was stricken simultaneously with pneumonia and polio at the age of four. Uncertain whether I had polio of the lungs, seven of the eight doctors who attended me—all practitioners of Western medicine—told my parents they should not feel optimistic about my survival. A Chinese fortune teller my mother consulted also gave a grim prognosis, but for an entirely different reason: I had been stricken because my name was offensive to the gods. My grandmother had named me "grandchild of wisdom," a name that the fortune teller said was too presumptuous for a

girl. So he advised my parents to change my name to "chaste virgin." All these pessimistic predictions notwithstanding, I hung onto life, if only by a thread. For three years, my body was periodically pierced with electric shocks as the muscles of my legs atrophied. Before my illness, I had been an active, rambunctious, precocious, and very curious child. Being confined to bed was thus a mental agony as great as my physical pain. Living in war-torn China, I received little medical attention; physical therapy was unheard of. But I was determined to walk. So one day, when I was six or seven, I instructed my mother to set up two rows of chairs to face each other so that I could use them as I would parallel bars. I attempted to walk by holding my body up and moving it forward with my arms while dragging my legs along behind. Each time I fell, my mother gasped, but I badgered her until she let me try again. After four nonambulatory years, I finally walked once more by pressing my hands against my thighs so my knees wouldn't buckle.

3 My father had been away from home during most of those years because of the war. When he returned, I had to confront the guilt he felt about my condition. In many East Asian cultures, there is a strong folk belief that a person's physical state in this life is a reflection of how morally or sinfully he or she lived in previous lives. Furthermore, because of the tendency to view the family as a single unit, it is believed that the fate of one member can be caused by the behavior of another. Some of my father's relatives told him that my illness had doubtless been caused by the wild carousing he did in his youth. A well-meaning but somewhat simple man, my father believed them.

4 Throughout my childhood, he sometimes apologized to me for having to suffer retribution for his former bad behavior. This upset me; it was bad enough that I had to deal with the anguish of not being able to walk, but to have to assuage his guilt as well was a real burden! In other ways, my father was very good to me. He took me out often, carrying me on his shoulders or back, to give me fresh air and sunshine. He did this until I was too large and heavy for him to carry. And ever since I can remember, he has told me that I am pretty.

5 After getting over her anxieties about my constant falls, my mother decided to send me to school. I had already learned to read some words of Chinese at the age of three by asking my parents to teach me the sounds and meaning of various characters in the daily newspaper. But between the ages of four and eight, I received no education since just staying alive was a full-time job. Much to her chagrin, my mother found no school in Shanghai, where we lived at the time, which would accept me as a student. Finally, as a last resort, she approached the American School, which agreed to enroll me only if my family kept an *amah* (a servant who takes care of children) by my side at all times. The tuition at the school was twenty U.S. dollars per month—a huge sum of money during those years of runaway inflation

in China—and payable only in U.S. dollars. My family afforded the high cost of tuition and the expense of employing a full-time *amah* for less than a year.

6 We left China as the Communist forces swept across the country in victory. We found an apartment in Hong Kong across the street from a school run by Seventh-Day Adventists. By that time I could walk a little, so the principal was persuaded to accept me. An *amah* now had to take care of me only during recess when my classmates might easily knock me over as they ran about the playground.

7 After a year and a half in Hong Kong, we moved to Malaysia, where my father's family had lived for four generations. There I learned to swim in the lovely warm waters of the tropics and fell in love with the sea. On land I was a cripple; in the ocean I could move with the grace of a fish. I liked the freedom of being in the water so much that many years later, when I was a graduate student in Hawaii, I became greatly enamored with a man just because he called me a "Polynesian water nymph."

8 As my overall health improved, my mother became less anxious about all aspects of my life. She did everything possible to enable me to lead as normal a life as possible. I remember how once some of her colleagues in the high school where she taught criticized her for letting me wear short skirts. They felt my legs should not be exposed to public view. My mother's response was, "All girls her age wear short skirts, so why shouldn't she?"

9 The years in Malaysia were the happiest of my childhood, even though I was constantly fending off children who ran after me calling, *"Baikah! Baikah!"* ("Cripple! Cripple!" in the Hokkien dialect commonly spoken in Malaysia). The taunts of children mattered little because I was a star pupil. I won one award after another for general scholarship as well as for art and public speaking. Whenever the school had important visitors my teacher always called on me to recite in front of the class.

10 A significant event that marked me indelibly occurred when I was twelve. That year my school held a music recital and I was one of the students chosen to play the piano. I managed to get up the steps to the stage without any problem, but as I walked across the stage, I fell. Out of the audience, a voice said loudly and clearly, "Ayah! A *baikah* shouldn't be allowed to perform in public." I got up before anyone could get on stage to help me and, with tears streaming uncontrollably down my face, I rushed to the piano and began to play. Beethoven's "Für Elise" had never been played so fiendishly fast before or since, but I managed to finish the whole piece. That I managed to do so made me feel really strong. I never again feared ridicule.

11 In later years I was reminded of this experience from time to time. During my fourth year as an assistant professor at the University of

California at Berkeley, I won a distinguished teaching award. Some weeks later I ran into a former professor who congratulated me enthusiastically. But I said to him, "You know what? I became a distinguished teacher by *limping* across the stage of Dwinelle 155!" (Dwinelle 155 is a large, cold, classroom that most colleagues of mine hate to teach in.) I was rude not because I lacked graciousness but because this man, who had told me that my dissertation was the finest piece of work he had read in fifteen years, had nevertheless advised me to eschew a teaching career.

12 "Why?" I asked.

13 "Your leg . . ." he responded.

14 "What about my leg?" I said, puzzled.

15 "Well, how would you feel standing in front of a large lecture class?"

16 "If it makes any difference, I want you to know I've won a number of speech contests in my life, and I am not the least bit self-conscious about speaking in front of large audiences. . . . Look, why don't you write me a letter of recommendation to tell people how brilliant I am, and let *me* worry about my leg!"

17 This incident is worth recounting only because it illustrates a dilemma that handicapped persons face frequently: those who care about us sometimes get so protective that they unwittingly limit our growth. This former professor of mine had been one of my greatest supporters for two decades. Time after time, he had written glowing letters of recommendation on my behalf. He had spoken as he did because he thought he had my best interest at heart; he thought that if I got a desk job rather than one that required me to be a visible, public person, I would be spared the misery of being stared at.

18 Americans, for the most part, do not believe as Asians do that physically handicapped persons are morally flawed. But they are equally inept at interacting with those of us who are not able-bodied. Cultural differences in the perception and treatment of handicapped people are most clearly expressed by adults. Children, regardless of where they are, tend to be openly curious about people who do not look "normal." Adults in Asia have no hesitation in asking visibly handicapped people what is wrong with them, often expressing their sympathy with looks of pity, whereas adults in the United States try desperately to be polite by pretending not to notice.

19 One interesting response I often elicited from people in Asia but have never encountered in America is the attempt to link my physical condition to the state of my soul. Many a time while living and traveling in Asia people would ask me what religion I belonged to. I would tell them that my mother is a devout Buddhist, that my father was baptized a Catholic but has never practiced Catholicism, and that I am an agnostic. Upon hearing this, people would try strenuously to convert me to their religion so that whichever God they believed in could bless me.

If I would only attend this church or that temple regularly, they urged, I would surely get cured. Catholics and Buddhists alike have pressed religious medallions into my palm, telling me if I would wear these, the relevant deity or saint would make me well. Once while visiting the tomb of Muhammad Ali Jinnah in Karachi, Pakistan, an old Muslim, after finishing his evening prayers, spotted me, gestured toward my legs, raised his arms heavenward, and began a new round of prayers, apparently on my behalf.

20 In the United States adults who try to act "civilized" toward handicapped people by pretending they don't notice anything unusual sometimes end up ignoring handicapped people completely. In the first few months I lived in this country, I was struck by the fact that whenever children asked me what was the matter with my leg, their adult companions would hurriedly shush them up, furtively look at me, mumble apologies, and rush their children away. After a few months of such encounters, I decided it was my responsibility to educate these people. So I would say to the flustered adults, "It's okay, let the kid ask." Turning to the child, I would say, "When I was a little girl, no bigger than you are, I became sick with something called polio. The muscles of my leg shrank up and I couldn't walk very well. You're much luckier than I am because now you can get a vaccine to make sure you never get my disease. So don't cry when your mommy takes you to get a polio vaccine, okay?" Some adults and their little companions I talked to this way were glad to be rescued from embarrassment; others thought I was strange.

21 Americans have another way of covering up their uneasiness: they become jovially patronizing. Sometimes when people spot my crutch, they ask if I've had a skiing accident. When I answer that unfortunately it is something less glamorous than that they say, "I bet you *could* ski if you put your mind to it!" Alternately, at parties where people dance, men who ask me to dance with them get almost belligerent when I decline their invitation. They say, "Of course you can dance if you *want* to!" Some have given me pep talks about how if I would only develop the right mental attitude, I would have more fun in life.

22 Different cultural attitudes toward handicapped persons came out clearly during my wedding. My father-in-law, as solid a representative of middle America as could be found, had no qualms about objecting to the marriage on racial grounds, but he could bring himself to comment on my handicap only indirectly. He wondered why his son, who had dated numerous high school and college beauty queens, couldn't marry one of them instead of me. My mother-in-law, a devout Christian, did not share her husband's prejudices, but she worried aloud about whether I could have children. Some Chinese friends of my parents, on the other hand, said that I was lucky to have found such a noble man, one who would marry me despite my handicap. I, for my

part, appeared in church in a white lace wedding dress I had designed and made myself—a miniskirt!

23 How Asian Americans treat me with respect to my handicap tells me a great deal about their degree of acculturation. Recent immigrants behave just like Asians in Asia; those who have been here longer or who grew up in the United States behave more like their white counterparts. I have not encountered any distinctly Asian American pattern of response. What makes the experience of Asian American handicapped people unique is the duality of responses we elicit.

24 Regardless of racial or cultural background, most handicapped people have to learn to find a balance between the desire to attain physical independence and the need to take care of ourselves by not overtaxing our bodies. In my case, I've had to learn to accept the fact that leading an active life has its price. Between the ages of eight and eighteen, I walked without using crutches or braces but the effort caused my right leg to become badly misaligned. Soon after I came to the United States, I had a series of operations to straighten out the bones of my right leg; afterwards though my leg looked straighter and presumably better, I could no longer walk on my own. Initially my doctors fitted me with a brace, but I found wearing one cumbersome and soon gave it up. I could move around much more easily—and more important, faster—by using one crutch. One orthopedist after another warned me that using a single crutch was a bad practice. They were right. Over the years my spine developed a double-S curve and for the last twenty years I have suffered from severe, chronic back pains, which neither conventional physical therapy nor a lighter work load can eliminate.

25 The only thing that helps my backaches is a good massage, but the soothing effect lasts no more than a day or two. Massages are expensive, especially when one needs them three times a week. So I found a job that pays better, but at which I have to work longer hours, consequently increasing the physical strain on my body—a sort of vicious circle. When I was in my thirties, my doctors told me that if I kept leading the strenuous life I did, I would be in a wheelchair by the time I was forty. They were right on target; I bought myself a wheelchair when I was forty-one. But being the incorrigible character that I am, I use it only when I am *not* in a hurry!

26 It is a good thing, however, that I am too busy to think much about my handicap or my backaches because pain can physically debilitate as well as cause depression. And there are days when my spirits get rather low. What has helped me is realizing that being handicapped is akin to growing old at an accelerated rate. The contradiction I experience is that often my mind races along as though I'm only twenty while my body feels about sixty. But fifteen or twenty years hence, unlike my peers who will have to cope with aging for the first time,

I shall be full of cheer because I will have already fought, and I hope won, that battle long ago.

27 Beyond learning how to be physically independent and, for some of us, living with chronic pain or other kinds of discomfort, the most difficult thing a handicapped person has to deal with, especially during puberty and early adulthood, is relating to potential sexual partners. Because American culture places so much emphasis on physical attractiveness, a person with a shriveled limb, or a tilt to the head, or the inability to speak clearly, experiences great uncertainty—indeed trauma—when interacting with someone to whom he or she is attracted. My problem was that I was not only physically handicapped, small, and short, but worse, I also wore glasses and was smarter than all the boys I knew! Alas, an insurmountable combination. Yet somehow I have managed to have intimate relationships, all of them with extraordinary men. Not surprisingly, there have also been countless men who broke my heart—men who enjoyed my company "as a friend," but who never found the courage to date or make love with me, although I am sure my experience in this regard is no different from that of many able-bodied persons.

28 The day came when my backaches got in the way of having an active sex life. Surprisingly that development was liberating because I stopped worrying about being attractive to men. No matter how headstrong I had been, I, like most women of my generation, had had the desire to be alluring to men ingrained into me. And that longing had always worked like a brake on my behavior. When what men think of me ceased to be compelling, I gained greater freedom to be myself.

29 I've often wondered if I would have been a different person had I not been physically handicapped. I really don't know, though there is no question that being handicapped has marked me. But at the same time I usually do not *feel* handicapped—and consequently, I do not act handicapped. People are therefore less likely to treat me as a handicapped person. There is no doubt, however, that the lives of my parents, sister, husband, other family members, and some close friends have been affected by my physical condition. They have had to learn not to hide me away at home, not to feel embarrassed by how I look or react to people who say silly things to me, and not to resent me for the extra demands my condition makes on them. Perhaps the hardest thing for those who live with handicapped people is to know when and how to offer help. There are no guidelines applicable to all situations. My advice is, when in doubt, ask, but ask in a way that does not smack of pity or embarrassment. Most important, please don't talk to us as though we are children.

30 So, has being physically handicapped been a handicap? It all depends on one's attitude. Some years ago, I told a friend that I had once said to an affirmative action compliance officer (somewhat sardonically

since I do not believe in the head count approach to affirmative action) that the institution which employs me is triply lucky because it can count me as non-white, female and handicapped. He responded, "Why don't you tell them to count you four times? . . . Remember, you're short, besides!"

✧ *Evaluating the Text*

1. What insight into cross-cultural perceptions of disabilities do you get from Chan's account? Specifically, how do Asian perceptions of disabilities differ from those in America?
2. To what extent did Chan have to overcome the well-meaning advice of family and friends and discount their perception of her diminished potential?
3. Chan has very strongly developed views; that is, she is an agnostic, doesn't believe in affirmative action, is uninhibited about sex, and has an unusual attitude toward the debilitating nature of her handicap. Which of her responses toward events made you aware of her unique personality?

✧ *Exploring Different Perspectives*

1. What personal attributes link Chan with Christy Brown in confronting disabilities in "The Letter 'A' "?
2. Discuss how Chan and Ruskin Bond in his story "The Eyes Are Not Here" treat the theme of disability.

✧ *Extending Viewpoints through Writing and Research*

1. To what extent are attitudes toward disability conditioned by cultural forces?
2. Do you know anyone who has a sense of irony and detachment similar to Chan's toward a disability or ailment? Write a short account of how this attitude enables him or her to cope with circumstances that might devastate another person.
3. Information on a book written by the author can be found at http://www.amazon.com/Asian-Americans-Interpretive-Immigrant-heritage/dp/.

Christy Brown

The Letter "A"

Christy Brown (1932–1981) was born in Dublin, the tenth child in a family of twenty-two. Brown was diagnosed as having cerebral palsy and being hopelessly retarded. An intense personal struggle and the loving attention and faith of his mother resulted in a surprising degree of rehabilitation. Brown's autobiography, My Left Foot *(1954), describing his struggle to overcome his massive handicap, was the basis for the 1989 Academy Award–winning film. Brown is also the author of an internationally acclaimed novel,* Down All the Days *(1970). "The Letter 'A,'" from his autobiography, describes the crucial moment when he first communicated signs of awareness and intelligence.*

Before You Read

Notice how Brown draws on his own experiences to raise the larger issue of how children with disabilities should be treated.

1 I was born in the Rotunda Hospital,[1] on June 5th, 1932. There were nine children before me and twelve after me, so I myself belong to the middle group. Out of this total of twenty-two, seventeen lived, but four died in infancy, leaving thirteen still to hold the family fort.

2 Mine was a difficult birth, I am told. Both mother and son almost died. A whole army of relations queued up outside the hospital until the small hours of the morning, waiting for news and praying furiously that it would be good.

3 After my birth Mother was sent to recuperate for some weeks and I was kept in the hospital while she was away. I remained there for some time, without name, for I wasn't baptized until my mother was well enough to bring me to church.

4 It was Mother who first saw that there was something wrong with me. I was about four months old at the time. She noticed that my head had a habit of falling backward whenever she tried to feed me. She attempted to correct this by placing her hand on the back of my neck to keep it steady. But when she took it away, back it would drop again. That was the first warning sign. Then she became aware of other defects as I got older. She saw that my hands were clenched nearly all

[1]Rotunda Hospital, a hospital in Dublin, Ireland.

of the time and were inclined to twine behind my back; my mouth couldn't grasp the teat of the bottle because even at that early age my jaws would either lock together tightly, so that it was impossible for her to open them, or they would suddenly become limp and fall loose, dragging my whole mouth to one side. At six months I could not sit up without having a mountain of pillows around me. At twelve months it was the same.

5 Very worried by this, Mother told my father her fears, and they decided to seek medical advice without any further delay. I was a little over a year old when they began to take me to hospitals and clinics, convinced that there was something definitely wrong with me, something which they could not understand or name, but which was very real and disturbing.

6 Almost every doctor who saw and examined me labeled me a very interesting but also a hopeless case. Many told Mother very gently that I was mentally defective and would remain so. That was a hard blow to a young mother who had already reared five healthy children. The doctors were so very sure of themselves that Mother's faith in me seemed almost an impertinence. They assured her that nothing could be done for me.

7 She refused to accept this truth, the inevitable truth—as it then seemed—that I was beyond cure, beyond saving, even beyond hope. She could not and would not believe that I was an imbecile, as the doctors told her. She had nothing in the world to go by, not a scrap of evidence to support her conviction that, though my body was crippled, my mind was not. In spite of all the doctors and specialists told her, she would not agree. I don't believe she knew why—she just knew, without feeling the smallest shade of doubt.

8 Finding that the doctors could not help in any way beyond telling her not to place her trust in me, or, in other words, to forget I was a human creature, rather to regard me as just something to be fed and washed and then put away again, Mother decided there and then to take matters into her own hands. I was *her* child, and therefore part of the family. No matter how dull and incapable I might grow up to be, she was determined to treat me on the same plane as the others, and not as the "queer one" in the back room who was never spoken of when there were visitors present.

9 That was a momentous decision as far as my future life was concerned. It meant that I would always have my mother on my side to help me fight all the battles that were to come, and to inspire me with new strength when I was almost beaten. But it wasn't easy for her because now the relatives and friends had decided otherwise. They contended that I should be taken kindly, sympathetically, but not seriously. That would be a mistake. "For your own sake," they told her, "don't look to this boy as you would to the others; it would only break

your heart in the end." Luckily for me, Mother and Father held out against the lot of them. But Mother wasn't content just to say that I was not an idiot: she set out to prove it, not because of any rigid sense of duty, but out of love. That is why she was so successful.

10 At this time she had the five other children to look after besides the "difficult one," though as yet it was not by any means a full house. They were my brothers, Jim, Tony, and Paddy, and my two sisters, Lily and Mona, all of them very young, just a year or so between each of them, so that they were almost exactly like steps of stairs.

11 Four years rolled by and I was now five, and still as helpless as a newly born baby. While my father was out at bricklaying, earning our bread and butter for us, Mother was slowly, patiently pulling down the wall, brick by brick, that seemed to thrust itself between me and the other children, slowly, patiently penetrating beyond the thick curtain that hung over my mind, separating it from theirs. It was hard, heart-breaking work, for often all she got from me in return was a vague smile and perhaps a faint gurgle. I could not speak or even mumble, nor could I sit up without support on my own, let alone take steps. But I wasn't inert or motionless. I seemed, indeed, to be convulsed with movement, wild, stiff, snakelike movement that never left me, except in sleep. My fingers twisted and twitched continually, my arms twined backwards and would often shoot out suddenly this way and that, and my head lolled and sagged sideways. I was a queer, crooked little fellow.

12 Mother tells me how one day she had been sitting with me for hours in an upstairs bedroom, showing me pictures out of a great big storybook that I had got from Santa Claus last Christmas and telling me the names of the different animals and flowers that were in them, trying without success to get me to repeat them. This had gone on for hours while she talked and laughed with me. Then at the end of it she leaned over me and said gently into my ear:

13 "Did you like it, Chris? Did you like the bears and the monkeys and all the lovely flowers? Nod your head for yes, like a good boy."

14 But I could make no sign that I had understood her. Her face was bent over mine hopefully. Suddenly, involuntarily, my queer hand reached up and grasped one of the dark curls that fell in a thick cluster about her neck. Gently she loosened the clenched fingers, though some dark strands were still clutched between them.

15 Then she turned away from my curious stare and left the room, crying. The door closed behind her. It all seemed hopeless. It looked as though there was some justification for my relatives' contention that I was an idiot and beyond help.

16 They now spoke of an institution.

17 "Never!" said my mother almost fiercely, when this was suggested to her. "I know my boy is not an idiot; it is his body that is shattered, not his mind. I'm sure of that."

18 Sure? Yet inwardly, she prayed God would give her some proof of her faith. She knew it was one thing to believe but quite another thing to prove.

19 I was now five, and still I showed no real sign of intelligence. I showed no apparent interest in things except with my toes—more especially those of my left foot. Although my natural habits were clean, I could not aid myself, but in this respect my father took care of me. I used to lie on my back all the time in the kitchen or, on bright warm days, out in the garden, a little bundle of crooked muscles and twisted nerves, surrounded by a family that loved me and hoped for me and that made me part of their own warmth and humanity. I was lonely, imprisoned in a world of my own, unable to communicate with others, cut off, separated from them as though a glass wall stood between my existence and theirs, thrusting me beyond the sphere of their lives and activities. I longed to run about and play with the rest, but I was unable to break loose from my bondage.

20 Then, suddenly, it happened! In a moment everything was changed, my future life molded into a definite shape, my mother's faith in me rewarded, and her secret fear changed into open triumph.

21 It happened so quickly, so simply after all the years of waiting and uncertainty, that I can see and feel the whole scene as if it had happened last week. It was the afternoon of a cold, gray December day. The streets outside glistened with snow, the white sparkling flakes stuck and melted on the windowpanes and hung on the boughs of the trees like molten silver. The wind howled dismally, whipping up little whirling columns of snow that rose and fell at every fresh gust. And over all, the dull, murky sky stretched like a dark canopy, a vast infinity of grayness.

22 Inside, all the family were gathered round the big kitchen fire that lit up the little room with a warm glow and made giant shadows dance on the walls and ceiling.

23 In a corner Mona and Paddy were sitting, huddled together, a few torn school primers before them. They were writing down little sums onto an old chipped slate, using a bright piece of yellow chalk. I was close to them, propped up by a few pillows against the wall, watching.

24 It was the chalk that attracted me so much. It was a long, slender stick of vivid yellow. I had never seen anything like it before, and it showed up so well against the black surface of the slate that I was fascinated by it as much as if it had been a stick of gold.

25 Suddenly, I wanted desperately to do what my sister was doing. Then—without thinking or knowing exactly what I was doing, I reached out and took the stick of chalk out of my sister's hand—with my left foot.

26 I do not know why I used my left foot to do this. It is a puzzle to many people as well as to myself, for, although I had displayed a curious interest in my toes at an early age, I had never attempted

before this to use either of my feet in any way. They could have been as useless to me as were my hands. That day, however, my left foot, apparently by its own volition, reached out and very impolitely took the chalk out of my sister's hand.

27 I held it tightly between my toes, and, acting on an impulse, made a wild sort of scribble with it on the slate. Next moment I stopped, a bit dazed, surprised, looking down at the stick of yellow chalk stuck between my toes, not knowing what to do with it next, hardly knowing how it got there. Then I looked up and became aware that everyone had stopped talking and was staring at me silently. Nobody stirred. Mona, her black curls framing her chubby little face, stared at me with great big eyes and open mouth. Across the open hearth, his face lit by flames, sat my father, leaning forward, hands outspread on his knees, his shoulders tense. I felt the sweat break out on my forehead.

28 My mother came in from the pantry with a steaming pot in her hand. She stopped midway between the table and the fire, feeling the tension flowing through the room. She followed their stare and saw me in the corner. Her eyes looked from my face down to my foot, with the chalk gripped between my toes. She put down the pot.

29 Then she crossed over to me and knelt down beside me, as she had done so many times before.

30 "I'll show you what to do with it, Chris," she said, very slowly and in a queer, choked way, her face flushed as if with some inner excitement.

31 Taking another piece of chalk from Mona, she hesitated, then very deliberately drew, on the floor in front of me, *the single letter "A."*

32 "Copy that," she said, looking steadily at me. "Copy it, Christy."

33 I couldn't.

34 I looked about me, looked around at the faces that were turned towards me, tense, excited faces that were at that moment frozen, immobile, eager, waiting for a miracle in their midst.

35 The stillness was profound. The room was full of flame and shadow that danced before my eyes and lulled my taut nerves into a sort of waking sleep. I could hear the sound of the water tap dripping in the pantry, the loud ticking of the clock on the mantel shelf, and the soft hiss and crackle of the logs on the open hearth.

36 I tried again. I put out my foot and made a wild jerking stab with the chalk which produced a very crooked line and nothing more. Mother held the slate steady for me.

37 "Try again, Chris," she whispered in my ear. "Again."

38 I did. I stiffened my body and put my left foot out again, for the third time. I drew one side of the letter. I drew half the other side. Then the stick of chalk broke and I was left with a stump. I wanted to fling it away and give up. Then I felt my mother's hand on my shoulder. I tried once more. Out went my foot. I shook, I sweated and strained every muscle. My hands were so tightly clenched that my fingernails

bit into the flesh. I set my teeth so hard that I nearly pierced my lower lip. Everything in the room swam till the faces around me were mere patches of white. But—I drew it—*the letter "A."* There it was on the floor before me. Shaky, with awkward, wobbly sides and a very uneven center line. But it *was* the letter "A." I looked up. I saw my mother's face for a moment, tears on her cheeks. Then my father stooped and hoisted me onto his shoulder.

39 I had done it! It had started—the thing that was to give my mind its chance of expressing itself. True, I couldn't speak with my lips. But now I would speak through something more lasting than spoken words—written words.

40 That one letter, scrawled on the floor with a broken bit of yellow chalk gripped between my toes, was my road to a new world, my key to mental freedom. It was to provide a source of relaxation to the tense, taut thing that was I, which panted for expression behind a twisted mouth.

✧ *Evaluating the Text*

1. What unusual signs alerted Christy's mother that he might be physically impaired? What did her response to the doctors' diagnosis reveal about her as a person and her attitude toward Christy?

2. What did Christy's mother hope to achieve by showing him pictures of animals and flowers? How did her friends and relatives react to her decision to treat Christy as if he were capable of mental development? How would Christy's day-to-day treatment have differed if his mother had not treated him as a member of the family?

3. Why does the narrative shift from Christy's mother's perspective to Christy's recollection of the day he was able to form the letter *A* with his left foot?

4. From the point of view of Christy's mother, father, and siblings, how did they know that his forming the letter *A* was a sign of intelligence and not merely an imitative gesture? How does the conclusion of this account suggest that this moment had deeper meaning for Christy than it did even for his family? What did this mean to him?

✧ *Exploring Different Perspectives*

1. Contrast the obstacles the narrators overcome in Brown's essay and in Sucheng Chan's memoir.

2. What cultural prejudices toward disability can be seen in Ireland according to Brown and in China as described by Sucheng Chan?

✧ *Extending Viewpoints through Writing and Research*

1. On any given day, how do you think Christy would have been treated if his mother had not made the decision to treat him as a member of the family? Write a brief account analyzing why over a period of time the difference in the way he was treated might have been capable of producing the unexpected development Christy describes. Include in your account such everyday events as meals and visits from friends.
2. Rent a copy of the 1989 Academy Award–winning film *My Left Foot,* based on Christy Brown's autobiography of the same name, and discuss which treatment, film or written word, more effectively dramatized the issues at stake and the feelings of Christy and his family at the moment when he drew the letter *A*.
3. If you have ever been temporarily physically incapacitated or have a disability, write an essay that will help your audience understand your plight and the visible and subtle psychological aspects of discrimination that the disabled must endure every day.

Douchan Gersi

Initiated into an Iban Tribe of Headhunters

Douchan Gersi is the producer and director of the television series called Explore, *seen on PBS and The Discovery Channel. He has traveled extensively throughout the world in search of tribal peoples. "Initiated into an Iban Tribe of Headhunters," from his book* Explorer *(1987), tells of the harrowing initiation process he underwent to become a member of the Iban tribe in Borneo. In 2003, Gersi published (in French) a study of the life of the Maharajas in India and in 1991 he wrote* Faces in the Smoke: An Eyewitness Experience of Voodoo, Shamanism, Psychic Healing, and Other Amazing Human Powers.

The Iban are a friendly and hospitable people who are a majority of the Sarawak population of northwest Borneo. They are well known for their textile weaving, woodcarving, and weaving of intricate mats and baskets. An accomplished Iban man not only would be proficient in argument and courageous in hunting, but also would be skillful in woodcarving. The traditional Iban dwelling is the longhouse (which is nearly always built by the bank of a navigable river), a semipermanent structure housing twenty or more families in separate apartments. The longhouse is decorated with drums, gongs, weavings, and hanging skulls from days gone by. The area in which they live is also prized for its orangutan population, a protected species that has resulted in a burgeoning tourism trade. The Iban have many festivals through which they maintain their cultural identity and heritage. Superstitions abound and the carved wood charms (often symbolized by crocodile and python figures) play a crucial role in protecting families from malevolent spirits.

Before You Read

Consider the ways in which rites of passage provide a means by which cultures divide "us" from "them."

The hopeful man sees success where others see shadows and storm.

—O. S. Marden

1 Against Tawa's [the family head who Gersi shared living space with in the longhouse] excellent advice I asked the chief if I could

become a member of their clan. It took him a while before he could give me an answer, for he had to question the spirits of their ancestors and wait for their reply to appear through different omens: the flight of a blackbird, the auguries of a chick they sacrificed. A few days after the question, the answer came:

2 "Yes . . . but!"

3 The "but" was that I would have to undergo their initiation. Without knowing exactly what physical ordeal was in store, I accepted. I knew I had been through worse and survived. It was to begin in one week.

4 Late at night I was awakened by a girl slipping into my bed. She was sweet and already had a great knowledge of man's morphology. Like all the others who came and "visited" me this way every night, she was highly skilled in the arts of love. Among the Iban, only unmarried women offer sexual hospitality, and no one obliged these women to offer me their favors. Sexual freedom ends at marriage. Unfaithfulness—except during yearly fertility celebrations when everything, even incest at times, is permitted—is punished as an offense against their matrimonial laws.

5 As a sign of respect to family and the elders, sexual hospitality is not openly practiced. The girls always came when my roommates were asleep and left before they awoke. They were free to return or give their place to their girlfriends.

6 The contrast between the violence of some Iban rituals and the beauty of their art, their sociability, their kindness, and their personal warmth has always fascinated me. I also witnessed that contrast among a tribe of Papuans (who, besides being headhunters, practice cannibalism) and among some African tribes. In fact, tribes devoted to cannibalism and other human sacrifices are often among the most sociable of people, and their art, industry, and trading systems are more advanced than other tribes that don't have these practices.

7 For my initiation, they had me lie down naked in a four-foot-deep pit filled with giant carnivorous ants. Nothing held me there. At any point I could easily have escaped, but the meaning of this rite of passage was not to kill me. The ritual was intended to test my courage and my will, to symbolically kill me by the pain in order for me to be reborn as a man of courage. I am not sure what their reactions would have been if I had tried to get out of the pit before their signal, but it occurred to me that although the ants might eat a little of my flesh, the Iban offered more dramatic potentials.

8 Since I wore, as Iban do, a long piece of cloth around my waist and nothing more, I had the ants running all over my body. They were everywhere. The pain of the ants' bites was intense, so I tried to relax to decrease the speed of my circulation and therefore the effects of the poison. But I couldn't help trying to get them away from my face

where they were exploring every inch of my skin. I kept my eyes closed, inhaling through my almost closed lips and exhaling through my nose to chase them away from there.

9 I don't know how long I stayed in the pit, waiting with anguish for the signal which would end my ordeal. As I tried to concentrate on my relaxing, the sound of the beaten gongs and murmurs of the assistants watching me from all around the pit started to disappear into a chaos of pain and loud heartbeat.

10 Then suddenly I heard Tawa and the chief calling my name. I removed once more the ants wandering on my eyelids before opening my eyes and seeing my friends smiling to indicate that it was over. I got out of the pit on my own, but I needed help to rid myself of the ants, which were determined to eat all my skin. After the men washed my body, the shaman applied an herbal mixture to ease the pain and reduce the swellings. I would have quit and left the village then had I known that the "pit" experience was just the hors d'oeuvre.

11 The second part of the physical test started early the next morning. The chief explained the "game" to me. It was Hide and Go Seek Iban-style. I had to run without any supplies, weapons, or food, and for three days and three nights escape a group of young warriors who would leave the village a few hours after my departure and try to find me. If I were caught, my head would be used in a ceremony. The Iban would have done so without hate. It was simply the rule of their life. Birth and death. A death that always engenders new life.

12 When I asked, "What would happen if someone refused this part of the initiation?" the chief replied that such an idea wasn't possible. Once one had begun, there was no turning back. I knew the rules governing initiations among the cultures of tradition but never thought they would be applied to me. Whether or not I survived the initiation, I would be symbolically killed in order to be reborn among them. I had to die from my present time and identity into another life. I was aware that, among some cultures, initiatory ordeals are so arduous that young initiates sometimes really die. These are the risks if one wishes to enter into another world.

13 I was given time to get ready and the game began. I ran like hell without a plan or, it seemed to me, a prayer of surviving. Running along a path I had never taken, going I knew not where, I thought about every possible way I could escape from the young warriors. To hide somewhere. But where? Climb a tree and hide in it? Find a hole and squeeze in it? Bury myself under rocks and mud? But all of these seemed impossible. I had a presentiment they would find me anyway. So I ran straight ahead, my head going crazy by dint of searching for a way to safely survive the headhunters.

14 I would prefer staying longer with ants, I thought breathlessly. It was safer to stay among them for a whole day since they were just

simple pain and fear compared to what I am about to undergo. I don't want to die.

15 For the first time I realized the real possibility of death—no longer in a romantic way, but rather at the hands of butchers.

16 Ten minutes after leaving the long house, I suddenly heard a call coming from somewhere around me. Still running, I looked all around trying to locate who was calling, and why. At the second call I stopped, cast my gaze about, and saw a woman's head peering out from the bushes. I recognized her as one of my pretty lovers. I hesitated, not knowing if she were part of the hunting party or a goddess come to save me. She called again. I thought, God, what to do? How will I escape from the warriors? As I stood there truly coming into contact with my impossible situation, I began to panic. She called again. With her fingers she showed me what the others would do if they caught me. Her forefinger traced an invisible line from one side of her throat to the other. If someone was going to kill me, why not her? I joined her and found out she was in a lair. I realized I had entered the place where the tribe's women go to hide during their menstruation. This area is taboo for men. Each woman has her own refuge. Some have shelters made of branches, others deep covered holes hidden behind bushes with enough space to eat and sleep and wait until their time is past.

17 She invited me to make myself comfortable. That was quite difficult since it was just large enough for one person. But I had no choice. And after all, it was a paradise compared to what I would have undergone had I not by luck crossed this special ground.

18 Nervously and physically exhausted by my run and fear and despair, I soon fell asleep. Around midnight I woke. She gave me rice- and meat. We exchanged a few words. Then it was her turn to sleep.

19 The time I spent in the lair with my savior went fast. I tried to sleep all day long, an escape from the concerns of my having broken a taboo. And I wondered what would happen to me if the headhunters were to learn where I spent the time of my physical initiation.

20 Then, when it was safe, I snuck back to the village . . . in triumph. I arrived before the warriors, who congratulated and embraced me when they returned. I was a headhunter at last.

21 I spent the next two weeks quietly looking at the Iban through new eyes. But strangely enough, instead of the initiation putting me closer to them, it had the opposite effect. I watched them more and more from an anthropological distance: my Iban brothers became an interesting clan whose life I witnessed but did not really share. And then suddenly I was bored and yearned for my own tribe. When Tawa had to go to an outpost to exchange pepper grains for other goods, I took a place aboard his canoe. Two days later I was in a small

taxi-boat heading toward Sibu, the first leg in civilization on my voyage home.

22 I think of them often. . . . I think about Tawa and the girl who saved my life, and all the others sitting on the veranda. How long will my adopted village survive before being destroyed like all the others in the way of civilization? And what has become of those who marked my flesh with the joy of their lives and offered me the best of their souls? If they are slowly vanishing from my memories, I know that I am part of the stories they tell. I know that my life among them will be perpetuated until the farthest tomorrow. Now I am a story caught in a living legend of a timeless people.

✧ *Evaluating the Text*

1. What do the unusual sexual customs of hospitality bestowed upon outsiders suggest about the different cultural values of the Iban? Do these customs suggest that the initiation would be harsher or milder than Gersi expected? Interpret this episode as it relates to the probable nature of Gersi's forthcoming initiation.

2. In a paragraph, explain the nature of the "hide and go seek" game that constituted the main test for a candidate. Explain why the use of the lighthearted term *game* is ironic in this context.

3. How does the reappearance of one of the girls who had earlier paid a nocturnal "visit" to Gersi result in his finding a safe hiding place? What does the nature of the hiding place reveal about the tribe's taboos?

4. Explain in what way the initiation resulted in Gersi feeling quite different than he had expected. That is, instead of feeling he was now part of the tribe, he actually felt more distant from them than he had felt before the initiation. To what factors do you attribute the unexpected sense of alienation? What did he discover about his own preconceptions during the initiation that stripped away certain romantic ideas he had about the Iban and the ability of any outsider to truly become a member of the tribe?

✧ *Exploring Different Perspectives*

1. Compare Gersi's sense of estrangement with Lydia Minatoya's dissatisfaction in "Transformation" after each writer has presumably been accepted into their respective communities.

2. What tribal symbols are important in Gersi's account and in Enid Schildkrout's article?

✧ *Extending Viewpoints through Writing and Research*

1. If you have ever been initiated into a fraternity or sorority or any other organization, compare the nature of Gersi's initiation with the one you experienced. In particular, try to identify particular stages in these initiations that mark the "death" of the outsider and the "rebirth" of the initiated member.

2. Examine any religious ritual, such as confirmation in the Catholic Church, and analyze it in terms of an initiation rite. For example, the ceremony of the Catholic Church by which one is confirmed as an adult member follows this pattern. A period of preparation is spent the year before confirmation. The ceremony has several stages, including confession, communion, and subsequent confirmation. Candidates are routinely quizzed prior to communion about their knowledge of basic theology and must be sponsored by a member in good standing of the Catholic community. For example, what is the significance of the newly chosen confirmation name? What responsibilities and obligations do candidates incur who complete the confirmation ceremony?

3. What was your reaction to learning that the culture Gersi describes is one that exists today (in Borneo) two days away from taxi-boats and civilization? Would you ever consider undertaking a journey to such a place? Describe the most exotic place you want to visit, and explain why you would want to go there.

4. A recent visit by students to the Iban with accompanying pictures can be found at http://www.Newsroom.unl.edu/releases/2008/07/21/unl+stud . . .

Enid Schildkrout

Body Art as Visual Language

Enid Schildkrout was chair and curator at the American Museum of Natural History and received her doctorate in social anthropology from Cambridge University in 1970. In the 1960s she did fieldwork in Ghana and continues to work with children of Ghanaian immigrants in New York City. The following essay first appeared in the journal Anthro Notes *(2001) and explores the diverse cultural meanings of body art.*

Before You Read

What different personal and social meanings can body art such as tattoos, piercing, makeup, and hairstyles express?

1 Body art is not just the latest fashion. In fact, if the impulse to create art is one of the defining signs of humanity, the body may well have been the first canvas. Alongside paintings on cave walls created by early humans over 30,000 years ago, we find handprints and ochre deposits suggesting body painting. Some of the earliest mummies known—like the "Ice Man" from the Italian-Austrian Alps, known as Otzi, and others from central Asia, the Andes, Egypt and Europe—date back to 5000 years. People were buried with ornaments that would have been worn through body piercings, and remains of others show intentionally elongated or flattened skulls. Head shaping was practiced 5000 years ago in Chile and until the 18th century in France. Stone and ceramic figurines found in ancient graves depict people with every kind of body art known today. People have always marked their bodies with signs of individuality, social status, and cultural identity.

The Language of Body Art

2 There is no culture in which people do not, or did not paint, pierce, tattoo, reshape, or simply adorn their bodies. Fashions change and forms of body art come and go, but people everywhere do something or other to "package" their appearance. No sane or civilized person goes out in the raw; everyone grooms, dresses, or adorns some part of their body to present to the world. Body art communicates a person's status in society; displays accomplishments; and encodes memories, desires, and life histories.

3 Body art is a visual language. To understand it one needs to know the vocabulary, including the shared symbols, myths, and social values that are written on the body. From tattoos to top hats, body art makes a statement about the person who wears it. But body art is often misunderstood and misinterpreted because its messages do not necessarily translate across cultures. Elaborately pictorial Japanese tattooing started among men in certain occupational groups and depicts the exploits of a gangster hero drawn from a Chinese epic. The tattoos have more meaning to those who know the stories underlying the images than they do to people unfamiliar with the tales. Traditional Polynesian tattooing is mainly geometric and denotes rank and political status but more recently has been used to define ethnic identity within Pacific island societies.

4 In an increasingly global world, designs, motifs, even techniques of body modification move across cultural boundaries, but in the process their original meanings are often lost. An animal crest worn as a tattoo, carved into a totem pole, or woven into a blanket may signify membership in a particular clan among Indians on the Northwest Coast of North America, but when worn by people outside these cultures, the designs may simply refer to the wearer's identification with an alternative way of life. Polynesian or Indonesian tattoo designs worn by Westerners are admired for the beauty of their graphic qualities, but their original cultural meanings are rarely understood. A tattoo from Borneo was once worn to light the path of a person's soul after death, but in New York or Berlin it becomes a sign of rebellion from "coat and tie" culture.

5 Because body art is such an obvious way of signaling cultural differences, people often use it to identify, exoticize, and ostracize others. Tattoos, scarification, or head shaping may be a sign of high status in one culture and low status in another, but to a total outsider these practices may appear to be simply "mutilation." From the earliest voyages of discovery to contemporary tourism, travelers of all sorts—explorers and missionaries, soldiers and sailors, traders and tourists—have brought back images of the people they meet. These depictions sometimes reveal as much about the people looking at the body art as about the people making and wearing it. Some early images of Europeans and Americans by non-Westerners emphasized elaborate clothing and facial hair. Alternatively, Western images of Africans, Polynesians and Native Americans focused on the absence of clothes and the presence of tattoos, body paint and patterns of scars. Representations of body art in engravings, paintings, photographs and film are powerful visual metaphors that have been used both to record cultural differences and to proclaim one group's supposed superiority over another.

Body Art: Permanent and Ephemeral

6 Most people think that permanent modification of the skin, muscles, and bones is what body art is all about. But if one looks at body art as a form of communication, there is no logical reason to separate permanent forms of body art, like tattoos, scarification, piercing, or plastic surgery, from temporary forms, such as makeup, clothing, or hairstyles. Punks and sideshow artists may have what appears to be extreme body art, but everyone does it in one way or another. All of these modifications convey information about a person's identity.

7 Nonetheless, some forms of body art are undeniably more permanent than others. The decision to display a tattoo is obviously different from the decision to change the color of one's lipstick or dye one's hair. Tattooing, piercing, and scarification are more likely to be ways of signaling one's place in society, or an irreversible life passage like the change from childhood to adulthood. Temporary forms of body art, like clothing, ornaments and painting, more often mark a moment or simply follow a fashion. But these dichotomies don't stand up to close scrutiny across cultures: tattoos and scarification marks are often done to celebrate an event and dying or cutting one's hair, while temporary, may signal a life-changing event, such as a wedding or a funeral.

Cultural Ideals of Beauty

8 Ideas of beauty vary from one culture to another. Some anthropologists and psychologists believe that babies in all cultures respond positively to certain kinds of faces. The beautiful body is often associated with the healthy body and non-threatening facial expressions and gestures. But this does not mean that beauty is defined the same way in all cultures. People's ideas about the way a healthy person should look are not the same in all cultures: some see fat as an indication of health and wealth while others feel quite the opposite. People in some cultures admire and respect signs of aging, while others do all they can to hide gray hair and wrinkles.

9 Notwithstanding the fact that parents often make decisions for their children, like whether or not to pierce the ears of infants, in general I would maintain that to be considered art and not just a marking, body art has to have some measure of freedom and intentionality in its creation. The brands put on enslaved people, or the numbers tattooed on concentration camp victims, or the scars left from an unwanted injury are body markings not body art.

Cultural Significance of Body Art

10 Body art takes on specific meanings in different cultures. It can serve as a link with ancestors, deities, or spirits. Besides being decorative,

tattoos, paint, and scars can mediate the relationships between people and the supernatural world. The decorated body can serve as a shield to repel evil or as a means of attracting good fortune. Tattoos in central Borneo had the same designs as objects of everyday use and shielded people from dangerous spirits. Selk'nam men in Tierra del Fuego painted their bodies to transform themselves into spirits for initiation ceremonies. Australian Aborigines painted similar designs on cave walls and their bodies to indicate the location of sacred places revealed in dreams.

11 Transitions in status and identity, for example, the transition between childhood and adulthood, are often seen as times of danger. Body art protects a vulnerable person, whether an initiate, a bride, or a deceased person, in this transitional phase. To ensure her good fortune, an Indian bride's hands and feet are covered in henna designs that also emphasize her beauty. For protection during initiation, a central African Chokwe girl's body is covered in white kaolin. In many societies, both the dead and those who mourn them are covered with paints and powders for decoration and protection.

12 Worldwide travel, large-scale migrations, and increasing access to global networks of communication mean that body art today is a kaleidoscopic mix of traditional practices and new inventions. Materials, designs, and practices move from one cultural context to another. Traditional body art practices are given new meanings as they move across cultural and social boundaries.

13 Body art is always changing, and in some form or another always engaging: it allows people to reinvent themselves—to rebel, to follow fashion, or to play and experiment with new identities. Like performance artists and actors, people in everyday life use body art to cross boundaries of gender, national identity, and cultural stereotypes.

14 Body art can be an expression of individuality, but it can also be an expression of group identity. Body art is about conformity and rebellion, freedom and authority. Its messages and meanings only make sense in the context of culture, but because it is such a personal art form, it continually challenges cultural assumptions about the ideal, the desirable, and the appropriately presented body.

Body Art Techniques

Body Painting

15 Body painting, the most ephemeral and flexible of all body art, has the greatest potential for transforming a person into something else—a spirit, a work of art, another gender, even a map to a sacred place including the afterlife. It can be simply a way of emphasizing a person's visual appeal, a serious statement of allegiance, or a protective and empowering coating.

16 Natural clays and pigments made from a great variety of plants and minerals are often mixed with vegetable oils and animal fat to make body paint. These include red and yellow ochre (iron rich clay), red cam wood, cinnabar, gold dust, many roots, fruits and flowers, cedar bark, white kaolin, chalk, and temporary skin dyes made from indigo and henna leaves. People all over the world adorn the living and also treat the dead with body paint.

17 The colors of body paint often have symbolic significance, varying from culture to culture. Some clays and body paints are felt to have protective and auspicious properties, making them ideal for use in initiation rituals, for weddings, and for funerals—all occasions of transition from one life stage to another.

18 Historically, body paints and dyes have been important trade items. Indians of North America exchanged many valuable items for vermillion, which is mercuric sulphide (an artificial equivalent of the natural dye made from cinnabar). Mixed with red lead by European traders, it could cause or sometimes caused mercury poisoning in the wearer.

Makeup

19 Makeup consists of removable substances—paint, powders, and dyes—applied to enhance or transform appearance. Commonly part of regular grooming, makeup varies according to changing definitions of beauty. For vanity and social acceptance, or for medicinal or ritual purposes, people regularly transform every visible part of their body. They have tanned or whitened skin; changed the color of their lips, eyes, teeth, and hair; and added or removed "beauty" spots.

20 From the 10th to the 19th century, Japanese married women and courtesans blackened their teeth with a paste made from a mixture of tea and sake soaked in iron scraps; black teeth were considered beautiful and sexually appealing.

21 Makeup can accentuate the contrast between men and women, camouflage perceived imperfections or signify a special occasion or ritual state. Makeup, like clothing and hairstyles, allows people to reinvent themselves in everyday life.

22 Rituals and ceremonies often require people to wear certain kinds of makeup, clothing, or hairstyles to indicate that a person is taking on a new identity (representing an ancestor or a spirit in a masquerade, for example) or transforming his or her social identity as in an initiation ceremony, wedding, graduation or naming ceremony. Male Japanese actors in Kabuki theater represent women by using strictly codified paints and motifs, and the designs and motifs of Chinese theatrical makeup indicate the identity of a character.

Hair

23 Hair is one the easiest and most obvious parts of the body subject to change, and combing and washing hair is part of everyday grooming in

most cultures. Styles of combing, braiding, parting, and wrapping hair can signify status and gender, age and ritual status, or membership in a certain group.

24 Hair often has powerful symbolic significance. Covering the head can be a sign of piety and respect, whether in a place of worship or all the time. Orthodox Jewish women shave their heads but also cover them with wigs or scarves. Muslim women in many parts of the world cover their heads, and sometimes cover their faces too, with scarves or veils. Sikh men in India never cut their hair and cover their heads with turbans. And the Queen of England is rarely seen without a hat.

25 Cutting hair is a ritual act in some cultures and heads are often shaved during rituals that signify the passage from one life stage to another. Hair itself, once cut, can be used as a symbolic substance. Being part, and yet not part, of a person, living or dead, hair can take on the symbolic power of the person. Some Native Americans formerly attached hair from enemies to war shirts, while warriors in Borneo formerly attached hair from captured enemies to war shields.

26 Reversing the normal treatment of hair, whatever that is in a particular culture, can be a sign of rebellion or of special status. Adopting the uncombed hair of the Rastafarians can be a sign of rebellion among some people, while for Rastafarians it is a sign of membership in a particular religious group. In many cultures people in mourning deliberately do not comb or wash their hair for a period of time, thereby showing that they are temporarily not part of normal everyday life.

27 What we do with our hair is a way of expressing our identity, and it is easy to look around and see how hair color, cut, style, and its very presence or absence, tells others much about how we want to be seen.

Body Shaping

28 The shape of the human body changes throughout life, but in many cultures people have found ways to permanently or temporarily sculpt the body. To conform to culturally defined ideals of male and female beauty, people have bound the soft bones of babies' skulls or children's feet, stretched their necks with rings, removed ribs to achieve tiny waists, and most commonly today, sculpted the body through plastic surgery.

29 Becoming fat is a sign of health, wealth and fertility in some societies, and fattening is sometimes part of a girl's coming of age ceremony. Tiny waists, small feet, and large or small breasts and buttocks have been prized or scorned as ideals of female beauty. Less common are ways of shaping men's bodies but developing muscles, shaping the head, or gaining weight are ways in which cultural ideals of male beauty and power have been expressed.

30 Head shaping is still done in parts of South America. For the Inka of South America and the Maya of Central America and Mexico, a specially

shaped head once signified nobility. Because the skull bones of infants and children are not completely fused, the application of pressure with pads, boards, bindings, or massage results in a gently shaped head that can be a mark of high status or local identity.

31 While Western plastic surgery developed first as a way of correcting the injuries of war, particularly after WW II, today people use plastic surgery to smooth their skin, remove unwanted fat, and reshape parts of their bodies.

Scarification

32 Permanent patterns of scars on the skin, inscribed onto the body through scarification, can be signs of beauty and indicators of status. In some cultures, a smooth, unmarked skin represents an ideal of beauty, but people in many other cultures see smooth skin as a naked, unattractive surface. Scarification, also called cicatrisation, alters skin texture by cutting the skin and controlling the body's healing process. The cuts are treated to prevent infection and to enhance the scars' visibility. Deep cuts leave visible incisions after the skin heals, while inserting substances like clay or ash in the cuts results in permanently raised wheals or bumps, known as keloids. Substances inserted into the wounds may result in changes in skin color, creating marks similar to tattoos. Cutting elaborate and extensive decorative patterns into the skin usually indicates a permanent change in a person's status. Because scarification is painful, the richly scarred person is often honored for endurance and courage. Branding is a form of scarification that creates a scar after the surface of the skin has been burned. Branding was done in some societies as a part of a rite of passage, but in western Europe and elsewhere branding, as well as some forms of tattoo, were widely used to mark captives, enslaved peoples, and criminals. Recently, some individuals and members of fraternities on U.S. college campuses have adopted branding as a radical form of decoration and self-identification.

Tattooing

33 Tattoo is the insertion of ink or some other pigment through the outer covering of the body, the epidermis, into the dermis, the second layer of skin. Tattooists use a sharp implement to puncture the skin and thus make an indelible mark, design, or picture on the body. The resulting patterns or figures vary according to the purpose of the tattoo and the materials available for its coloration.

34 Different groups and cultures have used a variety of techniques in this process. Traditional Polynesian tattooists punctured the skin by tapping a needle with a small hammer. The Japanese work by hand but with bundles of needles set in wooden handles. Since the late 19th century, the electric tattoo machine and related technological advances in equipment have revolutionized tattoo in the West, expanding the range of possible

designs, the colors available, and the ease with which a tattoo can be applied to the body. Prisoners have used materials as disparate as guitar strings and reconstructed electric shavers to create tattoos. Tattoos are usually intended as permanent markings, and it is only recently through the use of expensive laser techniques that they can be removed.

35 While often decorative, tattoos send important cultural messages. The "text" on the skin can be read as a commitment to some group, an emblem of a rite of passage, a personal or a fashion statement. In fact, cosmetic tattooing of eyebrows and eyeliner is one of the fastest growing of all tattoo enterprises. Tattoos can also signify bravery and commitment to a long, painful process—as is the case with Japanese full body tattooing or Māori body and facial patterns. Though there have been numerous religious and social injunctions against tattooing, marking the body in this way has been one of the most persistent and universal forms of body art.

Piercing

36 Body piercing, which allows ornaments to be worn in the body, has been a widespread practice since ancient times. Piercing involves long-term insertion of an object through the skin in a way that permits healing around the opening. Most commonly pierced are the soft tissues of the face, but many peoples, past and present, have also pierced the genitals and the chest. Ear, nose and lip ornaments, as well as pierced figurines, have been found in ancient burials of the Inka and Moche of Peru, the Aztecs and Maya of ancient Mexico, and in graves of central Asian, European and Mediterranean peoples.

37 The act of piercing is often part of a ritual change of status. Bleeding that occurs during piercing is sometimes thought of as an offering to gods, spirits or ancestors. Particular ornaments may be restricted to certain groups—men or women, rulers or priests—or may be inserted as part of a ceremony marking a change in status. Because ornaments can be made of precious and rare materials, they may signal privilege and wealth.

✧ *Evaluating the Text*

1. In what way has body art, including tatooing, piercing, and scarification, often served to signal important transitions in status and identity?
2. What forms can body art take in various cultures? What different aspects of physical appearance are often the sites of these transformations?
3. In what radically different ways is beauty defined in different cultures? What assumptions underlie these modifications?

✧ *Exploring Different Perspectives*

1. Compare how the issue of beauty is treated in Schildkrout's analysis and Ruskin Bond's story "The Eyes Are Not Here."
2. What paradox emerges from the way society views disability, as in Christy Brown's narrative, and in Schildkrout's discussion of cutting, shaping, and piercing of the body?

✧ *Extending Viewpoints through Writing and Research*

1. What body modifications—tatooing, piercing, or anything else—have you undergone or would consider? How could these be understood as symbolizing a rite of passage?
2. In a short essay, discuss the social forces that underlie the desire to decorate, modify, or even mutilate one's body.
3. How are any of the topics discussed by Schildkrout treated in typical fashion magazines? How does her approach as an anthropologist differ stylistically from those found in the fashion magazines?

To what extent does this picture illustrate Schildkrout's thesis?

Lydia Minatoya

Transformation

Lydia Minatoya was born in 1950 in Albany, New York. She received a doctorate in psychology from the University of Maryland in 1981 and taught and traveled throughout Asia. The following selection is drawn from Talking to High Monks in the Snow *(1992) and describes the concerns of her parents when choosing a name for her. She has also published* The Strangeness of Beauty *(1999).*

Before You Read

How might the name immigrant parents give to a child express a wish for the child's future?

1 Perhaps it begins with my naming. During her pregnancy, my mother was reading Dr. Spock. "Children need to belong," he cautioned. "An unusual name can make them the subject of ridicule." My father frowned when he heard this. He stole a worried glance at my sister. Burdened by her Japanese name, Misa played unsuspectingly on the kitchen floor.

2 The Japanese know full well the dangers of conspicuousness. "The nail that sticks out gets pounded down," cautions an old maxim. In America, Relocation was all the proof they needed.

3 And so it was, with great earnestness, my parents searched for a conventional name. They wanted me to have the full true promise of America.

4 "I will ask my colleague Froilan," said my father. "He is the smartest man I know."

5 "And he has poetic soul," said my mother, who cared about such things.

6 In due course, Father consulted Froilan. He gave Froilan his conditions for suitability.

7 "First, if possible, the full name should be alliterative," said my father. "Like Misa Minatoya." He closed his eyes and sang my sister's name. "Second, if not an alliteration, at least the name should have assonantal rhyme."

8 "Like Misa Minatoya?" said Froilan with a teasing grin.

9 "Exactly," my father intoned. He gave an emphatic nod. "Finally, most importantly, the name must be readily recognizable as

conventional." He peered at Froilan with hope. "Do you have any suggestions or ideas?"

10 Froilan, whose own American child was named Ricardito, thought a while.

11 "We already have selected the name for a boy," offered my father. "Eugene."

12 "Eugene?" wondered Froilan. "But it meets none of your conditions!"

13 "Eugene is a special case," said my father, "after Eugene, Oregon, and Eugene O'Neill. The beauty of the Pacific Northwest, the power of a great writer."

14 "I see," said Froilan, who did not but who realized that this naming business would be more complex than he had anticipated. "How about Maria?"

15 "Too common," said my father. "We want a *conventional* name, not a common one."

16 "Hmmm," said Froilan, wondering what the distinction was. He thought some more and then brightened. "Lydia!" he declared. He rhymed the name with media. "Lydia for *la bonita infanta!*"

17 And so I received my uncommon conventional name. It really did not provide the camouflage my parents had anticipated. I remained unalterably alien. For Dr. Spock had been addressing *American* families, and in those days, everyone knew all real American families were white.

18 Call it denial, but many Japanese Americans never quite understood that the promise of America was not truly meant for them. They lived in horse stalls at the Santa Anita racetrack and said the Pledge of Allegiance daily. They rode to Relocation Camps under armed guard, labeled with numbered tags, and sang "The Star-Spangled Banner." They lived in deserts or swamps, ludicrously imprisoned—where would they run if they ever escaped—and formed garden clubs, and yearbook staffs, and citizen town meetings. They even elected beauty queens.

19 My mother practiced her okoto and was featured in a recital. She taught classes in fashion design and her students mounted a show. Into exile she had carried an okoto and a sewing machine. They were her past and her future. She believed in Art and Technology.

20 My mother's camp was the third most populous city in the entire state of Wyoming. Across the barren lands, behind barbed wire, bloomed these little oases of democracy. The older generation bore the humiliation with pride. "*Kodomo no tame ni,*" they said. For the sake of the children. They thought that if their dignity was great, then their children would be spared. Call it valor. Call it bathos. Perhaps it was closer to slapstick: a sweet and bitter lunacy.

21 Call it adaptive behavior. Coming from a land swept by savage typhoons, ravaged by earthquakes and volcanoes, the Japanese have evolved a view of the world: a cooperative, stoic, almost magical way of thinking. Get along, work hard, and never quite see the things that can bring you pain. Against the tyranny of nature, of feudal lords, of wartime hysteria, the charm works equally well.

22 And so my parents gave me an American name and hoped that I could pass. They nourished me with the American dream: Opportunity, Will, Transformation.

23 When I was four and my sister was eight, Misa regularly used me as a comic foil. She would bring her playmates home from school and query me as I sat amidst the milk bottles on the front steps.

24 "What do you want to be when you grow up?" she would say. She would nudge her audience into attentiveness.

25 "A mother kitty cat!" I would enthuse. Our cat had just delivered her first litter of kittens and I was enchanted by the rasping tongue and soft mewings of motherhood.

26 "And what makes you think you can become a cat?" Misa would prompt, gesturing to her howling friends—wait for this; it gets better yet.

27 "This is America," I stoutly would declare. "I can grow up to be anything that I want!"

28 My faith was unshakable. I believed. Opportunity. Will. Transformation.

29 When we lived in Albany, I always was the teachers' pet. "So tiny, so precocious, so prettily dressed!" They thought I was a living doll and this was fine with me.

30 My father knew that the effusive praise would die. He had been through this with my sister. After five years of being a perfect darling, Misa had reached the age where students were tracked by ability. Then, the anger started. Misa had tested into the advanced track. It was impossible, the community declared. Misa was forbidden entry into advanced classes as long as there were white children being placed below her. In her defense, before an angry rabble, my father made a presentation to the Board of Education.

31 But I was too young to know of this. I knew only that my teachers praised and petted me. They took me to other classes as an example. "Watch now, as Lydia demonstrates attentive behavior," they would croon as I was led to an empty desk at the head of the class. I had a routine. I would sit carefully, spreading my petticoated skirt neatly beneath me. I would pull my chair close to the desk, crossing my swinging legs at my snowy white anklets. I would fold my hands carefully on the desk before me and stare pensively at the blackboard.

32 This routine won me few friends. The sixth-grade boys threw rocks at me. They danced around me in a tight circle, pulling at the

corners of their eyes. "Ching Chong Chinaman," they chanted. But teachers loved me. When I was in first grade, a third-grade teacher went weeping to the principal. She begged to have me skipped. She was leaving to get married and wanted her turn with the dolly.

33 When we moved, the greatest shock was the knowledge that I had lost my charm. From the first, my teacher failed to notice me. But to me, it did not matter. I was in love. I watched her moods, her needs, her small vanities. I was determined to ingratiate.

34 Miss Hempstead was a shimmering vision with a small upturned nose and eyes that were kewpie doll blue. Slender as a sylph, she tripped around the classroom, all saucy in her high-heeled shoes. Whenever I looked at Miss Hempstead, I pitied the Albany teachers whom, formerly, I had adored. Poor old Miss Rosenberg. With a shiver of distaste, I recalled her loose fleshy arms, her mottled hands, the scent of lavender as she crushed me to her heavy breasts.

35 Miss Hempstead had a pet of her own. Her name was Linda Sherlock. I watched Linda closely and plotted Miss Hempstead's courtship. The key was the piano. Miss Hempstead played the piano. She fancied herself a musical star. She sang songs from Broadway revues and shaped her students' reactions. "Getting to know you," she would sing. We would smile at her in a staged manner and position ourselves obediently at her feet.

36 Miss Hempstead was famous for her ability to soothe. Each day at rest time, she played the piano and sang soporific songs. Linda Sherlock was the only child who succumbed. Routinely, Linda's head would bend and nod until she crumpled gracefully onto her folded arms. A tousled strand of blonde hair would fall across her forehead. Miss Hempstead would end her song, would gently lower the keyboard cover. She would turn toward the restive eyes of the class. "Isn't she sweetness itself!" Miss Hempstead would declare. It made me want to vomit.

37 I was growing weary. My studiousness, my attentiveness, my fastidious grooming and pert poise: all were failing me. I changed my tactics. I became a problem. Miss Hempstead sent me home with nasty notes in sealed envelopes: Lydia is a slow child, a noisy child, her presence is disruptive. My mother looked at me with surprise, "*Nani desu ka?* Are you having problems with your teacher?" But I was tenacious. I pushed harder and harder, firmly caught in the obsessive need of the scorned.

38 One day I snapped. As Miss Hempstead began to sing her wretched lullabies, my head dropped to the desk with a powerful CRACK! It lolled there, briefly, then rolled toward the edge with a momentum that sent my entire body catapulting to the floor. Miss Hempstead's spine stretched slightly, like a cat that senses danger. Otherwise, she paid no heed. The linoleum floor was smooth and cool. It emitted a faint pleasant odor: a mixture of chalk dust and wax.

39 I began to snore heavily. The class sat electrified. There would be no drowsing today. The music went on and on. Finally, one boy could

not stand it. "Miss Hempstead," he probed plaintively, "Lydia has fallen asleep on the floor!" Miss Hempstead did not turn. Her playing grew slightly strident but she did not falter.

I lay on the floor through rest time. I lay on the floor through math drill. I lay on the floor while my classmates scraped around me, pushing their sturdy little wooden desks into the configuration for reading circle. It was not until penmanship practice that I finally stretched and stirred. I rose like Sleeping Beauty and slipped back to my seat. I smiled enigmatically. A spell had been broken. I never again had a crush on a teacher.

What clues in this picture of a student at her desk (who is not Minatoya) might allow you to imagine Lydia Minatoya when she was in her model student phase?

✧ *Evaluating the Text*

1. What expectations guided Minatoya's parents in choosing her name? Why does she believe that many Japanese Americans were in a state of denial about their true identity?
2. How do events involving her sister, Misa, set the stage for Lydia's entry into the public school system?
3. How did Minatoya's transformation lead her to revolt against the stereotyped role in which she was cast? What did she do?

✧ *Exploring Different Perspectives*

1. How do social cues alert the reader into how Christy Brown in "The Letter 'A' " and Minatoya are perceived?

2. How do the accounts by Minatoya and Douchan Gersi in "Initiated into an Iban Tribe of Headhunters" depict the narrator's disillusionment with what she or he thought would make her or him happy?

✧ *Extending Viewpoints through Writing and Research*

1. What expectations were involved with giving you your name? Do you like it or would you prefer to be called by another name or nickname?

2. Have you ever rebelled against a role into which you were cast? Describe your experiences.

Anwar F. Accawi

The Telephone

Anwar F. Accawi was born in a small village in Lebanon and was later educated in the United States. This 1997 essay describes the impact on his village when the first telephone was installed. He teaches at the University of Tennessee and has also written The Boy from the Tower of the Moon *(1999).*

Before You Read

What would your life have been like before the invention of the telephone?

1 When I was growing up in Magdaluna, a small Lebanese village in the terraced, rocky mountains east of Sidon, time didn't mean much to anybody, except maybe to those who were dying, or those waiting to appear in court because they had tampered with the boundary markers on their land. In those days, there was no real need for a calendar or a watch to keep track of the hours, days, months, and years. We knew what to do and when to do it, just as the Iraqi geese knew when to fly north, driven by the hot wind that blew in from the desert, and the ewes knew when to give birth to wet lambs that stood on long, shaky legs in the chilly March wind and baaed hesitantly, because they were small and cold and did not know where they were or what to do now that they were here. The only timepiece we had need of then was the sun. It rose and set, and the seasons rolled by, and we sowed seed and harvested and ate and played and married our cousins and had babies who got whooping cough and chickenpox—and those children who survived grew up and married *their* cousins and had babies who got whooping cough and chickenpox. We lived and loved and toiled and died without ever needing to know what year it was, or even the time of day.

2 It wasn't that we had no system for keeping track of time and of the important events in our lives. But ours was a natural—or rather, a divine—calendar, because it was framed by acts of God. Allah himself set down the milestones with earthquakes and droughts and floods and locusts and pestilences. Simple as our calendar was, it worked just fine for us.

3 Take, for example, the birth date of Teta Im Khalil, the oldest woman in Magdaluna and all the surrounding villages. When I first met her, we had just returned home from Syria at the end of the Big

War and were living with Grandma Mariam. Im Khalil came by to welcome my father home and to take a long, myopic look at his foreign-born wife, my mother. Im Khalil was so old that the skin of her cheeks looked like my father's grimy tobacco pouch, and when I kissed her (because Grandma insisted that I show her old friend affection), it was like kissing a soft suede glove that had been soaked with sweat and then left in a dark closet for a season. Im Khalil's face got me to wondering how old one had to be to look and taste the way she did. So, as soon as she had hobbled off on her cane, I asked Grandma, "How old is Teta Im Khalil?"

4 Grandma had to think for a moment; then she said, "I've been told that Teta was born shortly after the big snow that caused the roof on the mayor's house to cave in."

5 "And when was that?" I asked.

6 "Oh, about the time we had the big earthquake that cracked the wall in the east room."

7 Well, that was enough for me. You couldn't be more accurate than that, now, could you? Satisfied with her answer, I went back to playing with a ball made from an old sock stuffed with other, much older socks.

8 And that's the way it was in our little village for as far back as anybody could remember: people were born so many years before or after an earthquake or a flood; they got married or died so many years before or after a long drought or a big snow or some other disaster. One of the most unusual of these dates was when Antoinette the seamstress and Saeed the barber (and tooth puller) got married. That was the year of the whirlwind during which fish and oranges fell from the sky. Incredible as it may sound, the story of the fish and oranges was true, because men—respectable men, like Abu George the blacksmith and Abu Asaad the mule skinner, men who would not lie even to save their own souls—told and retold that story until it was incorporated into Magdaluna's calendar, just like the year of the black moon and the year of the locusts before it. My father, too, confirmed the story for me. He told me that he had been a small boy himself when it had rained fish and oranges from heaven. He'd gotten up one morning after a stormy night and walked out into the yard to find fish as long as his forearm still flopping here and there among the wet navel oranges.

9 The year of the fish-bearing twister, however, was not the last remarkable year. Many others followed in which strange and wonderful things happened: milestones added by the hand of Allah to Magdaluna's calendar. There was, for instance, the year of the drought, when the heavens were shut for months and the spring from which the entire village got its drinking water slowed to a trickle. The spring was about a mile from the village, in a ravine that opened at one end into a small, flat clearing covered with fine gray dust and hard, marble-sized

goat droppings, because every afternoon the goatherds brought their flocks there to water them. In the year of the drought, that little clearing was always packed full of noisy kids with big brown eyes and sticky hands, and their mothers—sinewy, overworked young women with protruding collarbones and cracked, callused brown heels. The children ran around playing tag or hide-and-seek while the women talked, shooed flies, and awaited their turns to fill up their jars with drinking water to bring home to their napping men and wet babies. There were days when we had to wait from sunup until late afternoon just to fill a small clay jar with precious, cool water.

10 Sometimes, amid the long wait and the heat and the flies and the smell of goat dung, tempers flared, and the younger women, anxious about their babies, argued over whose turn it was to fill up her jar. And sometimes the arguments escalated into full-blown, knockdown-dragout fights; the women would grab each other by the hair and curse and scream and spit and call each other names that made my ears tingle. We little brown boys who went with our mothers to fetch water loved these fights, because we got to see the women's legs and their colored panties as they grappled and rolled around in the dust. Once in a while, we got lucky and saw much more, because some of the women wore nothing at all under their long dresses. God, how I used to look forward to those fights. I remember the rush, the excitement, the sun dancing on the dust clouds as a dress ripped and a young white breast was revealed, then quickly hidden. In my calendar, that year of drought will always be one of the best years of my childhood, because it was then, in a dusty clearing by a trickling mountain spring, I got my first glimpses of the wonders, the mysteries, and the promises hidden beneath the folds of a woman's dress. Fish and oranges from heaven . . . you can get over that.

11 But, in another way, the year of the drought was also one of the worst of my life, because that was the year that Abu Raja, the retired cook who used to entertain us kids by cracking walnuts on his forehead, decided it was time Magdaluna got its own telephone. Every civilized village needed a telephone, he said, and Magdaluna was not going to get anywhere until it had one. A telephone would link us with the outside world. At the time, I was too young to understand the debate, but a few men—like Shukri, the retired Turkish-army drill sergeant, and Abu Hanna the vineyard keeper—did all they could to talk Abu Raja out of having a telephone brought to the village. But they were outshouted and ignored and finally shunned by the other villagers for resisting progress and trying to keep a good thing from coming to Magdaluna.

12 One warm day in early fall, many of the villagers were out in their fields repairing walls or gathering wood for the winter when the shout went out that the telephone-company truck had arrived at Abu Raja's

dikkan, or country store. There were no roads in those days, only footpaths and dry streambeds, so it took the telephone-company truck almost a day to work its way up the rocky terrain from Sidon—about the same time it took to walk. When the truck came into view, Abu George, who had a huge voice and, before the telephone, was Magdaluna's only long-distance communication system, bellowed the news from his front porch. Everybody dropped what they were doing and ran to Abu Raja's house to see what was happening. Some of the more dignified villagers, however, like Abu Habeeb and Abu Nazim, who had been to big cities like Beirut and Damascus and had seen things like telephones and telegraphs, did not run the way the rest did; they walked with their canes hanging from the crooks of their arms, as if on a Sunday afternoon stroll.

13 It did not take long for the whole village to assemble at Abu Raja's *dikkan*. Some of the rich villagers, like the widow Farha and the gendarme Abu Nadeem, walked right into the store and stood at the elbows of the two important-looking men from the telephone company, who proceeded with utmost gravity, like priests at Communion, to wire up the telephone. The poorer villagers stood outside and listened carefully to the details relayed to them by the not-so-poor people who stood in the doorway and could see inside.

14 "The bald man is cutting the blue wire," someone said.

15 "He is sticking the wire into the hole in the bottom of the black box," someone else added.

16 "The telephone man with the mustache is connecting two pieces of wire. Now he is twisting the ends together," a third voice chimed in.

17 Because I was small and unaware that I should have stood outside with the other poor folk to give the rich people inside more room (they seemed to need more of it than poor people did), I wriggled my way through the dense forest of legs to get a firsthand look at the action. I felt like the barefoot Moses, sandals in hand, staring at the burning bush on Mount Sinai. Breathless, I watched as the men in blue, their shirt pockets adorned with fancy lettering in a foreign language, put together a black machine that supposedly would make it possible to talk with uncles, aunts, and cousins who lived more than two days' ride away.

18 It was shortly after sunset when the man with the mustache announced that the telephone was ready to use. He explained that all Abu Raja had to do was lift the receiver, turn the crank on the black box a few times, and wait for an operator to take his call. Abu Raja, who had once lived and worked in Sidon, was impatient with the telephone man for assuming that he was ignorant. He grabbed the receiver and turned the crank forcefully, as if trying to start a Model T Ford. Everybody was impressed that he knew what to do. He even called the operator by her first name: "Centralist." Within moments, Abu Raja

was talking with his brother, a concierge in Beirut. He didn't even have to raise his voice or shout to be heard.

19 If I hadn't seen it with my own two eyes and heard it with my own two ears, I would not have believed it—and my friend Kameel didn't. He was away that day watching his father's goats, and when he came back to the village that evening, his cousin Habeeb and I told him about the telephone and how Abu Raja had used it to speak with his brother in Beirut. After he heard our report, Kameel made the sign of the cross, kissed his thumbnail, and warned us that lying was a bad sin and would surely land us in purgatory. Kameel believed in Jesus and Mary, and wanted to be a priest when he grew up. He always crossed himself when Habeeb, who was irreverent, and I, who was Presbyterian, were around, even when we were not bearing bad news.

20 And the telephone, as it turned out, was bad news. With its coming, the face of the village began to change. One of the first effects was the shifting of the village's center. Before the telephone's arrival, the men of the village used to gather regularly at the house of Im Kaleem, a short, middle-aged widow with jet-black hair and a raspy voice that could be heard all over the village, even when she was only whispering. She was a devout Catholic and also the village *shlikki*—whore. The men met at her house to argue about politics and drink coffee and play cards or backgammon. Im Kaleem was not a true prostitute, however, because she did not charge for her services—not even for the coffee and tea (and, occasionally, the strong liquor called arrack) that she served the men. She did not need the money; her son, who was overseas in Africa, sent her money regularly. (I knew this because my father used to read her son's letters to her and take down her replies, as Im Kaleem could not read and write.) Im Kaleem was no slut either—unlike some women in the village—because she loved all the men she entertained, and they loved her, every one of them. In a way, she was married to all the men in the village. Everybody knew it—the wives knew it; the itinerant Catholic priest knew it; the Presbyterian minister knew it—but nobody objected. Actually, I suspect the women (my mother included) did not mind their husbands' visits to Im Kaleem. Oh, they wrung their hands and complained to one another about their men's unfaithfulness, but secretly they were relieved, because Im Kaleem took some of the pressure off them and kept the men out of their hair while they attended to their endless chores. Im Kaleem was also a kind of confessor and troubleshooter, talking sense to those men who were having family problems, especially the younger ones.

21 Before the telephone came to Magdaluna, Im Kaleem's house was bustling at just about any time of day, especially at night, when its windows were brightly lit with three large oil lamps, and the loud voices of the men talking, laughing, and arguing could be heard in the street below—a reassuring, homey sound. Her house was an island of

Ruskin Bond

The Eyes Are Not Here

Ruskin Bond was born in India in 1934 and is an acclaimed short story writer, poet, and novelist. In 1992, he received the Sahitya Akademi award for English writing in India. The following story—"The Eyes Are Not Here"—first appeared in Contemporary Indian Short Stories in English, *edited by Shiv K. Kumar (1991).*

Before You Read

What interesting travel experiences have you had that taught you something about yourself?

1 I had the compartment to myself up to Rohana, and then a girl got in. The couple who saw her off were probably her parents; they seemed very anxious about her comfort, and the woman gave the girl detailed instructions as to where to keep her things, when not to lean out of the windows, and how to avoid speaking to strangers. They said their good-byes; the train pulled out of the station.

2 As I was totally blind at the time, my eyes sensitive only to light and darkness, I was unable to tell what the girl looked like; but I knew she wore slippers from the way they slapped against her heels. It would take me some time to discover something about her looks, and perhaps I never would. But I liked the sound of her voice, and even the sound of her slippers.

3 "Are you going all the way to Dehra?" I asked.

4 I must have been sitting in a dark corner, because my voice startled her. She gave a little exclamation and said, "I didn't know anyone else was here."

5 Well, it often happens that people with good eyesight fail to see what is right in front of them. They have too much to take in, I suppose. Whereas people who cannot see (or see very little) have to take in only the essentials, whatever registers most tellingly on their remaining senses.

6 "I didn't see you either," I said. "But I heard you come in."

7 I wondered if I would be able to prevent her from discovering that I was blind. I thought "Provided I keep to my seat, it shouldn't be too difficult."

8 The girl said, "I'm getting down at Saharanpur. My aunt is meeting me there."

9 "Then I had better not be too familiar," I said. "Aunts are usually formidable creatures."

10 "Where are you going?" she asked.

11 "To Dehra, and then to Mussoorie."

12 "Oh, how lucky you are, I wish I were going to Mussoorie. I love the hills. Especially in October."

13 "Yes, this is the best time," I said, calling on my memories. "The hills are covered with wild dahlias, the sun is delicious, and at night you can sit in front of a logfire and drink a little brandy. Most of the tourists have gone, and the roads are quiet and almost deserted. Yes, October is the best time."

14 She was silent, and I wondered if my words had touched her, or whether she thought me a romantic fool. Then I made a mistake.

15 "What is it like?" I asked.

16 She seemed to find nothing strange in the question. Had she noticed already that I could not see? But her next question removed my doubts.

17 "Why don't you look out of window?" she asked.

18 I moved easily along the berth and felt for the window ledge. The window was open, and I faced it, making a pretence of studying the landscape. I heard the panting of the engine, the rumble of the wheels, and, in my mind's eye, I could see the telegraph-posts flashing by.

19 "Have you noticed," I ventured, "that the trees seem to be moving while we seem to be standing still?"

20 "That always happens," she said. "Do you see any animals?" Hardly any animals left in the forests near Dehra.

21 I turned from the window and faced the girl, and for a while we sat in silence.

22 "You have an interesting face," I remarked. I was becoming quite daring, but it was a safe remark. Few girls can resist flattery.

23 She laughed pleasantly, a clear, ringing laugh.

24 "It's nice to be told I have an interesting face. I'm tired of people telling me I have a pretty face."

25 Oh, so you do have a pretty face, thought I, and aloud I said: "Well, an interesting face can also be pretty."

26 "You are a very gallant young man," she said. "But why are you so serious?"

27 I thought then, that I would try to laugh for her; but the thought of laughter only made me feel troubled and lonely.

28 "We'll soon be at your station," I said.

29 "Thank goodness it's a short journey. I can't bear to sit in a train for more than two or three hours."

30 Yet I was prepared to sit there for almost any length of time, just to listen to her talking. Her voice had the sparkle of a mountain stream. As soon as she left the train, she would forget our brief encounter;

but it would stay with me for the rest of the journey, and for some time after.

31 The engine's whistle shrieked, the carriage wheels changed their sound and rhythm.

32 The girl got up and began to collect her things. I wondered if she wore her hair in a bun, or if it was plaited, or if it hung loose over her shoulders, or if it was cut very short.

33 The train drew slowly into the station. Outside, there was the shouting of porters and vendors and a high-pitched female voice near the carriage door which must have belonged to the girl's aunt.

34 "Good-bye," said the girl.

35 She was standing very close to me, so close that the perfume from her hair was tantalizing. I wanted to raise my hand and touch her hair; but she moved away, and only the perfume still lingered where she had stood.

'You may break, you may shatter the vase if you will,
But the scent of the roses will linger there still . . .'

36 There was some confusion in the doorway. A man, getting into the compartment, stammered an apology. Then the door banged shut, and the world was shut out again. I returned to my berth. The guard blew his whistle and we moved off. Once again, I had a game to play and a new fellow-traveller.

37 The train gathered speed, the wheels took up their song, the carriage groaned and shook. I found the window and sat in front of it, staring into the daylight that was darkness for me.

38 So many things were happening outside the window. It could be a fascinating game, guessing what went on out there.

39 The man who had entered the compartment broke into my reverie.

40 "You must be disappointed," he said, "I'm sorry I'm not as attractive a travelling companion as the one who just left."

41 "She was an interesting girl," I said. "Can you tell me—did she keep her hair long or short?"

42 "I don't remember," he said, sounding puzzled. "It was her eyes I noticed, not her hair. She had beautiful eyes—but they were of no use to her, she was completely blind. Didn't you notice?"

✧ *Evaluating the Text*

1. What game does the narrator play with his traveling companion?
2. In view of what the narrator discovers at the end of the story, how has Bond placed clues all along for the reader that make sense only when you know the ending?
3. Why is the ending of the story ironic and somewhat poignant?

✧ *Exploring Different Perspectives*

1. How does the account by Christy Brown in "The Letter 'A' " provide another perspective on the way people with disabilities are viewed?
2. Compare the different ways in which Sucheng Chan in "You're Short, Besides!" and the narrator in Bond's story handle their respective disabilities.

✧ *Extending Viewpoints through Writing and Research*

1. What is your favorite game to play to pass the time while traveling? Describe the appeal it has for you.
2. Have ever heard someone's voice such as on a radio show, created a picture of him or her in your mind, and then had the occasion to see this person? How did your mental image correspond or differ with the way the person looked?

Connecting Cultures

Sucheng Chan, "You're Short, Besides!"

What ironic paradox emerges from Valerie Steele and John S. Major's (see "China Chic: East Meets West" in Chapter 8) discussion of foot binding and Chinese attitudes toward disability in Chan's narrative?

Christy Brown, "The Letter 'A' "

Compare and contrast the attitudes of the parents toward their children in Brown's account and in Viramma's "A Pariah's Life" in Chapter 5.

Douchan Gersi, "Initiated into an Iban Tribe of Headhunters"

Contrast Gersi's sense of estrangement with Tepilit Ole Saitoti's feeling of acceptance after undergoing initiation rituals as he describes in "The Initation of a Maasai Warrior" in Chapter 3.

Enid Schildkrout, "Body Art as Visual Language"

What insight does Schildkrout's discussion of the symbolism of hair give you into Meeta Kaur's narrative in "Journey by Inner Light" in Chapter 1?

Lydia Minatoya, "Transformation"

In what ways do both Minatoya's account and Poranee Natadecha-Sponsel's analysis in "Individualism as an American Cultural Value" in Chapter 6 emphasize the issue of how identity is defined in American culture?

Anwar F. Accawi, "The Telephone"

In what ways is Accawi's account similar to that of Helena Norberg-Hodge in "Learning from Ladakh" in Chapter 4 in terms of the outside world intruding into a local environment?

Ruskin Bond, "The Eyes Are Not Here"

How do both Bond in this short story and Kate Chopin in her story "Désirée's Baby" in Chapter 5 require the reader to reassess their assumptions at the end of the story?

3

How Culture Shapes Gender Roles

Because of our social circumstances, male and female are really two cultures and their life experiences are utterly different.
—Kate Millett (b. 1934, U.S. feminist writer)
Sexual Politics (1969)

Culture plays an enormous part in shaping our expectations attached to sex roles. This process, sometimes called *socialization,* determines how each of us assimilates our culture's ideas of what it means to act as a male or female. We tend to acquire a sense of our own sexual identity in conjunction with societal expectations. Yet these expectations differ strikingly from culture to culture. For example, in male-dominated Islamic Middle Eastern societies, the gender roles and relationships between men and women are very different from those in modern Western societies.

The characteristics that define gender roles have varied widely throughout history in cultures as diverse as those in Europe, Asia, the Middle East, and the Americas. The responsibilities and obligations that collectively define what it means to be a woman or a man in different societies have changed dramatically in those societies, which have themselves changed in recent times. The movement toward equality between the sexes—a transformation that has been only partially realized—has allowed women to assume positions of leadership and perform tasks in the workplace, the professions, and in society that were traditionally reserved for men. The works in this chapter address the changing cultural expectations attached to being a man or a woman as well as the psychological and social stresses produced by these changes in redrawing the boundaries of gender roles, marriage, and parenthood.

How you see yourself is determined in large part by the social meanings attached to specific behavior for men and women in your culture—beginning with the fairy tales told to children, extending through the conceptions of masculinity and femininity promulgated by the media, and including opportunities available in the workplace.

The authors in this chapter provide insight into the way in which we acquire specific sexual identities, because of the cultural expectations, pressures, and values that shape the choices we make. How we feel about ourselves and our life experiences reveals the powerful role gender stereotypes play in shaping our personal development. Some writers in this chapter speak out against the constricting effects of these rigid cultural expectations that enforce inflexible images of masculine and feminine behavior. These restrictive stereotypes legitimize and perpetuate gender inequality.

Judith Ortiz Cofer, in "The Myth of the Latin Woman," describes how different cultural expectations in her native Puerto Rico and the United States result in her being stereotyped as a "hot-blooded Latina." Don Kulick and Thaïs Machado-Borges in "Leaky" perceptively analyze the cultural pressures that compel Brazilian women to undergo cosmetic surgery and follow extreme diets to achieve a socially acceptable appearance. Latifa Ali with Richard Shears in "Betrayed" narrates the harrowing experience she had in trying to escape from Iraq rather than being the victim of an honor killing by her family. Tepilit Ole Saitoti in "The Initiation of a Maasai Warrior," the first autobiographical account by a Maasai, recalls the significance of the circumcision ceremony he underwent as a young boy. Waris Dirie, in "The Tragedy of Female Circumcision," describes how traumatic this experience was for her and argues movingly for its elimination. Andrew Sullivan, in "My Big Fat Straight Wedding," discusses the reasons why same-sex marriages ought to be considered a right. A columnist, Nicholas D. Kristof, who had purchased the freedom of child sex workers in Cambodia, offers some hope in "Striking the Brothels' Bottom Line."

To help you understand how the works in this chapter relate to each other, you might use one or several of the following guidelines before writing about gender.

1. How personally is the author involved with the subject?
2. Does the author dramatize the choices with true-to-life examples or hypothetical instances?
3. What is the author's chief purpose in writing about this issue—to explain, to explore, or to persuade?
4. How has your view of this issue been changed by the author's treatment?
5. Does the author believe that language can be used to empower or to disempower?

6. Does the author mainly focus on the liabilities or advantages of being male or female?

Recommended Films on This Theme

- *Casablanca* (United States, 1942) The classic romantic film of espionage set in Nazi-occupied French Morocco brings two former lovers together;
- *Brief Encounter* (England, 1946) The story of a doomed love affair between a married physician and a married housewife during the 1940s;
- *La Cage aux Folles* (France, 1978) A hilarious tale of a gay Saint-Tropez nightclub owner (and his lover) who pretend to be a married middle-class couple when his son gets engaged to a girl from a conservative family;
- *Monsoon Wedding* (India/United States, 2001) The tale of a girl living in New Delhi who has been promised in an arranged marriage to an Indian computer programmer living in the United States, but who has been carrying on a romance with the host of an American television show.

Judith Ortiz Cofer

The Myth of the Latin Woman

Judith Ortiz Cofer, a poet and novelist, was born in 1952 in Hormigueros, Puerto Rico. After her father, a career navy officer, retired, the family settled in Georgia where Cofer attended Augusta College. During college she married and, with her husband and daughter, moved to Florida where she finished a master's degree in English at Florida Atlantic University. A fellowship allowed her to pursue graduate work at Oxford University, after which she returned to Florida and began teaching English and writing poetry. Her first volume of poetry, Peregrina *(1985), won the Riverstone International Poetry Competition and was followed by two more poetry collections,* Reaching for the Mainland *(1987) and* Terms of Survival *(1988). Her first novel,* The Line of the Sun *(1989), was listed as one of 1989's "twenty-five books to remember" by the New York City Public Library System. Her recent works include a collection of short stories,* An Island Like You: Stories of the Barrio *(1995), and* The Year of Our Revolution *(1998). Cofer is a Professor of English and Creative Writing at the University of Georgia. In the following essay, drawn from her collection* The Latin Deli: Prose and Poetry *(1993), Cofer explores the destructive effects of the Latina stereotype. Most recently, she has written* Call Me Maria: A Novel *(2004) and the poetry collection* A Love Story Beginning in Spanish *(2005).*

Before You Read

As you read, notice how Cofer's desire to succeed as a writer is a reaction to the repeated instances in which she is misperceived because of her ethnicity.

1 On a bus trip to London from Oxford University where I was earning some graduate credits one summer, a young man, obviously fresh from a pub, spotted me and as if struck by inspiration went down on his knees in the aisle. With both hands over his heart he broke into an Irish tenor's rendition of "Maria" from *West Side Story*. My politely amused fellow passengers gave his lovely voice the round of gentle applause it deserved. Though I was not quite as amused, I managed my version of an English smile: no show of teeth, no extreme contortions of the facial muscles—I was at this time of my life practicing reserve and cool. Oh, that British control, how I coveted it. But "Maria"

had followed me to London, reminding me of a prime fact of my life: you can leave the island, master the English language, and travel as far as you can, but if you are a Latina, especially one like me who so obviously belongs to Rita Moreno's gene pool, the island travels with you.

2 This is sometimes a very good thing—it may win you that extra minute of someone's attention. But with some people, the same things can make *you* an island—not a tropical paradise but an Alcatraz, a place nobody wants to visit. As a Puerto Rican girl living in the United States and wanting like most children to "belong," I resented the stereotype that my Hispanic appearance called forth from many people I met.

3 Growing up in a large urban center in New Jersey during the 1960s, I suffered from what I think of as "cultural schizophrenia." Our life was designed by my parents as a microcosm of their *casas* on the island. We spoke in Spanish, ate Puerto Rican food bought at the *bodega,* and practiced strict Catholicism at a church that allotted us a one-hour slot each week for mass, performed in Spanish by a Chinese priest trained as a missionary for Latin America.

4 As a girl I was kept under strict surveillance by my parents, since my virtue and modesty were, by their cultural equation, the same as their honor. As a teenager I was lectured constantly on how to behave as a proper *senorita*. But it was a conflicting message I received, since the Puerto Rican mothers also encouraged their daughters to look and act like women and to dress in clothes our Anglo friends and their mothers found too "mature" and flashy. The difference was, and is, cultural; yet I often felt humiliated when I appeared at an American friend's party wearing a dress more suitable to a semi-formal than to a playroom birthday celebration. At Puerto Rican festivities, neither the music nor the colors we wore could be too loud.

5 I remember Career Day in our high school, when teachers told us to come dressed as if for a job interview. It quickly became obvious that to the Puerto Rican girls "dressing up" meant wearing their mothers' ornate jewelry and clothing, more appropriate (by mainstream standards) for the company Christmas party than as daily office attire. That morning I had agonized in front of my closet, trying to figure out what a "career girl" would wear. I knew how to dress for school (at the Catholic school I attended, we all wore uniforms), I knew how to dress for Sunday mass, and I knew what dresses to wear for parties at my relatives' homes. Though I do not recall the precise details of my Career Day outfit, it must have been a composite of these choices. But I remember a comment my friend (an Italian American) made in later years that coalesced my impressions of that day. She said that at the business school she was attending, the Puerto Rican girls always stood out for wearing "everything at once." She meant, of course, too much jewelry, too many accessories. On that day at school we were simply made the negative models by the nuns, who were themselves not credible fashion

experts to any of us. But it was painfully obvious to me that to the others, in their tailored skirts and silk blouses, we must have seemed "hopeless" and "vulgar." Though I now know that most adolescents feel out of step much of the time, I also know that for the Puerto Rican girls of my generation that sense was intensified. The way our teachers and classmates looked at us that day in school was just a taste of the cultural clash that awaited us in the real world, where prospective employers and men on the street would often misinterpret our tight skirts and jingling bracelets as a "come-on."

6 Mixed cultural signals have perpetuated certain stereotypes—for example, that of the Hispanic woman as the "hot tamale" or sexual firebrand. It is a one-dimensional view that the media have found easy to promote. In their special vocabulary, advertisers have designated "sizzling" and "smoldering" as the adjectives of choice for describing not only the foods but also the women of Latin America. From conversations in my house I recall hearing about the harassment that Puerto Rican women endured in factories where the "boss-men" talked to them as if sexual innuendo was all they understood, and worse, often gave them the choice of submitting to their advances or being fired.

7 It is custom, however, not chromosomes, that leads us to choose scarlet over pale pink. As young girls, it was our mothers who influenced our decisions about clothes and colors—mothers who had grown up on a tropical island where the natural environment was a riot of primary colors, where showing your skin was one way to keep cool as well as to look sexy. Most important of all, on the island, women perhaps felt freer to dress and move more provocatively since, in most cases, they were protected by the traditions, mores, and laws of a Spanish/Catholic system of morality and machismo whose main rule was: *You may look at my sister, but if you touch her I will kill you*. The extended family and church structure could provide a young woman with a circle of safety in her small pueblo on the island; if a man "wronged" a girl, everyone would close in to save her family honor.

8 My mother has told me about dressing in her best party clothes on Saturday nights and going to the town's plaza to promenade with her girlfriends in front of the boys they liked. The males were thus given an opportunity to admire the women and to express their admiration in the form of *piropos*: erotically charged street poems they composed on the spot. (I have myself been subjected to a few *piropos* while visiting the island, and they can be outrageous, although custom dictates that they must never cross into obscenity.) This ritual, as I understand it, also entails a show of studied indifference on the woman's part; if she is "decent," she must not acknowledge the man's impassioned words. So I do understand how things can be lost in translation. When a Puerto Rican girl dressed in her idea of what is attractive meets a man from the mainstream culture who has been trained to react to

certain types of clothing as a sexual signal, a clash is likely to take place. I remember the boy who took me to my first formal dance leaning over to plant a sloppy, over-eager kiss painfully on my mouth; when I didn't respond with sufficient passion, he remarked resentfully: "I thought you Latin girls were supposed to mature early," as if I were expected to *ripen* like a fruit or vegetable, not just grow into womanhood like other girls.

9 It is surprising to my professional friends that even today some people, including those who should know better, still put others "in their place." It happened to me most recently during a stay at a classy metropolitan hotel favored by young professional couples for weddings. Late one evening after the theater, as I walked toward my room with a colleague (a woman with whom I was coordinating an arts program), a middle-aged man in a tuxedo, with a young girl in satin and lace on his arm, stepped directly into our path. With his champagne glass extended toward me, he exclaimed "Evita!"[1]

10 Our way blocked, my companion and I listened as the man half-recited, half-bellowed "Don't Cry for Me, Argentina." When he finished, the young girl said: "How about a round of applause for my daddy?" We complied, hoping this would bring the silly spectacle to a close. I was becoming aware that our little group was attracting the attention of the other guests. "Daddy" must have perceived this too, and he once more barred the way as we tried to walk past him. He began to shout-sing a ditty to the tune of "La Bamba"—except the lyrics were about a girl named Maria whose exploits rhymed with her name and gonorrhea. The girl kept saying "Oh, Daddy" and looking at me with pleading eyes. She wanted me to laugh along with the others. My companion and I stood silently waiting for the man to end his offensive song. When he finished, I looked not at him but at his daughter. I advised her calmly never to ask her father what he had done in the army. Then I walked between them and to my room. My friend complimented me on my cool handling of the situation, but I confessed that I had really wanted to push the jerk into the swimming pool. This same man—probably a corporate executive, well-educated, even worldly by most standards—would not have been likely to regale an Anglo woman with a dirty song in public. He might have checked his impulse by assuming that she could be somebody's wife or mother, or at least *somebody* who might take offense. But, to him, I was just an Evita or a Maria: merely a character in his cartoon-populated universe.

11 Another facet of the myth of the Latin woman in the United States is the menial, the domestic—Maria the housemaid or countergirl. It's true that work as domestics, as waitresses, and in factories is all that's

[1]A musical about Eva Duarte de Peron, the former first lady of Argentina.

available to women with little English and few skills. But the myth of the Hispanic menial—the funny maid, mispronouncing words and cooking up a spicy storm in a shiny California kitchen—has been perpetuated by the media in the same way that "Mammy" from *Gone with the Wind* became America's idea of the black woman for generations. Since I do not wear my diplomas around my neck for all to see, I have on occasion been sent to that "kitchen" where some think I obviously belong.

12 One incident has stayed with me, though I recognize it as a minor offense. My first public poetry reading took place in Miami, at a restaurant where a luncheon was being held before the event. I was nervous and excited as I walked in with notebook in hand. An older woman motioned me to her table, and thinking (foolish me) that she wanted me to autograph a copy of my newly published slender volume of verse, I went over. She ordered a cup of coffee from me, assuming that I was the waitress. (Easy enough to mistake my poems for menus, I suppose.) I know it wasn't an intentional act of cruelty. Yet of all the good things that happened later, I remember that scene most clearly, because it reminded me of what I had to overcome before anyone would take me seriously. In retrospect I understand that my anger gave my reading fire. In fact, I have almost always taken any doubt in my abilities as a challenge, the result most often being the satisfaction of winning a convert, of seeing the cold, appraising eyes warm to my words, the body language change, the smile that indicates I have opened some avenue for communication. So that day as I read, I looked directly at that woman. Her lowered eyes told me she was embarrassed at her faux pas, and when I willed her to look up at me, she graciously allowed me to punish her with my full attention. We shook hands at the end of the reading and I never saw her again. She has probably forgotten the entire incident, but maybe not.

13 Yet I am one of the lucky ones. There are thousands of Latinas without the privilege of an education or the entrees into society that I have. For them life is a constant struggle against the misconceptions perpetuated by the myth of the Latina. My goal is to try to replace the old stereotypes with a much more interesting set of realities. Every time I give a reading, I hope the stories I tell, the dreams and fears I examine in my work, can achieve some universal truth that will get my audience past the particulars of my skin color, my accent, or my clothes.

14 I once wrote a poem in which I called all Latinas "God's brown daughters." This poem is really a prayer of sorts, offered upward, but also, through the human-to-human channel of art, outward. It is a prayer for communication and for respect. In it, Latin women pray "in Spanish to an Anglo God/with a Jewish heritage," and they are "fervently hoping/that if not omnipotent,/at least He be bilingual."

✧ *Evaluating the Text*

1. What characteristics define, from Cofer's perspective, the "Maria" stereotype in terms of style, clothes, and behavior? How has this stereotype been a source of harassment for Cofer?
2. How has the desire to destroy this stereotype and its underlying attitudes motivated Cofer to write the kinds of works she has?
3. How does Cofer use her personal experiences as a springboard to understanding sexual stereotyping of Latinas?

✧ *Exploring Different Perspectives*

1. What constraints operate in Puerto Rican culture to guard the modesty of women compared to those in Iraq/Kurdistan as described by Latifa Ali (with Richard Shears) in "Betrayed"?
2. Compare Cofer's experiences with the aspirations of women in Brazil as described by Don Kulick and Thaïs Machado-Borges in "Leaky."

✧ *Extending Viewpoints through Writing and Research*

1. Have you ever been in a situation where someone who is unaware of your ethnic, racial, or religious background disparaged the group to which you belong? What did you do?
2. Create a character sketch of a male chauvinist.

Don Kulick and Thaïs Machado-Borges

Leaky

Don Kulick is a professor of anthropology at New York University who has conducted field work in Papua New Guinea, Italy, Sweden, and Brazil. His most recent book with Deborah Cameron is The Language and Sexuality Reader *(2006). Thaïs Machado-Borges is a research fellow at the Institute of Latin American Studies at Stockholm University, Sweden, and is the author of* Only for You! Brazilians and the Telenovela Flow *(2003). The following article originally appeared in* Fat: The Anthropology of an Obsession, *edited by Don Kulick and Anne Meneley (2005), and explores the popularity of cosmetic surgery and dieting in Brazil in order to emulate First World values in a Third World environment.*

Before You Read

Why would cosmetic surgery and being thin be a value in a Third World country?

1 During the 1990s—a decade when over half the population of several countries officially became overweight, and when in the world as a whole more people became obese than malnourished—the only known group of people anywhere on earth to have grown thinner, other than famine victims, were rich Brazilian women in cities.

2 What, one might wonder, is their secret? It could be that in addition to starving themselves and paying vast amounts of money for personal trainers, plastic surgery, and liposuctions, many rich Brazilian women also take diet medicines that they insist make them leak fat.

3 This essay is not about those leaky women. It is, instead, about middle-class women who want to be like them. It is about how fat in any society is never just about weight or health or looks. Instead, fat is a symbol, a mirror we can gaze into to glimpse the things society tells us are the fairest of them all—and the things society tells us are the grossest, least fair of them all. Looking closely at how people think about fat tells us a lot about how they think about the world in which they live. In this sense, a desire to leak fat is a desire to leak out more than fat, something other than fat, something else besides fat.

Fat That Flows

4 One hot summer afternoon on the southeastern coast of Brazil, in 1999, Thaïs was relaxing on the porch of her friend Thelma's summer house.

5 Thelma is a staff administrator in her late forties. She is tall and white, and has a full but by no means heavy figure. A glass of cold Brazilian beer in hand, Thelma had just brought up the topic of a new diet pill that was all the rage throughout Brazil.

6 "I'm dying to buy Flowcal," she said to her friend Maria, who was similarly equipped with a glass of beer. "I read that it is the only diet medicine that does not have side effects."[1]

7 Maria, a white secretary in her fifties with a figure similar to Thelma's, agreed: "I know! It really sounds wonderful," she said. "They say that once you start to take it, it has an immediate effect!"

8 "It will be on sale in a few weeks," Thelma said. "But you know, I'm going to check and see if I can buy some of it now on the black market so I can start taking it right away. I read that it will cost about two hundred reals a box [about U.S. $150], and that one box only lasts a month."

9 "That's expensive," Maria said. "And you have to take it every day if you want it to work."

10 "But Flowcal dissolves the fat in your body," Thelma explained. "It doesn't let the body accumulate fat. So you eat normally but you get thinner."

11 "I know," Maria said, and she repeated what she had heard others say: "It alters something in the body so that it won't absorb fat. All fat is eliminated."

12 Now it was Angela, Maria's seventeen-year-old daughter, who enthused: "Is that true? God, I want to take some of these pills as well!"

13 Her mother cut her off. "No way, Angela. Can you imagine? At that price! The only one in this family who is going to take it is me."

14 Thaïs sat with these women on the porch cradling her own glass of beer, trying hard to disguise her amazement at the intensity with which they discussed Flowcal. In a country obsessed with beautiful, svelte, sensual bodies, Flowcal was a sensation. The first month it was available, Brazilians flocked to drugstores and bought 300,000 boxes. Flowcal was so popular because it seemed to offer the incredible possibility of losing weight not by *not* eating but, instead, *by* eating.

15 "You eat normally, but you get thinner," Thelma gushed. Flowcal, according to these women and many others, was a miracle.

16 "I've heard that the more fat you eat, the stronger the effect," Thaïs's friend Debora told her. Debora's seventy-year-old mother reacted like everyone else.

---

[1]The names of diet medicines and products presented in this chapter have been changed.

17 "Could it really be possible to lose weight without going on a diet?" she asked, clasping her hands as if in prayer. "That is truly a miracle!"

18 A miracle indeed. Based on our own personal conviction that something that sounds too good to be true is, more often than not, too good to be true, we remain skeptical in the face of claims like those of Thelma, Maria, and Debora. But we are anthropologists, not nutritionists or chemists. We are far from qualified to judge the veracity of the claims made for Flowcal in the mass media, and by many of the women we knew.

19 What interests us more than the truthfulness of the claims is the fact that the women believed them at all, especially with such conviction and gusto. Why were women like Thelma and Maria in such a frenzy about a diet product?

First World or Third World?

20 Anthropology teaches us that while a person's desires may feel intensely personal, they are shaped by the culture in which that person lives. It may seem a far-fetched claim initially, but Thelma and Maria's enthusiasm for the alleged transformative effects of Flowcal has to do with the fact that they live in a country wracked by a profound identity crisis.

21 Brazil has the tenth largest economy in the world and is one of the richest countries on earth. But it is a rich country full of poor people. Brazil has the dubious distinction of having one of the most unequal distributions of wealth in the world: the richest 20 percent of the population earns twenty-nine times as much as the poorest. Compare this to Mexico, where the richest 20 percent of the population earns sixteen times as much as the poorest, or the U.S., where the richest 20 percent of the population earns nine times as much as the poorest.

22 In the U.S., where there are also sharp contrasts between the rich and the poor, nearly 70 percent of the population fall into the middle class, and about 20 percent are at the poverty line or below (usually defined as $1,400 a month for a family of four). This means that the U.S. has an upper class that consists of about 10 percent of the population.

23 Brazil, too, has an upper class that consists of about 10 percent of the population. The difference is that the middle class accounts for only about 20 percent of the population. Seventy percent of the Brazilian population is poor, and roughly 30 percent of Brazilians live in abject poverty. That is, they earn less than $100 a month. Another 40 percent make less than $300 a month.

24 These remarkable economic inequalities are linked to equally remarkable racial inequalities. Generally speaking, the whiter you are in Brazil, the richer you are. Of the poorest 10 percent of Brazilians,

60 percent are black or brown. Of the richest 10 percent, 83 percent are white. In education, nonwhites complete fewer years of study than whites. The average income of nonwhites is a little less than half that of whites. Afro-Brazilians have a life expectancy fourteen years shorter than that for whites, they have an infant mortality rate 30 percent higher, and they have more than double the proportion of illiterates.

25 In addition to the prevalence of poverty and illiteracy throughout the country, Brazil's government, judiciary, and labor market are caught in a tension between old-style hierarchical thinking—where you can acquire favors, rights, and privileges because of who you are and who you know—and individualistic, egalitarian ideals. It was only in 1989 that Brazil, for the first time in its history as an independent state, became a real democracy with free, fair, and competitive elections. The country's constitution asserts that Brazil is a modern, democratic country where all citizens should be treated equally. At the same time, however, the traditional, hierarchical heritage still persists in all kinds of contexts.

26 This close coexistence of wealth and poverty, hierarchy and egalitarianism has put many Brazilians in a quandary. Is their country a First World country—that is, is Brazil rich, advanced, modern, and white? Or is it a Third World country—that is, backward, dirty, poor, and of color? There are a lot of jokes in Brazil about the country's flag, which, in a way, symbolically embodies the problem. In the middle of the flag are printed the proud words "Order and Progress." Most Brazilians see those words as a hope or, more cynically, as a cruel taunt, rather than as a description of the way the country is organized or governed.

27 This quandary about whether Brazil is "really" a First World or a Third World country is particularly perplexing and pressing for people of the middle class, precisely because they are in the middle. They aren't rich, so they can't take for granted the power and privileges that automatically come with wealth. But they aren't poor, either—and they certainly don't want to be. But the extreme instability of the Brazilian economy (the country has changed and devalued its currency six times in the past twenty years) makes their position a tense and fragile one. And they know it.

28 The way that people in Brazil, particularly people in the middle class, cope with this situation is to live their lives as though they personally are First World citizens, even if people around them are not. They do this by buying things that come from the First World, or encourage associations with it (cars, clothes, electronic devices, computers), traveling to the First World (charter trips to Europe and to the United States, where Disney World in Florida is the preferred destination), and thinking about and manipulating their bodies in ways that make them seem rich, advanced, and white.

Making Bodies

29 Nowhere in the world is the cult of the body beautiful as developed as it is in Brazil. Brazil has more plastic surgeons per capita than anywhere else in the world. In 2001 there were 350,000 cosmetic surgery operations in a population of 170 million. This is an impressive number for a nation where 60 percent of the working population earns less than 150 U.S. dollars per month.

30 The general attitude in Brazil toward cosmetic surgery borders on reverence. Expressions such as "the power of scalpels," "the magic of cosmetic surgeries," and the "march toward scientific progress" are seen and heard everywhere. Brazil's most famous plastic surgeon, Ivo Pitanguy—whose claim to fame is a buttock lift that has been copied worldwide—is a household name. There are several glossy lifestyle magazines devoted to cosmetic surgery, with names like *Plastic Surgery and Beauty* and *Body and Plastic Surgery*. These sell almost as many copies per month as *Playboy*—which, by the way, is one of Brazil's biggest selling magazines. One recurring *Playboy* cover girl, a dancer named Carla Perez, won a discount from her surgeon because she was a great advertisement for his work. She took advantage of the discount to pay for breast implants for her mother, sister, and sister-in-law.

31 Brazil's contestant to the 2001 Miss Universe Pageant, twenty-two-year-old Juliana Borges, scandalized many non-Brazilians by speaking freely and frequently about the number and kinds of plastic surgeries she had undergone. These included breast implants, bioplastic sculpting in her cheekbones, silicone remolding in her chin, a sharpened jaw, pinned-back ears, and liposuction in her waistline and back.

32 "The same way someone has to study to become a doctor," Borges told reporters, "someone has to train. I have to work on my figure to get it where I want it . . . It's something I needed for my profession, for my work. I have a doctorate in body measurements."

33 An eighteen-year-old middle-class girl named Claudia, whom Thaïs knew, subscribed to the same philosophy. After months of pleading, she finally convinced her parents to pay for breast reduction surgery. Claudia told Thaïs that she had several reasons for wanting this surgery: her breasts were too big, they were too heavy, and she could not wear T-shirts or dresses without using a bra.

34 "*Frente-unicas* [a kind of bodice that leaves the back bare] were in fashion and I was completely out of it. I couldn't wear anything!" Claudia said, exasperated. Now that she had managed to convince her parents to pay for the operation—in twelve monthly installments—she felt as though one of her dreams had come true. "I think I will be another person after this surgery!" she said.

35 Claudia was not the only one to anticipate the surgery with excitement. One week before the procedure, her mother provided Thaïs with details.

36 "They've booked it for 7:30 A.M.," her mother explained. "But we have to be there one hour before that. The doctor said it will take about three hours, because first they do one breast and then the other. She will receive a general anesthesia, because it's a complicated procedure. They do the nipple first: I think they cut it and then they sew it. They build the whole breast anew. The doctor said that Claudia had so many glands. Too many glands. They'll have to go."

37 From an American or European perspective, the willingness with which people like Claudia and her mother talk about plastic surgery may seem surprising. Whereas cosmetic surgery in the U.S. or Europe is still seen as a private matter, and one that is slightly embarrassing or at least socially awkward, in Brazil surgeries like Claudia's are very public matters. Not only did everyone in Claudia's family know about her surgery, all her friends and colleagues did too.

38 Thaïs mentioned this to a mutual friend, Joana, who had introduced her to Claudia. Joana offered an interesting explanation.

39 "This procedure means one thing to them," Joana told Thaïs. "Status. To have plastic surgery is to show that you have the money to afford it. It's chic to talk about it. That's why Claudia and her family are talking so openly about it. It shows that they have money."

40 Indeed, some weeks later Thaïs heard a conversation between Joana and Claudia's mother. They were talking about the Italian porn star Cicciolina, who was playing a minor nonspeaking role in a popular *telenovela* that was being broadcast at the time. Inevitably, the subject of pornographic films arose.

41 Claudia's mother was perplexed. "I don't understand those films," she declared. "The women have enormous breasts. It's ugly! Those huge breasts bouncing. It must be because they don't have the money to pay for surgery."

. . .

White Bodies

42 In Brazil, modifying one's body through surgery is about more than just becoming more beautiful and desirable. It is even about more than showing that you care about yourself, which is a phrase that frequently crops up whenever cosmetic surgery is discussed in the Brazilian mass media. (For example, Juliana Borges—Miss Brazil—explained that "I'm happy to show that any woman, even if she doesn't feel very pretty or very perfect, can make the effort to do this and fulfill a dream she would like to realize. I think this is now within reach.")

43 Instead, modifying your body in Brazil is fundamentally about displaying your wealth. But since money is associated with race (a well-known Brazilian proverb is *"O dinheiro embranquece"*—"Money whitens"), changing one's body is also about approximating whiteness.

44 Brazil is a country born out of a mixture of native peoples, Portuguese colonists, and African slaves. Slave traders shipped about four million slaves across the Atlantic to Brazil between the mid-sixteenth century to the mid-nineteenth century. This was more than one-third of all slaves transported across the Atlantic. (Compare this figure of four million to the figure of 661,000, which is the approximate number of slaves brought to the United States.)

45 What the slaves who were brought to Brazil encountered was a country with a tiny population of colonists—mostly men—and some indigenous people, many of whom were also slaves. The scarcity of white women, and the fact that white male colonialists could do what they wanted with their slaves, meant that very quickly a racially mixed population developed, with people who ranged across the color spectrum from black to white with complex gradations in between.

46 This mixture has always troubled the white elite. It became especially worrisome at the turn of the last century, after Brazil finally abolished slavery (the last country in the Western Hemisphere to do so) in 1888. At that point the Brazilian elite despaired over the enormous numbers of black people in the country. They believed that racial mixture had condemned Brazil to eternal backwardness and hopelessness.

47 Two related solutions to this problem were found. The first was to encourage, through various campaigns, more white people to emigrate to Brazil from Europe. From the late 1800s onward, the immigration of white people from Italy, Spain, Portugal, Poland, and Germany increased exponentially.

48 The second solution was the development of a policy of "whitening" the population. This basic idea here was that racial mixing, at the end of the day, wasn't perhaps such a bad thing after all. Miscegenation was not harmful to Brazil: on the contrary, the mixture of races ultimately benefited the Portuguese settlers. It made their mixed-race descendants better able to survive and thrive in the tropical Brazilian climate. Now, though, it was said, the dark past was over and the future belonged to those who were the whitest, partly because it was believed that white genes were stronger in the long run, and partly because people "naturally" wanted partners with lighter skin, since whiter skin was considered more attractive and desirable.

49 Although the grosser forms of this kind of racist thinking are no longer widely espoused in Brazil, the fact that race is not so much an either/or matter—as it is in the United States, where you are either black *or* white—means that individuals, to a certain extent, can assert their own racial affiliation on a broad racial continuum. But the fact that whiteness remains connected to wealth, power, and privilege also means that most people opt *up* the racial ladder toward whiteness, rather than down, toward blackness. It is something of a joke in Brazil

that there are about 160 euphemisms one can choose from to avoid having to utter the words "I am black."

"Everything Is Tastier with No-Cal"

50 What has all this got to do with diet products like Flowcal? Let us explain this by looking closely at a television commercial for another diet product. The product being advertised here is No-Cal, a sugar substitute. The commercial features two well-known actresses and a popular actor. The women are in their thirties, and they are famous primarily for always playing rich, desirable characters in *telenovelas*. The man is in his late forties or early fifties, dignified, stately, and also known for always playing rich, desirable characters in *telenovelas*. All three are white. They have pale, light complexions and straight, dark hair.

51 The commercial opens with a mid-shot of Carolina Ferraz, one of the actresses. She is sitting leisurely in a dining chair, in front of a table covered with a white cloth. The whole setting is very white and bright. Behind her one sees a huge window and a green, unfocused background. This could be a restaurant, a spa, or even Carolina Ferraz's private home. She is wearing a white cardigan, her hair is tied in a ponytail, and her only adornment is a small pair of discreet, expensive-looking earrings. She is holding a cup of ice cream in one hand and a spoon in the other. She looks at the camera and says, "You are probably wondering: how come Carolina is so thin, when she eats this much?"

52 The shot cuts to the other actress, Silvia Pfeiffer. She is also sitting in a chair in front of a white table. The background is also unfocused, very light and bright. It suggests the atmosphere of an expensive restaurant. Silvia Pfeiffer has short hair, pearl earrings, and a white dress or top that leaves her shoulders visible. She is filmed in a mid-shot, from the waist up. Looking placidly at the camera, she answers Carolina's question: "She uses No-Cal!"

53 We cut back to Carolina Ferraz and the same setting as in the first shot. "With No-Cal"—Carolina smiles—"I take away the calories of my juice, of my coffee, of my dessert."

54 Now the scene changes to a mid-shot of José Mayer, the actor. He is standing, wearing a white T-shirt and an open white shirt. He faces the camera. "Isn't it nice," he asks, "to cut calories but still eat tasty food?" He raises a little cup of coffee—which is also white—as if toasting the camera, takes a sip, and winks.

55 Silvia Pfeiffer, in close-up: "Do you want advice? No-Cal has almost *no* calories."

56 José Mayer, in extreme close-up: "You don't need to get rid of taste in order to get rid of calories."

57 Silvia Pfeiffer, in extreme close-up: "And besides that, with No-Cal, your coffee tastes much better."

58 Carolina Ferraz, in close-up: "Everything," she says suggestively, "is tastier with No-Cal."

59 Carolina smiles at the camera, and the forty-second commercial ends.

60 In a way, this commercial is no different from hundreds of others broadcast around the globe, trying to tempt people into using products that they are probably better off without. But there is more to this commercial than the hawking of a sugar substitute. A specific *Brazilian* message is being conveyed here, one that highlights all of the concerns we have been discussing so far, including First Worldness, wealth, and whiteness.

61 The first thing to notice is that everything in the commercial is white: the clothes, the decor, the people, even the cup from which José Mayer sips coffee. Whiteness like this is a very common way in Brazil of representing wealth. In *telenovelas,* those mainstays of Brazilian television, for example, it is very common to see living rooms of the upper and upper middle classes furnished with predominantly white, somewhat futuristic furniture that gives the rooms a light and bright atmosphere.

62 There is also an economy to this aesthetic of using whiteness to represent privileged milieus. White furniture, settings, and clothes require more work to be kept clean. Having a white living room implies that one also has the money to afford people (usually nonwhite maids, washers, and cleaners) to keep the white white.

63 Another connection between whiteness, wealth, and the First World is the association one might make between whiteness and hospitals, clinics, and doctors. A commercial like this, filmed entirely in a white ambience, encourages viewers to associate No-Cal with science, advanced technology, and First World know-how.

64 Of course, diet products like No-Cal and the very idea of going on a diet in the first place are, in themselves, associated with wealth. A sugar substitute such as the one in this commercial costs much more than sugar. The commercial is structured around the idea that *you*—provided that *you* have the money—will be able to sip *your* artificially sweetened coffee, drink *your* juice, and eat *your* dessert without gaining any weight. But in a country like Brazil, where experts estimate that thirty-two million people—that is, one in five Brazilians—go hungry every day, this kind of pre-occupation to avoid calories is, to put it mildly, a class-specific concern.

Leaking Out the Third World

65 All of which brings us back at last to Flowcal. A few days before the national celebration of Carnival—the time of the year when Brazilians of all ages, colors, and classes get down and shake their purposefully

scantily clad bodies for up to a whole week—Thelma, who wanted to be ready, finally managed to purchase a box of Flowcal and start taking it. She and her friend Maria told Thaïs in gory detail how the diet pill worked.

66 Thelma, Maria shrieked with excitement, was "leaking fat"!

67 "We were sitting in Thelma's living room, talking about life," Maria said. "Then the phone rang and Thelma got up to answer it. That's when I saw that her pants and the sofa where she was sitting were stained with something that looked like oil. Thelma didn't even notice it! She was leaking fat and she couldn't help it."

68 Thelma, who was thrilled, continued Maria's description.

69 "And I remember that that day my stomach was almost empty. But the more fat food you eat, the stronger the effect. Fat food can give you diarrhea. If you eat something fat, then you have to be prepared and stay at home! And when you go to the bathroom, if you look, it looks just like when you pour oil into water. You can actually see little lumps of dissolved fat!"

70 The ironic thing is that what Thelma and Maria described may in fact have been a side effect of Flowcal, not a sign of its efficacy. The patient information leaflet that comes with the pills lists common side effects: "oily spotting, gas with discharge, urgent need to go to the bathroom, oily or fatty stools, an oily discharge, increased number of bowel movements, and inability to control bowel movements."

71 No matter, though. The two friends were clearly not interested in the fine print. They wanted results and they got them, even if it meant a stained sofa and oily trousers.

72 The results they wanted were not just the loss of fat: what they wanted to lose by taking Flowcal and beginning to literally leak was any connection to the Third World, poverty, and people of color. They wanted all of that expelled from their bodies and flushed away from their sight.

73 Flowcal is talked about as a modern drug and a miraculous cure for misplaced fat. Like other cutting-edge diet products, Flowcal originates in the First World, in this case from a laboratory in Switzerland—a country that many Brazilians consider to be the epitome of a developed and wealthy First World nation. An aura of scientific complexity and modernity emanates from products like Flowcal, and they are presented in advertisements and everyday conversations as having an almost magical power. And indeed their true effects are more magical than real. By spending more than most of their fellow countrymen earn in a month for a box of diet pills that give them diarrhea and oily discharges, women like Thelma and Maria can luxuriate in the fantasy that they live lives similar to the rich Brazilian women in cities who keep getting thinner as the rest of the globe gets fatter. Flowcal puts them in touch with Carolina Ferraz and Silvia Pfeiffer. It makes them

attractive for José Mayer. When they swallow a Flowcal, Thelma and Maria are swallowing particular Brazilian fantasies of class, race, order, and progress. Flowcal is the whole First World in a little blue pill.

✧ *Evaluating the Text*

1. In what ways have cosmetic surgery and the concept of "white bodies" revealed current Brazilian social aspirations?
2. How do Kulick and Machado-Borges use advertising campaigns, interviews, and statistics to document the changing social values that Brazilians pursue?
3. Why does a product like Flowcal, even with its unpleasant side effects, symbolize the almost magical transformation that women in Brazil strive to achieve?

✧ *Exploring Different Perspectives*

1. How do both female circumcision as discussed by Waris Dirie in "The Tragedy of Female Circumcision" and cosmetic surgery as analyzed in "Leaky" come to define women in different cultures?
2. To what extent is race a key factor in the accounts by Kulick and Machado-Borges and by Judith Ortiz Cofer in "The Myth of the Latin Woman"?

✧ *Extending Viewpoints through Writing and Research*

1. Would any of the procedures or products discussed in this essay be something you would consider? Would your reasons be the same as those of the Brazilians? Why or why not? Is the point of having plastic surgery in the United States to show that you have the money to afford it? Why or why not?
2. To what extent does American advertising package class aspirations in racial terms? Find and analyze an ad that does this through the images and messages it projects.
3. What contemporary American products such as Alli™ promise the same results (and caution regarding the same side effects) as the Brazilian counterpart Flowcal?

How does this billboard advertising cosmetic surgery in an affluent area of Rio de Janeiro tell you how widespread this practice is in Brazil?

Latifa Ali with Richard Shears

Betrayed

Latifa Ali grew up in Australia but returned to her native Kurdistan in northern Iraq, where her family had planned a marriage for her and was unaware of the fact that she had been raped by her cousin. This chapter from her autobiography Betrayed *(2009) relates her terrifying ordeal as she sought to escape, with help from Americans, from her father who would have killed her under the honor code. Richard Shears is the Australian and South East Asian correspondent for London's* Daily Mail *newspaper.*

Before You Read

Have you ever had a secret whose exposure would have put you in danger?

1 "You've got a problem," he said, understanding immediately. "A real big problem."

2 I didn't need to be told that, but it helped to hear that someone else appreciated it—and didn't spit in my face.

3 "What can I do to help?" he asked as I went on to describe my father's very real threat to kill me.

4 I told Matt that if there was some way of getting in touch with the Australian Embassy in Iraq, I'd be able to give them my passport details and they would be able to verify my citizenship—and do something to help me escape.

5 Matt told me to wait while he wandered off to another office, where there was an Internet connection. He returned with a printout of the embassy, its address, email and phone number. Of course, I knew its location because I had driven close to it with my sleazy Baghdad cousin but what I had not possessed was a phone number.

6 "Why don't you call them right away?" he said, nodding towards a telephone.

7 I couldn't believe what was happening. Was it really going to be as simple as that?

8 It took time to talk my way past a receptionist and I was then put through to a consular official. I told him that I was an Australian citizen of Kurdish heritage and I was trapped in Dohuk. I knew I was blurting it out and I felt Matt touch my shoulder and whisper: "Relax."

9 The official's next words stunned me. "You have to come in to the embassy and explain this to us."

10 "I can't do that!" I cried. "Don't you understand? I'm way up here in the north. I have no money nor any means of getting to you! I would need a man to drive me to Baghdad and there's no way that any man would do this without knowing the reason for my description. I can't tell him that I want to escape. Aren't you aware of Kurdish culture?"

11 On hearing my response on the phone I heard Matt mutter: "Doesn't this guy know there's a war on? You can't drive around Iraq like you're on a darn picnic."

12 I asked the official to take down my old home address in Sydney and my passport details so he could verify who I was. The response I had was: "Unless you can come in to the embassy, there's nothing we can do."

13 "Please, please! Even if I could get to you, my family would know I've gone missing and they'll kill me. I wouldn't even reach you. They'd catch me on the way and that would be the end of me. Please understand. I'm an Australian and I'm begging you to help me."

14 "There's nothing I can do unless you come in. Look, I'm busy and cannot continue this conversation. Try to come in."

15 Then he hung up on me.

16 I burst into tears. Matt told me that he would relay my precarious position to his superiors, assuring me that it would be treated with the greatest confidence.

17 "We'll do what we can to get you out of here," he said. But his words had little impact. After the broken promises by David and Zana, after the dismissive tone of the embassy official, I held out little hope of ever leaving Kurdistan before my secret was discovered. Matt had held out a helping hand but I held out little hope of it coming to anything.

18 As each day passed I went about my duties, trying to remain happy but crying inside. Joyce was a great friend and in time I revealed my position to her. She was horrified and very concerned. But she assured me that if I had placed my trust in Matt and the other officers, they wouldn't let me down. Word obviously got around, but not in a gossipy way. The officers in the unit were genuinely interested in helping me and said they were looking at ways and means of doing so. As well as Matt, I was constantly being reassured by Joyce and an officer from Texas who spent all day chewing tobacco (and spitting it into a jar which he carried around).

19 Three weeks after I had started with the unit, I heard my aunties talking in the kitchen. Although I was in my bedroom their voices carried over the gap at the top of the dividing wall.

20 "What is going on with our Australian niece?" I heard one of them say. "She is receiving all these offers from men who have rich families and she is turning them all down. We shall have to do something."

21 Then I heard my grandmother's voice. "We were hoping to marry her off soon after she arrived. She's become too much for us to handle,

sitting around in her bedroom all the time. She's become a great nuisance to us all."

22 Sitting around in my bedroom! It was my grandmother who had confined me to that room when I wasn't doing the housework. And she seemed to have overlooked the fact that I was now away each day working for the Americans.

23 Then came a comment from my Aunty Whaffa . . . : "I think it's time to have her checked before we marry her off."

24 Dear God, they were plotting to drag me off for a medical check. I had heard that there was a hospital in Dohuk where brides-to-be were taken at the insistence of the families of some men to ensure that they were virgins. I remembered the gorgeous Pela, the girl from Sweden who had been killed by relatives. She was "inspected" after her death and found to have been killed needlessly. She was still a virgin. Even suspicion was enough to bring about her "honor killing." What a misnomer such deaths were. They were murder, as plain as that.

25 "Is there someone her father wants her to marry?" I heard one of the aunties say.

26 "Oh yes," said another. "He's already discussed it with me. He has his eye on Ibrahim's son, Heval." I vaguely knew who they were talking about—my father's first cousin. But it was worse than that. Much worse. For his father was Etab's father—the man who had joined in the honor killing of his daughter. Now I recalled all the compliments my father had paid to Heval over the months, vaguely suspecting that they were meant for me, but I had tried to dismiss them, believing that this was another one of those round-about approaches that had been made for my hand.

27 "We will have her checked and arrange with my son for the marriage within a few months," I heard my grandmother say. "He wants her married before she is 25 and her birthday is at the end of the year."

28 "I still don't understand why she has been refusing these wonderful men. It is a great embarrassment to us all," said a voice, to which another responded: "It will not be for much longer."

29 "And perhaps we should do something about what she is wearing to work, or have that employment stopped altogether. Have you noticed how she is dressing? You can see her shape in those clothes."

30 I could hear that Jamilla, my stepmother, was in the kitchen with them, but she said nothing in my defense. She had no authority over the other women. She was the newcomer, even though, as the wife of the owner, she was officially the "lady of the house."

31 I was now well aware that I was in a race against time—receiving help to escape from the Americans or being forced to have a medical check-up at the "virgin hospital." That night, I felt so sick about my precarious position that I could not face the evening meal.

32 The following day, red eyed from lack of sleep and tears, Matt was quick to pick up that something dramatic had happened. When I told

him of the conversations I had heard he cried: "Oh shit. It's full speed ahead for us, then."

33 Matt went off and pulled strings with his superiors. It was arranged that I should be taken to the office of the Coalition Provisional Authority (CPA). The headquarters was housed in a building adjoining one of the city's big hotels and it was there I was introduced to one of the senior co-ordinators, who I will call Rob, for security reasons. A tall man in his 40s with steely gray hair, he was dressed in civvies as he held out his hand. He had already been briefed about my case, but brought out a yellow note pad and jotted down all my details—full name, passport number, background in Australia, when I left, when I arrived in Kurdistan. He also noted at my request—I wanted this to be made clear to anyone prepared to help me—that I was not a virgin. And that my father had slapped and beaten me and had threatened to kill me if I brought any shame to the family. I began to tell him through my tears about honor killings, but he interrupted. "Yes, I'm well aware of them," he said. "Yours is indeed a very serious case and rest assured, we will get you out."

34 "But please do it as soon as you can," I urged. "I know my time is getting short. They are already talking about taking me for a medical check-up and then all will be lost. I might not even make it out of the hospital."

35 "I'll get onto the Australian Embassy immediately."

36 When I told him of the reaction I had received previously, he shook his head in dismay. "Hanging up on you without trying to seek a solution? That should never have happened," he said.

37 The days rolled by. I tried my best to keep away from my aunties. I looked into my father's face, seeking a clue to his thoughts. He had remained silent about Heval and I wondered if that was because a wedding was being quietly arranged behind my back. I didn't even know Heval apart from his name. Each night I repeated the same prayer: "Please God, help the Americans to help me. Help them to get me out of here."

38 Then one day as I was translating a document from Arabic to English, despite my still relatively limited knowledge of Arabic, one of the officers, Daniel, said quietly: "Start making preparations. You're getting out. Begin by putting your important belongings in a bag and bringing them in, a bit at a time so you don't raise any suspicion at home."

39 I spun around. "Do you really mean it? Am I really going to be leaving?"

40 He grinned. "You betcha!"

41 So the next morning I sorted through my belongings in my bedroom, placing pieces of my jewelry, photos, my music and some light clothing that I could squeeze up into a shoulder bag without raising the suspicion of my watchful grandmother or the taxi-driver cousin

who was still calling to collect me each morning. My hands shook with excitement as I packed in the bright red top I had owned since I was 17 and which I had been forbidden to wear in Kurdistan for it was the sign of a loose woman. I was careful not to put in too much for I knew I would have several more days to sneak things out.

42 The next day, I told myself, I would smuggle out more of my jewelry and my diary, which contained so many truths about my grandmother and my aunties. I didn't want to leave the diary at the military unit overnight because, even though I trusted all around me, I was still worried that it might fall into the wrong hands. So I locked it away in the closet, planning to remove it some time in the coming days. I stared at the shoes and the clothes my aunties had bought for me. They could definitely stay behind!

43 As my cousin drove me to the headquarters that morning, the bag with my belongings at my feet in the back seat of the taxi, I kept telling myself to remain calm—and to be prepared for another disappointment. If another let-down came, though, I knew it would be disaster for me. Time had run out.

44 At the office, I dropped the bag at my feet while I waited for the opportunity to ask where I could store it.

45 "You have your stuff? Great!" It was Daniel! "You'll be leaving in five minutes."

46 It took a second or two for his words to sink in. Then I was hit by a flash of doubt. Leaving for where? Was I being sacked? Were they going to take me home because I was, as I'd heard my aunties say so often in the past, "too much trouble"? And why so soon, when they had told me that it would be a week or so before anything could be done? Surely, something had gone terribly wrong.

47 Before I could say anything, he added: "There's a vehicle waiting for you. You're going to be taken to Mosul and from there to Baghdad and then—home, baby!"

48 He read the delight in my eyes and my intention, as I pushed back the chair, to throw my arms around him with thanks. He backed away slightly. "Hey girl, don't make it too obvious! There's only a handful of us who know what's happening. Your case has been top secret—and I mean top secret."

49 "Except from me," said a new voice. It was Matt, who had come into the office, grinning. "Back to kangaroo land for you," he said, throwing me a wink. "Told ya we'd be getting you out."

50 Then they gave me my instructions. A very careful plan had been mapped out to ensure there were no leaks back to my father. They would be using a Kurdish driver employed by the military to take me to what I would tell him was the home of a make-believe aunty and from there I would be transferred to another vehicle. I would not be giving the driver the address, though.

51 "How will I know where it is, then?" I asked.

52 "I'll give you instructions with my finger," said Daniel. "When you see which way I point as we travel, you tell the driver to go that way."

53 I had just enough time to hurry into an adjoining dormitory to say goodbye to another staff member, Trevor, who had been most friendly and helpful to me. I asked if it was in order for him to know I was going and was told to be quick. So I ran into the dormitory and gave Trevor a hug and a kiss and told him this was goodbye. "I know," he said. "They told me a short time ago."

54 We were both in tears. Then he reached into his backpack and pulled out a small package. "You might need this. It's the best I can do."

55 As we headed away from the villa in a white colored, unmarked, four-wheel drive, I opened the gift. It was $US300, Trevor's monthly allowance for food and other expenses. He also gave me his email address. These people are just incredible, I thought, as we headed through the streets. Daniel was in the front seat and every now and then he would casually lift his hand to his face and use his thumb to indicate a right turn and a finger to indicate a left, instructions I then passed to the driver who assumed I knew exactly where I was going. I glanced back occasionally, terrified that we were being followed, but there were no suspicious vehicles behind us.

56 When Daniel dropped his hand quickly, it was the signal for us to stop. Then, according to my instructions, I told the driver to let me out and to take Daniel on to another military compound. I wanted to kiss Daniel's neck in thanks but of course that couldn't be done. It was just a "thanks and see you," kind of goodbye, with a discreet touch of my hand on his shoulder.

57 As the car disappeared, I found myself standing alone in the street with my own small bag and another that the military and CPA had given to me. There were houses beside me, but there was no one in sight. What should I do? Was this a sick joke? Despite my belief in the Americans, I had been betrayed so many times that the thought came over me. I couldn't bear to imagine what my punishment would be if I was eventually brought back to my father's door by a good Samaritan Kurd who had found me wandering the streets. But suddenly I found myself surrounded by three American men, not soldiers, but armed to the teeth. They were dressed in flak jackets and had weapons in holsters on their legs and their belts. I knew who they were, having had them pointed out to me on previous trips into town with men from the unit. They were freelancers from the Blackwater security firm, a mainstay of support for the US army. They bundled me into one of three black four-wheel drivers that had driven up behind me and had parked in such a way that they blocked the street off from any vehicle that might have managed to follow me here. I recalled vaguely seeing

them parked in a side street as I was driven to this spot. I was indeed at the center of a grand escape operation.

58 In the car was a familiar figure. It was Rob, from the CPA. He gave me a big grin. "You're on your way," he said. "Took a little bit of work, but here you are."

59 As we sped from that street and began to head south, one of the Blackwater men, Ed, said: "You're safe now. Everything's under control."

60 "I just need one thing from you," said Rob, handing me a piece of paper and a tape recorder. "Just need you to repeat these words so we have a record that all is in order."

61 It was a simple legal document declaring that I was leaving Kurdistan—and Iraq—under my own free will. What an inner thrill I had to read those words: my own free will. At last.

62 There were Kurdish checkpoints ahead at which police normally checked the identity of every person passing through. But because we were able to show that we were in an official US vehicle—the model was easily recognizable and Ed held out an ID as we approached—we were waved through without question. I just had to be sure I lay down flat across the back seat, with clothing over me. There would have been hell to pay if I, a Kurdish woman, was found traveling in an American military vehicle.

63 I was told I would be flown to Baghdad from a military compound set up at Mosul airport. The area was surrounded by razor wire and sandbags, just like the compound in Dohuk, and on the runway I could see a Hercules aircraft. I couldn't believe that this was happening. It was all so fast and unexpected. I'd left my father's home for work that morning and now I was in a US compound in Mosul, staring at an aircraft that would soon be flying me to Baghdad on my way out of this wretched place.

64 But it was not going to happen immediately. I was told I might have to wait for a day or two while final arrangements were made for my transportation. I was shown to a temporary building, like a trailer, which would be my quarters until everything was ready for my flight. It was fitted out with everything that I might need—including novels written in English and even a Harry Potter book! I felt as though I was already back in the West. There were snacks and a small TV and a single bed. Creature comforts indeed.

65 Opening the bag the men at the Dohuk base had given me, I found they had thought of everything for a girl making an emergency escape; personal medical items, a nightgown, toothbrush, toothpaste, shampoo, conditioner, comb, T-shirt, a notepad and pen, a small hand-towel, a packet of chips and a small container of juice.

66 Looking through these simple items I felt a great wave of love overwhelming me—their love for me and mine for them.

67 I dined with some of the Americans that night in the food hall, enjoying a choice of sausages, hot dogs, Asian food, fruits and all kinds of desserts. To my delight, one of the soldiers who was eating there had been based in Dohuk and we managed to have a quiet chat. He, like the others, was sad that I was leaving, but at the same time delighted for my sake. As instructed I had to pretend that I was an Iraqi journalist, but I had to make sure I kept my distance from two or three other journalists, Europeans, who were staying at the base, waiting to take the same flight to Baghdad. I might have had trouble bluffing my way past their questions about who I worked for and what stories I'd been covering and so on. Despite ensuring I stayed away from the other journalists, I was happy to be shown around the base by one of the soldiers—a move for which I was to be criticized later for showing myself when my escape was so top secret that only a few people knew about it.

68 As this was wartime, there were no set flight schedules. Aircraft had to come and go when it was decided everything was perfectly safe and flight paths were revealed at the last minute, so the following morning I was still told that my departure was on hold. I was uneasy about having to wait around.

69 A third day arrived. It was then that one of my escorts, a soldier called Donnie, said to me over breakfast:

70 "I don't know what that bitch has against you."

71 I stared at him. "That bitch who's in admin," he explained, although I did not know who he was talking about. "She's a Kurdish American but she has all the say-so around here. She's refusing to let you leave."

72 He paused for a moment. Then said: "She's insisting you be returned to your family."

✧ *Evaluating the Text*

1. What factors made Ali's situation so precarious as a Muslim woman raised as a Westerner but now living with her father and his mother in Kurdistan?
2. Why was it necessary for Ali to prepare her departure in secret and take her jewelry and diary with her?
3. Who blocked Ali's attempt to escape and why was this ironic?

✧ *Exploring Different Perspectives*

1. How does Latifa Ali's memoir and Andrew Sullivan's essay "My Big Fat Straight Wedding" communicate the problems arising from wanting to marry someone not acceptable to society?

2. What insight do the accounts by Ali and Waris Dirie ("The Tragedy of Female Circumcision") provide into fundamentalist Islamic societies' need to define and control female sexuality?

✧ *Extending Viewpoints through Writing and Research*

1. Why is it ironic that Ali's struggle with Iraqi culture and customs takes place in a society where a "war on terror" has been declared?
2. Research the rationale underlying the ancient custom of honor killing. Identify instances in which this is taking place in the United States today.

Tepilit Ole Saitoti

The Initiation of a Maasai Warrior

Named for the language they speak—Maa, a distinct, but unwritten African tongue—the Maasai of Kenya and Tanzania, a tall, handsome, and proud people, still live much as they always have, herding cattle, sheep, and goats in and around the Great Rift Valley. This personal narrative is unique—the first autobiographical account written by a Maasai, which vividly documents the importance of the circumcision ceremony that serves as a rite of passage into warrior rank. Tepilit Ole Saitoti studied animal ecology in the United States and has returned to Kenya, where he is active in conservation projects. His experiences formed the basis for a National Geographic Society film, Man of Serengeti *(1971). This account first appeared in Saitoti's autobiography,* The Worlds of a Maasai Warrior *(1986).*

The Maasai are a nomadic pastoral people of East Africa. Maasai society is patrilineal; polygyny (having two or more wives at the same time) is practiced. Boys are initiated into a warrior age-group responsible for herding and other tribal labors. Only after serving as a warrior may a man marry. The Maasai traditionally live in the kraal, a compound within which are mud houses (eight to fifteen huts per kraal). The settlements are surrounded by a thorn bush fence and in the evening, cattle, goats, and other domestic animals are brought inside the kraal for protection against wild animals. The Maasai drink cow's milk every day and when they do not have enough, they mix cow's blood with the milk (the Maasai believe the blood makes them strong). The wealth of the Maasai is measured by the number of cattle they have acquired and they believe that God has entrusted his cattle with them. As young boys reach fifteen, they are initiated into manhood in a ceremony in which they wear headdresses of ostrich plumes and eagle feathers, shave their heads, are circumcised, and become morani *or warriors. They then color their skin red and braid their ocher-colored hair and with their fellow initiates learn survival skills. The image most people have of these warriors is of a tall, thin man holding a spear in one hand with a red cloth wrapped around his waist or thrown over his shoulders.*

Before You Read

Consider what rituals in our society signify a person has left childhood behind and how those differ from those of the Maasai.

1 "Tepilit, circumcision means a sharp knife cutting into the skin of the most sensitive part of your body. You must not budge; don't move a muscle or even blink. You can face only one direction until the operation is completed. The slightest movement on your part will mean you are a coward, incompetent and unworthy to be a Maasai man. Ours has always been a proud family, and we would like to keep it that way. We will not tolerate unnecessary embarrassment, so you had better be ready. If you are not, tell us now so that we will not proceed. Imagine yourself alone remaining uncircumcised like the water youth [white people]. I hear they are not circumcised. Such a thing is not known in Maasailand; therefore, circumcision will have to take place even if it means holding you down until it is completed."

2 My father continued to speak and every one of us kept quiet. "The pain you will feel is symbolic. There is a deeper meaning in all this. Circumcision means a break between childhood and adulthood. For the first time in your life, you are regarded as a grownup, a complete man or woman. You will be expected to give and not just to receive. To protect the family always, not just to be protected yourself. And your wise judgment will for the first time be taken into consideration. No family affairs will be discussed without your being consulted. If you are ready for all these responsibilities, tell us now. Coming into manhood is not simply a matter of growth and maturity. It is a heavy load on your shoulders and especially a burden on the mind. Too much of this—I am done. I have said all I wanted to say. Fellows, if you have anything to add, go ahead and tell your brother, because I am through. I have spoken."

3 After a prolonged silence, one of my half-brothers said awkwardly, "Face it, man . . . it's painful. I won't lie about it, but it is not the end. We all went through it, after all. Only blood will flow, not milk." There was laughter and my father left.

4 My brother Lellia said, "Men, there are many things we must acquire and preparations we must make before the ceremony, and we will need the cooperation and help of all of you. Ostrich feathers for the crown and wax for the arrows must be collected."

5 "Are you *orkirekenyi?*" One of my brothers asked. I quickly replied no, and there was laughter. *Orkirekenyi* is a person who has transgressed sexually. For you must not have sexual intercourse with any circumcised woman before you yourself are circumcised. You must wait until you are circumcised. If you have not waited, you will be fined. Your father, mother, and the circumciser will take a cow from you as punishment.

6 Just before we departed, one of my closest friends said, "If you kick the knife, you will be in trouble." There was laughter. "By the way, if you have decided to kick the circumciser, do it well. Silence him once and for all." "Do it the way you kick a football in school." "That will fix

him," another added, and we all laughed our heads off again as we departed.

7 The following month was a month of preparation. I and others collected wax, ostrich feathers, honey to be made into honey beer for the elders to drink on the day of circumcision, and all the other required articles.

8 Three days before the ceremony my head was shaved and I discarded all my belongings, such as my necklaces, garments, spear, and sword. I even had to shave my pubic hair. Circumcision in many ways is similar to Christian baptism. You must put all the sins you have committed during childhood behind and embark as a new person with a different outlook on a new life.

9 The circumciser came the following day and handed the ritual knives to me. He left drinking a calabash of beer. I stared at the knives uneasily. It was hard to accept that he was going to use them on my organ. I was to sharpen them and protect them from people of ill will who might try to blunt them, thus rendering them inefficient during the ritual and thereby bringing shame on our family. The knives threw a chill down my spine; I was not sure I was sharpening them properly, so I took them to my closest brother for him to check out, and he assured me that the knives were all right. I hid them well and waited.

10 Tension started building between me and my relatives, most of whom worried that I wouldn't make it through the ceremony valiantly. Some even snarled at me, which was their way of encouraging me. Others threw insults and abusive words my way. My sister Loiyan in particular was more troubled by the whole affair than anyone in the whole family. She had to assume my mother's role during the circumcision. Were I to fail my initiation, she would have to face the consequences. She would be spat upon and even beaten for representing the mother of an unworthy son. The same fate would befall my father, but he seemed unconcerned. He had this weird belief that because I was not particularly handsome, I must be brave. He kept saying, "God is not so bad as to have made him ugly and a coward at the same time."

11 Failure to be brave during circumcision would have other unfortunate consequences: the herd of cattle belonging to the family still in the compound would be beaten until they stampeded; the slaughtered oxen and honey beer prepared during the month before the ritual would go to waste; the initiate's food would be spat upon and he would have to eat it or else get a severe beating. Everyone would call him Olkasiodoi, the knife kicker.

12 Kicking the knife of the circumciser would not help you anyway. If you struggle and try to get away during the ritual, you will be held down until the operation is completed. Such failure of nerve would haunt you in the future. For example, no one will choose a person who kicked the knife for a position of leadership. However, there have been

instances in which a person who failed to go through circumcision successfully became very brave afterwards because he was filled with anger over the incident; no one dares to scold him or remind him of it. His agemates, particularly the warriors, will act as if nothing had happened.

13 During the circumcision of a woman, on the other hand, she is allowed to cry as long as she does not hinder the operation. It is common to see a woman crying and kicking during circumcision. Warriors are usually summoned to help hold her down.

14 For women, circumcision means an end to the company of Maasai warriors. After they recuperate, they soon get married, and often to men twice their age.

15 The closer it came to the hour of truth, the more I was hated, particularly by those closest to me. I was deeply troubled by the withdrawal of all the support I needed. My annoyance turned into anger and resolve. I decided not to budge or blink, even if I were to see my intestines flowing before me. My resolve was hardened when newly circumcised warriors came to sing for me. Their songs were utterly insulting, intended to annoy me further. They tucked their wax arrows under my crotch and rubbed them on my nose. They repeatedly called me names.

16 By the end of the singing, I was fuming. Crying would have meant I was a coward. After midnight they left me alone and I went into the house and tried to sleep but could not. I was exhausted and numb but remained awake all night.

17 At dawn I was summoned once again by the newly circumcised warriors. They piled more and more insults on me. They sang their weird songs with even more vigor and excitement than before. The songs praised warriorhood and encouraged one to achieve it at all costs. The songs continued until the sun shone on the cattle horns clearly. I was summoned to the main cattle gate, in my hand a ritual cowhide from a cow that had been properly slaughtered during my naming ceremony. I went past Loiyan, who was milking a cow, and she muttered something. She was shaking all over. There was so much tension that people could hardly breathe.

18 I laid the hide down and a boy was ordered to pour ice-cold water, known as *engare entolu* (ax water), over my head. It dripped all over my naked body and I shook furiously. In a matter of seconds I was summoned to sit down. A large crowd of boys and men formed a semicircle in front of me; women are not allowed to watch male circumcision and vice versa. That was the last thing I saw clearly. As soon as I sat down, the circumciser appeared, his knives at the ready. He spread my legs and said, "One cut," a pronouncement necessary to prevent an initiate from claiming that he had been taken by surprise. He splashed a white liquid, a ceremonial paint called *enturoto,* across my face.

Almost immediately I felt a spark of pain under my belly as the knife cut through my penis' foreskin. I happened to choose to look in the direction of the operation. I continued to observe the circumciser's fingers working mechanically. The pain became numbness and my lower body felt heavy, as if I were weighed down by a heavy burden. After fifteen minutes or so, a man who had been supporting from behind pointed at something, as if to assist the circumciser. I came to learn later that the circumciser's eyesight had been failing him and that my brothers had been mad at him because the operation had taken longer than was usually necessary. All the same, I remained pinned down until the operation was over. I heard a call for milk to wash the knives, which signaled the end, and soon the ceremony was over.

19 With words of praise, I was told to wake up, but I remained seated. I waited for the customary presents in appreciation of my bravery. My father gave me a cow and so did my brother Lellia. The man who had supported my back and my brother-in-law gave me a heifer. In all I had eight animals given to me. I was carried inside the house to my own bed to recuperate as activities intensified to celebrate my bravery.

20 I laid on my own bed and bled profusely. The blood must be retained within the bed, for according to Maasai tradition, it must not spill to the ground. I was drenched in my own blood. I stopped bleeding after about half an hour but soon was in intolerable pain. I was supposed to squeeze my organ and force blood to flow out of the wound, but no one had told me, so the blood coagulated and caused unbearable pain. The circumciser was brought to my aid and showed me what to do, and soon the pain subsided.

21 The following morning, I was escorted by a small boy to a nearby valley to walk and relax, allowing my wound to drain. This was common for everyone who had been circumcised, as well as for women who had just given birth. Having lost a lot of blood, I was extremely weak. I walked very slowly, but in spite of my caution I fainted. I tried to hang on to bushes and shrubs, but I fell, irritating my wound. I came out of unconsciousness quickly, and the boy who was escorting me never realized what had happened. I was so scared that I told him to lead me back home. I could have died without there being anyone around who could have helped me. From that day on, I was selective of my company while I was feeble.

22 In two weeks I was able to walk and was taken to join other newly circumcised boys far away from our settlement. By tradition Maasai initiates are required to decorate their headdresses with all kinds of colorful birds they have killed. On our way to the settlement, we hunted birds and teased girls by shooting them with our wax blunt arrows. We danced and ate and were well treated wherever we went. We were protected from the cold and rain during the healing period. We were not allowed to touch food, as we were regarded as unclean, so

whenever we ate we had to use specially prepared sticks instead. We remained in this pampered state until our wounds healed and our headdresses were removed. Our heads were shaved, we discarded our black cloaks and bird headdresses and embarked as newly shaven warriors, Irkeleani.

23 As long as I live I will never forget the day my head was shaved and I emerged a man, a Maasai warrior. I felt a sense of control over my destiny so great that no words can accurately describe it. I now stood with confidence, pride, and happiness of being, for all around me I was desired and loved by beautiful, sensuous Maasai maidens. I could now interact with women and even have sex with them, which I had not been allowed before. I was now regarded as a responsible person.

24 In the old days, warriors were like gods, and women and men wanted only to be the parent of a warrior. Everything else would be taken care of as a result. When a poor family had a warrior, they ceased to be poor. The warrior would go on raids and bring cattle back. The warrior would defend the family against all odds. When a society respects the individual and displays confidence in him the way the Maasai do their warriors, the individual can grow to his fullest potential. Whenever there was a task requiring physical strength or bravery, the Maasai would call upon their warriors. They hardly ever fall short of what is demanded of them and so are characterized by pride, confidence, and an extreme sense of freedom. But there is an old saying in Maasai: "You are never a free man until your father dies." In other words, your father is paramount while he is alive and you are obligated to respect him. My father took advantage of this principle and held a tight grip on all his warriors, including myself. He always wanted to know where we all were at any given time. We fought against his restrictions, but without success. I, being the youngest of my father's five warriors, tried even harder to get loose repeatedly, but each time I was punished severely.

25 Roaming the plains with other warriors in pursuit of girls and adventure was a warrior's pastime. We would wander from one settlement to another, singing, wrestling, hunting, and just playing. Often I was ready to risk my father's punishment for this wonderful freedom.

26 One clear day my father sent me to take sick children and one of his wives to the dispensary in the Korongoro Highlands. We rode in the L.S.B. Leakey lorry. We ascended the highlands and were soon attended to in the local hospital. Near the conservation offices I met several acquaintances, and one of them told me of an unusual circumcision that was about to take place in a day or two. All the local warriors and girls were preparing to attend it.

27 The highlands were a lush green from the seasonal rains and the sky was a purple-blue with no clouds in sight. The land was overflowing with milk, and the warriors felt and looked their best, as they always did

when there was plenty to eat and drink. Everyone was at ease. The demands the community usually made on warriors during the dry season when water was scarce and wells had to be dug were now not necessary. Herds and flocks were entrusted to youths to look after. The warriors had all the time for themselves. But my father was so strict that even at times like these he still insisted on overworking us in one way or another. He believed that by keeping us busy, he would keep us out of trouble.

28 When I heard about the impending ceremony, I decided to remain behind in the Korongoro Highlands and attend it now that the children had been treated. I knew very well that I would have to make up a story for my father upon my return, but I would worry about that later. I had left my spear at home when I boarded the bus, thinking that I would be coming back that very day. I felt lighter but now regretted having left it behind; I was so used to carrying it wherever I went. In gales of laughter resulting from our continuous teasing of each other, we made our way toward a distant kraal. We walked at a leisurely pace and reveled in the breeze. As usual we talked about the women we desired, among other things.

29 The following day we were joined by a long line of colorfully dressed girls and warriors from the kraal and the neighborhood where we had spent the night, and we left the highland and headed to Ingorienito to the rolling hills on the lower slopes to attend the circumcision ceremony. From there one could see Oldopai Gorge, where my parents lived, and the Inaapi hills in the middle of the Serengeti Plain.

30 Three girls and a boy were to be initiated on the same day, an unusual occasion. Four oxen were to be slaughtered, and many people would therefore attend. As we descended, we saw the kraal where the ceremony would take place. All those people dressed in red seemed from a distance like flamingos standing in a lake. We could see lines of other guests heading to the settlements. Warriors made gallant cries of happiness known as *enkiseer*. Our line of warriors and girls responded to their cries even more gallantly.

31 In serpentine fashion, we entered the gates of the settlement. Holding spears in our left hands, we warriors walked proudly, taking small steps, swaying like palm trees, impressing our girls, who walked parallel to us in another line, and of course the spectators, who gazed at us approvingly.

32 We stopped in the center of the kraal and waited to be greeted. Women and children welcomed us. We put our hands on the children's heads, which is how children are commonly saluted. After the greetings were completed, we started dancing.

33 Our singing echoed off the kraal fence and nearby trees. Another line of warriors came up the hill and entered the compound, also singing and moving slowly toward us. Our singing grew in intensity.

Both lines of warriors moved parallel to each other, and our feet pounded the ground with style. We stamped vigorously, as if to tell the next line and the spectators that we were the best.

34 The singing continued until the hot sun was overhead. We recessed and ate food already prepared for us by other warriors. Roasted meat was for those who were to eat meat, and milk for the others. By our tradition, meat and milk must not be consumed at the same time, for this would be a betrayal of the animal. It was regarded as cruel to consume a product of the animal that could be obtained while it was alive, such as milk, and meat, which was only available after the animal had been killed.

35 After eating we resumed singing, and I spotted a tall, beautiful *esiankiki* (young maiden) of Masiaya whose family was one of the largest and richest in our area. She stood very erect and seemed taller than the rest.

36 One of her breasts could be seen just above her dress, which was knotted at the shoulder. While I was supposed to dance generally to please all the spectators, I took it upon myself to please her especially. I stared at and flirted with her, and she and I danced in unison at times. We complemented each other very well.

37 During a break, I introduced myself to the *esiankiki* and told her I would like to see her after the dance. "Won't you need a warrior to escort you home later when the evening threatens?" I said. She replied, "Perhaps, but the evening is still far away."

38 I waited patiently. When the dance ended, I saw her departing with a group of other women her age. She gave me a sidelong glance, and I took that to mean come later and not now. With so many others around, I would not have been able to confer with her as I would have liked anyway.

39 With another warrior, I wandered around the kraal killing time until the herds returned from pasture. Before the sun dropped out of sight, we departed. As the kraal of the *esiankiki* was in the lowlands, a place called Enkoloa, we descended leisurely, our spears resting on our shoulders.

40 We arrived at the woman's kraal and found that cows were now being milked. One could hear the women trying to appease the cows by singing to them. Singing calms cows down, making it easier to milk them. There were no warriors in the whole kraal except for the two of us. Girls went around into warriors' houses as usual and collected milk for us. I was so eager to go and meet my *esiankiki* that I could hardly wait for nightfall. The warriors' girls were trying hard to be sociable, but my mind was not with them. I found them to be childish, loud, bothersome, and boring.

41 As the only warriors present, we had to keep them company and sing for them, at least for a while, as required by custom. I told the other

warrior to sing while I tried to figure out how to approach my *esiankiki*. Still a novice warrior, I was not experienced with women and was in fact still afraid of them. I could flirt from a distance, of course. But sitting down with a woman and trying to seduce her was another matter. I had already tried twice to approach women soon after my circumcision and had failed. I got as far as the door of one woman's house and felt my heart beating like a Congolese drum; breathing became difficult and I had to turn back. Another time I managed to get in the house and succeeded in sitting on the bed, but then I started trembling until the whole bed was shaking, and conversation became difficult. I left the house and the woman, amazed and speechless, and never went back to her again.

42 Tonight I promised myself I would be brave and would not make any silly, ridiculous moves. "I must be mature and not afraid," I kept reminding myself, as I remembered an incident involving one of my relatives when he was still very young and, like me, afraid of women. He went to a woman's house and sat on a stool for a whole hour; he was afraid to awaken her, as his heart was pounding and he was having difficulty breathing.

43 When he finally calmed down, he woke her up, and their conversation went something like this:

44 "Woman, wake up."

45 "Why should I?"

46 "To light the fire."

47 "For what?"

48 "So you can see me."

49 "I already know who you are. Why don't *you* light the fire, as you're nearer to it than me?"

50 "It's your house and it's only proper that you light it yourself."

51 "I don't feel like it."

52 "At least wake up so we can talk, as I have something to tell you."

53 "Say it."

54 "I need you."

55 "I do not need one-eyed types like yourself."

56 "One-eyed people are people too."

57 "That might be so, but they are not to my taste."

58 They continued talking for quite some time, and the more they spoke, the braver he became. He did not sleep with her that night, but later on he persisted until he won her over. I doubted whether I was as strong-willed as he, but the fact that he had met with success encouraged me. I told my warrior friend where to find me should he need me, and then I departed.

59 When I entered the house of my *esiankiki*, I called for the woman of the house, and as luck would have it, my lady responded. She was waiting for me. I felt better, and I proceeded to talk to her like a professional. After much talking back and forth, I joined her in bed.

60 The night was calm, tender, and loving, like most nights after initiation ceremonies as big as this one. There must have been a lot of courting and lovemaking.

61 Maasai women can be very hard to deal with sometimes. They can simply reject a man outright and refuse to change their minds. Some play hard to get, but in reality are testing the man to see whether he is worth their while. Once a friend of mine while still young was powerfully attracted to a woman nearly his mother's age. He put a bold move on her. At first the woman could not believe his intention, or rather was amazed by his courage. The name of the warrior was Ngengeiya, or Drizzle.

62 "Drizzle, what do you want?"

63 The warrior stared her right in the eye and said, "You."

64 "For what?"

65 "To make love to you."

66 "I am your mother's age."

67 "The choice was either her or you."

68 This remark took the woman by surprise. She had underestimated the saying "There is no such thing as a young warrior." When you are a warrior, you are expected to perform bravely in any situation. Your age and size are immaterial.

69 "You mean you could really love me like a grownup man?"

70 "Try me, woman."

71 He moved in on her. Soon the woman started moaning with excitement, calling out his name. "Honey Drizzle, Honey Drizzle, you *are* a man." In a breathy, stammering voice, she said, "A real man."

72 Her attractiveness made Honey Drizzle ignore her relative old age. The Maasai believe that if an older and a younger person have intercourse, it is the older person who stands to gain. For instance, it is believed that an older woman having an affair with a young man starts to appear younger and healthier, while the young man grows older and unhealthy.

73 The following day when the initiation rites had ended, I decided to return home. I had offended my father by staying away from home without his consent, so I prepared myself for whatever punishment he might inflict on me. I walked home alone.

✧ *Evaluating the Text*

1. How is the candidate's life, reputation, and destiny dependent on the bravery he shows during the circumcision ceremony? What consequences would his family have to suffer if he were to flinch or shudder? What responsibilities does Saitoti assume and what privileges is he allowed upon successful completion of the ceremony?

How does this image of a young Maasai warrior illustrate Saitoti's description?

2. What is Saitoti's attitude toward his father? What assumptions about a son's responsibilities account for how Saitoti's father treats him?

3. Several Maasai customs reveal the profound symbiotic relationship they have with nature and the animal world. For example, what is the rationale behind their practice of not eating milk and meat together? Why is Saitoti careful not to allow the blood from his wound to spill onto the ground?

✧ *Exploring Different Perspectives*

1. Compare the experiences of Saitoti with those of Waris Dirie in "The Tragedy of Female Circumcision" in terms of the contrasting objectives of circumcision.

2. Compare the concepts of what it means to be male in the accounts by Saitoti and Andrew Sullivan in "My Big Fat Straight Wedding."

✧ *Extending Viewpoints through Writing and Research*

1. How does the Maasai ritual Saitoti describes deepen the bond between the community and the initiate in ways that are quite similar to the bar mitzvah in Judaism and the confirmation ceremony

in Christianity? In a short essay, explore how any of these rites of passage affirm the culture, unite the candidate with his or her community, and ensure the continuation of traditions.

2. In what sense are Saitoti's interactions with his friends and the opposite sex quite typical of a teenage boy despite cultural differences between the Maasai and contemporay Americans?

3. How does the idea of the warrior in Maasai society correspond to being a soldier in Western culture? What similarities and differences can you discover between the initiations they undergo and the responsibilites that they accept?

Waris Dirie

The Tragedy of Female Circumcision

Waris Dirie was born in Somalia and as a child underwent female circumcision, a custom that is also practiced in the Sudan, Saudi Arabia, Egypt, Libya, and Yemen. The following selection that describes her experience and later fame as a supermodel first appeared in Marie Claire *magazine in March 1996. In 1997, Dirie became a United Nations ambassador for the abolition of female genital mutilation (FGM). Her autobiography* Desert Flower: The Extraordinary Journey of a Desert Nomad, *written with Cathleen Miller, was published in 1998. More recently, Dirie has written* Desert Children *with Corinna Milborn and translated by Sheelagh Alabaster in 2007. Although many countries view female circumcision as a cultural belief that has been practiced for generations, in 2009, the Ugandan parliament (Uganda is a country located in West Africa) unanimously passed a bill banning female genital mutilation with penalties of possible imprisonment for those who continue to practice it.*

Before You Read

What have you heard or what do you know about the practice of female circumcision?

1 In my profession as a model, people sometimes tell me I'm beautiful, but they don't know what lies beneath the surface. Let me tell you who I am and where I come from.

2 I was born in Somalia, East Africa, one of 12 children. I don't really know how old I am. I'm around 28. In Africa, there is no time, no watch, no calendar. My family is nomadic. When I was a child, we moved around every day, looking for food and water. We slept on the ground in the open air. I spent my time running around barefoot, with the whole desert before me. There was nothing to plan, no tomorrow. We lived every day as it came.

3 I had never heard anything about the western world, but somehow I knew there was something else outside Africa. I had never even seen a white person. But I always wanted to be different, so I asked my cousin, "Where do you go to become white?" They said, "If you leave Africa, you become white because there is no sun."

4 When I was about 5 years old, my father decided it was time for me to be circumcised. I remember it so clearly that if I think about it, I'll throw up. The woman who did it called herself a "professional cutter," but she was just an old gypsy who traveled around with her bag. My mother sat me down and said, "Be a good girl; don't move. I don't have the energy to hold you down." The old woman held a dirty razor blade, and I could see the dried blood on it from the person she had cut before me. I opened my legs, closed my eyes, and blocked my mind. I did it for my mother. The woman didn't just cut the clitoris—she cut everything, including the labia. She then sewed me up tightly with a needle. All I could feel was pain. After I had been cut, I lay on the floor in agony. They tied my legs together to stop me from walking, so that I wouldn't rip open. I was on my back for a month. I couldn't eat, I couldn't think, I could not do anything. I turned black, blue, and yellow. I couldn't urinate—the pee just dripped out of me. After three weeks my mother found someone else to open me up a tiny bit to give me a space to pee because I was getting so sick. I bled for the next two, three months. I nearly died. I wanted to die at the time—I had given up on life.

5 One of my younger sisters and two of my cousins died from the procedure. My mother has had it done, like her mother, grandmothers, and great-grandmothers before her. You can't escape it. They catch you, tie you down, and then do it. It's done for men. They think if you haven't been circumcised, you're going to sleep around. They cut you so that you won't be horny. It has nothing to do with religion. Neither the Bible nor the Koran talks about female circumcision anywhere. Men invented the custom so that sexual pleasure is nonexistent for women—sex is just for men. When you marry, the man forces himself in or cuts you with a knife. When you give birth, they unsew you. Once the baby has come out, they sew you back up again. It continues like this. A woman who has ten children is sewn up and opened like a piece of material.

6 One day, when I was about 13, my father came to me on the sand. "I have found a man for you," he said. "You are getting married. Aren't you happy?" He had sold me for five camels to a 60-year-old man. I met this man the next day. He looked so old. I thought, "There has got to be more to life." That was the second I decided to leave Africa. I told my mother. I was her favorite. "Do what you want," she said. "Be safe, be happy, and don't forget me." She gave me the biggest hug and cried.

7 I left that night for Mogadishu, the Somali capital, where I knew I had an aunt. I ran through the desert for about ten days, pushing myself to keep going until I was ready to drop. I had nothing on me, just a piece of cloth on my waist. When it was dark and tribesmen were asleep, I would drink milk from their camels. When I reached Mogadishu, I just stood there like a zombie, I was so scared. I told

people I was looking for my aunt, and eventually I found her. One day, one of my uncles came to see her. He was the Somali ambassador in England and was looking for a girl to work at his residence in London. When I heard this, I begged my aunt to convince him to take me. I had no idea where I would be going, but I knew it would be out of Africa. My uncle agreed.

8 I had never seen an airplane before. Looking back, it was hilarious, because I remember that in the plane, I was desperate to go to the toilet. I only knew how to pee outside in the bush. Eventually, I couldn't hold it any longer. I had watched people go to the little cabin at the back of the plane, so I did the same, but I was frightened that if I touched something, the plane would blow up. I didn't know how to flush, so I filled the toilet with cups of water so it wouldn't look like I had just peed!

9 I arrived in London in December. I was about 14. I worked as a servant in my uncle's residence for four years. Every day, I would get up at 6 A.M., then cook and clean without stopping until midnight. I never had a day off.

10 The culture shock for me in England was huge. I didn't speak English. I couldn't read or write. But I knew right from the start that I was different from white women. I was aware that what had been done to me when I was 5 doesn't happen in western culture. I was angry and completely frustrated. I wanted to be the same as the girls around me. I kept saying to myself, "Why me? Why?" It was something I had to learn to live with.

11 Men would often bother me. I used to accompany my little cousin to school every day and men would stare at me, or blow me kisses. I'd ignore them, not knowing what was going on. One man in particular approached me all the time. I thought he was disgusting and dirty like the others. One day, he followed me home and introduced himself to my aunt. He said he was a photographer and wanted to take pictures of me. My aunt refused. I was disappointed.

12 I had heard about Iman, the Somalian supermodel. I had covered my wall with photographs of her that I'd cut from magazines. To me, she looked like a typical Somali woman, but when I came to the western world, I found out that she was rich and famous.

13 Shortly afterward, my ambassador uncle's term of office ended and he wanted to take me back to Somalia. But I didn't want to go back. The day before we were due to leave London, I buried my passport in the garden and told him I had lost it. He was furious because there was no time to issue another one, and the family was forced to leave without me.

14 I was free at last. That day, I went to Oxford Street, London's main shopping street, and spotted a Somali woman—I know what my people look like. I told her that I had nowhere to stay. She was living at

the YMCA and helped me get a room there. The next day, I got a day job scrubbing floors at McDonald's and started night school.

15 Meanwhile, I kept in touch with the photographer and he took some pictures of me. One day, a modeling agency called. They wanted to sign me on. At my first job casting, for a calendar, the photographer asked me to take off my top. I stormed out. That night, the modeling agency tracked me down and yelled, "What on earth are you doing? Do you know how much you could earn on this job?" I had no idea. In England, the Pirelli calendar with its topless supermodels has a cult status. But I thought I'd have to have sex with the photographer and preferred to go back to my McDonald's, scrubbing the floor. When I realized all I had to do was smile at the camera for 2500 pounds ($4000), I went back the next day and took my shirt off. I got the job and my photograph was chosen for the cover of the calendar. That day changed my life.

16 I've been modeling ever since. I find it ridiculous that people pay me just for how I look. When I landed a job at Revlon, the cosmetics company, the ad I was in had a headline that said: "The most beautiful women in the world wear Revlon." I thought, "Wait a minute, I'm not that pretty. I'm OK." It took a long time for me to say "Thank you" when someone said, "You're so pretty." My mother, on the other hand, is beautiful. She is beautiful inside.

17 I hadn't been back to Somalia for 15 years when BBC television approached me last year and said they wanted to do a documentary on my life. I said to them, "Let's make a deal. I'll do the program only if you take me back to Africa so I can see my family again." It's too dangerous for me to go back there alone because of the civil war. They agreed.

18 Being back there after so long was incredible—I had missed my family so much. In the West, you hear only about the bad in Africa, the starvation and war, but to me, Africa is still a magical place. But I wish Africans had clean water to drink, could grow trees and send their children to school.

19 None of my family understands how I make a living, except my mother. She's proud of me. I begged her to come back with me to London, but she doesn't want to leave Somalia. When it was time for me to go, I was overwhelmed with emotion. It had felt so good to be back in Africa—I am at home there.

20 As for the future, I'm very romantic about getting married and having kids. But it took me a long time to start dating. First of all, sex is not important to me. Second, I need to know a man well before I get close. When I see a man, or when he touches me, I want him to keep a distance. Men are loving and say, "It's OK. I'm not going to eat you. What's the matter? Don't you like sex?" They don't understand because I don't tell them what happened to me.

21 I now have a beautiful boyfriend and, yes, I fall in love and can have a physical relationship like everyone else. Being circumcised doesn't mean I've lost every feeling in my body. But female circumcision changes your whole life, not just sex. And I still have health problems associated with it. Every month, my periods are very heavy and last a long time. I have to lock myself up for three days because it hurts so badly. I went to doctors everywhere and they all said, "There's nothing we can do." I've been opened up, but it still doesn't help. It used to make me really, really depressed, but I have to live with it. I try to enjoy my life and I consider myself very lucky. There's nothing I can do about what happened to me. I can't turn back the clock.

22 Whoever came up with female circumcision should be tortured, because it is torture. It has got nothing at all to do with male circumcision, where they just cut off an extra piece of skin. Female circumcision is mutilation. It is brutal, cruel, and unnecessary.

23 It's very painful for me to talk about this subject because it is so deeply personal. And I don't want anybody's sympathy. But it's time for me to tell the world and swallow my pride in order to save my sisters in Africa. I want to be an ambassador on their behalf because they can't stick up for themselves. I've seen them suffer from it and die from it. I was strong enough to survive and I want to make a difference. I can talk because I've experienced the pain. I want female circumcision to stop. Now! Today! If only I could make that happen, I would drop everything. Even if I just save one woman from this torture, it would be worth it.

✧ *Evaluating the Text*

1. What role does female circumcision play in Somalian culture? What insight does Dirie provide into the trauma she experienced both at the time and for years after?

2. Dirie writes, "Neither the Bible nor the Koran talks about female circumcision anywhere." Why does she mention this and how does it negate arguments for female circumcision?

3. How did Dirie's life as a supermodel provide her with opportunities that transformed her life and put her in a position to be heard on this issue?

✧ *Exploring Different Perspectives*

1. Compare the Somalian cultural attitude toward women with what Latifa Ali reveals in "Betrayed."

2. Contrast the role that female circumcision plays in Somalian culture with the role male circumcision plays among the Maasai as described by Tepilit Ole Saitoti in "The Initiation of a Maasai Warrior."

✧ *Extending Viewpoints through Writing and Research*

1. What factors explain the difference placed on female virginity in Somalian culture and contemporary U.S. society?
2. What current efforts, if any, are being made to outlaw or police the continued practice of female circumcision among immigrants in the United States? You might consult the Web site http://www.fgmnetwork.org.

Andrew Sullivan

My Big Fat Straight Wedding

Andrew Sullivan (b. 1963) is a British political commentator and author who has lived in the United States since 1984. He is the former editor of The New Republic, *author and blogger for* The Atlantic. *In the following essay from* The Atlantic Online *(September 2008), Sullivan explores issues connected with his marriage to Aaron Tone.*

Before You Read

Should gay marriage be accepted as a constitutional right? Why or why not?

1 What if gays were straight?

2 The question is absurd—gays are defined as not straight, right?—yet increasingly central to the debate over civil-marriage rights. Here is how California's Supreme Court put it in a key passage in its now-famous May 15 ruling that gay couples in California must be granted the right to marry, with no qualifications or euphemisms:

> These core substantive rights include, most fundamentally, the opportunity of an individual to establish—with the person with whom the individual has chosen to share his or her life—an *officially recognized and protected family* possessing mutual rights and responsibilities and entitled to the same respect and dignity accorded a union traditionally designated as marriage.

What's notable here is the starting point of the discussion: an "individual." The individual citizen posited by the court is defined as prior to his or her sexual orientation. He or she exists as a person before he or she exists as straight or gay. And the right under discussion is defined as "the opportunity of an individual" to choose another "person" to "establish a family" in which reproduction and children are not necessary. And so the distinction between gay and straight is essentially abolished. For all the debate about the law in this decision, the debate about the terms under discussion has been close to nonexistent. And yet in many ways, these terms are at the core of the decision, and are the reason why it is such a watershed. The ruling, and the language it uses, represents the removal of the premise of the last generation in favor of a premise accepted as a given by the next.

3 The premise used to be that homosexuality was an activity, that gays were people who chose to behave badly; or, if they weren't choosing to behave badly, were nonetheless suffering from a form of sickness or, in the words of the Vatican, an "objective disorder." And so the question of whether to permit the acts and activities of such disordered individuals was a legitimate area of legislation and regulation.

4 But when gays are seen as the same as straights—as individuals; as normal, well-adjusted, human individuals—the argument changes altogether. The question becomes a matter of how we treat a minority with an involuntary, defining characteristic along the lines of gender or race. And when a generation came of age that did not merely grasp this intellectually, but knew it from their own lives and friends and family members, then the logic for full equality became irresistible.

5 This transformation in understanding happened organically. It began with the sexual revolution in the 1970s, and then came crashing into countless previously unaware families, as their sons and uncles and fathers died in vast numbers from AIDS in the 1980s and 1990s. It emerged as younger generations came out earlier and earlier, and as their peers came to see gay people as fellows and siblings, rather than as denizens of some distant and alien subculture. It happened as lesbian couples became parents and as gay soldiers challenged the discrimination against them. And it percolated up through the popular culture—from *Will & Grace* and *Ellen* to almost every reality show since *The Real World*.

6 What California's court did, then, was not to recognize a new right to same-sex marriage. It was to acknowledge an emergent cultural consensus. And once that consensus had been accepted, the denial of the right to marry became, for many, a constitutional outrage. The right to marry, after all, is, as the court put it, "one of the basic, inalienable civil rights guaranteed to an individual." Its denial was necessarily an outrage—and not merely an anomaly—because the right to marry has such deep and inalienable status in American constitutional law.

7 The political theorist Hannah Arendt, addressing the debate over miscegenation laws during the civil-rights movement of the 1950s, put it clearly enough:

> The right to marry whoever one wishes is an elementary human right compared to which "the right to attend an integrated school, the right to sit where one pleases on a bus, the right to go into any hotel or recreation area or place of amusement, regardless of one's skin or color or race" are minor indeed. Even political rights, like the right to vote, and nearly all other rights enumerated in the Constitution, are secondary to the inalienable human rights to "life, liberty and the pursuit of happiness" proclaimed in the Declaration of Independence; and to this category the right to home and marriage unquestionably belongs.

Note that Arendt put the right to marry before even the right to vote. And this is how many gay people of the next generation see it. Born into straight families and reared to see homosexuality as a form of difference, not disability, they naturally wonder why they would be excluded from the integral institution of their own families' lives and history. They see this exclusion as unimaginable—as unimaginable as straight people would if they were told that they could not legally marry someone of their choosing. No other institution has an equivalent power to include people in their own familial narrative or civic history as deeply or as powerfully as civil marriage does. And the next generation see themselves as people first and gay second.

8 Born in a different era, I reached that conclusion through more pain and fear and self-loathing than my 20-something fellow homosexuals do today. But it was always clear to me nonetheless. It just never fully came home to me until I too got married.

9 It happened first when we told our families and friends of our intentions. Suddenly, they had a vocabulary to describe and understand our relationship. I was no longer my partner's "friend" or "boyfriend"; I was his fiancé. Suddenly, everyone involved themselves in our love. They asked how I had proposed; they inquired when the wedding would be; my straight friends made jokes about marriage that simply included me as one of them. At that first post-engagement Christmas with my in-laws, I felt something shift. They had always been welcoming and supportive. But now I was family. I felt an end—a sudden, fateful end—to an emotional displacement I had experienced since childhood.

10 The wedding occurred last August in Massachusetts in front of a small group of family and close friends. And in that group, I suddenly realized, it was the heterosexuals who knew what to do, who guided the gay couple and our friends into the rituals and rites of family. Ours was not, we realized, a different institution, after all, and we were not different kinds of people. In the doing of it, it was the same as my sister's wedding and we were the same as my sister and brother-in-law. The strange, bewildering emotions of the moment, the cake and reception, the distracted children and weeping mothers, the morning's butterflies and the night's drunkenness: this was not a gay marriage; it was a marriage.

11 And our families instantly and for the first time since our early childhood became not just institutions in which we were included, but institutions that we too owned and perpetuated. My sister spoke of her marriage as if it were interchangeable with my own, and my niece and nephew had no qualms in referring to my husband as their new uncle. The embossed invitations and the floral bouquets and the fear of fluffing our vows: in these tiny, bonding gestures of integration, we all came to see an alienating distinction become a unifying difference.

12 It was a moment that shifted a sense of our own identity within our psyches and even our souls. Once this happens, the law eventually follows. In California this spring, it did.

✧ *Evaluating the Text*

1. In Sullivan's view, why must the law change to reflect an emerging cultural consensus?
2. How have past developments, as reflected in the experience in many families and in popular culture, acknowledged this trend?
3. What personal dimension did Sullivan's experience bring to this social issue?

✧ *Exploring Different Perspectives*

1. In what sense does the meaning of marriage play an important role in Sullivan's essay and in Latifa Ali's account in "Betrayed"?
2. In what respects do both Sullivan and Judith Ortiz Cofer (in "The Myth of the Latin Woman") argue for more realistic and compassionate treatment of minorities?

✧ *Extending Viewpoints through Writing and Research*

1. What current developments have continued to raise the issue of same-sex marriage in different states?
2. State legislatures put through bills to pass same-sex marriage, but why, in your opinion, do voters, through referendums in those states, decide against it?

Nicholas Kristof

Striking the Brothels' Bottom Line

Nicholas D. Kristof was born in 1959 in Chicago. He is an American journalist, author, and op-ed columnist for the New York Times *who has won two Pulitzer Prizes. In the following essay, which first appeared January 11, 2009, Kristof continues to report on human rights abuses and sex trafficking in Cambodia.*

Before You Read
What do you know about sex trafficking?

Poipet, Cambodia

1 In trying to figure out how we can defeat sex trafficking, a starting point is to think like a brothel owner.

2 My guide to that has been Sok Khorn, an amiable middle-aged woman who is a longtime brothel owner here in the wild Cambodian town of Poipet. I met her five years ago when she sold me a teenager, Srey Mom, for $203 and then blithely wrote me a receipt confirming that the girl was now my property. At another brothel nearby, I purchased another imprisoned teenager for $150.

3 Astonished that in the 21st century I had bought two human beings, I took them back to their villages and worked with a local aid group to help them start small businesses. I've remained close to them over the years, but the results were mixed.

4 The second girl did wonderfully, learning hairdressing and marrying a terrific man. But Srey Mom, it turned out, was addicted to methamphetamine and fled back to the brothel world to feed her craving.

5 I just returned again to Ms. Khorn's brothel to interview her, and found something remarkable. It had gone broke and closed, like many of the brothels in Poipet. One lesson is that the business model is more vulnerable than it looks. There are ways we can make enslaving girls more risky and less profitable, so that traffickers give up in disgust.

6 For years, Ms. Khorn had been grumbling to me about the brothel—the low margins, the seven-day schedule, difficult customers,

grasping policemen and scorn from the community. There was also a personal toll, for her husband had sex with the girls, infuriating her, and the couple eventually divorced bitterly. Ms. Khorn was also troubled that her youngest daughter, now 13, was growing up surrounded by drunken, leering men.

7 Then in the last year, the brothel business became even more challenging amid rising pressure from aid groups, journalists and the United States State Department's trafficking office. The office issued reports shaming Cambodian leaders and threatened sanctions if they did nothing.

8 Many of the brothels are owned by the police, which complicates matters, but eventually authorities in Cambodia were pressured enough that they ordered a partial crackdown.

9 "They didn't tell me to close down exactly," said another Poipet brothel owner whom I've also interviewed periodically. "But they said I should keep the front door closed."

10 About half the brothels in Poipet seem to have gone out of business in the last couple of years. After Ms. Khorn's brothel closed, her daughter-in-law took four of the prostitutes to staff a new brothel, but it's doing poorly and she is thinking of starting a rice shop instead. "A store would be more profitable," grumbled the daughter-in-law, Sav Channa.

11 "The police come almost every day, asking for $5," she said. "Any time a policeman gets drunk, he comes and asks for money. . . . Sometimes I just close up and pretend that this isn't a brothel. I say that we're all sisters."

12 Ms. Channa, who does not seem to be imprisoning anyone against her will, readily acknowledged that some other brothels in Poipet torture girls, enslave them and occasionally beat them to death. She complained that their cruelty gives them a competitive advantage.

13 But brutality has its own drawbacks as a business model, particularly during a crackdown, pimps say. Brothels that imprison and torture girls have to pay for 24-hour guards, and they lose business because they can't allow customers to take girls out to hotel rooms. Moreover, the Cambodian government has begun prosecuting the most abusive traffickers.

14 "One brothel owner here was actually arrested," complained another owner in Poipet, indignantly. "After that, I was so scared, I closed the brothel for a while."

15 To be sure, a new brothel district has opened up on the edge of Poipet—in the guise of "karaoke lounges" employing teenage girls. One of the Mama-sans there offered that while she didn't have a young virgin girl in stock, she could get me one.

16 Virgin sales are the profit center for many brothels in Asia (partly because they stitch girls up and resell them as virgins several times over), and thus these sales are their economic vulnerability as well. If

we want to undermine sex trafficking, the best way is to pressure governments like Cambodia's to organize sting operations and arrest both buyers and sellers of virgin girls. Cambodia has shown it is willing to take at least some action, and that is one that would strike at the heart of the business model.

17 Sexual slavery is like any other business: raise the operating costs, create a risk of jail, and the human traffickers will quite sensibly shift to some other trade. If the Obama administration treats 21st-century slavery as a top priority, we can push many of the traffickers to quit in disgust and switch to stealing motorcycles instead.

18 I invite you to comment on this column on my blog, *On the Ground*. Please also join me on Facebook, watch my YouTube videos and follow me on Twitter.

✧ *Evaluating the Text*

1. How does Kristof use an unusual approach in his investigation of sex trafficking in Cambodia?
2. What do you learn about Kristof's history of trying to combat this crime? What results did his intervention produce?
3. What positive signs does Kristof cite to suggest that the situation may be improving?

✧ *Exploring Different Perspectives*

1. Compare the premium placed on virginity as a commodity in this essay and in Latifa Ali's account in "Betrayed."
2. Compare the cultural attitudes toward women that emerge in the accounts by Kristof in Cambodia and Waris Dirie in Somalia.

✧ *Extending Viewpoints through Writing and Research*

1. What current news stories around the world and in the United States have continued to bring this issue to public awareness? You might check Kristof's column in the *New York Times* or his blog at www.nytimes.com/ontheground.
2. Has the Wilberforce Act passed by Congress in 2009, which strengthened sanctions on countries that tolerate sex trafficking, produced any positive results?

Connecting Cultures

Judith Ortiz Cofer, "The Myth of the Latin Woman"

How do both Cofer's account and that of Andrew X. Pham in "Foreign-Asians" in Chapter 7 show the writers struggling with unwarranted assumptions by others?

Don Kulick and Thaïs Machado-Borges, "Leaky"

Compare the role that skin color plays in establishing social rank in "Leaky" and in Kate Chopin's story, "Désirée's Baby" in Chapter 5.

Latifa Ali with Richard Shears, "Betrayed"

How do both this account and Serena Nanda's "Arranging a Marriage in India" in Chapter 8 explore conflicts between traditional values and present-day realities?

Tepilit Ole Saitoti, "The Initiation of a Maasai Warrior"

What insights do Saitoti and Joe Bageant ("Valley of the Gun" in Chapter 1) offer into how one becomes accepted as an adult in one's group?

Waris Dirie, "The Tragedy of Female Circumcision"

To what extent is female circumcision as described by Dirie comparable to foot binding in China as described by Valerie Steele and John S. Major in "China Chic: East Meets West" in Chapter 8?

Andrew Sullivan, "My Big Fat Straight Wedding"

How do the accounts by Sullivan and Serena Nanda in "Arranging a Marriage in India" in Chapter 8 address the evolution of traditional marriage practices?

Nicholas D. Kristof, "Striking the Brothels' Bottom Line"

How does Kristof's essay reveal the new form slavery has taken when compared with Frederick Douglass's "My Bondage and My Freedom" in Chapter 7?

4

Working Lives

People who work sitting down get paid more
than people who work standing up.

—Ogden Nash (1902–1971)
U.S. writer of humorous verse

The way we identify ourselves in terms of the work we do is far-reaching. Frequently, the first question we ask when we meet someone is, "What do you do?" Through work we define ourselves and others; yet cultural values also play a part in influencing how we feel about the work we do.

In addition to providing a means to live, work has an important psychological meaning in our culture. Some societies value work more than leisure; in other cultures, the reverse is true and work is viewed as something you do just to provide the necessities of life. In the United States, the work you perform is intertwined with a sense of identity and self-esteem.

Work in most societies involves the exchange of goods and services. In tribal cultures, as distinct from highly industrialized cultures, there is little job specialization, although age and gender determine what tasks one performs. Economies may range from the barter system, in which goods are traded, to more complex market economies based on the reciprocal exchange of goods and services for money. The transformation of resources is a key element in creating jobs and a stable economy.

The attitude people have toward the work they do varies within and between cultures. Helena Norberg-Hodge in "Learning from Ladakh" describes the catastrophic changes in the lives of this traditional community wrought by materialism. In Japan, Tomoyuki Iwashita, in "Why I Quit the Company," explains how the seeming security of lifetime employment does not offset sacrificing one's life for the corporation. Jack Owens in "Don't Shoot! We're Republicans!" communicates the drama and danger of being an FBI agent. Bill Geist in "The Land of Lost Luggage!" humorously describes a small town in Alabama to which all lost luggage makes its way to be sold. Vivienne

Walt and Amanda Bower in "Follow the Money" explore the unpublicized but very real worldwide economy created by migrant workers who send money back home. In "A Coming Storm," Kris Holloway writes of her experiences while in the Peace Corps in Mali assisting a midwife. Jose Antonio Burciaga in "My Ecumenical Father" evokes the unusual interfaith tolerance of his father who worked at a Jewish temple.

To help you understand how the writings in this chapter relate to each other, you might use one or several of the following guidelines before writing about work.

1. Which of the author's values seem closest to your own?
2. What stylistic means does the writer use to evoke the working environment?
3. Does the writer support his or her conclusions with personal experiences that are appropriate and effective?
4. What changes does the author suggest or recommend?
5. How would you characterize the author's tone and degree of emotional involvement with the issue?
6. Does the author connect the subject to a broader political or social issue?

Recommended Films on This Theme

- *Jean de Florette* (France, 1987) The story of two scheming farmers in a drought-striken province who block the spring so that they can purchase their neighbor's farm for little cost;
- *The Office* (United Kingdom, 2001) An amusing film that follows the staff and manager of an office about to be downsized;
- *Osama* (Afghanistan, 2003) The story about a 12-year-old who disguises herself as a boy in order to work and support her family;
- *Blood Diamonds* (United States/Sierra Leone-2006) An inside look at the exploitative industry of diamond mining in Sierra Leone.

Helena Norberg-Hodge

Learning from Ladakh

Helena Norberg-Hodge was born in Sweden in 1946. She is a linguist by training, speaks six languages, and is the first Westerner to master the Ladakhi language. Ladakh, or "Little Tibet," is a desert land high up in the Western Himalayas that, for more than a thousand years, has been the home to a thriving culture based on frugality and cooperation. Encroachments by Western consumerism in the late 1970s and 1980s altered the natural balance and brought threats from pollution, inflation, unemployment, and greed.

Norberg-Hodge is the founder and director of the International Society for Ecology and Culture, and in 1986 she shared the Right Livelihood Award, known as the "Alternative Nobel Prize." Ancient Futures: Learning from Ladakh *(1991), from which the following selection has been taken, has been translated into forty-two languages.*

Before You Read

Consider how a money-based economy could alter the relationships between people in a community that had been based on cooperative labor.

We don't have any poverty here.

—Tsewang Paljor, 1975

If you could only help us Ladakhis, we're so poor.

—Tsewang Paljor, 1983

1 In the traditional culture, villagers provided for their basic needs without money. They had developed skills that enabled them to grow barley at 12,000 feet and to manage yaks and other animals at even higher elevations. People knew how to build houses with their own hands from the materials of the immediate surroundings. The only thing they actually needed from outside the region was salt, for which they traded. They used money in only a limited way, mainly for luxuries.

2 Now, suddenly, as part of the international money economy, Ladakhis find themselves ever more dependent—even for vital needs—on a system that is controlled by faraway forces. They are vulnerable to decisions made by people who do not even know that Ladakh exists. If the value of the dollar changes, it will ultimately have

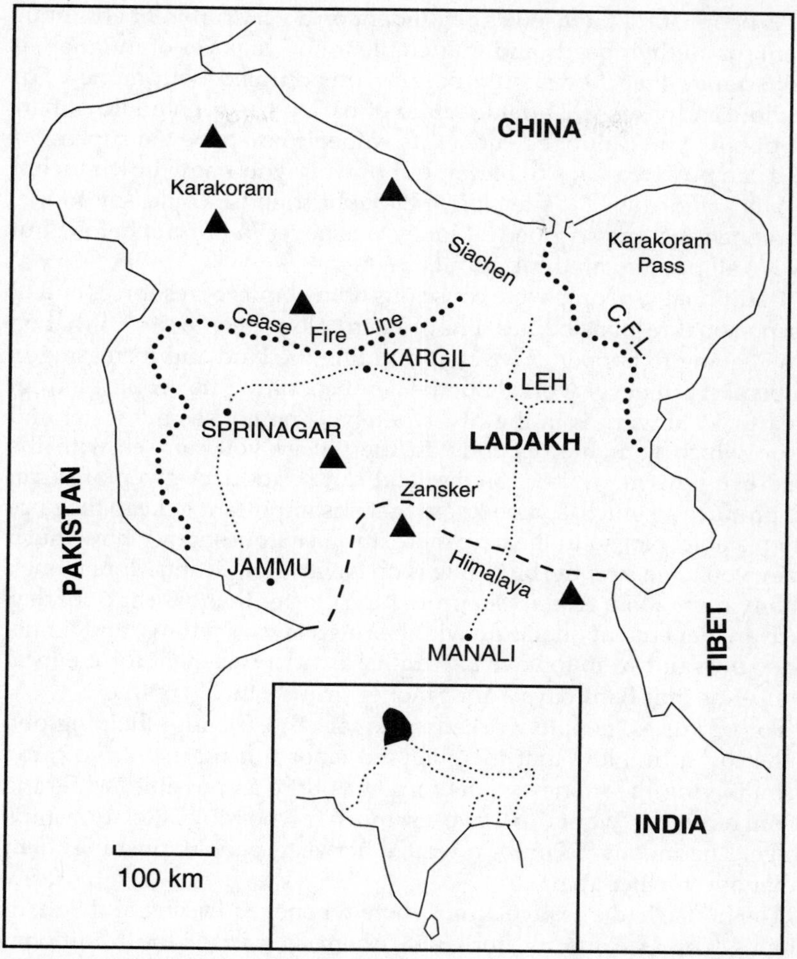

How does this map provide a geographical context for Norberg-Hodge's essay?

an effect on the Indian rupee. This means that Ladakhis, who need money to survive, are now under the control of the managers of international finance. Living off the land, they had been their own masters.

3 At first, people were not aware of the fact that the new economy creates dependence; money appeared to be only an advantage. Since it traditionally had been a good thing, bringing luxuries from far away, more of it seemed to be an unconditional improvement. Now you can buy all sorts of exotic things that you could not before, like three-minute noodles and digital watches.

4 As people find themselves dependent on a very different economic system for all their needs and vulnerable to the vagaries of inflation, it is not strange that they should become preoccupied with money. For two thousand years in Ladakh, a kilo of barley has been a kilo of barley, but now you cannot be sure of its value. If you have ten rupees today, it can buy two kilos of barley, but how do you know how much it will buy tomorrow? "It's terrible," Ladakhi friends would say to me, "everyone is getting so greedy. Money was never important before, but now it's all people can think about."

5 Traditionally, people were conscious of the limits of resources and of their personal responsibilities. I have heard older people say: "What on earth is going to happen if we start dividing the land and increasing in numbers? It can never work." But the new economy cuts people off from the earth. Paid work is in the city, where you cannot see the water and soil on which your life depends. In the village you can see with the naked eye how many mouths the land can support. A given area can only produce so much, so you know that it is important to keep the population stable. Not so in the city; there it is just a question of how much money you have, and the birth rate is no longer significant. More money will buy more food. And it can grow much faster than wheat or barley, which are dependent on nature with her own laws, rhythms, and limits. Money does not seem to have any limits; an advertisement for the local Jammu-Kashmir Bank says, "Your money grows quickly with us."

6 For centuries, people worked as equals and friends—helping one another by turn. Now that there is paid labor during the harvest, the person paying the money wants to pay as little as possible, while the person receiving wants to have as much as possible. Relationships change. The money becomes a wedge between people, pushing them further and further apart.

7 The house had a festive atmosphere whenever Tsering and Sonam Dolma's friends came to work with them as part of the traditional *lhangsde* practice. Sonam used to cook special food for the occasion. But in the last couple of years, the practice has gradually disappeared and their farm near Leh is increasingly dependent on paid labor. Sonam complains bitterly about rising prices and resents having to pay high wages. The festive atmosphere of friends working together has gone; these laborers are strangers, sometimes Nepalis or Indians from the plains who have no common language.

8 The changing economy makes it difficult to remain a farmer. Previously, with cooperative labor between people, farmers had no need for money. Now, unable to pay larger and larger wages for farm hands, some are forced to abandon the villages to earn money in the city. For those who stay, the pressure increases to grow food for profit, instead of food for themselves. Cash cropping becomes the norm as farmers

are pushed by the forces of development to become dependent on the market economy.

9 The new economy also increases the gap between rich and poor. In the traditional economy there were differences in wealth, but its accumulation had natural limits. You could only care for so many yaks or store so many kilos of barley. Money, on the other hand, is easily stored in the bank, and the rich get richer and the poor get poorer.

10 I knew a man named Lobzang who had an antique shop in Leh. Like many Ladakhi shopkeepers, he had given up farming and come to Leh to make money, but his wife and children still lived in the village. He wanted the best for his children, and as soon as he could afford the housing, he planned to bring them to town to get the benefits of an education and, in particular, to learn English.

11 I had just dropped into his shop to say hello when an old man from Lobzang's village came in to sell his butter jars. It was a full day's journey on foot and by bus from the village. The old man probably planned to spend a couple of days with relatives in Leh, buying supplies to take back to the village with the money from the butter jars. He looked dignified in his traditional burgundy woolen robes. He put two jars on the counter. They had the warm patina that comes from generations of constant handling. They were made of fine-grained apricot wood and had a simple elegance that would certainly appeal to tourists. "They're lovely," I said. "What will you keep your butter in without them?" "We keep it in used milk tins," he said.

12 They argued about the price. Apparently a few weeks earlier, Lobzang had promised him a much higher price than he was willing to offer now. He pointed to some cracks in the jars and refused to raise his offer. I knew he would get ten times as much when he sold the jars to the tourists. The old man threw me an imploring look, but what could I say? He left the shop with a disappointed stoop to his shoulders and enough money to buy a few kilos of sugar.

13 "You shouldn't have said they were lovely," Lobzang scolded me. "I had to give him more."

14 "But he's from your own village. Do you have to bargain so hard with him?"

15 "I hate it, but I have to. Besides, a stranger would have given him even less."

✧ *Evaluating the Text*

1. How has the introduction of a money-based economy distorted relationships between people and made them dependent on things they didn't even know existed?

2. How does the incident of the shopkeeper and his former neighbor illustrate the change for the worse that has overtaken the Ladakhis since money became the medium of exchange?

✧ *Exploring Different Perspectives*

1. Contrast the homegrown capitalism Norberg-Hodge describes with the remittances of money sent by workers to their home countries in "Follow the Money" by Vivienne Walt and Amanda Bower.
2. How does money override the personal meanings of possessions in the accounts by Norberg-Hodge and Bill Geist in "The Land of Lost Luggage!"?

✧ *Extending Viewpoints through Writing and Research*

1. Have you ever participated in a barter situation where you traded goods for services? How were your relationships different from those based solely on an exchange of money?
2. In your opinion, were the Ladakhis better off before the introduction of money? Explain your answer.
3. The author's discussion of consumerism in Ladakh can be found at http://www.isec.org.uk/articles/pressure.html.

Tomoyuki Iwashita

Why I Quit the Company

Tomoyuki Iwashita signed on to work for a prominent Japanese corporation just after graduating from college. The life of the typical "salaryman" did not appeal to him for reasons he explains in "Why I Quit the Company," which originally appeared in the New Internationalist, *May 1992. He is currently a journalist based in Tokyo.*

Before You Read

Consider the insights this piece offers into corporate life in Japan and why a well-paid worker would drop out.

1 When I tell people that I quit working for the company after only a year, most of them think I'm crazy. They can't understand why I would want to give up a prestigious and secure job. But I think I'd have been crazy to stay, and I'll try to explain why.

2 I started working for the company immediately after graduating from university. It's a big, well-known trading company with about 6,000 employees all over the world. There's a lot of competition to get into this and other similar companies, which promise young people a wealthy and successful future. I was set on course to be a Japanese "yuppie."

3 I'd been used to living independently as a student, looking after myself and organizing my own schedule. As soon as I started working all that changed. I was given a room in the company dormitory, which is like a fancy hotel, with a twenty-four-hour hot bath service and all meals laid on. Most single company employees live in a dormitory like this, and many married employees live in company apartments. The dorm system is actually a great help because living in Tokyo costs more than young people earn—but I found it stifling.

4 My life rapidly became reduced to a shuttle between the dorm and the office. The working day is officially eight hours, but you can never leave the office on time. I used to work from nine in the morning until eight or nine at night, and often until midnight. Drinking with colleagues after work is part of the job; you can't say no. The company building contained cafeterias, shops, a bank, a post office, a doctor's office, a barber's. . . . I never needed to leave the building. Working, drinking, sleeping, and standing on a horribly crowded commuter

train for an hour and a half each way: This was my life. I spent all my time with the same colleagues; when I wasn't involved in entertaining clients on the weekend, I was expected to play golf with my colleagues. I soon lost sight of the world outside the company.

5 This isolation is part of the brainwashing process. A personnel manager said: "We want excellent students who are active, clever, and tough. Three months is enough to train them to be devoted businessmen." I would hear my colleagues saying: "I'm not making any profit for the company, so I'm not contributing." Very few employees claim all the overtime pay due to them. Keeping an employee costs the company 50 million yen ($400,000) a year, or so the company claims. Many employees put the company's profits before their own mental and physical well-being.

6 Overtiredness and overwork leave you little energy to analyze or criticize your situation. There are shops full of "health drinks," cocktails of caffeine and other drugs, which will keep you going even when you're exhausted. *Karoshi* (death from overwork) is increasingly common and is always being discussed in the newspapers. I myself collapsed from working too hard. My boss told me: "You should control your health; it's your own fault if you get sick." There is no paid sick leave; I used up half of my fourteen days' annual leave because of sickness.

7 We had a labor union, but it seemed to have an odd relationship with the management. A couple of times a year I was told to go home at five o'clock. The union representatives were coming around to investigate working hours; everyone knew in advance. If it was "discovered" that we were all working overtime in excess of fifty hours a month our boss might have had some problem being promoted; and our prospects would have been affected. So we all pretended to work normal hours that day.

8 The company also controls its employees' private lives. Many company employees under thirty are single. They are expected to devote all their time to the company and become good workers; they don't have time to find a girlfriend. The company offers scholarships to the most promising young employees to enable them to study abroad for a year or two. But unmarried people who are on these courses are not allowed to get married until they have completed the course! Married employees who are sent to train abroad have to leave their families in Japan for the first year.

9 In fact, the quality of married life is often determined by the husband's work. Men who have just gotten married try to go home early for a while, but soon have to revert to the norm of late-night work. They have little time to spend with their wives and even on the weekend are expected to play golf with colleagues. Fathers cannot find time to communicate with their children and child rearing is largely left to

mothers. Married men posted abroad will often leave their family behind in Japan; they fear that their children will fall behind in the fiercely competitive Japanese education system.

10 Why do people put up with this? They believe this to be a normal working life or just cannot see an alternative. Many think that such personal sacrifices are necessary to keep Japan economically successful. Perhaps, saddest of all, Japan's education and socialization processes do not equip people with the intellectual and spiritual resources to question and challenge the status quo. They stamp out even the desire for a different kind of life.

11 However, there are some signs that things are changing. Although many new employees in my company were quickly brainwashed, many others, like myself, complained about life in the company and seriously considered leaving. But most of them were already in fetters—of debt. Pleased with themselves for getting into the company and anticipating a life of executive luxury, these new employees throw their money around. Every night they are out drinking. They buy smart clothes and take a taxi back to the dormitory after the last train has gone. They start borrowing money from the bank and soon they have a debt growing like a snowball rolling down a slope. The banks demand no security for loans; it's enough to be working for a well-known company. Some borrow as much as a year's salary in the first few months. They can't leave the company while they have such debts to pay off.

12 I was one of the few people in my intake of employees who didn't get into debt. I left the company dormitory after three months to share an apartment with a friend. I left the company exactly one year after I entered it. It took me a while to find a new job, but I'm working as a journalist now. My life is still busy, but it's a lot better than it was. I'm lucky because nearly all big Japanese companies are like the one I worked for, and conditions in many small companies are even worse.

13 It's not easy to opt out of a life-style that is generally considered to be prestigious and desirable, but more and more young people in Japan are thinking about doing it. You have to give up a lot of superficially attractive material benefits in order to preserve the quality of your life and your sanity. I don't think I was crazy to leave the company. I think I would have gone crazy if I'd stayed.

✧ *Evaluating the Text*

1. What features of Iwashita's account address the crucial issue of his company's attempt to totally control the lives of employees?
2. What psychological effects led him to actually quit his secure job?
3. In what important respects do Japanese corporate employees differ from their American counterparts? In what ways are they similar?

✧ *Exploring Different Perspectives*

1. In what respects did Iwashita find himself being exploited in much the same way as the Ladakhis described in Helena Norberg-Hodge's account?
2. What parallels can you discover between Iwashita's situation in Japan and the low-wage migrant workers described by Vivienne Walt and Amanda Bower?

✧ *Extending Viewpoints through Writing and Research*

1. Drawing on work experiences you have had, discuss any similarities and differences you found on the question of conformity and subservience to the company. Analyze the different motivations that drive Japanese and American workers.
2. If you were in Iwashita's situation, would you have made the same decision he did? Why or why not?

Jack Owens

"Don't Shoot! We're Republicans!"

Jack Owens worked for thirty years as a Federal Bureau of Investigation (FBI) special agent. In the following excerpt drawn from his autobiography Don't Shoot, We're Republicans!: The True Story of the FBI Agent Who Did Things His Way *(2009), he recalls his early days as an agent setting up roadblocks and the surprising encounter it produced.*

Before You Read

What kinds of missions do you think FBI agents perform?

Prologue

1 You become a junkie in the Federal Bureau of Investigation, get high on adrenalin, black coffee, and sleeping with your ears open. You do all night surveillances in a dark car surfing the good time FM, and killing the dome light so you can open the door and pee out. For variety, you get out of the car, stretch, and pee on the Bureau tires. You stay awake talking to your partner about what an asshole your boss is. The FBI lives on gripes and stale air. Show me a better way to spend thirty years.

2 One night, because we had nothing more pressing and we were itching for adventure, three carloads of agents drove out of Birmingham and up the west side of Alabama into northeast Mississippi, hunting two fugitives who were joined at the hip. One, a dude named Singleton, was wanted for killing a convenience store manager in Alabama during a robbery, shooting him for the fun of it. Singleton collected coins and was a regular at numismatic shows, where he stole coins he couldn't buy. The other fugitive I'll call Thompson, a run-of-the-mill car thief. It was June, 1978. I'd been an agent for nine years and was certain I knew everything there was to know about everything.

3 It was darker than the inside of a snake's butt in rural Mississippi. We were a long way from home in a caravan of dull cars, feeling our way over unfamiliar roads, talking loud, comparing notes on the office stenos, invincible and full of ourselves. Every time we got out of the cars or rolled down the windows, elephant mosquitoes came at us like lava. No one wanted to stir. I longed for peanut butter and beer, resigned to a long night of it.

4 My partner was Luther Brannon, an Alabama native who'd once driven a school bus in Talladega County, hauling Pat, my future second wife, to her primary grades. Luther, who could be a hardass, had once stopped the bus in order to kick his kid brother Arlan off for misbehaving. The incident so affected Arlan he became a mortician.

5 Luther Brannon was six years older than me, a difference that had never meant squat to us. We were friends as well as colleagues, saw the world as one big landscape of University of Alabama football victories. Luther and I loved the Crimson Tide more than we hated Auburn. The only glitch in our relationship was Luther's thick, wavy black hair, which left me cold and bitter. I was receding on top and would have killed Luther for his hair. He was a supervisor, one of the few desk jockeys in the FBI who was worth a spit, so I didn't hold that against him. Luther never ordered the agents on his squad to do anything that he wouldn't do himself, which was why he was holed up with me in some deep south moonscape.

6 I sat shotgun in the Bureau Pontiac, Luther had the wheel. The engine idled while we parked off the side of the highway a ways east of cotton country in the Mississippi Delta. Luther checked a road map with a pin light, consulted it out of boredom because he always knew where he was.

7 The FBI radio barked with a warning from agents miles away that the two fugitives were headed toward us in a wrecker towing a Mustang. You could usually trust what you heard on the Bureau radio, so Luther and I pulled across the road to block both lanes. The two FBI cars behind us did the same. We were lined up and exposed on the highway like toes in a sandal.

8 I put the emergency blue light on the dash and flipped it on, turned the interior of the Bureau car into a blue light special at K-Mart. Luther and I squinted as the bright light rotated in and out of our eyes.

9 The FBI radio went silent. What the hell did that mean? Where were the fugitives?

10 I ran my fingers along the stock of the M-79 grenade launcher resting on my lap. The business end was wide and looked like a grouper with indigestion. It was loaded with a round that could take out the windshield of a car and anyone behind it. The 79 smelled of Hoppies cleaning fluid and oil.

11 I looked down the highway. Headlights appeared in the distance. I clicked off the safety on the 79. I had to pee. Luther picked up the radio mic. "Quarter mile away," he said into the radio, which might have been heard in Natchez or in Detroit and not by the agents in the two cars directly behind us. You never knew about the reach of Bureau radios. They were influenced by sunspots, menstrual cycles, rings around the moon, the tides down on the Gulf. Coaches in the press box and cons on death row had better communications than the FBI.

12 The headlights down the road grew as the tall wrecker bore down on us at high speed. Luther grunted. He never said much, whether he was leading an arrest team or laying sheet rock. Luther had a knack for home improvement and laying pipe.

13 The wrecker didn't slow one bit. It wasn't going to stop. We could back off the highway and get out of the way, or we could stay put. My side of the car faced the wrecker, so I was hoping Luther would decide to back into the next county.

14 I looked at Luther. Our car didn't move. Luther took his hands off the steering wheel and gripped his .38 service revolver. We were in a Pontiac, playing chicken with a wrecker. I braced for impact.

15 The wrecker swerved off the side of the road, towing a fish-tailing Mustang. The agents behind us opened up on the wrecker as it flew by, fired a dozen rounds, a hundred rounds, I didn't know. The wrecker dissolved into a row of oversized taillights up the Mississippi hardtop, the half-dead Mustang in its wake.

16 Luther let loose a stream of profanities, gunned the Pontiac up the road after the wrecker. The other Bureau cars fell in behind us. We were going 90, but the wrecker stretched its lead. No way a wrecker with a tow could haul like that. We ate some sharp turns on the two-lane and the blue light flew off the dash. I left it on the floor. Never liked the damn things.

17 The Pontiac came out of a curve and Luther buried the brakes to keep from running past the wrecker and out of Mississippi. We stopped next to the driver's side of the abandoned wrecker, its doors open, engine running. FBI bullet holes peppered the door.

18 I jumped out and aimed the M-79 into the empty cab of the wrecker. I had an urge to waste the interior just for the hell of it. I didn't though. It wasn't worth the endless paper work explaining to FBIHQ why I'd gone to war against the empty front seat of a truck. There wasn't hide nor hair of the fugitives. No blood in the cab. No nothing.

19 Luther joined me, gun drawn. We stood there getting our bearings. There were thick woods in front of us. A wall of trees absorbed the headlights of the wrecker and the Bureau Pontiac. The other Bureau cars pulled in and lit up the place further. The woods were black as Mississippi tar. The fugitives had run off. We debated whether to pursue the fugitives or find an all night diner. Pursuit won, but the vote was close.

20 More FBI arrived, local cops too, and Mississippi State Police. Luther and I and a dozen other agents spread out and walked into the thicket of briars and needles. The long Bureau flashlights made us easy targets. We walked for a quarter mile or so, kept our voices down but made noise anyway, stepping on underbrush, announcing ourselves. The whole scene sucked. We had little hope of finding the fugitives in

the dark. Plus, there were critters in the woods, just as there are fish in the ocean. I don't like to go into the woods or the ocean. Roughing it for me is running out of ice.

21 Luther called a halt to the search. We walked back to the highway to await daylight, then had another go with dogs and helicopters. I was glad to be out of the woods.

22 The sun brought heat, bloodhounds, and the FBI air force, piloted by agents flying a helicopter and a single engine plane over parts of Mississippi, Alabama, and Tennessee. There was no trace of the fugitives. The hounds lost their noses, the Bureau planes went to hangar. We stood down, exhausted. I had fire ants, mosquito bites, and a poison ivy leaf up my sleeve. I was not happy.

23 It was mid-afternoon when news came from McNairy County, Tennessee, just above the border with Alabama, that one of the fugitives, Thompson, had ridden a motorcycle into a rain-drenched field of honeysuckle trying to make his escape. The mud closed in on his tires and slowed him down. In desperation, he gunned the engine and attempted to run down a McNairy County Deputy Sheriff, who agilely stepped to the side of the cycle and swung the stock of a shotgun at Thompson's head, knocking him off the bike and into the mud, unconscious.

24 Six months later, the second fugitive, Singleton, was spotted by agents at a coin show in Huntsville, Alabama. He escaped again, fleeing to his girlfriend's place at a small motel in Florence, Alabama. He came out of the room later that night to get more beer and to call his wife. Luther Brannon had an arrest team waiting for him. I was downstate attending to something else and missed the fun, darn it. Singleton, who'd vowed never to be taken alive, was taken alive.

25 When Luther and the other agents arrived back in Birmingham, I joined them for a celebration at a local joint. Luther picked up the tab as usual. You can't have this kind of fun practicing law.

Don't Shoot! We're Republicans!

26 June, 1983. Another night roadblock in the sticks. Another rural highway, this time in Alabama instead of Mississippi. I trust the agents who are with me; we've made arrests as a team before. At the top of the food chain in the posse is Luther Brannon, a damned fine street agent turned supervisor. Luther is unflappable. I'm glad he's running this fugitive hunt.

27 Our backs are to Logan Martin Lake a few miles away. There are eight agents in four cars, two to a car. We're in the outback of Talladega County east of Birmingham not far from where my wife grew up with her three sisters near the city of Talladega itself. The area where we set up the roadblock is a patchwork of farm land and low hills that feel

like ocean swells when you drive eighty up and down them. Mt. Cheaha, the highest point in Alabama at 2400 feet, is off to the east in the Talladega National Forest.

28 I'm behind the wheel and Luther is riding shotgun, and has the shotgun to prove it. Unlike many arrests where you wait and wait some more, there will be no delays tonight because the bad guy is close. Other FBI units in the county report by radio that the fugitive is heading in our direction and is about two miles away. When he's right on top of us, we'll pull across the highway, put the blue lights on the dashes and stop him.

29 The FBI radio adds a twist, reports there are two cars coming up the highway traveling close together. The fugitive is in the lead vehicle, followed by an accomplice. There is always some little hook to spike your adrenalin.

30 The guy we're looking for is a white male with bank robbery etched into his résumé of sins. He is *A & D*—armed and dangerous. There is no information at this moment to further assess the bad guy in the second vehicle. The informant who provided the information that set the roadblock trap in motion is a *reliable* source, meaning that previous information he provided to the FBI turned out to be true. We've paid him before and we'll pay him again tonight.

31 Four headlights appear and disappear as they surf the Talladega County hills looking like giant fireflies. They're a half mile away. Luther and I are in the lead car. I pull the BuCar[1] across the highway. The three BuCars behind us follow suit. This time there are cars coming at Luther and me instead of a big wrecker towing a Mustang. I turn on the blue light and blue lights spring to life behind us. Luther and I bail out of the car and use the hood for cover.

32 The two vehicles bear down on us with blinding head beams. I squint, watch and hear the bad guys brake to a stop just feet ahead of us. It's a standoff as we stare into the lights. No one moves. I point my .38 revolver at the driver of the first car. Agents crouch on both sides of me, asses and elbows in shotguns.

33 *FBI! Get out of the cars now!* Luther shouts.

34 The driver door on the first car opens. The guy eases out from behind the wheel with his hands up. It's the fugitive we're looking for, no doubt at all. Luther commands him to walk around to the front of his car and stand in the beams. He complies. Agents run at him and throw him to the ground face down. They handcuff his hands behind his back, palms out, the Bureau way.

35 Which leaves the second car.

36 *Open the door and get out of the car!* Luther shouts.

---

[1]BuCar is short for Bureau car.

37 Nothing happens. The door doesn't open. I'm tense, ready to rush the car. Shotguns are pointed at its windshield. Both front doors of the second vehicle slowly open simultaneously. A dome light illuminates the interior of the car. Two elderly ladies are hunkered down in the front seat dressed in their Sunday finery and looking horrified. Their hands are jammed in the air against the interior roof of their car. They surrender without a fight.

38 I walk up to the driver side with my .38 on them even though they are bluehairs. Old, well-dressed women can shoot you just as dead as a 200-pound man. Luther keeps his shotgun pointed to cover me. He and I walk up on the ladies. The driver says in a high-pitched voice:

39 *Don't shoot! We're Republicans!*

40 The two ladies from Talladega County had just been to a meeting of the Republican faithful to discuss politics. In their seventies, they were activists and believed in the emergence of the GOP as a force in rural Alabama. They just happened to be on a country road behind a car carrying a bad guy and ran smack dab into an FBI roadblock and a host of shotguns. They were certain that being Republicans would save them. They were right.

✧ *Evaluating the Text*

1. How does Owens's experience in setting up a roadblock in Mississippi reveal his uncertainty, excitement, and satisfaction in being an FBI agent?
2. How does the second roadblock in Alabama result in a humorous misunderstanding?
3. How does Owens's relationship with his partner Luther Brannon convey a sense of the way agents depend on each other?

✧ *Exploring Different Perspectives*

1. Compare the experiences of Luther Brannon and Owens as a team with the experiences of Kris Holloway and Monique in Mali, in "A Coming Storm."
2. What insight into rural Alabama is provided by Owens's account and Bill Geist's report in "The Land of Lost Luggage!"?

✧ *Extending Viewpoints through Writing and Research*

1. How does Owens's account of his FBI experiences add to your understanding of what FBI agents actually do?
2. Would this kind of career appeal to you? Why or why not?

Bill Geist

The Land of Lost Luggage!

Bill Geist was born in 1945 in Illinois. He served as a combat photographer in Vietnam and since 1987 has been a correspondent contributing to CBS news shows. He appears regularly on CBS Sunday Morning *with Charles Osgood.*

In the following essay from Way Off the Road: Discovering the Peculiar Charms of Small Town America *(2007), we discover what happens to all our lost luggage.*

Before You Read

Have you lost your luggage when traveling? Describe your experiences.

Scottsboro, Alabama, Pop: 14,762

1 Millions of bags are checked at airports every day, thousands of which are never to be seen again.

2 But where do they go? Oddly enough, almost all flock to the same destination: a remote village in the Appalachian foothills where indigenous peoples celebrate the misfortunes of air travelers, enjoying deep discounts on their losses in . . . The Land of Lost Luggage!

3 I'd heard tales of this mysterious locale, but figured it for folklore, until I saw it with my own eyes: the Unclaimed Baggage Center in Scottsboro, Alabama, an orphanage of sorts for virtually all lost bags. But despair not. Here, your luggage and its contents will find good homes.

4 In Scottsboro, they call luggage lost by the airlines "unclaimed baggage," as though it was you who flew to the wrong place (Kansas City), and not your bags (Kuala Lumpur). As though you hadn't waited in vain at the luggage carousel, staring with growing desperation at that black hole upchucking the bags of the lucky ones. As though you hadn't waited around half the day to see if your luggage might be on the next flight, then filled out all the paperwork, stopped at a 7-Eleven to buy a toothbrush, and made a dozen fruitless calls to the airline, spending hours on hold listening to instrumental versions of "Feelings." As though you hadn't attended your friend's out-of-town wedding in the "Let's Go Mets" T-shirt you wore on the plane.

5 Or maybe it's the bags' fault. The airlines like to say a bag "fails to make a flight," or they'll call it "mishandled baggage," as in "a small percentage of the two billion bags checked every year are mishandled."

6 But how, and why, on earth does your Samsonite or American Tourister end up in a small town in northeastern Alabama? Well, for openers, it's not yours anymore. Bryan Owens, owner of the United Baggage Center (UBC), buys your lost luggage from the airlines after they've "tried" unsuccessfully for about ninety days to reunite you and your bag. (Can't you see a TV show where Maury Povich reunites lost suitcases with their tearful owners?)

7 Bryan, a dapper middle-aged businessman, buys the bags by the pound or yard, sight unseen. They arrive in a steady flow of trailer trucks at the UBC, where they're opened and the contents sorted, some of it going to charity, some to the cleaners, some directly onto store shelves. "We stock seven thousand never-seen-before items in the store every day," Bryan says, carefully avoiding the word "new." "We throw out the pornography and liquor," he says. Where?

8 The idea of benefiting from the losses of others is as old as morticians and pawnbrokers, as fresh as personal injury lawyers and television newscasters, but what ingenious, entrepreneurial mind came up with this idea?

9 "My father, Doyle, started the business in 1970," Bryan recalls, "with a borrowed pickup truck and a $300 loan, and he was off to buy his first load of unclaimed bags. From buses. We had a few card tables set up and had clothes dumped on the tables and sold them that way." An industry was born, a monopoly.

10 No more card tables. The UBC is a vast, modern department store on the order of, say, a Target. But with better stuff: Prada, Tiffany, Hermès, Dolce & Gabbana, Evan Picone, Dior, Gucci—just a few of the designer tags I notice on a wide variety of items that, while not new and not available in a variety of sizes, are half the price of new. "People tend to take their best things on trips," notes Bryan, who happens to be wearing someone else's Cartier wristwatch.

11 "You just don't find things like this in stores in northeastern Alabama, trust me," says one knowledgeable consumer. Lost luggage is a planetary problem and Bryan buys it the world over. "Exotic international outfits," says another shopper, "from Africa to India to China." Where to wear them in northeastern Alabama is your problem.

12 And the UBC is way more interesting than your normal stores. Along with the thousands of clothing items, digital cameras, stereos, books, perfumes, golf clubs, rugs (Oriental to purple shag), and other relatively standard fare, you come across some of the damnedest things imaginable, and unimaginable. Who takes a kitchen faucet on a plane trip? Who loses a full-size Windsurfer? An ornate, double-decked, carved wood Greek Orthodox church table? A ten-foot Swiss Alps horn? Major appliances: a TV, a clothes dryer? Who leaves behind their wheelchair? Was there a faith healer on board?

13 You hope the musician who lost the trumpet wasn't on his way to a gig. You hope the tuba being tested by a customer to the delight of fellow shoppers wasn't lost on the way to wherever tuba players go. Likewise, the accordion. I tried to play "Stars Fell on Alabama" and "Sweet Home Alabama" on a mishandled didgeridoo,[1] accompanied by two other shoppers on the lost maracas . . . but we saw early on we weren't going anywhere, so the group broke up.

14 You hope the woman (presumably) who lost her Las Vegas show-girl outfit—bra, bikini bottoms, headpiece, all encrusted with hundreds of multicolored glass jewels—was able to run out to a local department store and replace it.

15 And you sincerely hope the many brides who lost their wedding dresses were on their way home from the ceremonies. God! Those baggage handlers should do hard time, seriously. The $2,500 maximum payment per lost bag just doesn't cut it.

16 "We open up these bags and never know what we'll find," Bryan says. "Every day is like Christmas around here." They might find another glass eye, perhaps another mummified falcon, another $17,000 diamond necklace. "It's a bit like an archaeological dig. It's a cross-section of what's going on in society. You open up a bag, you know what the most popular novels are, what the current fashions are, what kind of electronic gizmos people are carrying with them. You can tell a lot about the society by what people pack." Bryan says there are some big surprises and absolute shocks. "We opened up one bag packed full of Egyptian artifacts dating back to 1500 BC; we had a camera designed for the space shuttle; an F-16 guidance system; a six-carat diamond solitaire ring worth about $20,000; a huge emerald, forty-one carats, so big we didn't think it could be real."

17 An original oil painting was sold here for $50 and later appraised at $20,000. "We missed that one," Bryan says. "Another customer bought a suitcase, tossed it in her attic, and a couple of years later pulled it out and found $2,000 in a little side pouch."

18 Most shoppers come for lesser goods, least of all the half-used lipsticks and other people's underpants. Gross. "We have the largest cleaning and dry-cleaning facility in the area," Bryan assures us. Still . . .

19 And there's a popular new line: prohibited items confiscated from air travelers by Transportation Security Administration agents. Bryan buys these too. "We get in fingernail clippers, nail files, and knives almost by the ton. Tear gas, firearms." Yes, the UBC has all your weaponry needs.

---

[1]didgeridoo: A wind instrument made from a hollowed-out branch blown into on one side to produce a low-pitched tone. It is used by Aborigines in Australia.

20 Do they ever try to reunite the items with their rightful owners? Nope. It's finders keepers, losers weepers. Do the losers ever come here seeking their own lost stuff? Yes, but they never seem to find it, although strange things do happen.

21 "I was looking at a painting," says Rob, a customer, "and I immediately recognized the subject as a hot air balloon owned by a friend of mine. I bought it, delivered it to my friend and his wife, and they started crying. It turned out the painting was done by their daughter, who was in art school in Los Angeles and lost the painting at LAX. She was crushed. It was a Christmas gift to her parents. It's a little mystical, don't you think?"

22 Ron said his neighbor here in Scottsboro left a new blazer on a flight, and when the UBC sorters recognized his name inside the jacket they called him. Wonder if he had to buy it back? And there's the tale of the man who bought ski boots here for his wife and she found her maiden name inscribed inside the boots, which had been lost on a flight years ago.

23 Other towns are built on the steel industry, or autos, or crops, or music, or computer technology. Lost luggage has made this rather poor little town on the Tennessee River a major tourist destination attracting way more visitors than they get over at NASA's Space and Rocket Center in Huntsville. The UBC has a coffee shop, a souvenir stand, and a concierge to answer questions like where to spend the night and where there's a golf course he can play while she shops. Lost luggage mini-vacations!

24 The UBC claims a million shoppers a year, a figure that may be distorted somewhat by A. Z. Proctor, a retiree who comes to the UBC three times a day. "You'd be surprised what some people take with them on planes," he says.

25 Allan Garner, another shopper, has been coming three to four times a week for thirty years. "I like stuff that's broken in," he says. "You go buy something new and you're gonna mess it up so why not buy something already messed up?" Follow?

26 He's seen some highly unusual items come and go. "I remember when Jesse Jackson was running for president his suits came in here. Had his name in them. And one time when MC Hammer was touring his backdrop came in here from his concert stage." (Lost cargo comes here too.) Great buy, but tough to blend into your home decor I would think.

27 Scottsboro, Alabama, is an entire town dressed in other people's stuff, which doesn't really seem to bother them all that much.

28 Do any of them ever feel like, I don't know, vultures? Nope. "Sometimes I think about it and I feel sorry for them that they lost it," says Marilyn, a regular shopper at UBC, "but since it's already lost, it's OK. I haven't had any nightmares, you know?"

29 One person's loss is another's gain. I watch a teenage girl, a fair-skinned redhead, excitedly admire a red dress, a bejeweled sheath—what you'd call a cocktail dress or a prom dress if she were old enough for either.

30 "It's so beautiful!" she cries.

31 "Where you gonna wear it?" cautions Mom.

32 "Can I at least try it on?" she pleads with her mother, who refers her to Dad, who says it's probably OK to just go ahead and try it.

33 "It's so beautiful Mom, look at it," says the infatuated daughter. "I'd be so unhappy if I'd lost this." She must have been going someplace really special.

34 The girl goes into the changing room and emerges . . . changed . . . suddenly looking grown-up, beautiful . . . and she's beaming. Her parents seem a bit taken aback by the sight.

35 Here in Scottsboro, what's lost is found, and the unhappiness of loss gives way to the joy of a fourteen-year-old girl who bought her first evening dress with her lawn-mowing money, for $12, in . . . The Land of Lost Luggage!

✧ *Evaluating the Text*

1. How has the United Baggage Center in Scottsboro, Alabama, made a business out of reselling lost luggage?
2. What unusual incidents of owners reunited with their lost luggage does Geist mention?
3. How does Geist's tone add to the readers's enjoyment of his essay?

✧ *Exploring Different Perspectives*

1. How does consumerism play a role in the accounts by Geist and Helena Norberg-Hodge in "Learning from Ladakh"?
2. How do both accounts by Geist and by Vivienne Walt and Amanda Bower in "Follow the Money" reveal the surprising dividends of castaway items and marginalized people?

✧ *Extending Viewpoints through Writing and Research*

1. Would you want to buy or wear someone's items from their lost luggage? Why or why not?
2. If you could find out that items that you lost in your luggage could be repurchased, would you go to the center at Scottsboro, Alabama, to retrieve them? Why or why not?

Vivienne Walt and Amanda Bower

Follow the Money

Vivienne Walt is a staff writer for Time *magazine and has worked as a foreign correspondent for twenty-five years. Amanda Bower also writes for* Time *and has worked as a freelance journalist throughout the world. In the following essay, which initially appeared in the Europe Edition of* Time International *(December 2005), the authors report on the important economic effect of the money sent home by migrant workers in France, Mexico, and other countries.*

Before You Read

How much do you know about the phenomenon of migrant workers around the world sending money home to support their families?

1 Waly Diabira pats the cover on his bed in the cramped fifth-floor room he shares with two men in a red-brick dormitory building for immigrants near Paris' Left Bank. "My father slept on this same bed, in this same room, for many years," he says. In 1950, his father, Mamadou Diabira, left their tiny village in Mali and caught a steamboat to Europe, where he worked as a street cleaner in Paris for about 25 years, receiving a certificate of thanks signed by then mayor Jacques Chirac. Waly, a 32-year-old building cleaner, only got to know his father when he sneaked into France at 18 on a boat from Morocco; he now works legally in France. A large photograph hangs above Waly's narrow bed, of his 2-year-old daughter, whom he has never met. The migrant tradition has continued into the next generation, fueled by the same force that kept his father rooted in France for decades—the need to send money home. Similar stories swell the immigrant population in Paris and other cities across France, and are multiplied millions of times across the world.

2 Such tales are nothing new. The color TV in a remote Turkish farmstead and the concrete-walled house amid shacks of corrugated iron have often been paid for by absent family members. Plenty of church halls in Ireland have been funded by passing the plate around congregations in Boston and New York. But the scale of money flows is new. Mass migration has produced a giant worldwide economy all its own, which has accelerated so fast during the past few years that the figures have astounted the experts. This year [2005], remittances—the cash that migrants send home—is set to exceed $232 billion, nearly 60% higher

than the number just four years ago, according to the World Bank, which tracks the figures. Of that, about $166.9 billion goes to poor countries, nearly double the amount in 2000. In many of those countries, the money from migrants has now overshot exports, and exceeds direct foreign aid from other governments. "The way these numbers have increased is mind-boggling," says Dilip Ratha, a senior economist for the World Bank and co-author of a new Bank report on remittances. Ratha says he was so struck by the figures that he rechecked his research several times, wondering if he might have miscalulated. Indeed, he believes the true figure for remittances this year is probably closer to $350 billion, since migrants are estimated to send one-third of their money using unofficial methods, including taking it home by hand. That money is never reported to tax officials, and appears on no records.

3 One reason for the growth in recorded remittances has its origins in the global war on terrorism. To stop terrorist networks using informal transfer systems like hawala in Africa, the Middle East and South Asia (where it's referred to as hundi), European and U.S. officials have cracked down on them. That has shifted payments to easier-to-track official channels. Some migrants, however, still use methods that elude the bean counters. In Hong Kong, Endang Muna Saroh, 35, works as a nanny to two children in a comfortable residential neighborhood, and sends $200 home every month to her mother and 10-year-old son in Surabaya, Indonesia, wiring the money to her brother-in-law's bank account. The country receives recorded remittances such as this worth a total of $1.8 billion a year. Yet like many migrants, Endang also saved hundreds of dollars to carry by hand to her family in August, when she flew home for her first visit in four years.

4 In Paris, Waly keeps a notebook on his bedside table, in which he writes lists of the cash amounts he gives each month to couriers. They fly to Mali—where remittances account for 3.2% of the country's national income—with wads of euros stuffed in their pockets and luggage. With about 300 people from his village of Ambadedi working in Paris—an estimated one-quarter of Ambadedi's entire population—the community has a well-organized network to transfer money, much of which is aimed at avoiding the hefty commissions from banks. "I write careful notes," Waly says. "'Here's €20 for my mother, €30 to my sister, and so on.' " Of the €1,000 he earns each month cleaning office buildings in Paris, he sends about €500 home, and then pays €240 for his share of the monthly rental. That experience is repeated across the world. The life of squirreling away money is grueling: it involves years-long separation from families, miserable living conditions, and the threat of deportation for the many who are working illegally. All the same, remittances play a vital role in recycling money from the rich world to the poor one. "Migration is going up," says Ratha. "We had better not wish it away, because it's very much there to stay."

5 On three continents, migrants and their families described how the transfers worked. Nine years ago, Cornelio Zamora left his home in Zacapoaxtla, Mexico, paying a smuggler $2,500 to take him across the Rio Grande into the U.S. He had been unable to support his wife and four children on the $7 a day he earned as a bus driver. Working as a house painter in San Jose, California, Zamora, 48, now sends about $700 a month home. His wife says she has based all family decisions—where to send the children to school, what house to live in—on Zamora's monthly earnings "on the other side."

6 In migrants' countries of origin, escalating desires—for things like better education and bigger homes—help drive the remittances. Ironically, economists calculate that the poorer the migrants are, the more money they dispatch. "There is enormous social pressure to send money home," says Khalid Koser, a geography professor at University College London, who in October co-authored a report for the Global Commission on International Migration in Geneva, which researches governments' immigration policies. Koser found that many migrants scrape by in first-world cities, depriving themselves of basic comforts in order to "keep people alive" back home. "There are many people sending 40% of their income in remittances," he says, adding that many families save to pay the passage of a migrant to richer parts of Asia, or to Europe or the U.S. Ruhel Daked, a 26-year-old Bangladeshi, earns €1,300 a month working as a chef in Paris. Yet despite his modestly comfortable salary, he bunks with two other Bangladeshis in a dormitory building for immigrants, with one toilet shared among many men, because he says he has one goal: "To save! Save as much as I can. That is why I am here."

7 In visits to migrants' hometowns, the impact on their families and communities is clear. Waly's village of Ambadedi has sent thousands of migrants to Paris since his father Mamadou first headed there. Set atop the steep northern bank of the Senegal River, the village at first glance looks like countless others in West Africa. Goats and donkeys meander down the dirt lanes, and women scrub clothes in the river. But Ambadedi has cherished luxuries that are absent from other remote parts of Mali. There is a generator that lights up most of the houses every night. A water tower feeds water to several collection points. And television antennas bristle from the rooftops of two-story concrete houses—a far cry from the mud hut in which old Mamadou was raised. Villagers have even started dreaming about building a bridge across the river to connect Ambadedi to the nearest highway, says Sekou Drame, Mamadou's brother-in-law, as he escorts a *Time* reporter back to the wooden pirogue that will ferry him across the river's muddy flow. "It depends on God," he says. "And our families in France."

8 In Mexico, the Zamora family home is another tangible indicator of the impact of remittances. Zamora's work in California has paid for

a new three-bedroom house, the first his family has ever owned. The changes his cash has brought to his family within one generation are dizzying; one daughter has trained as a nurse, another as a teacher, and his son as a radio technician. "The first time I wore shoes, I was 14 years old," Zamora says. "I don't want my family to go through that." It's a similar story in Indonesia where Endang's monthly money transfers from four years' work as a nanny in Hong Kong finally paid off last July, when her 10-year-old son, her mother and several relatives moved into a renovated two-story concrete house in Surabaya, bought with Endang's savings for about $9,700. In Paris, Daked, the Bangladeshi chef, says his parents recently bought a family home with the funds he has sent home since sneaking into Europe in 1997; he estimated his total remittances at about €38,000 in eight years.

9 Vital though the flow of remittances may be, it cannot, on its own, lift entire nations out of poverty. Those who study the impact of remittances argue that the money allows poor countries to put off basic decisions of economic management, like reforming their tax-collection systems and building decent schools. "Everyone loves money that flows in with no fiscal implications," says Devesh Kapur, a specialist on migration and professor of government at the University of Texas in Austin. "They see it as a silver bullet." But bullets wound; and skilled workers often understandably put the interests of their families before those of their countries, choosing to work abroad so they can send remittances back home. About eight out of 10 college graduates from Haiti and Jamaica live outside their countries, and about half the college graduates of Sierra Leone and Ghana have also emigrated, according to the Paris-based Organization for Economic Co-operation and Development.

10 Remittances to poor countries can also mask the fact that they don't produce much at home. In the western Mali district of Kayes—where Waly's village of Ambadedi is located and where most migrants hail from—the region has done so well that farmers use remittances as a crutch. Studies have shown that they spend less time on their land than farmers in other parts of Mali: there is more money to be made by migrating to Europe. "You see poverty other places, but here, you see money," says Abdel Kader Coulibaly, a bank manager in Kayes. He says migrants' families spend all they get, rather than investing it to generate income locally. "All the money ends up with shopkeepers and traders from Bamako [the capital]," he says.

11 The trick now is to find programs that maximize the benefits of remitted cash while avoiding some of its downside. Some migrants are now using their economic clout to perform work usually done by big aid organizations. Ambadedi's workers' association in Paris, for example, funds some village projects with its members' own earnings. But the association also solicits help from the French government and

the European Union. "We have a project under way to purify the village water supply," says Ibrahim Diabira, 55, a relative of Waly, who works in Paris as a building cleaner and helps run the village association in the French capital. Elsewhere, host nations have created temporary legal work programs, in which migrants earn legal wages with benefits, before returning home. That way, migrants retain close links to their countries while developing skills abroad. "When they go back, they will take augmented skills, savings and networks," says Kapur. (He himself left his native India 22 years ago and settled in the U.S.)

12 In Paris, Waly is planning to return home in January to see his 2-year-old daughter for the first time, and to spend time with his wife. But he won't stay long. "Frankly, people would die there if we didn't work here," he says. Come spring, he will be back in Paris, cleaning offices, and changing the way the world spreads its wealth around.

✧ *Evaluating the Text*

1. How does the story of Waly Diabira exemplify experiences that are typical of migrant workers around the world?
2. What motivates migrant workers to put the interests of their families in their home countries above their own comfort?
3. What relationship do the authors discover about the workers' level of poverty and how much they send back to their families?

✧ *Exploring Different Perspectives*

1. How does this account by Vivienne Walt and Amanda Bower and that of Helena Norberg-Hodge in "Learning from Ladakh" represent very different approaches to generating income?
2. How does Walt and Bower's account and Holloway's essay ("A Coming Storm") reveal innovative ways for dealing with intractable social problems?

✧ *Extending Viewpoints through Writing and Research*

1. If you were forced to relocate to another country, would you send money back to your family and relatives in your home country? Why or why not?
2. What experiences have you had with immigrants in your community, and what have you learned about their family situations and backgrounds?

Kris Holloway

A Coming Storm

Kris Holloway worked as a Peace Corps volunteer in Mali, West Africa (1989–1991), where she met and befriended Monique Dembele, a midwife whose experiences are reflected in the following excerpt from Monique and the Mango Rains: Two Years with a Midwife in Mali *(2006). In this account, we come to know a woman who sought to better the lives of women and children in a remote and impoverished village in Mali.*

Before You Read

What do you know what functions midwives perform?

1 The rains had come. The clack and lurch of donkey carts laden with people and basins of food bound for the fields became constant. Paths were congested. Everyone had a *dàba* (stubby-handled hoe) across his or her shoulders, the sharp wide blade facing back, the handle forward across the chest. Time to sow by hand the precious seeds saved from last year's harvest. Every year it was a bit of a gamble, deciding when to sow the seeds. Plant too late and growing time would be lost. Too early, before the earth receives sufficient rainfall, and the shoots would die. Many villagers had not the stock to reseed, and no one could afford to make the same mistake twice. I had learned that Malians could be a laid-back folk, except about rain. As Monique said, "Rain means that people live."

2 Everyone was exhausted at night from the day's labor. Gone were the sounds of the balafon and the radio. Even the belotte players ceased their nightly game. In the midst of this toil and quiet came *Tabasci* or *Eid al-Adha* in Arabic, "Festival of the Sacrifice." This Muslim holiday (also fondly known in Mali as *La Fête des Moutons* or "Festival of the Sheep") takes place every year, seventy days after the end of Ramadan, to celebrate the Prophet Abraham's willingness to sacrifice his only son Ishmael at God's command. It also celebrates the return of the faithful from the Hajj, the annual pilgrimage to Mecca, which few Malians I knew made, but was revered nonetheless. Sheep, which villagers had been fattening up for months, were sliced, skinned, gutted, chopped, and sautéed all in one day. Bowl upon bowl of rice and sauce laden with fresh mouton, a feast five times more than what any family could consume, was delivered to all family compounds. Monique and

Elise didn't have to cook a meal for days. Children, dressed in their finest attire, came in and out of the compound giving benedictions and blessings. In turn, we invited them to eat and gave them a few coins or *Sogosogo bonbons,* a local cough drop that served as candy. It felt like abundance, food and health and blessings, in a time of not enough.

3 The birthing house was humid, stifling hot, and crowded. In the darkened front hall, women lined the cracked walls, some sitting, some standing, all with bulging bellies, all with toddlers hugging their legs, all waiting to be seen for prenatal consultations by Monique.

4 I murmured greetings as I made my way toward the examination room. So many women here, despite the fact that it was the rainy season, the season of constant, never-ending toil. I looked down, carefully stepping over legs, baskets, and children, and almost collided with Korotun.

5 "I ni sogoma, Fatumata," she said, and then scolded, "you missed my prenatal visit."

6 "Sorry, I had no idea there would be so many women this early." I was also tired. Bintou, a short, light-skinned woman, had gone into labor late in the evening. I had stayed with Monique in Bintou's airless hut, in the middle of a compound teeming with children, as she slowly labored on a straw mat spread out on the smooth dirt floor. Though Bintou's cervix had dilated early in the evening, she was not able to push; the contractions came and went, but she could not put force behind them. After midnight Monique insisted I get some rest, and off I went, leaving her and Bintou alone in the darkened womb of mud.

7 "Of course we are here early, we must get to our fields, after all. Anyway, Monique says everything is fine. But you had better not be late when it is time for me to give birth."

8 She pointed her finger at me for emphasis.

9 "I won't, Korotun, I won't."

10 I entered the last room on the left. Monique was leaning over a large upright metal scale, fiddling with the silver weights on the twin bars while a very pregnant woman stood motionless. Monique's temples, and Basil's sleeping head flat against her back, were beaded in moisture.

11 "Good, good," Monique said, giving the smaller weight a final tap. "You are gaining."

12 She wiped her forehead with her arm and asked the woman to lie down, then lifted the woman's shirt. The swollen belly was taut, but wrinkled and scarred; she had given birth before, many times. Using her hands as guides, Monique felt and pushed, measuring from the pubic bone to the top of the body inside.

13 "And the baby is growing too."

14 Her fingers searched through shifting skin to determine the baby's position. Strapping on a fetascope, a funny instrument that looked more

musical than medical with a large cone protruding from its forehead band, she leaned over and pressed the cone down in several places until she found the baby's heartbeat.

15 "Your baby's head is down, which is good. He sounds strong," She took her ledger and pen off the windowsill and began to write.

16 Finally Monique looked at me. Her eyes were puffy and lined, evidence of a long night.

17 "Fatumata, hello. The blood pressure cuff is over there, if you want to help the next mother."

18 I grabbed the cuff and called to the next woman, who was standing just outside the doorway. She was a young woman from the Dembele quartier. I had seen her a number of times, pounding millet under the hangar. I wrapped the blood pressure cuff around her arm and began pumping it up.

19 "All done, Salimata," Monique said to the woman still lying down on the bed, "but watch the salt. Your blood pressure is higher than before. Drink lots of clean water. Now that you are in your last month of pregnancy, I want you to come in each week. Any questions?"

20 Salimata shook her head.

21 I listened to the rhythmic thumping of blood, watched the needle bounce, then let the air in the cuff hiss out.

22 "One-fifteen over seventy-five," I announced as I unwrapped the cuff, and then took the woman's pulse. "Seventy-two."

23 "Good." Monique recorded the numbers. Salimata sat up on the bed while the young Dembele woman got up on the scale.

24 "I feel a storm coming," Monique said and glanced up at the ripped edge of the roof and the holes. No repairs had been made in years. One bad tempest could peel off the entire top of the building.

25 Out the slatted window the sky was a brilliant blue, but a gray band hugged the western horizon. It was my first full rainy season here, but I, too, was learning to feel the coming rain. The air was pregnant with it. The heat and water, too heavy for the sky to hold, would soon be dropped.

26 There were at least twenty more women to see.

27 Salimata stood and rearranged her pagne. Monique motioned for the young woman to lie down, and then came over to the window.

28 "The mother, Bintou, died last night, Fatumata," she whispered. "After giving birth."

29 "Oh, Monique. I'm so sorry." I leaned back against the wall with a thud.

30 "She finally pushed her baby out, but afterwards the bleeding would not stop. I tried everything, everything . . ."

31 Monique rubbed her eyes, retied sleeping Basil, and returned to her work.

32 I stared out the slatted window. I had yet to hear of Monique losing a mother, though statistically I knew women in Mali died in labor

every day, especially teen mothers whose bodies weren't ready yet for the toll of childbirth, and many-times-over mothers, like Bintou, whose bodies were worn out from it. I knew what Monique must have done last night. If putting the baby to Bintou's breast hadn't stopped the flow of blood after birth, she would have given her a shot of Pitocin, a drug that made the uterus contract and was Monique's only recourse in the event of hemorrhage. It obviously hadn't been enough.

33 In the handful of births I had attended, all the women and their babies had been fine, meaning that they lived, not that they were free of complications. During the pushing, some women tore horribly and then had to get stitched up. Many lost a lot of blood and many sustained a variety of infections after birth. Having spent all of my post-puberty years actively avoiding pregnancy and therefore childbirth, I was reading an old copy of *Our Bodies, Ourselves* by the Boston Women's Health Collective to educate myself. Much of the information Monique had already taught me: a woman must eat iron-rich foods and have regular prenatal check-ups; she must be in a comfortable position for the birth, be surrounded by supportive caregivers, be hydrated, and relax between contractions.

34 From what I was reading, it seemed that this age-old wisdom had been forgotten in hospitals in the U.S., where technology and interventions were the norm. I was astounded at the rate of Cesarean sections (around one quarter of all births) in such a healthy, rich country (could they all really be necessary?), and at the control that the medical establishment had assumed over the birthing process. In contrast, birth in Nampossela was a family and community event and lacked almost all modern medical interventions. Monique had simple tools, clean hands, and a sharp mind. But if a woman needed an IV, or a Cesarean section, or a fetal monitor, it was not an option. If Monique had had access to more emergency medical care, could she have saved Bintou? I didn't know. But I hoped that giving birth didn't have to happen at one extreme or the other—that a happy medium existed between the two.

35 In Mali, the rainy season was the hardest time to be pregnant and give birth, and not just because women like Bintou were forced to labor in their small, stuffy huts. Fieldwork was physically exhausting and infectious diseases abundant. Perhaps Bintou had been malnourished, fighting malaria or some other infection. Perhaps her uterus could no longer contract after bearing six children. Perhaps her husband or her heavy workload did not allow her to rest during her pregnancy or did not allow her to attend prenatal consultations, where she could have learned about taking care of herself. At least if we repair this maternity ward, I thought to myself, women can stay here before their births, and after to rest. A well-rested mother had less postpartum bleeding; she was stronger and healed faster.

36 I turned back from the window. Monique had measured the young woman's taut, smooth belly, felt for the baby's position, and was strapping on the fetascope.

37 I looked at the flawless, bright skin of the soon-to-be mother on the bed and thought of the lined, wizened leather of Salimata's stomach. Salimata stood in the doorway talking to the other women. Undoubtedly they knew about Bintou's death. Were they talking about it? About how death could just as easily visit them? Did they understand what they could do to stack the odds in their favor? Or was it simply the will of God?

38 "Fatumata," a small voice said from behind me. I turned to see Oumou, the well digger's wife, peeking through the doorway, over the heads of children.

39 She stepped a little closer, nervously smiling through her right hand, which partially covered her mouth. She had huge eyes, a long oval chin, and a flattened nose. I never stood too close to her, partly because of her shyness, partly due to the fear that she would topple over on me. Oumou had tall legs for a short woman, tall legs that bent forward so that her torso hovered backwards over and behind her rear. A hefty baby on her back made the list more alarming. She looked as if she might fall on her back at any moment.

40 "Come on in," Monique said.

41 Oumou shuffled forward, two little children hiding between her legs, and stood quietly next to me. She patted her belly under the swirls of white and green pagne. "I am here for . . ."

42 "You're pregnant?"

43 "Uh-hum," she said with her hand back over her mouth.

44 I looked at her from a couple of angles. I couldn't tell the difference between early pregnancy and its first swell of promise, and the leftover droopy bulge from previous children. Monique finished with the young woman and penned Oumou's name on what was now the last line in the ledger. The spaces to the right of her name were empty: a clean, hopeful slate.

45 Out of the corner of my eye I caught sight of Oumou falling backwards. I spun around with arms outstretched, but she was only sitting down. I let out a breath, my arms falling to my sides. Then I wrapped the blood pressure cuff around her bicep. Her children stayed at her legs. Monique called in another woman; I maneuvered to make room. Sweat fell off my brow, splattering the blood pressure gauge. Between the humidity and the warmth of the bodies, the unventilated building had to be 110 degrees.

46 After another hour of weighing and measuring, assessing nutrition, and extracting promises of rest and no heavy lifting, the crowd of women noticeably lessened, but not just because of us. They were leaving before the storm. A breeze found its way inside and fluttered the

collar of my dress. Monique sighed. I stepped out into the emptying corridor and walked toward the open door, drawn by the hint of coolness. Dark clouds raced in the sky.

47 Outside, women were walking fast as they carried their laundry, fetched water, or balanced firewood on their heads. Men sped by on bicycles. Drivers hollered at their donkeys to move the carts faster (donkeys being donkeys, this had little effect). A group of girls approached, coming from the fields, singing, and dancing, energized by the electric feel of the air. Dust swirled by in eddies, wrapping around their legs before dissolving and mixing together again downwind.

48 "Fatumata," Oumou called as she walked out of the hallway and into the doorway.

49 "You're still here? I thought you had left."

50 "I was waiting for you to finish your work." Her eyes filled with water. "Yesterday, I lost Soloman."

51 "Oh, Oumou, another child died?" She had buried Gwewa only months ago.

52 "I cannot have more children, Fatumata, please." Her hand stilled her mouth but could not hide her desperation.

53 Monique quietly joined us; it was obvious that she had already heard the news.

54 "I lose them. I had nine. Now I am left with five and this one," Oumou pointed to her belly. "Too many have died, and yet my husband, Daouda, he wants to have more. I can't have more, Fatumata."

55 I searched for words in Bambara, "There are plastic things that Daouda can put on himself, and pills you can take."

56 "I do not have money."

57 "We'll see, Oumou," Monique said. "There may be something we can do, where you don't need to have money."

58 I wondered how much Monique knew about modern contraception.

59 "Hmm," Oumou said and nodded. "Daouda cannot know."

60 With that, she left. We watched her walk into the village, along the now deserted path, silent children in tow. They buried their faces in her tattered dress to escape the wind. Korotun wanted children, Oumou didn't. Both wanted control over situations where they currently had little.

61 I was startled out of my thoughts by a clap of thunder that rattled the roof. Within seconds, another clap of thunder, this time closer, shook the entire birthing house. Beads of rain struck the tin like pebbles. The interval between the drops shortened, working into a dull roar. Monique darted into the nearest room, and I heard the screech of iron on concrete as she shut down the window slats. Then she raced out, Basil hollering on her back. I ran into another room and slammed its window slats with a bang. The downpour ignited. The noise was deafening, as if herds of miniature beasts were crisscrossing at breakneck speed

along the roof. I stared out the front door. Stray trees were pitched in battle with the wind, caught in a frenzied dance. Everything faded in and out of view behind sheets of water. The ground was a blur of ricocheting spray and dust in the throes of becoming mud. Monique ran up, slammed and bolted the door. Then we both ran to the wall farthest from the direction of the rain.

62 The wind came in waves, shaking the birthing house, threatening to break through the bricks. Rain drove through any open crack in the windows and leaked through the space around the closed front door. It blew in where the roof was not secured well. Dark water stains quickly spread down the walls and writhed across the uneven floor in what looked like tentacles. I gasped as I heard a loud, painful creak from the opposite end of the hall and saw the edge of the metal roof catch in the storm's fury and bend upwards. Taking advantage of this failing, the rain poured in. The sky was a blur the color of pavement.

63 "What a storm!" Monique yelled as she held Basil, covering him with her body and staring at the curled up roof. We huddled together, eyes wide, all senses on alert.

64 For over an hour I willed the roof to stay down as the storm churned outside. Then, as abruptly as it had come, it ended.

65 The damage was extensive. All the equipment was soaked. The old foam mattresses resembled giant sponges, weighing down the metal frames and streaming water. Wet papers stuck together, blue ink smudged and blurred, making ghostly sentences.

66 "We really must repair this building," I said.

67 "Yes. There is no question that it is not safe, even for consultations, while the rains are coming," she said.

68 We splashed through the large puddle around the door and opened it.

69 Already sunny again, the steam rose from the swollen ground littered with shattered palms, broken tree limbs, and straw roofs blown off homes and granaries. Countless muddy rivulets joined and split, all moving toward the sacred stream. I was accustomed to the stream being no more than a dried bed. Now it surged and flowed, cutting off the fields to the village's east. Its banks crumbled. What a trade. Life-giving rains came at the expense of devastating erosion; precious topsoil was washed away by the very thing needed to make it flourish. But for now, the world was refreshed, the oppressive heat dissipated. In the distance men readied their donkey carts for the fields, eager to plant their seeds.

✧ *Evaluating the Text*

1. How do we know that Kris Holloway has great respect and appreciation for Monique's skill as a midwife?

2. Why is the case of Bintou, who dies after giving birth, an example of the discouraging reality that women face in Mali?
3. How does Holloway frame her account by describing the threatening deluge of the storm?

✧ *Exploring Different Perspectives*

1. Compare the challenging work environments described by Kris Holloway and Tomoyuki Iwashita in "Why I Quit the Company."
2. Given a choice, would you rather be an FBI agent in Alabama as discussed by Jack Owens in "Don't Shoot! We're Republicans!" or a midwife's assistant in Mali as described by Kris Holloway? Explain your answer.

✧ *Extending Viewpoints through Writing and Research*

1. What similarities and differences in prenatal care and childbirth exist in American society when compared with that of women in Mali?
2. What is the most exotic place you ever visited? Would the prospect of giving birth to a child there be appealing to you? Why or why not?

Jose Antonio Burciaga

My Ecumenical Father

Jose Antonio Burciaga (1940–1996) was born in El Chuco, Texas, and grew up in El Paso, Texas. After serving in the United States Air Force, he earned an arts degree from the University of Texas at El Paso in 1968. He founded a Chicano publishing company; started a comedy troupe, Cultural Clash; and wrote numerous poems, stories, and essays. The following is drawn from Drink Cultura *(1993) and describes his experiences growing up in El Paso, Texas, where his father worked as a custodian in a synagogue.*

Before You Read

Do you know someone who maintains ties with his or her own culture and at the same time respects and understands another?

1 ¡Feliz Navidad! Merry Christmas! Happy Hanukkah! As a child, my season's greetings were tricultural—Mexicano, Anglo and Jewish.

2 Our devoutly Catholic parents raised three sons and three daughters in the basement of a Jewish synagogue, Congregation B'nai Zion in El Paso, Texas. José Cruz Burciaga was the custodian and *shabbat goy*. A shabbat goy is Yiddish for a Gentile who, on the Sabbath, performs certain tasks forbidden to Jews under orthodox law.

3 Every year around Christmas time, my father would take the menorah out and polish it. The eight-branched candleholder symbolizes Hanukkah, the commemoration of the first recorded war of liberation in that part of the world.

4 In 164 B.C., the Jewish nation rebelled against Antiochus IV Epiphanes, who had attempted to introduce pagan idols into the temples. When the temple was reconquered by the Jews, there was only one day's supply of oil for the Eternal Light in the temple. By a miracle, the oil lasted eight days.

5 My father was not only in charge of the menorah but for 10 years he also made sure the Eternal Light remained lit.

6 As children we were made aware of the differences and joys of Hanukkah, Christmas and Navidad. We were taught to respect each celebration, even if they conflicted. For example, the Christmas carols taught in school. We learned the song about the twelve days of Christmas, though I never understood what the hell a partridge was doing in a pear tree in the middle of December.

7 We also learned a German song about a boy named Tom and a bomb—*O Tannenbaum*. We even learned a song in the obscure language of Latin, called "Adeste Fideles," which reminded me of, *Ahh! d'este deo,* a Mexican pasta soup. Though 75% of our class was Mexican-American, we never sang a Christmas song in *Español*. Spanish was forbidden.

8 So our mother—a former teacher—taught us "Silent Night" in Spanish: *Noche de paz, noche de amor*. It was so much more poetic and inspirational.

9 While the rest of El Paso celebrated Christmas, Congregation B'nai Zion celebrated Hanukkah. We picked up Yiddish and learned a Hebrew prayer of thanksgiving. My brothers and I would help my father hang the Hanukkah decorations.

10 At night, after the services, the whole family would rush across the border to Juarez and celebrate the *posadas,* which takes place for nine days before Christmas. They are a communal re-enactment of Joseph and Mary's search for shelter, just before Jesus was born.

11 To the posadas we took candles and candy left over from the Hanukkah celebrations. The next day we'd be back at St. Patrick's School singing, "I'm dreaming of a white Christmas."

12 One day I stopped dreaming of the white Christmases depicted on greeting cards. An old immigrant from Israel taught me Jesus was born in desert country just like that of the West Texas town of El Paso.

13 On Christmas Eve, my father would dress like Santa Claus and deliver gifts to his children, nephews, godchildren and the little kids in orphanages. The next day, minus his disguise, he would take us to Juarez, where we delivered gifts to the poor in the streets.

14 My father never forgot his childhood poverty and forever sought to help the less fortunate. He taught us to measure wealth not in money but in terms of love, spirit, charity and culture.

15 We were taught to respect the Jewish faith and culture. On the Day of Atonement, when the whole congregation fasted, my mother did not cook, lest the food odors distract. The respect was mutual. No one ever complained about the large picture of Jesus in our living room.

16 Through my father, leftover food from B'nai B'rith luncheons, Bar Mitzvahs and Bat Mitzvahs found its way to Catholic or Baptist churches or orphanages. Floral arrangements in the temple that surrounded a Jewish wedding *huppah* canopy many times found a second home at the altar of St. Patrick's Cathedral or San Juan Convent School. Surplus furniture, including old temple pews, found their way to a missionary Baptist Church in *El Segundo Barrio*.

17 It was not uncommon to come home from school at lunch time and find an uncle priest, an aunt nun and a Baptist minister visiting our home at the same time that the Rabbi would knock on our door. It was

just as natural to find the president of B'nai Zion eating beans and tortillas in our kitchen.

18 My father literally risked his life for the Jewish faith. Twice he was assaulted by burglars who broke in at night. Once he was stabbed in the hand. Another time he stayed up all night guarding the sacred Torahs after anti-Semites threatened the congregation. He never philosophized about his ecumenism, he just lived it.

19 Cruz, as most called him, was a man of great humor, a hot temper and a passion for dance. He lived the Mexican Revolution and rode the rails during the Depression. One of his proudest moments came when he became a U.S. citizen.

20 September 23, 1985, sixteen months after my mother passed away, my father followed. Like his life, his death was also ecumenical. The funeral was held at Our Lady of Peace, where a priest said the mass in English. My cousins played mandolin and sang in Spanish. The president of B'nai Zion Congregation said a prayer in Hebrew. Members of the congregation sat with Catholics and Baptists.

21 Observing Jewish custom, the cortege passed by the synagogue one last time. Fittingly, father was laid to rest on the Sabbath. At the cemetery, in a very Mexican tradition, my brothers, sisters and I each kissed a handful of dirt and threw it on the casket.

22 I once had the opportunity to describe father's life to the late, great Jewish American writer Bernard Malamud. His only comment was, "Only in America!"

✧ *Evaluating the Text*

1. What functions did Burciaga's father perform for the Jewish temple? In what way did he and his family embody the idea stated in the title?

2. Why is it significant that Burciaga was not permitted to sing in Spanish, although he learned German and Latin songs in school?

3. How does Burciaga's description of his father's funeral consolidate important ideas in this essay?

✧ *Exploring Different Perspectives*

1. Compare Burciaga's father's work experiences with those described by Tomoyuki Iwashita in "Why I Quit the Company."

2. In what ways was Burciaga's father's experience closer to that of the Ladakhis (see "Learning from Ladakh" by Helena Norberg-Hodge) before the onset of consumerism?

✧ *Extending Viewpoints through Writing and Research*

1. What holiday or festival outside your own culture have you attended or witnessed? Describe it in a short essay for an audience who has never seen it.
2. What do you think Bernard Malamud meant at the end of the essay when he said, "Only in America"?

Connecting Cultures

Helena Norberg-Hodge, "Learning from Ladakh"

Compare an economy based on consumerism as described by Norberg-Hodge with one based on reciprocity as described by David R. Counts in "Too Many Bananas" in Chapter 6.

Tomoyuki Iwashita, "Why I Quit the Company"

Compare the economy of Japan as pictured by Iwashita with that of China as portrayed by Fareed Zakharia in "The Challenger" in Chapter 6.

Jack Owens, "Don't Shoot! We're Republicans!"

Compare the methods and values of those charged with enforcing the law in Owens's account with those described by Gino Del Guercio in "The Secrets of Voodoo in Haiti" in Chapter 6.

Bill Geist, "The Land of Lost Luggage!"

How does the entreprenurial instinct underlie the accounts by Geist and Ray Kroc in "Grinding It Out: The Making of McDonald's" in Chapter 7?

Vivienne Walt and Amanda Bower, "Follow the Money"

Compare the accounts by Walt and Bower with Gordon Parks in "Flavio's Home" in Chapter 5 in terms of people trying to support their families.

Kris Holloway, "A Coming Storm"

Compare the experience of midwives in Holloway's account set in Mali and that of Viramma in "A Pariah's Life" in Chapter 5.

Jose Antonio Burciaga, "My Ecumenical Father"

Compare Burciaga's father's experience working in a Jewish temple on holidays with those of Ethel G. Hofman in "An Island Passover" in Scotland in Chapter 7.

5

Race, Class, and Caste

I am an invisible man. . . . I am a man of substance, of flesh and bone, fiber and liquids—and I might even be said to possess a mind. I am invisible, understand, simply because people refuse to see me.

—Ralph Ellison (1914–1994), African American author, from the prologue to *Invisible Man* (1952)

Every society can be characterized in terms of social class. Although the principles by which class is identified vary widely from culture to culture, from the amount of money you earn in the United States to what kind of accent you speak with in England, to what religious caste you are born into in India, class serves to set boundaries around individuals in terms of opportunities and possibilities. The concept of class in its present form has been in force for only a few hundred years in Western cultures. In prior times, for example, in medieval Europe, your position and chances in life were determined at birth by the *estate* into which you were born, whether that of peasant, clergy, or noble.

Conflicts based on inequalities of social class are often intertwined with those of race because minorities usually receive the least education, have the least political clout, earn the least income, and find work in occupations considered menial without the possibility of advancement. In some societies, such as that in India, for example, an oppressive caste system based on tradition has, until recently, been responsible for burdening the "untouchables" with the most onerous tasks.

Class conditions our entire lives by limiting, more than we might like to admit, who we can be friends with, what our goals are, and even who we can marry.

Class reflects the access one has to important resources, social privileges, choices, and a sense of control over one's own life. Although caste in India is something one cannot change, social stratification in the United States is less rigid and upward mobility is possible through a variety of means such as work, financial success, marriage, and education. More frequently, however, a de facto class system can be said to exist in terms of health care, salaries, housing, and opportunities for education that varies greatly for the rich and the poor.

The writers in this chapter explore many of the less obvious connections between social class and the control people exercise over their lives. Mary Crow Dog and Richard Erdoes recount in "Civilize Them with a Stick" the racism experienced by Native Americans attending a government-run boarding school. Although officially outlawed, the caste known as untouchables lead lives similar to that described by Viramma in her autobiographical account, "A Pariah's Life." Immaculée Ilibagiza re-creates in "Left to Tell" the terrifying time when she and other Tutsi women hid to escape being murdered by a crazed mob of Hutus during Rwanda's civil war. In "What Is Poverty?" Jo Goodwin Parker brings home the day-to-day consequences of being poverty-stricken in the southern United States. Gordon Parks describes in "Flavio's Home" the horrendous condition of the *favelas* (slums) on the outskirts of Rio de Janeiro and the life of a courageous young boy trying to provide for his family. A timeless story, "Désirée's Baby," by Kate Chopin, offers a complex and thoughtful exploration of the consequences of endemic sexism and racism in Louisiana at the turn of the last century.

To help you understand how the works in this chapter relate to each other, you might use one or several of the following guidelines before writing about race, class, and caste.

1. What does the writer believe is the most important aspect of his or her experience?
2. How does the author frame the event that proved to be so important in his or her life?
3. Based on reading any of the works in this chapter, which of your past experiences would you want to reflect on and write about—would it be in the form of an essay, short story, poem, or play?
4. How does social class, race, or caste play an important role in these works?
5. Is the author realistic or overly sentimental about the subject?
6. Does the author examine the issue in terms of the forces that shape history?

Recommended Films on This Theme

- *Mildred Pierce* (United States, 1945) A classic film about an ambitious working-class divorcee who discovers her spoiled daughter murdered her lover;

- *Trading Places* (United States, 1983) A hilarious spoof about two commodity brokers who use a street hustler to discover whether heredity or environment determines success;
- *Children of Heaven* (Iran, 1997) The story of a young boy who loses his sister's shoes and must conceal this from their parents by sharing the remaining pair with her;
- *Twilight Samurai* (Japan, 2002) A story of an unemployed samurai in nineteenth-century Japan who cares for his senile mother and two daughters.

Mary Crow Dog and Richard Erdoes

Civilize Them with a Stick

Mary Crow Dog (who later took the name Mary Brave Bird) was born in 1956 and grew up on a South Dakota reservation in a one-room cabin without running water or electricity. She joined the new movement of tribal pride sweeping Native American communities in the 1960s and 1970s and was at the siege of Wounded Knee, South Dakota, in 1973. She married the American Indian Movement (AIM) leader Leonard Crow Dog, the movement's chief medicine man. Her powerful autobiography Lakota Woman, *written with Richard Erdoes, one of America's leading writers on Native American affairs and the author of eleven books, became a national best-seller and won the American Book Award for 1991. Her second book,* Ohitika Woman *(1993), was also written with Richard Erdoes. In "Civilize Them with a Stick," from* Lakota Woman, *the author recounts her personal struggle as a young student at a boarding school run by the Bureau of Indian Affairs.*

Before You Read

Notice how the quote from the Department of Interior (1901) that precedes Mary Crow Dog's essay provides an ironic contrast to the conditions she describes.

> *. . . Gathered from the cabin, the wickiup, and the tepee,*
> *partly by cajolery and partly by threats;*
> *partly by bribery and partly by force,*
> *they are induced to leave their kindred*
> *to enter these schools and take upon themselves*
> *the outward appearance of civilized life.*
>
> —Annual report of the Department of Interior, 1901

1 It is almost impossible to explain to a sympathetic white person what a typical old Indian boarding school was like; how it affected the Indian child suddenly dumped into it like a small creature from another world, helpless, defenseless, bewildered, trying desperately and instinctively to survive and sometimes not surviving at all. I think such children were like the victims of Nazi concentration camps trying to tell average, middle-class Americans what their experience had been like. Even now, when these schools are much improved, when the

buildings are new, all gleaming steel and glass, the food tolerable, the teachers well trained and well intentioned, even trained in child psychology—unfortunately the psychology of white children, which is different from ours—the shock to the child upon arrival is still tremendous. Some just seem to shrivel up, don't speak for days on end, and have an empty look in their eyes. I know of an eleven-year-old on another reservation who hanged herself, and in our school, while I was there, a girl jumped out of the window, trying to kill herself to escape an unbearable situation. That first shock is always there. . . .

2 The mission school at St. Francis was a curse for our family for generations. My grandmother went there, then my mother, then my sisters and I. At one time or other every one of us tried to run away. Grandma told me once about the bad times she had experienced at St. Francis. In those days they let students go home only for one week every year. Two days were used up for transportation, which meant spending just five days out of three hundred and sixty-five with her family. And that was an improvement. Before grandma's time, on many reservations they did not let the students go home at all until they had finished school. Anybody who disobeyed the nuns was severely punished. The building in which my grandmother stayed had three floors, for girls only. Way up in the attic were little cells, about five by five by ten feet. One time she was in church and instead of praying she was playing jacks. As punishment they took her to one of those little cubicles where she stayed in darkness because the windows had been boarded up. They left her there for a whole week with only bread and water for nourishment. After she came out she promptly ran away, together with three other girls. They were found and brought back. The nuns stripped them naked and whipped them. They used a horse buggy whip on my grandmother. Then she was put back into the attic—for two weeks.

3 My mother had much the same experiences but never wanted to talk about them, and then there I was, in the same place. The school is now run by the BIA—the Bureau of Indian Affairs—but only since about fifteen years ago. When I was there, during the 1960s, it was still run by the Church. The Jesuit fathers ran the boys' wing and the Sisters of the Sacred Heart ran us—with the help of the strap. Nothing had changed since my grandmother's days. I have been told recently that even in the '70s they were still beating children at that school. All I got out of school was being taught how to pray. I learned quickly that I would be beaten if I failed in my devotions or, God forbid, prayed the wrong way, especially prayed in Indian to Wakan Tanka, the Indian Creator.

4 The girls' wing was built like an F and was run like a penal institution. Every morning at five o'clock the sisters would come into our large dormitory to wake us up, and immediately we had to kneel down at the sides of our beds and recite the prayers. At six o'clock we

were herded into the church for more of the same. I did not take kindly to the discipline and to marching by the clock, left-right, left-right. I was never one to like being forced to do something. I do something because I feel like doing it. I felt this way always, as far as I can remember, and my sister Barbara felt the same way. An old medicine man once told me: "Us Lakotas are not like dogs who can be trained, who can be beaten and keep on wagging their tails, licking the hand that whipped them. We are like cats, little cats, big cats, wildcats, bobcats, mountain lions. It doesn't matter what kind, but cats who can't be tamed, who scratch if you step on their tails." But I was only a kitten and my claws were still small.

5 Barbara was still in the school when I arrived and during my first year or two she could still protect me a little bit. When Barb was a seventh-grader she ran away together with five other girls, early in the morning before sunrise. They brought them back in the evening. The girls had to wait for two hours in front of the mother superior's office. They were hungry and cold, frozen through. It was wintertime and they had been running the whole day without food, trying to make good their escape. The mother superior asked each girl, "Would you do this again?" She told them that as punishment they would not be allowed to visit home for a month and that she'd keep them busy on work details until the skin on their knees and elbows had worn off. At the end of her speech she told each girl, "Get up from this chair and lean over it." She then lifted the girls' skirts and pulled down their underpants. Not little girls either, but teenagers. She had a leather strap about a foot long and four inches wide fastened to a stick, and beat the girls, one after another, until they cried. Barb did not give her that satisfaction but just clenched her teeth. There was one girl, Barb told me, the nun kept on beating and beating until her arm got tired.

6 I did not escape my share of the strap. Once, when I was thirteen years old, I refused to go to Mass. I did not want to go to church because I did not feel well. A nun grabbed me by the hair, dragged me upstairs, made me stoop over, pulled my dress up (we were not allowed at the time to wear jeans), pulled my panties down, and gave me what they called "swats"—twenty-five swats with a board around which Scotch tape had been wound. She hurt me badly.

7 My classroom was right next to the principal's office and almost every day I could hear him swatting the boys. Beating was the common punishment for not doing one's homework, or for being late to school. It had such a bad effect upon me that I hated and mistrusted every white person on sight, because I met only one kind. It was not until much later that I met sincere white people I could relate to and be friends with. Racism breeds racism in reverse.

8 The routine at St. Francis was dreary. Six A.M., kneeling in church for an hour or so; seven o'clock, breakfast; eight o'clock, scrub the floor,

peel spuds, make classes. We had to mop the dining room twice every day and scrub the tables. If you were caught taking a rest, doodling on the bench with a fingernail or knife, or just rapping, the nun would come up with a dish towel and just slap it across your face, saying, "You're not supposed to be talking, you're supposed to be working!" Monday mornings we had cornmeal mush, Tuesday oatmeal, Wednesday rice and raisins, Thursday cornflakes, and Friday all the leftovers mixed together or sometimes fish. Frequently the food had bugs or rocks in it. We were eating hot dogs that were weeks old, while the nuns were dining on ham, whipped potatoes, sweet peas, and cranberry sauce. In winter our dorm was icy cold while the nuns' rooms were always warm.

9 I have seen little girls arrive at the school, first-graders, just fresh from home and totally unprepared for what awaited them, little girls with pretty braids, and the first thing the nuns did was chop their hair off and tie up what was left behind their ears. Next they would dump the children into tubs of alcohol, a sort of rubbing alcohol, "to get the germs off." Many of the nuns were German immigrants, some from Bavaria, so that we sometimes speculated whether Bavaria was some sort of Dracula country inhabited by monsters. For the sake of objectivity I ought to mention that two of the German fathers were great linguists and that the only Lakota–English dictionaries and grammars which are worth anything were put together by them.

10 At night some of the girls would huddle in bed together for comfort and reassurance. Then the nun in charge of the dorm would come in and say, "What are the two of you doing in bed together? I smell evil in this room. You girls are evil incarnate. You are sinning. You are going to hell and burn forever. You can act that way in the devil's frying pan." She would get them out of bed in the middle of the night, making them kneel and pray until morning. We had not the slightest idea what it was all about. At home we slept two and three in a bed for animal warmth and a feeling of security.

11 The nuns and the girls in the two top grades were constantly battling it out physically with fists, nails, and hair-pulling. I myself was growing from a kitten into an undersized cat. My claws were getting bigger and were itching for action. About 1969 or 1970 a strange young white girl appeared on the reservation. She looked about eighteen or twenty years old. She was pretty and had long, blond hair down to her waist, patched jeans, boots, and a backpack. She was different from any other white person we had met before. I think her name was Wise. I do not know how she managed to overcome our reluctance and distrust, getting us into a corner, making us listen to her, asking us how we were treated. She told us that she was from New York. She was the first real hippie or Yippie we had come across. She told us of people called the Black Panthers, Young Lords,

and Weathermen. She said, "Black people are getting it on. Indians are getting it on in St. Paul and California. How about you?" She also said, "Why don't you put out an underground paper, mimeograph it. It's easy. Tell it like it is. Let it all hang out." She spoke a strange lingo but we caught on fast.

12 Charlene Left Hand Bull and Gina One Star were two full-blood girls I used to hang out with. We did everything together. They were willing to join me in a Sioux uprising. We put together a newspaper which we called the *Red Panther.* In it we wrote how bad the school was, what kind of slop we had to eat—slimy, rotten, blackened potatoes for two weeks—the way we were beaten. I think I was the one who wrote the worst article about our principal of the moment, Father Keeler. I put all my anger and venom into it. I called him a goddam wasičun son of a bitch. I wrote that he knew nothing about Indians and should go back to where he came from, teaching white children whom he could relate to. I wrote that we knew which priests slept with which nuns and that all they ever could think about was filling their bellies and buying a new car. It was the kind of writing which foamed at the mouth, but which also lifted a great deal of weight from one's soul.

13 On Saint Patrick's Day, when everybody was at the big powwow, we distributed our newspapers. We put them on windshields and bulletin boards, in desks and pews, in dorms and toilets. But someone saw us and snitched on us. The shit hit the fan. The three of us were taken before a board meeting. Our parents, in my case my mother, had to come. They were told that ours was a most serious matter, the worst thing that had ever happened in the school's long history. One of the nuns told my mother, "Your daughter really needs to be talked to." "What's wrong with my daughter?" my mother asked. She was given one of our *Red Panther* newspapers. The nun pointed out its name to her and then my piece, waiting for mom's reaction. After a while she asked, "Well, what have you got to say to this? What do you think?"

14 My mother said, "Well, when I went to school here, some years back, I was treated a lot worse than these kids are. I really can't see how they can have any complaints, because we was treated a lot stricter. We could not even wear skirts halfway up our knees. These girls have it made. But you should forgive them because they are young. And it's supposed to be a free country, free speech and all that. I don't believe what they done is wrong." So all I got out of it was scrubbing six flights of stairs on my hands and knees, every day. And no boy-side privileges.

15 The boys and girls were still pretty much separated. The only time one could meet a member of the opposite sex was during free time, between four and five-thirty, in the study hall or on benches or the volleyball court outside, and that was strictly supervised. One day

Charlene and I went over to the boys' side. We were on the ball team and they had to let us practice. We played three extra minutes, only three minutes more than we were supposed to. Here was the nuns' opportunity for revenge. We got twenty-five swats. I told Charlene, "We are getting too old to have our bare asses whipped that way. We are old enough to have babies. Enough of this shit. Next time we fight back." Charlene only said, "Hoka-hay!"

16 We had to take showers every evening. One little girl did not want to take her panties off and one of the nuns told her, "You take those underpants off—or else!" But the child was ashamed to do it. The nun was getting her swat to threaten the girl. I went up to the sister, pushed her veil off, and knocked her down. I told her that if she wanted to hit a little girl she should pick on me, pick one her own size. She got herself transferred out of the dorm a week later.

17 In a school like this there is always a lot of favoritism. At St. Francis it was strongly tinged with racism. Girls who were near-white, who came from what the nuns called "nice families," got preferential treatment. They waited on the faculty and got to eat ham or eggs and bacon in the morning. They got the easy jobs while the skins, who did not have the right kind of background—myself among them—always wound up in the laundry room sorting out ten bushel baskets of dirty boys' socks every day. Or we wound up scrubbing the floors and doing all the dishes. The school therefore fostered fights and antagonism between whites and breeds, and between breeds and skins. At one time Charlene and I had to iron all the robes and vestments the priests wore when saying Mass. We had to fold them up and put them into a chest in the back of the church. In a corner, looking over our shoulders, was a statue of the crucified Savior, all bloody and beaten up. Charlene looked up and said, "Look at that poor Indian. The pigs sure worked him over." That was the closest I ever came to seeing Jesus.

18 I was held up as a bad example and didn't mind. I was old enough to have a boyfriend and promptly got one. At the school we had an hour and a half for ourselves. Between the boys' and the girls' wings were some benches where one could sit. My boyfriend and I used to go there just to hold hands and talk. The nuns were very uptight about any boy-girl stuff. They had an exaggerated fear of anything having even the faintest connection with sex. One day in religion class, an all-girl class, Sister Bernard singled me out for some remarks, pointing me out as a bad example, an example that should be shown. She said that I was too free with my body. That I was holding hands which meant that I was not a good example to follow. She also said that I wore unchaste dresses, skirts which were too short, too suggestive, shorter than regulations permitted, and for that I would be punished. She dressed me down before the whole class, carrying on and on about my unchastity.

19 I stood up and told her, "You shouldn't say any of those things, miss. You people are a lot worse than us Indians. I know all about you, because my grandmother and my aunt told me about you. Maybe twelve, thirteen years ago you had a water stoppage here in St. Francis. No water could get through the pipes. There are water lines right under the mission, underground tunnels and passages where in my grandmother's time only the nuns and priests could go, which were off-limits to everybody else. When the water backed up they had to go through all the water lines and clean them out. And in those huge pipes they found the bodies of newborn babies. And they were white babies. They weren't Indian babies. At least when our girls have babies, they don't do away with them that way, like flushing them down the toilet, almost.

20 "And that priest they sent here from Holy Rosary in Pine Ridge because he molested a little girl. You couldn't think of anything better than dump him on us. All he does is watch young women and girls with that funny smile on his face. Why don't you point him out for an example?"

21 Charlene and I worked on the school newspaper. After all we had some practice. Every day we went down to Publications. One of the priests acted as the photographer, doing the enlarging and developing. He smelled of chemicals which had stained his hands yellow. One day he invited Charlene into the darkroom. He was going to teach her developing. She was developed already. She was a big girl compared to him, taller too. Charlene was nicely built, not fat, just rounded. No sharp edges anywhere. All of a sudden she rushed out of the darkroom, yelling to me, "Let's get out of here! He's trying to feel me up. That priest is nasty." So there was this too to contend with—sexual harassment. We complained to the student body. The nuns said we just had a dirty mind.

22 We got a new priest in English. During one of his first classes he asked one of the boys a certain question. The boy was shy. He spoke poor English, but he had the right answer. The priest told him, "You did not say it right. Correct yourself. Say it over again." The boy got flustered and stammered. He could hardly get out a word. But the priest kept after him: "Didn't you hear? I told you to do the whole thing over. Get it right this time." He kept on and on.

23 I stood up and said, "Father, don't be doing that. If you go into an Indian's home and try to talk Indian, they might laugh at you and say, 'Do it over correctly. Get it right this time!'"

24 He shouted at me, "Mary, you stay after class. Sit down right now!"

25 I stayed after class, until after the bell. He told me, "Get over here!"

26 He grabbed me by the arm, pushing me against the blackboard, shouting, "Why are you always mocking us? You have no reason to do this."

27 I said, "Sure I do. You were making fun of him. You embarrassed him. He needs strengthening, not weakening. You hurt him. I did not hurt you."

28 He twisted my arm and pushed real hard. I turned around and hit him in the face, giving him a bloody nose. After that I ran out of the room, slamming the door behind me. He and I went to Sister Bernard's office. I told her, "Today I quit school. I'm not taking any more of this, none of this shit anymore. None of this treatment. Better give me my diploma. I can't waste any more time on you people."

29 Sister Bernard looked at me for a long, long time. She said, "All right, Mary Ellen, go home today. Come back in a few days and get your diploma." And that was that. Oddly enough, that priest turned out okay. He taught a class in grammar, orthography, composition, things like that. I think he wanted more respect in class. He was still young and unsure of himself. But I was in there too long. I didn't feel like hearing it. Later he became a good friend of the Indians, a personal friend of myself and my husband. He stood up for us during Wounded Knee and after. He stood up to his superiors, stuck his neck way out, became a real people's priest. He even learned our language. He died prematurely of cancer. It is not only the good Indians who die young, but the good whites, too. It is the timid ones who know how to take care of themselves who grow old. I am still grateful to that priest for what he did for us later and for the quarrel he picked with me—or did I pick it with him?—because it ended a situation which had become unendurable for me. The day of my fight with him was my last day in school.

✧ *Evaluating the Text*

1. What aspects of life at the government boarding school most clearly illustrate the government's desire to transform Native Americans? How did Mary Crow Dog react to the experiences to which she was subjected at the government-run school?

2. What historical insight did the experiences of Mary Crow Dog's mother and grandmother provide into those of Mary Crow Dog herself?

3. Why was the incident of the underground newspaper a crucial one for Mary Crow Dog?

✧ *Exploring Different Perspectives*

1. How do the works by Mary Crow Dog and Kate Chopin (see "Désirée's Baby") illustrate the effects of racism?

2. In what sense are Native Americans comparable to the untouchables or outcasts as described by Viramma in "A Pariah's Life"?

✧ *Extending Viewpoints through Writing and Research*

1. What experiences have you had that made you aware of institutionalized racism?

2. How did this essay give you insight into the vast difference between the traditional culture of Native Americans and their lives in the present?

Viramma

A Pariah's Life

Viramma is an agricultural worker and midwife in Karani, a village in southeast India. She is a member of the caste formerly known as Pariahs, or untouchables, and now more commonly called Dalits, from the Sanskrit for "downtrodden" or "oppressed." She has told her life story over a period of ten years to Josiane and Jean-Luc Racine. She communicates an impression of great strength and fatalism (of her twelve children, only three survive). Her account, translated by Will Hobson, which first appeared in Granta *(Spring 1997) is a vivid portrait of one at the margin of society. The autobiographical book* Viramma: Life of an Untouchable *was published in 1997.*

Before You Read

Consider the unusual superstitions and rituals by which Viramma lives her life and her status as an untouchable in Indian society.

1 I am the midwife here. I was born in the village of Velpakkam in Tamil Nadu, and when I married, I came to Karani, my husband's village. I was still a child then. I am a farm worker and, like all my family, I am a serf, bonded to Karani's richest landowner. We are Pariahs. We live apart from the other castes; we eat beef, we play the drums at funerals and weddings because only we can touch cow hide; we work the land. My son Anbin corrects me when I say "Pariah"; he says we should use the word "Harijan."[1] Every day people from the political parties come to the village and tell us to demand higher wages, to fight the caste system. And they mean well. But how would we survive? We have no land, not even a field.

2 We midwives help women during labour and are paid twenty rupees a month by the state. When a woman goes into labour, her relatives come and find me: "Eldest sister-in-law! The woman's in pain at home!" So I drop everything; I go and see her, examine her, turn her round one way, then the other; I pester her a bit and then tell her more or less when the child is going to be born. And it always turns out as I said it would. When the child is born, I cut the cord with a knife and tell one of the other women attending to find a hoe and a crowbar and

[1]*Harijan*: "loved ones of God." The name change was suggested by Mahatma Gandhi.

to dig a hole in the channel near the house. I wait for the placenta to come out and go and bury it immediately. Then I take care of the mother. I stretch her out on a mat, propped up with pillows, wash the baby with soap and hot water and lay it down next to its mother. Then I put a sickle and some margosa leaves at the head of the mat, so spirits don't come near them—those rogue spirits love to prowl around the lanes in the evening or at night, eating any food left lying on the ground and trying to possess people.

3 It's well known that they follow us everywhere we go, when we're hoeing or planting out; when we're changing our sanitary towels; when we're washing our hair. They sense that we're going to visit a woman in labour and then they possess us. That's why we put down the sickle and the margosa leaves. After the birth I'll visit the mother quite often, to make sure everything's going all right. If impurities have stayed in the womb, I'll cook the leaves of the "cow's itch" plant, extract the juice and make the mother drink it three times.

4 That's how a birth happens here. We Pariahs prefer to have babies at home. I tell the nurse if the newborns are boys or girls, and she goes and enters them in the registers at Pondicherry hospital. In the past, we'd take women to hospital only in emergencies. We went there in an ox-cart or a rickshaw, and often the woman died on the way. Nowadays doctors visit the villages and give medicines and tonics to women when they become pregnant. In the sixth or seventh month they're meant to go to the dispensary for a check-up. A nurse also comes to the village. Yes, everything has changed now.

5 I had my twelve children alone; I didn't let anyone near me. "Leave me in peace," I always said to the nurses. "It will come out on its own! Why do you want to rummage around in there?" I always give birth very gently—like stroking a rose. It never lasts long: I'm not one of those women whose labours drag on all night, for days even.

6 When I'm giving birth I first make a point of preparing a tray for Ettiyan—the god of death's assistant—and his huge men, with their thick moustaches and muscly shoulders. On the tray I put green mangoes, coconuts and other fruit as well as some tools: a hoe, a crowbar, a basket, so that they can set to work as soon as the child comes out of the sack in our womb. Yes! I've seen enough to know what I'm talking about. I've had a full bushel of children! Everything we eat goes into that sack: that's how the child grows. Just think what a mystery it is. With the blood he collects over ten months, Isvaran [the god Siva] moulds a baby in our womb. Only he can do that. Otherwise how could a sperm become a child?

7 I've always had plenty of milk. It used to flow so much that the front of my sari was all stiff. It's well known that we breastfeed our children for a long time. That prevents us from having another child immediately. If we were always pregnant, how could we work and eat?

Rich women can stretch their legs and take a rest. But to get my rice, I have to work: planting out, hoeing, grazing the cows, collecting wood. When we've got a little one in our arms, it's the same: we take it everywhere, and we worry, because while we're working we don't really know what it's doing, where it is. That's why we try to wait at least three years, until the child grows up, walks and can say, "Dad," "Mum," "That's our cow." That's what we take as a sign. Then we can start "talking" again, "doing it." If we time it like this, the child will be strong and chubby.

8 But Isvaran has given me a baby a year. Luckily my blood has stayed the same; it hasn't turned, and my children have never been really emaciated. Of course that also depends on the way you look after them. For me, that used to be my great worry! I managed to feed them well. As soon as I had a little money, I'd buy them sweets. I'd make them rice whenever I could, some *dosai,* some *idli.* I'd put a little sugar in cow's milk. . . . That's how I took care of them. There are some women who just let their children be without giving them regular meals. Human beings can only live if you put at least a little milk in their mouths when they're hungry! It happens with us that some women skip their children's mealtimes when they're working. But how do you expect them to grow that way?

9 Isvaran has done his work well; he's put plenty of children in my womb: beautiful children, born in perfect health. It's only afterwards that some have died. One of diarrhea, another of apoplexy. All of them have walked! Two of my children even came to the peanut harvest. I pierced their noses to put a jewel in. I plaited their hair and put flowers in it and pretty *potteu* on their foreheads, made with paste. I took good care of my little ones. I never neglected them. I dressed them neatly. If high-caste people saw them running in the street, they'd talk to them kindly, thinking that they were high-caste children.

10 How many children have I had? Wait . . . I've had twelve. The first was a girl, Muttamma. Then a boy, Ganesan. After that, a girl, Arayi. *Ayo!* After that I don't remember any more. But I've definitely had twelve: we registered them at the registry office. Yes, when there's a birth, you have to go there and declare it. "Here Sir, I've had a boy or a girl and I name it Manivelu, Nataraja or Perambata." Down there they enter all that into a big ledger. *Ayo!* If we went to that office, perhaps they could tell us how many children I've had and their names as well. *Ayo!* Look at that, I don't remember any more. They're born; they die. I haven't got all my children's names in my head: all I have left are Miniyamma, my fourth child; Anbin, my eighth; and Sundari, my eleventh.

11 A pregnant woman is prey to everything that roams around her: ghosts, ghouls, demons, the evil spirits of people who have committed suicide or died violent deaths. She has to be very careful, especially if

she is a Pariah. We Pariah women have to go all over the place, grazing the cattle, collecting wood. We're outside the whole time, even when the sun's at its height. Those spirits take advantage of this: they grab us and possess us so we fall ill, or have miscarriages. Something like that happened to me when I was pregnant with my second child.

12 One of my nephews died suddenly, the day after his engagement. One night when I was asleep I saw him sitting on me—I felt him! My husband told me that I had squeezed him very tight in my arms, that I'd been delirious and mumbling something. The following day we decided that the boy needed something, and that's why he'd come. My husband went to get bottles of arrack and palm wine. I arranged the offerings in the middle of the house: betel, areca nuts, lime, a big banana leaf with a mountain of rice, some salt fish, some toast, a cigar, bottles of alcohol, a jar of water and a beautiful oil lamp. In the meantime my husband went to find the priest from the temple of Perumal [Vishnu]—he's the one responsible for funerals. The priest asked us to spread river sand next to the offerings. He called on Yama, the god of death, and drew the sign of Yama in the sand. We ate that evening as usual and went to sleep in a corner. You must never sleep opposite the door, because a spirit might slap you when it comes in if it finds you in its way. You have to be brave when a spirit arrives! In fact you won't see it; you only hear its footsteps, like the sound of little bells, *djang, djang,* when an ox-cart goes by. It goes *han! han! han!* as if it's craving something. It always comes with its messengers, all tied to each other with big ropes. You hear them walking with rhythmic, heavy steps: *ahum! ahum! ahum!*

13 We were very afraid. As soon as the spirit came in, the lamp went out in a flash, even though it was full of oil. We heard it walking about and eating its fill and then suddenly it fled. We heard it running away very fast. When day broke soon after it had gone, we rushed to see what had happened. The rice was scattered, everywhere. On the sand we found a cat's paw-print, and part of Yama's sign had been rubbed out. The spirit had come in the form of a cat! While we were waiting for the priest to come, we collected the offerings in a big wicker basket. The priest himself was very satisfied and said that the spirit wouldn't come back. But I fell ill soon after and had a miscarriage.

14 There are worse spirits, though: the *katteri,* for example, who spy on women when they are pregnant. You have to be very careful with them. There are several sorts of *katteri*: Rana Katteri, who has bleeding wounds and drinks blood; or Irsi Katteri, the foetus eater—she's the one who causes miscarriages. As soon as she catches the smell of a foetus in a woman's womb, she's there, spying, waiting for her chance. We can tell immediately that it's that bitch at work if there are black clots when a baby aborts: she sucks up the good blood and leaves only the bad.

15 My first three children were born at my mother's house. Their births went well, and they died in good shape. It was the spirit living

in that house who devoured them. My grandfather knew about sorcery. People came to see him; they used to say that he called up the spirit, talked to it and asked it to go along with him when he went out. It lived with him, basically. When my grandfather died, we tried to drive it away but it was no use; it used to come back in the form of my grandfather; it joined in conversations, calling my grandmother by her name like her dead husband used to. And my grandmother used to answer back, "Ah! The only answer I'll give you is with my broom, you dog! I recognize you! I know who you are! Get out of here!" It would just throw tamarind seeds at her face. When a sorcerer came from Ossur to try and get rid of it, it turned vicious. The sorcerer told us he couldn't do anything against it. The spirit had taken root in that ground. It was old and cunning: we were the ones who had to go. It destroyed everything! Everything! A garlic clove couldn't even grow! My father had to sell his paddy field. I gave birth three times there: none of those children survived. The spirit ate them as and when they were born. Nothing prospered. That's how it is with the spirits.

16 All my children have been buried where they died: the first ones at Velpakkam, the others at Karani. My mother insisted we burn the first-born and throw her ashes in the river so a sorcerer didn't come and get them. The ashes or bones of first-borns are coveted by magicians. A tiny bit of ash or hair is enough for them. You see them with a hoe on their shoulder prowling around where a first-born has been burnt or buried. We made sure that everything disappeared. We have a saying that if you dissolve the ashes completely in water, you'll immediately have another child.

17 Until they grow up, we mothers always have a fire in our belly for our children: we must feed them, keep them from sickness, raise them to become men or women who can work. One of my three sisters died of a kind of tuberculosis. She had been married and she left a son. I brought him up after her death, but like his mother, he was often ill. Before she died, my sister had prayed that he would become strong, so I took up her prayers. I went into three houses and in each one I asked for a cubit of fabric. I put the three bits of fabric on the ground and laid the child on them. Then I went into three other houses and exchanged the child for three measures of barley, saying, "The child is yours; the barley is mine." Of course afterwards I would get the child back. Then I went to three other houses to collect handfuls of dirt. I mixed the three handfuls, spread them out and rolled the baby in them, saying, "Your name will be Kuppa! You are Kuppa! You have been born of dirt!" Then I pierced his nostril with a silver thread which I twisted into a ring. That worked very well for him! He's still alive and he still wears that ring in his nose today.

18 What is more important for us women than children? If we don't draw anything out of our womb, what's the use of being a woman?

A woman who has no son to put a handful of rice in her mouth, no daughter to close her eyes, is an unhappy woman. She or her parents must have failed in their dharma. I have been blessed in that way: Isvaran has filled my womb. Ah, if all my children were alive, they'd do all the trades in the world! One would be a labourer, another a carpenter. I would have made one of them study. We could have given two daughters away in marriage and enjoyed our grandchildren. I would be able to go and rest for a month with each of my sons. Yes, we would have been proud of our children.

✧ *Evaluating the Text*

1. In what specific ways does the caste into which Viramma was born determine every aspect of her life?
2. Folk beliefs and superstitions play a very important role in Viramma's world. What are some of these and how does her belief in them provide an explanation for the things that have happened to her?
3. From a Western perspective, Viramma's attitude toward childbearing is unusual. However, she earns her living as a midwife and has become reconciled to the death of most of her own children. What cultural values unique to India does she embody?

✧ *Exploring Different Perspectives*

1. How do the accounts by Viramma and Immaculée Ilibagiza in "Left to Tell" illuminate the role that being a scapegoat plays in each culture?
2. Is caste in India as described by Viramma the same as race in America as depicted by Kate Chopin in her story "Désirée's Baby"?

✧ *Extending Viewpoints through Writing and Research*

1. Have you ever known anyone whose explanation for events was rooted in superstition? What were the events and what were the superstitions that explained them?
2. What is your own attitude toward having large families? Do you think people should have as many children as they want? Why or why not? As a research project, you might investigate the one-child-per-family policy in China.
3. For information on the caste known as Dalits, or untouchables, see http://www.ncdhr.org.in.

Immaculée Ilibagiza

Left to Tell

Immaculée Ilibagiza grew up in Rwanda and studied engineering at the National University. In 1994, Rwanda was engulfed by genocide and most of her family who were Tutsis were killed by the Hutus. She survived by hiding with five other women in a small bathroom of a local pastor's home for 91 days while machete-wielding mobs hunted for them. In 1998, she emigrated to the United States and began working for the United Nations. In the following chapter from Left to Tell *(2006), she describes how her faith sustained her during the first few days of this ordeal. More recently, she has published* Led by Faith: Rising from the Ashes of the Rwandan Genocide *(2008) and* Our Lady of Kibeho: Heaven Speaks to the World from the Heart of Africa *(2008).*

Before You Read

What characteristics distinguish genocide from events where large numbers of people are killed?

1 I closed the door behind Vianney and Augustine and joined the other Tutsi women.

2 Pastor Murinzi carried a flashlight and led us down the dark hallway to his bedroom. Our eyes followed the beam of light along the walls until it landed on a door that I assumed opened to the yard.

3 "This is where you'll stay," he said, swinging the door open to reveal our new home: a small bathroom about four feet long and three feet wide. The light shimmered as it bounced off the white enamel tiles on the bottom half of the walls. There was a shower stall at one end and a toilet at the other—the room wasn't big enough for a sink. And there was a small air vent/window near the ceiling that was covered with a piece of red cloth, which somehow made the room feel even smaller.

4 I couldn't imagine how all six of us could possibly fit in this space, but the pastor herded us through the door and packed us in tight. "While you're in here, you must be absolutely quiet, and I mean *silent*," he said. "If you make any noise, you will die. If they hear you, they will find you, and then they will kill you. No one must know that you're here, not even my children. Do you understand?"

5 "Yes, Pastor," we mumbled in unison.

6 "And don't flush the toilet or use the shower." He shone his light along the wall above the toilet. "There's another bathroom on the other side of that wall, which uses the same plumbing. So if you absolutely must flush, wait until you hear someone using the other bathroom, then do so at *exactly* the same time. Do you understand?"

7 "Yes, Pastor."

8 The flashlight clicked off, and his last words were spoken in the dark. "I think that they're going to keep killing for another week, maybe less. If you're careful, you might live through this. I'd hate for the killers to get you . . . I know what they would do."

9 He shut the door and left us standing in blackness, our bodies pressing against one another. The musky heat of our breath, sweat, and skin mingled together and made us feel faint.

10 We tried to sit, but there wasn't enough room for all of us to move at the same time. The four tallest had to push our backs against the wall and slide to the tile floor, then pull the smaller girls down on top of us. It was past 3 A.M. and we were all wide-awake, yet we didn't dare speak. We sat as best we could, listening to the crickets outside and to our own labored breathing.

11 I prayed silently, asking God to protect Vianney and Augustine and keep my parents and Damascene safe. I thanked Him for delivering us to the bathroom—I truly believed that God had guided Pastor Murinzi to bring us here, and for the first time in days, I felt safe. If *I* hadn't noticed the bathroom we were currently in after so many visits to the house, no one else would.

12 I asked God to bless Pastor Murinzi for risking his own safety to help us . . . but then I winced at the prayer. A flush of anger burned my cheeks as I remembered how he'd sent my brother and our friend into the night. I prayed that God would eventually help me forgive the pastor.

13 The moon emerged from behind a cloud, and a thin streak of pale light slipped through a crack in the red curtain, providing enough illumination for me to make out the faces of my companions. Sitting beside me was Athanasia, a pretty, dark-skinned 14-year-old with big beautiful eyes that caught the moonlight. Sitting on top of her was 12-year-old Beata, still wearing her school uniform, who looked lost and very frightened. I pulled her onto my lap, cradling her in my arms until she closed her eyes.

14 Across from me was Therese, who, at 55, was the eldest of the group. She wore a colorful, traditional Rwandan wrap-dress popular with married women. She looked more worried than any of us, probably because she only had two of her six children—Claire and Sanda—with her. Claire was very light-skinned, and even though she was my age, she was nervous and withdrawn and wouldn't make eye contact. Her little sister Sanda was only seven, and the youngest of the group.

She was cute, sweet, and surprisingly calm. She never once cried or looked frightened, even when the rest of us were trembling—I think she must have been in shock the entire time we were in that bathroom.

15 The pastor's repeated warnings to be quiet had burned into us. We sat in an uncomfortable heap, too afraid to adjust our positions or to even breathe too heavily. We waited for the gray light of dawn to fill the room, then carefully pried ourselves apart to take turns standing and stretching. A two- or three-minute break was all we allowed ourselves before resuming our awkward positions on the floor.

16 When morning broke, the birds in the pastor's shade tree began singing. I was jealous of them, thinking, *How lucky you are to have been born birds and have freedom—after all, look at what we humans are doing to ourselves.*

17 We were so exhausted, hungry, cramped, and hot that our first day in the bathroom passed in a painful haze. It was impossible to sleep—if I dozed off, I was immediately awoken by a leg cramp or someone's elbow knocking against my ribs.

18 In the early evening, we heard Pastor Murinzi talking to someone outside. "No, no, no," he said. "I don't know what you're talking about—I'm a good Hutu, and I'd never hide Tutsis. There are no Tutsis here . . . they left last night."

19 We stared at each other with our eyes wide open. We were terrified.

20 "I don't want any trouble with the government," the pastor continued. "You people know me, and you should protect this house . . . those Tutsi rebels might attack me for being such a good Hutu."

21 Whoever the pastor was talking to left, and we relaxed. Pastor Murinzi had just lied to save us—I felt assured that he wouldn't hand us over to the killers. He had little choice now, because if he turned us in, the killers would know that he'd hidden us. They'd call him a moderate, a traitor to his tribe, and would kill him as surely as they'd kill us.

22 I breathed easier and hugged young Beata, who was lying across my lap. I remembered how my mother sometimes held me in her lap when I was young and frightened. The memory of Mom saddened me—this was the first time in my life that I didn't know the whereabouts of my parents or brothers. I slipped into a half sleep and dreamed of Vianney, Augustine, and Damascene knocking on the pastor's gate, while behind them, our house was burning. I saw my parents sitting on Dad's motorcycle, and my mother asking, "What will happen to my boys?"

23 While I was dreaming, Pastor Murinzi opened the door, and without saying a word, shoved a plate of cold potatoes and beans into the room. It was late, maybe 11 P.M., and none of us had had anything to eat or drink for nearly two days.

24 We attacked the plate, grabbing the food with our dirty fingers and stuffing it into our mouths.

25 When the pastor returned five minutes later with forks, we'd already devoured every bit of food. He stared at the plate, and then looked at us with pity. A moment later he tossed a very thin mattress into the room. "You've traveled down a long road. Now try to get some rest," he said, and closed the door.

26 When we awoke the next day, we took turns stretching our aching muscles. Moving even an inch was a major production because we couldn't talk to one another. We quickly worked out forms of sign language that would become our silent shorthand for the remainder of our stay in the bathroom.

27 I grimaced at the pain in my cramped legs, thinking that I'd have quite a tale of hardship to tell after the war. "Listen to what I had to endure," I'd boast to my friends. "I spent an entire day and night trapped in a tiny bathroom with five strangers. What a hero I am!"

28 No sooner had I begun my little fantasy than I was jolted back to reality by images of my family: my parents fleeing our burning house, Damascene slipping sadly away, and Vianney and Augustine wandering in the open with nowhere to hide. Thank God that Aimable was safely away from Rwanda in another country! But what about the thousands of displaced Tutsis who had sought refuge at our house? What had become of them? Had they found shelter, or were they lying somewhere bleeding to death? I felt silly and selfish for indulging in my self-pity when thousands were undoubtedly suffering far more.

29 It was my turn to stretch when a commotion erupted outside. There were dozens, maybe hundreds, of voices, some yelling, others chanting. We knew immediately that the killers had arrived.

30 "Let us hunt them in the forests, lakes, and hills; let us find them in the church; let us wipe them from the face of the earth!"

31 I stood on my tiptoes and peeked out the window through a little hole in the curtain. The other ladies grabbed at me, trying to pull me down. Athanasia shook her head wildly, silently mouthing, "Get down! They're looking for us! Get down before they see you!"

32 I ignored them, knocking their hands away and peering through the hole. I immediately regretted my decision because I was petrified by what I saw.

33 Hundreds of people surrounded the house, many of whom were dressed like devils, wearing skirts of tree bark and shirts of dried banana leaves, and some even had goat horns strapped onto their heads. Despite their demonic costumes, their faces were easily recognizable, and there was murder in their eyes.

34 They whooped and hollered. They jumped about, waving spears, machetes, and knives in the air. They chanted a chilling song of genocide while doing a dance of death: "Kill them, kill them, kill them all; kill them big and kill them small! Kill the old and kill the young . . . a

baby snake is still a snake, kill it, too, let none escape! Kill them, kill them, kill them all!"

35 It wasn't the soldiers who were chanting, nor was it the trained militiamen who had been tormenting us for days. No, these were my neighbors, people I'd grown up and gone to school with—some had even been to our house for dinner.

36 I spotted Kananga, a young man I'd known since childhood. He was a high school dropout my dad had tried to help straighten out. I saw Philip, a young man who'd been too shy to look anyone in the eye, but who now seemed completely at home in this group of killers. At the front of the pack I could make out two local schoolteachers who were friends of Damascene. I recognized dozens of Mataba's most prominent citizens in the mob, all of whom were in a killing frenzy, ranting and screaming for Tutsi blood. The killers leading the group pushed their way into the pastor's house, and suddenly the chanting was coming from all directions.

37 "Find them, find them, kill them all!"

38 My head was spinning; I fell backward onto the ladies. I couldn't breathe. "Dear God, save us . . ." I whispered, but couldn't remember the words to any of my prayers. A wave of despair washed over me, and I was overwhelmed by fear.

39 That's when the devil first whispered in my ear. *Why are you calling on God? Look at all of them out there . . . hundreds of them looking for you. They are legion, and you are one. You can't possibly survive—you won't survive. They're inside the house, and they're moving through the rooms. They're close, almost here . . . they're going to find you, rape you, cut you, kill you!*

40 My heart was pounding. What was this voice? I squeezed my eyes shut as tightly as I could to resist the negative thoughts. I grasped the red and white rosary my father had given me, and silently prayed with all my might: *God, in the Bible You said that You can do anything for anybody. Well, I am one of those anybodies, and I need You to do something for me now. Please, God, blind the killers when they reach the pastor's bedroom—don't let them find the bathroom door, and don't let them see us! You saved Daniel in the lions' den, God, You stopped the lions from ripping him apart . . . stop these killers from ripping us apart, God! Save us, like You saved Daniel!*

41 I prayed more intensely than I'd ever prayed before, but still the negative energy wracked my spirit. The voice of doubt was in my ear again as surely as if Satan himself were sitting on my shoulder. I literally felt the fear pumping through my veins, and my blood was on fire. *You're going to die, Immaculée!* the voice taunted. *You compare yourself to Daniel? How conceited you are . . . Daniel was pure of heart and loved by God—he was a prophet, a saint! What are you? You are nothing . . . you deserve suffering and pain . . . you deserve to die!*

42 I clutched my rosary as though it were a lifeline to God. In my mind and heart I cried out to Him for help: *Yes, I am nothing, but You are*

forgiving. I am human and I am weak, but please, God, give me Your forgiveness. Forgive my trespasses . . . and please send these killers away before they find us!

43 My temples pounded. The dark voice was in my head, filling it with fearful, unspeakable images. *Dead bodies are everywhere. Mothers have seen their babies chopped in half, their fetuses ripped from their wombs . . . and you think you should be spared? Mothers prayed for God to spare their babies and He ignored them—why should He save you when innocent babies are being murdered? You are selfish, and you have no shame. Listen, Immaculée . . . do you hear them? The killers are outside your door—they're here for you.*

44 My head was burning, but I did hear the killers in the hall, screaming, "Kill them! Kill them all!"

45 *No! God is love,* I told the voice. *He loves me and wouldn't fill me with fear. He will not abandon me. He will not let me die cowering on a bathroom floor. He will not let me die in shame!*

46 I struggled to form an image of God in my mind, envisioning two pillars of brilliant white light burning brightly in front of me, like two giant legs. I wrapped my arms around the legs, like a frightened child clinging to its mother. I begged God to fill me with His light and strength, to cast out the dark energy from my heart: *I'm holding on to Your legs, God, and I do not doubt that You can save me. I will not let go of You until You have sent the killers away.*

47 The struggle between my prayers and the evil whispers that I was sure belonged to the devil raged in my mind. I never stopped praying . . . and the whispering never relented.

48 In the evening, the pastor opened the door and found us all in a sort of trance. I was bathed in sweat, exhausted, clutching my rosary in both hands, and oblivious to my surroundings. I was still mouthing prayer after prayer while staring vacantly at the others. Therese was using one hand to cover her eyes and the other to hold her Bible firmly on top of her head. And young Beata was crouching on her knees, arms in front of her, hands clasped in prayer.

49 The pastor called our names, but not one of us heard him. Finally, he shook us to awaken us from our stupor. I looked up at him, blinking, confused, and completely taken aback when he began laughing at us.

50 "What are you ladies doing? For heaven's sake, relax. The killers left seven hours ago. I can't believe you're all still praying."

51 To me, those seven hours had passed in what seemed like a few minutes, yet I was utterly drained. In all my years of praying, I'd never focused so completely on God, or been so keenly aware of the presence of darkness. I'd seen evil in the eyes of the killers, and had felt evil all around me while the house was being searched. And I'd listened to the dark voice, letting it convince me that we were about to be slaughtered.

Every time I succumbed to my fear and believed the lies of that poisonous whispering, I felt as though the skin were being peeled from my scalp. It was only by focusing on God's positive energy that I was able to pull myself through that first visit by the killers. My father had always said that you could never pray too much . . . now I could see that he was right.

52 I realized that my battle to survive this war would have to be fought inside of me. Everything strong and good in me—my faith, hope, and courage—was vulnerable to the dark energy. If I lost my faith, I knew that I wouldn't be able to survive. I could rely only on God to help me fight.

53 The visit by the killers had left us all spent. Pastor Murinzi brought us a plate of food, but despite our hunger, we were too tired to eat. The food was untouched when he returned around midnight.

54 The pastor returned again in the middle of the night during a heavy storm. The rain beat down so loudly against the iron roof that he was able to talk freely without the fear of being overheard. "We were lucky today. They searched all over the house and looked in every room. They looked in the yard and dug through the dung heap behind the cow pen. They crawled into the ceiling and under the furniture—they even stuck their machetes into my suitcases to make sure that I wasn't hiding Tutsi babies. They were crazed, like rabid animals. Their eyes were glazed and red . . . I think they'd been smoking drugs.

55 "But when they reached my bedroom, they saw that it was neat, so they didn't want to mess it up. They said that they'd leave the bedroom for now but warned that they'd search it next time when they came back."

56 "Next time!" we gasped.

57 I couldn't imagine reliving the same ordeal. Surely God wouldn't put us through that suffering twice!

58 "You never know when they're going to come back," the pastor said. "They could come at any time, and God help us all if they find you."

59 His parting sentence echoed in my mind, keeping me awake all night and throughout the next day.

60 Pastor Murinzi returned the next evening in a panic. "A friend told me that the leader of a death squad thinks the killers did a bad job searching the house yesterday," he hissed. "Some of you were seen in the house a few days ago, and there are rumors that you're hiding here. A different group of killers is being sent to search more thoroughly."

61 I moaned as my body went limp. I simply didn't have the strength to live through another of the killers' hunting expeditions. *God, why don't You just lead them to us now and get it over with?* I entreated. *Why do You let us suffer like this? Why do You torture us?*

62 How could we escape again? The house that once seemed so huge had become my cell, a death trap. I could think of only one escape:

I wanted to go to heaven. *Oh, God, I prayed soundlessly, I have no heart left to fight. I'm ready to give up . . . please give me strength and protect me from the demons that are all around me. Show me how to make the killers blind again.*

63 I raised my head and opened my eyes. When I saw the pastor standing in the doorway, a crystal clear image flashed through my mind. "I have an idea," I told him in a hushed but insistent voice. "Can you push your wardrobe in front of the bathroom door? It's tall and wide enough to completely cover it, so if the killers can't see the door, they'll never find us. It will be as though they're blind!"

64 Pastor Murinzi thought for a moment and then shook his head. "No, it wouldn't change anything; in fact, it would probably make matters worse. If they look behind the wardrobe and find the door, they will be even more vicious with you."

65 "Oh, no! Pastor, please, you must . . ." I was certain that God had sent me a sign. In my soul, I knew that if the wardrobe were in front of the door, we'd be saved. But the pastor was immovable, so I did something I'd never done in my life: I got on my knees and bowed down to him. "Please, I'm begging you," I said. "I know in my heart that if you don't put the wardrobe in front of the door, they're going to find us the next time they search. Don't worry about making them angry—they can only kill us once. Please do this for us . . . God will reward you if you do."

66 I don't know if it was the sight of me begging on my knees or the fear that I'd be overheard that convinced him, but he relented. "All right, all right. Keep your voice down, Immaculée. I'll move it right now. I hope it helps, but I doubt it will."

67 He disappeared, and a moment later we heard the wardrobe sliding in front of the bathroom door. The other ladies looked at me and whispered, "That was such a good idea—what put it into your head?"

68 I couldn't remember if I'd ever seen the pastor's wardrobe before, but I knew for certain that the idea to move it came to me when I prayed for help.

69 "God," I simply replied.

✧ *Evaluating the Text*

1. In what context was the author compelled to hide with five other women in a bathroom to avoid being killed?

2. What does Ilibagiza hear that makes it quite clear the mob is looking specifically for her? What had already happened to Ilibagiza's family?

3. What impression do you get of the pastor who hides her and the other women in his house?

✧ *Exploring Different Perspectives*

1. Compare the accounts by Ilibagiza and by Mary Crow Dog and Richard Erdoes (see "Civilize Them with a Stick") in terms of the persecution each experienced.
2. Compare the way Ilibagiza and Jo Goodwin Parker (see "What Is Poverty?") take you inside the minds of the authors to fully understand their feelings.

✧ *Extending Viewpoints through Writing and Research*

1. How does Ilibagiza's religious faith sustain her through the harrowing ordeal she experiences?
2. As a research project, investigate the repercussions of the Rwandan civil war for both the Hutus and the Tutsis and the way this event has been captured by films such as *Hotel Rwanda* (2004).

Jo Goodwin Parker

What Is Poverty?

Jo Goodwin Parker's poignant and realistic account of the shame, humiliation, and outrage of being poor was first given as a speech in Deland, Florida, on December 27, 1965, and was published in America's Other Children: Public Schools Outside Suburbia, *edited by George Henderson (1971). Parker reveals in graphic detail the hard choices she was forced to make in an ever-losing battle to preserve the health of her three children.*

Before You Read

Have you known anyone who was poverty-striken?

1 You ask me what is poverty? Listen to me. Here I am, dirty, smelly, and with no "proper" underwear on and with the stench of my rotting teeth near you. I will tell you. Listen to me. Listen without pity. I cannot use your pity. Listen with understanding. Put yourself in my dirty, worn out, ill-fitting shoes, and hear me.

2 Poverty is getting up every morning from a dirt- and illness-stained mattress. The sheets have long since been used for diapers Poverty is living in a smell that never leaves. This is a small of urine, sour milk, and spoiling food sometimes joined with the strong smell smell of long-cooked onions. Onions are cheap. If you have smelled this smell, you did not know how it came. It is the smell of the outdoor privy. It is the smell of young children who cannot walk the long dark way in the night. It is the smell of rotting garbage. I could bury it, but where is the shovel? Shovels cost money.

3 Poverty is being tired. I have always been tired. They told me at the hospital when the last baby came that I had chronic anemia caused from poor diet, a bad case of worms, and that I needed a corrective operation. I listened politely—the poor are always polite. The poor always listen. They don't say that there is no money for iron pills, or better food, or worm medicine. The idea of an operation is frightening and costs so much that, if I had dared, I would have laughed. Who takes care of my children? Recovery from an operation takes a long time. I have three children. When I left them with "Granny" the last time I had a job, I came home to find the baby covered with fly specks, and a diaper that had not been changed since I left. When the dried diaper came off, bits of my baby's flesh came with it. My other child

was playing with a sharp bit of broken glass, and my oldest was playing alone at the edge of a lake. I made twenty-two dollars a week, and a good nursery school costs twenty dollars a week for three children. I quit my job.

4 Poverty is dirt. You say in your clean clothes coming from your clean house, "Anybody can be clean." Let me explain about housekeeping with no money. For breakfast I give my children grits with no oleo or cornbread without eggs and oleo. This does not use up many dishes. What dishes there are, I wash in cold water and with no soap. Even the cheapest soap has to be saved for the baby's diapers. Look at my hands, so cracked and red. Once I saved for two months to buy a jar of Vaseline for my hands and the baby's diaper rash. When I had saved enough, I went to buy it and the price had gone up two cents. The baby and I suffered on. I have to decide every day if I can bear to put my cracked, sore hands into the cold water and strong soap. But you ask, why not hot water? Fuel costs money. If you have a wood fire it costs money. If you burn electricity, it costs money. Hot water is a luxury. I do not have luxuries. I know you will be surprised when I tell you how young I am. I look so much older. My back has been bent over the wash tubs every day for so long, I cannot remember when I ever did anything else. Every night I wash every stitch my school age child has on and just hope her clothes will be dry by morning.

5 Poverty is staying up all night on cold nights to watch the fire, knowing one spark on the newspaper covering the walls means your sleeping children die in flames. In summer poverty is watching gnats and flies devour your baby's tears when he cries. The screens are torn and you pay so little rent you know they will never be fixed. Poverty means insects in your food, in your nose, in your eyes, and crawling over you when you sleep. Poverty is hoping it never rains because diapers won't dry when it rains and soon you are using newspapers. Poverty is seeing your children forever with runny noses. Paper handkerchiefs cost money and all your rags you need for other things. Even more costly are antihistamines. Poverty is cooking without food and cleaning without soap.

6 Poverty is asking for help. Have you ever had to ask for help, knowing your children will suffer unless you get it? Think about asking for a loan from a relative, if this is the only way you can imagine asking for help. I will tell you how it feels. You find out where the office is that you are supposed to visit. You circle that block four or five times. Thinking of your children, you go in. Everyone is very busy. Finally, someone comes out and you tell her that you need help. That never is the person you need to see. You go see another person, and after spilling the whole shame of your poverty all over the desk between you, you find that this isn't the right office after all—you must repeat the whole process, and it never is any easier at the next place.

7 You have asked for help, and after all it has a cost. You are again told to wait. You are told why, but you don't really hear because of the red cloud of shame and the rising black cloud of despair.

8 Poverty is remembering. It is remembering quitting school in junior high because "nice" children had been so cruel about my clothes and my smell. The attendance officer came. My mother told him I was pregnant. I wasn't, but she thought that I could get a job and help out. I had jobs off and on, but never long enough to learn anything. Mostly I remember being married. I was so young then. I am still young. For a time, we had all the things you have. There was a little house in another town, with hot water and everything. Then my husband lost his job. There was unemployment insurance for a while and what few jobs I could get. Soon, all our nice things were repossessed and we moved back here. I was pregnant then. This house didn't look so bad when we first moved in. Every week it gets worse. Nothing is ever fixed. We now had no money. There were a few odd jobs for my husband, but everything went for food then, as it does now. I don't know how we lived through three years and three babies, but we did. I'll tell you something, after the last baby I destroyed my marriage. It had been a good one, but could you keep on bringing children in this dirt? Did you ever think how much it costs for any kind of birth control? I knew my husband was leaving the day he left, but there were no good-bys between us. I hope he has been able to climb out of this mess somewhere. He never could hope with us to drag him down.

9 That's when I asked for help. When I got it, you know how much it was? It was, and is, seventy-eight dollars a month for the four of us; that is all I ever can get. Now you know why there is no soap, no needles and thread, no hot water, no aspirin, no worm medicine, no hand cream, no shampoo. None of these things forever and ever and ever. So that you can see clearly, I pay twenty dollars a month rent, and most of the rest goes for food. For grits and cornmeal, and rice and milk and beans. I try my best to use only the minimum electricity. If I use more, there is that much less for food.

10 Poverty is looking into a black future. Your children won't play with my boys. They will turn to other boys who steal to get what they want. I can already see them behind the bars of their prison instead of behind the bars of my poverty. Or they will turn to the freedom of alcohol or drugs, and find themselves enslaved. And my daughter? At best, there is for her a life like mine.

11 But you say to me, there are schools. Yes, there are schools. My children have no extra books, no magazines, no extra pencils, or crayons, or paper and the most important of all, they do not have health. They have worms, they have infections, they have pink-eye all summer. They do not sleep well on the floor, or with me in my one bed. They do not suffer from hunger, my seventy-eight dollars keeps

us alive, but they do suffer from malnutrition. Oh yes, I do remember what I was taught about health in school. It doesn't do much good. In some places there is a surplus commodities program. Not here. The county said it cost too much. There is a school lunch program. But I have two children who will already be damaged by the time they get to school.

12 But, you say to me, there are health clinics. Yes, there are health clinics and they are in the towns. I live out here eight miles from town. I can walk that far (even if it is sixteen miles both ways), but can my little children? My neighbor will take me when he goes; but he expects to get paid, *one way or another*. I bet you know my neighbor. He is that large man who spends his time at the gas station, the barbershop, and the corner store complaining about the government spending money on the immoral mothers of illegitimate children.

13 Poverty is an acid that drips on pride until all pride is worn away. Poverty is a chisel that chips on honor until honor is worn away. Some of you say that you would do *something* in my situation, and maybe you would, for the first week or the first month, but for year after year after year?

14 Even the poor can dream. A dream of a time when there is money. Money for the right kinds of food, for worm medicine, for iron pills, for toothbrushes, for hand cream, for a hammer and nails and a bit of screening, for a shovel, for a bit of paint, for some sheeting, for needles and thread. Money to pay *in money* for a trip to town. And, oh, money for hot water and money for soap. A dream of when asking for help does not eat away the last bit of pride. When the office you visit is as nice as the offices of other governmental agencies, when there are enough workers to help you quickly, when workers do not quit in defeat and despair. When you have to tell your story to only one person, and that person can send you for other help and you don't have to prove your poverty over and over again.

15 I have come out of my despair to tell you this. Remember I did not come from another place or another time. Others like me are all around you. Look at us with an angry heart, anger that will help you help me. Anger that will let you tell of me. The poor are always silent. Can you be silent too?

✧ *Evaluating the Text*

1. What trade-offs does Parker face in trying to keep her children clean and fed? Or whether she should work and send her three children to nursery school or leave them with her mother?

2. How does Parker answer those who make suggestions about how she might improve her situation?

3. What damages and consequences for her children does Parker foresee because she is unable to help them now?

✧ *Exploring Different Perspectives*

1. Compare Parker's circumstances to those of Flavio's family in the favelas of Rio de Janeiro as described by Gordon Parks.

2. How does poverty function as a caste system in much the same way as being an untouchable is in India, as described by Viramma in "A Pariah's Life"?

✧ *Extending Viewpoints through Writing and Research*

1. How did this essay change your ideas about what it means to be poor in the United States?

2. Have you known someone who had to rely on disability compensation, welfare, or unemployment benefits? If so, to what extent were his or her experiences similar to those described by Parker?

Gordon Parks

Flavio's Home

Gordon Parks (1912–2006) was a filmmaker, composer, and writer for whom photography was an enduring passion. He was the first African American photographer hired by Life *and* Vogue *magazines. In the following essay, drawn from* Voices in the Mirror *(1990), we accompany him to the favelas outside Rio de Janeiro and come to know a courageous twelve-year-old boy, Flavio. Parks's later works include* A Hungry Heart: A Memoir *(2005).*

Before You Read

Do ads depicting Rio de Janeiro mention the favelas that surround this major city?

1 I've never lost my fierce grudge against poverty. It is the most savage of all human afflictions, claiming victims who can't mobilize their efforts against it, who often lack strength to digest what little food they scrounge up to survive. It keeps growing, multiplying, spreading like a cancer. In my wanderings I attack it wherever I can—in barrios, slums and favelas.[1]

2 Catacumba was the name of the favela where I found Flavio da Silva. It was wickedly hot. The noon sun baked the mud-rot of the wet mountainside. Garbage and human excrement clogged the open sewers snaking down the slopes. José Gallo, a *Life* reporter, and I rested in the shade of a jacaranda tree halfway up Rio de Janeiro's most infamous deathtrap. Below and above us were a maze of shacks, but in the distance alongside the beach stood the gleaming white homes of the rich.

3 Breathing hard, balancing a tin of water on his head, a small boy climbed toward us. He was miserably thin, naked but for filthy denim shorts. His legs resembled sticks covered with skin and screwed into his feet. Death was all over him, in his sunken eyes, cheeks and jaundiced coloring. He stopped for breath, coughing, his chest heaving as water slopped over his bony shoulders. Then jerking sideways like a

[1]favela: Slums on the outskirts of Rio de Janeiro, Brazil, inhabited by seven hundred thousand people.

mechanical toy, he smiled a smile I will never forget. Turning, he went on up the mountainside.

4 The detailed *Life* assignment in my back pocket was to find an impoverished father with a family, to examine his earnings, political leanings, religion, friends, dreams and frustrations. I had been sent to do an essay on poverty. This frail boy bent under his load said more to me about poverty than a dozen poor fathers. I touched Gallo, and we got up and followed the boy to where he entered a shack near the top of the mountainside. It was a leaning crumpled place of old plankings with a rusted tin roof. From inside we heard the babblings of several children. José knocked. The door opened and the boy stood smiling with a bawling naked baby in his arms.

5 Still smiling, he whacked the baby's rump, invited us in and offered us a box to sit on. The only other recognizable furniture was a sagging bed and a broken baby's crib. Flavio was twelve, and with Gallo acting as interpreter, he introduced his younger brothers and sisters: "Mario, the bad one; Baptista, the good one; Albia, Isabel and the baby Zacarias." Two other girls burst into the shack, screaming and pounding on one another. Flavio jumped in and parted them. "Shut up, you two." He pointed at the older girl. "That's Maria, the nasty one." She spit in his face. He smacked her and pointed to the smaller sister. "That's Luzia. She thinks she's pretty."

6 Having finished the introductions, he went to build a fire under the stove—a rusted, bent top of an old gas range resting on several bricks. Beneath it was a piece of tin that caught the hot coals. The shack was about six by ten feet. Its grimy walls were a patchwork of misshapen boards with large gaps between them, revealing other shacks below stilted against the slopes. The floor, rotting under layers of grease and dirt, caught shafts of light slanting down through spaces in the roof. A large hole in the far corner served as a toilet. Beneath that hole was the sloping mountainside. Pockets of poverty in New York's Harlem, on Chicago's south side, in Puerto Rico's infamous El Fungito seemed pale by comparison. None of them had prepared me for this one in the favela of Catacumba.

7 Flavio washed rice in a large dishpan, then washed Zacarias's feet in the same water. But even that dirty water wasn't to be wasted. He tossed in a chunk of lye soap and ordered each child to wash up. When they were finished he splashed the water over the dirty floor, and, dropping to his knees, he scrubbed the planks until the black suds sank in. Just before sundown he put beans on the stove to warm, then left, saying he would be back shortly. "Don't let them burn," he cautioned Maria. "If they do and Poppa beats me, you'll get it later." Maria, happy to get at the licking spoon, switched over and began to stir the beans. Then slyly she dipped out a spoonful and swallowed them. Luzia eyed her. "I see you. I'm going to tell on you for stealing our supper."

8 Maria's eyes flashed anger. "You do and I'll beat you, you little bitch." Luzia threw a stick at Maria and fled out the door. Zacarias dropped off to sleep. Mario, the bad one, slouched in a corner and sucked his thumb. Isabel and Albia sat on the floor clinging to each other with a strange tenderness. Isabel held onto Albia's hair and Albia clutched at Isabel's neck. They appeared frozen in an act of quiet violence.

9 Flavio returned with wood, dumped it beside the stove and sat down to rest for a few minutes, then went down the mountain for more water. It was dark when he finally came back, his body sagging from exhaustion. No longer smiling, he suddenly had the look of an old man and by now we could see that he kept the family going. In the closed torment of that pitiful shack, he was waging a hopeless battle against starvation. The da Silva children were living in a coffin.

10 When at last the parents came in, Gallo and I seemed to be part of the family. Flavio had already told them we were there. "Gordunn Americano!" Luzia said, pointing at me. José, the father, viewed us with skepticism. Nair, his pregnant wife, seemed tired beyond speaking. Hardly acknowledging our presence, she picked up Zacarias, placed him on her shoulder and gently patted his behind. Flavio scurried about like a frightened rat, his silence plainly expressing the fear he held of his father. Impatiently, José da Silva waited for Flavio to serve dinner. He sat in the center of the bed with his legs crossed beneath him, frowning, waiting. There were only three tin plates. Flavio filled them with black beans and rice, then placed them before his father. José da Silva tasted them, chewed for several moments, then nodded his approval for the others to start. Only he and Nair had spoons; the children ate with their fingers. Flavio ate off the top of a coffee can. Afraid to offer us food, he edged his rice and beans toward us, gesturing for us to take some. We refused. He smiled, knowing we understood.

11 Later, when we got down to the difficult business of obtaining permission from José da Silva to photograph his family, he hemmed and hawed, wallowing in the pleasant authority of the decision maker. He finally gave in, but his manner told us that he expected something in return. As we were saying good night Flavio began to cough violently. For a few moments his lungs seemed to be tearing apart. I wanted to get away as quickly as possible. It was cowardly of me, but the bluish cast of his skin beneath the sweat, the choking and spitting were suddenly unbearable.

12 Gallo and I moved cautiously down through the darkness trying not to appear as strangers. The Catacumba was no place for strangers after sundown. Desperate criminals hid out there. To hunt them out, the police came in packs, but only in daylight. Gallo cautioned me. "If you get caught up here after dark it's best to stay at the da Silvas' until morning." As we drove toward the city the large white buildings

of the rich loomed up. The world behind us seemed like a bad dream. I had already decided to get the boy Flavio to a doctor, and as quickly as possible.

13 The plush lobby of my hotel on the Copacabana waterfront was crammed with people in formal attire. With the stink of the favela in my clothes, I hurried to the elevator hoping no passengers would be aboard. But as the door was closing a beautiful girl in a white lace gown stepped in. I moved as far away as possible. Her escort entered behind her, swept her into his arms and they indulged in a kiss that lasted until they exited on the next floor. Neither of them seemed to realize that I was there. The room I returned to seemed to be oversized; the da Silva shack would have fitted into one corner of it. The steak dinner I had would have fed the da Silvas for three days.

14 Billowing clouds blanketed Mount Corcovado as we approached the favela the following morning. Suddenly the sun burst through, silhouetting Cristo Redentor, the towering sculpture of Christ with arms extended, its back turned against the slopes of Catacumba. The square at the entrance to the favela bustled with hundreds of favelados. Long lines waited at the sole water spigot. Others waited at the only toilet on the entire mountainside. Women, unable to pay for soap, beat dirt from their wash at laundry tubs. Men, burdened with lumber, picks and shovels and tools important to their existence threaded their way through the noisy throngs. Dogs snarled, barked and fought. Woodsmoke mixed with the stench of rotting things. In the mist curling over the higher paths, columns of favelados climbed like ants with wood and water cans on their heads.

15 We came upon Nair bent over her tub of wash. She wiped away sweat with her apron and managed a smile. We asked for her husband and she pointed to a tiny shack off to her right. This was José's store, where he sold kerosene and bleach. He was sitting on a box, dozing. Sensing our presence, he awoke and commenced complaining about his back. "It kills me. The doctors don't help because I have no money. Always talk and a little pink pill that does no good. Ah, what is to become of me?" A woman came to buy bleach. He filled her bottle. She dropped a few coins and as she walked away his eyes stayed on her backside until she was out of sight. Then he was complaining about his back again.

16 "How much do you earn a day?" Gallo asked.

17 "Seventy-five cents. On a good day maybe a dollar."

18 "Why aren't the kids in school?"

19 "I don't have money for the clothes they need to go to school."

20 "Has Flavio seen a doctor?"

21 He pointed to a one-story wooden building. "That's the clinic right there. They're mad because I built my store in front of their place. I won't tear it down so they won't help my kids. Talk, talk, talk and

pink pills." We bid him good-bye and started climbing, following mud trails, jutting rock, slime-filled holes and shack after shack propped against the slopes on shaky pilings. We sidestepped a dead cat covered with maggots. I held my breath for an instant, only to inhale the stench of human excrement and garbage. Bare feet and legs with open sores climbed above us—evils of the terrible soil they trod every day, and there were seven hundred thousand or more afflicted people in favelas around Rio alone. Touching me, Gallo pointed to Flavio climbing ahead of us carrying firewood. He stopped to glance at a man descending with a small coffin on his shoulder. A woman and a small child followed him. When I lifted my camera, grumbling erupted from a group of men sharing beer beneath a tree.

22 "They're threatening," Gallo said, "Keep moving. They fear cameras. Think they're evil eyes bringing bad luck." Turning to watch the funeral procession, Flavio caught sight of us and waited. When we took the wood from him he protested, saying he was used to carrying it. He gave in when I hung my camera around his neck. Then, beaming, he climbed on ahead of us.

23 The fog had lifted and in the crisp morning light the shack looked more squalid. Inside the kids seemed even noisier. Flavio smiled and spoke above their racket. "Someday I want to live in a real house on a real street with good pots and pans and a bed with sheets." He lit the fire to warm leftovers from the night before. Stale rice and beans—for breakfast and supper. No lunch; midday eating was out of the question. Smoke rose and curled up through the ceiling's cracks. An air current forced it back, filling the place and Flavio's lungs with fumes. A coughing spasm doubled him up, turned his skin blue under viscous sweat. I handed him a cup of water, but he waved it away. His stomach tightened as he dropped to his knees. His veins throbbed as if they would burst. Frustrated, we could only watch; there was nothing we could do to help. Strangely, none of his brothers or sisters appeared to notice. None of them stopped doing whatever they were doing. Perhaps they had seen it too often. After five interminable minutes it was over, and he got to his feet, smiling as though it had all been a joke. "Maria, it's time for Zacarias to be washed!"

24 "But there's rice in the pan!"

25 "Dump it in another pan—and don't spill water!"

26 Maria picked up Zacarias, who screamed, not wanting to be washed. Irritated, Maria gave him a solid smack on his bare bottom. Flavio stepped over and gave her the same, then a free-for-all started with Flavio, Maria and Mario slinging fists at one another. Mario got one in the eye and fled the shack calling Flavio a dirty son-of-a-bitch. Zacarias wound up on the floor sucking his thumb and escaping his washing. The black bean and rice breakfast helped to get things back to normal. Now it was time to get Flavio to the doctor.

27 The clinic was crowded with patients—mothers and children covered with open sores, a paralytic teenager, a man with an ear in a state of decay, an aged blind couple holding hands in doubled darkness. Throughout the place came wailings of hunger and hurt. Flavio sat nervously between Gallo and me. "What will the doctor do to me?" he kept asking.

28 "We'll see. We'll wait and see."

29 In all, there were over fifty people. Finally, after two hours, it was Flavio's turn and he broke out in a sweat, though he smiled at the nurse as he passed through the door to the doctor's office. The nurse ignored it; in this place of misery, smiles were unexpected.

30 The doctor, a large, beady-eyed man with a crew cut, had an air of impatience. Hardly acknowledging our presence, he began to examine the frightened Flavio. "Open your mouth. Say 'Ah.' Jump up and down. Breathe out. Take off those pants. Bend over. Stand up. Cough. Cough louder. Louder." He did it all with such cold efficiency. Then he spoke to us in English so Flavio wouldn't understand. "This little chap has just about had it." My heart sank. Flavio was smiling, happy to be over with the examination. He was handed a bottle of cough medicine and a small box of pink pills, then asked to step outside and wait.

31 "This the da Silva kid?"

32 "Yes."

33 "What's your interest in him?"

34 "We want to help in some way."

35 "I'm afraid you're too late. He's wasted with bronchial asthma, malnutrition and, I suspect, tuberculosis. His heart, lungs and teeth are all bad." He paused and wearily rubbed his forehead. "All that at the ripe old age of twelve. And these hills are packed with other kids just as bad off. Last year ten thousand died from dysentery alone. But what can we do? You saw what's waiting outside. It's like this every day. There's hardly enough money to buy aspirin. A few wealthy people who care help keep us going." He was quiet for a moment. "Maybe the right climate, the right diet, and constant medical care might . . ." He stopped and shook his head. "Naw. That poor lad's finished. He might last another year—maybe not." We thanked him and left.

36 "What did he say?" Flavio asked as we scaled the hill.

37 "Everything's going to be all right, Flav. There's nothing to worry about."

38 It had clouded over again by the time we reached the top. The rain swept in, clearing the mountain of Corcovado. The huge Christ figure loomed up again with clouds swirling around it. And to it I said a quick prayer for the boy walking beside us. He smiled as if he had read my thoughts. "Papa says 'El Cristo' has turned his back on the favela."

39 "You're going to be all right, Flavio."

How does this photo of the favela in Rio de Janeiro capture the desperate circumstances in which Flavio and his family live?

40 "I'm not scared of death. It's my brothers and sisters I worry about. What would they do?"

41 "You'll be all right, Flavio."

✧ *Evaluating the Text*

1. What picture does Parks present of the work Flavio must do to look after his family?
2. Where is Parks staying in Rio de Janeiro and why does he include a description of his accommodations?
3. According to Parks, what sort of future awaits Flavio?

✧ *Exploring Different Perspectives*

1. How does the scarcity of nourishing food play a role in the accounts of Parks and Jo Goodwin Parker in "What Is Poverty?"
2. How do Parks and Mary Crow Dog and Richard Erdoes (see "Civilize Them with a Stick") use descriptions of contrasting environments to get their point across?

✧ *Extending Viewpoints through Writing and Research*

1. Have you ever met anyone who was as courageous as Flavio in very difficult circumstances? Describe this person.
2. What changes has the Brazilian government planned to make since the announcement that Brazil will host the Olympic games?

Kate Chopin

Désirée's Baby

1 *Kate Chopin (1851–1904) was born Katherine O'Flaherty, the daughter of a successful St. Louis businessman and his French Creole wife. After her father died in 1855, Kate was raised by her mother and great-grandmother. When she was nineteen, she married Oscar Chopin and accompanied him to New Orleans where he established himself as a cotton broker. After his business failed, they moved to his family plantation in Louisiana where he opened a general store. After his sudden death in 1883, Chopin managed the plantation for a year, but then decided to return to St. Louis with her six children. She began to submit stories patterned on the realistic fiction of Guy de Maupassant to local papers and national magazines, including the* Saturday Evening Post *and* Atlantic Monthly. *Her stories of Creole life were widely praised for their realistic delineation of Creole manners and customs and were later collected in* Bayou Folk *(1894) and* A Night in Acadie *(1897). Her novel* The Awakening *(1899), although widely praised as a masterpiece for its frank depiction of its heroine's sexual awakening and need for self-fulfillment, created a public controversy. Chopin's uncompromising delineation of the pressures of class and race in Louisiana at the time are clearly seen in the poignant story "Désirée's Baby"(1899).*

Before You Read

Consider the extent to which the character of Désirée serves as a vehicle for the expression of Chopin's views on race and class.

1 As the day was pleasant, Madame Valmondé drove over to L'Abri to see Désirée and the baby.

2 It made her laugh to think of Désirée with a baby. Why, it seems but yesterday that Désirée was little more than a baby herself; when Monsieur in riding through the gateway of Valmondé had found her lying asleep in the shadow of the big stone pillar.

3 The little one awoke in his arms and began to cry for "Dada." That was as much as she could do or say. Some people thought she might have strayed there of her own accord, for she was of the toddling age. The prevailing belief was that she had been purposely left by a party of Texans, whose canvas-covered wagons, late in the day, had crossed the ferry that Coton Maïs kept, just below the plantation. In time Madame

Valmondé abandoned every speculation but the one that Désirée had been sent to her by a beneficent Providence to be the child of her affection, seeing that she was without child of the flesh. For the girl grew to be beautiful and gentle, affectionate and sincere—the idol of Valmondé.

4 It was no wonder, when she stood one day against the stone pillar in whose shadow she had lain asleep, eighteen years before, that Armand Aubigny riding by and seeing her there, had fallen in love with her. That was the way all the Aubignys fell in love, as if struck by a pistol shot. The wonder was that he had not loved her before; for he had known her since his father brought him home from Paris, a boy of eight, after his mother died there. The passion that awoke in him that day, when he saw her at the gate, swept along like an avalanche, or like a prairie fire, or like anything that drives headlong over all obstacles.

5 Madame Valmondé bent her portly figure over Désirée and kissed her, holding her an instant tenderly in her arms. Then she turned to the child.

6 "This is not the baby!" she exclaimed, in startled tones. French was the language spoken at Valmondé in those days.

7 "I knew you would be astonished," laughed Désirée, "at the way he has grown. The little *cochon de lait!*[1] Look at his legs, mamma, and his hands and fingernails,—real fingernails. Zandrine had to cut them this morning. Isn't it true, Zandrine?"

8 The woman bowed her turbaned head majestically, "Mais si, Madame."

9 "And the way he cries," went on Désirée, "is deafening. Armand heard him the other day as far away as La Blanche's cabin."

10 Madame Valmondé had never removed her eyes from the child. She lifted it and walked with it over to the window that was lightest. She scanned the baby narrowly, then looked as searchingly at Zandrine, whose face was turned to gaze across the fields.

11 "Yes, the child has grown, has changed" said Madame Valmondé, slowly, as she replaced it beside its mother. "What does Armand say?"

12 Désirée's face became suffused with a glow that was happiness itself.

13 "Oh, Armand is the proudest father in the parish, I believe, chiefly because it is a boy, to bear his name; though he says not—that he would have loved a girl as well. But I know it isn't true. I know he says that to please me. And mamma," she added, drawing Madame Valmondé's head down to her, and speaking in a whisper, "he hasn't punished one of them—not one of them—since baby is born. Even Négrillon, who pretended to have burnt his leg that he might rest from work—he only laughed, and said Négrillon was a great scamp. Oh, mama, I'm so happy; it frightens me."

[1]*cochon de lait*: Literally "pig of milk." A big feeder.

14 What Désirée said was true. Marriage, and later the birth of his son, had softened Armand Aubigny's imperious and exacting nature greatly. This was what made the gentle Désirée so happy, for she loved him desperately. When he frowned she trembled, but loved him. When he smiled, she asked no greater blessing of God. But Armand's dark, handsome face had not often been disfigured by frowns since the day he fell in love with her.

15 When the baby was about three months old, Désirée awoke one day to the conviction that there was something in the air menacing her peace. It was at first too subtle to grasp. It had only been a disquieting suggestion; an air of mystery among the blacks; unexpected visits from far-off neighbors who could hardly account for their coming. Then a strange, an awful change in her husband's manner, which she dared not ask him to explain. When he spoke to her, it was with averted eyes, from which the old love light seemed to have gone out. He absented himself from home; and when there, avoided her presence and that of her child, without excuse. And the very spirit of Satan seemed suddenly to take hold of him in his dealings with the slaves. Désirée was miserable enough to die.

16 She sat in her room, one hot afternoon, in her *peignoir,* listlessly drawing through her fingers the strands of her long, silky brown hair that hung about her shoulders. The baby, half naked, lay asleep upon her own great mahogany bed, that was like a sumptuous throne, with its satin-lined half canopy. One of La Blanche's little quadroon boys—half naked too—stood fanning the child slowly with a fan of peacock feathers. Désirée's eyes had been fixed absently and sadly upon the baby, while she was striving to penetrate the threatening mist that she felt closing about her. She looked from her child to the boy who stood beside him; and back again, over and over. "Ah!" It was a cry that she could not help, which she was not conscious of having uttered. The blood turned like ice in her veins, and a clammy moisture gathered upon her face.

17 She tried to speak to the little quadroon boy; but no sound would come, at first. When he heard his name uttered, he looked up, and his mistress was pointing to the door. He laid aside the great, soft fan, and obediently stole away, over the polished floor, on his bare tiptoes.

18 She stayed motionless, with gaze riveted upon her child, and her face the picture of fright.

19 Presently her husband entered the room, and without noticing her, went to a table and began to search among some papers which covered it.

20 "Armand," she called to him, in a voice which must have stabbed him, if he was human. But he did not notice. "Armand," she said again. Then she rose and tottered towards him. "Armand," she panted once more, clutching his arm, "look at our child. What does it mean? Tell me."

21 He coldly but gently loosened her fingers from about his arm and thrust the hand away from him. "Tell me what it means!" she cried despairingly.

22 "It means," he answered lightly, "that the child is not white; it means that you are not white."

23 A quick conception of all that this accusation meant for her nerved her with unwonted courage to deny it. "It is a lie; it is not true, I am white! Look at my hair, it is brown; and my eyes are gray, Armand, you know they are gray. And my skin is fair," seizing his wrist. "Look at my hand, whiter than yours, Armand," she laughed hysterically.

24 "As white as La Blanche's," he returned cruelly, and went away leaving her alone with their child.

25 When she could hold a pen in her hand, she sent a despairing letter to Madame Valmondé.

26 "My mother, they tell me I am not white. Armand has told me I am not white. For God's sake tell them it is not true. You must know it is not true. I shall die. I must die. I cannot be so unhappy, and live."

27 The answer that came was as brief:

28 "My own Désirée: Come home to Valmondé; back to your mother who loves you. Come with your child."

29 When the letter reached Désirée she went with it to her husband's study, and laid it open upon the desk before which he sat. She was like a stone image: silent, white, motionless after she placed it there.

30 In silence he ran his cold eyes over the written words. He said nothing. "Shall I go, Armand?" she asked in tones sharp with agonized suspense.

31 "Yes, go."

32 "Do you want me to go?"

33 "Yes, I want you to go."

34 He thought Almighty God had dealt cruelly and unjustly with him; and felt, somehow, that he was paying Him back in kind when he stabbed thus into his wife's soul. Moreover he no longer loved her, because of the unconscious injury she had brought upon his home and his name.

35 She turned away like one stunned by a blow, and walked slowly towards the door, hoping he would call her back.

36 "Good-by, Armand," she moaned.

37 He did not answer her. That was his last blow at fate.

38 Désirée went in search of her child. Zandrine was pacing the sombre gallery with it. She took the little one from the nurse's arms with no word of explanation, and descending the steps, walked away, under the live-oak branches.

39 It was an October afternoon; the sun was just sinking. Out in the still fields the Negroes were picking cotton.

40 Désirée had not changed the thin white garment nor the slippers which she wore. Her hair was uncovered and the sun's rays brought a golden gleam from its brown meshes. She did not take the broad, beaten road which led to the far-off plantation of Valmondé. She walked across a deserted field, where the stubble bruised her tender feet, so delicately shod, and tore her thin gown to shreds.

41 She disappeared among the reeds and willows that grew thick along the banks of the deep, sluggish bayou; and she did not come back again.

42 Some weeks later there was a curious scene enacted at L'Abri. In the centre of the smoothly swept back yard was a great bonfire. Armand Aubigny sat in the wide hallway that commanded a view of the spectacle; and it was he who dealt out to a half dozen negroes the material which kept this fire ablaze.

43 A graceful cradle of willow, with all its dainty furbishings, was laid upon the pyre, which had already been fed with the richness of a priceless *layette*. Then there were silk gowns, and velvet and satin ones added to these; laces, too, and embroideries; bonnets and gloves; for the *corbeille*[2] had been of rare quality.

44 The last thing to go was a tiny bundle of letters; innocent little scribblings that Désirée had sent to him during the days of their espousal. There was the remnant of one back in the drawer from which he took them. But it was not Désirée's; it was part of an old letter from his mother to his father. He read it. She was thanking God for the blessing of her husband's love:

45 "But, above all," she wrote, "night and day, I thank the good God for having so arranged our lives that our dear Armand will never know that his mother, who adores him, belongs to the race that is cursed with the brand of slavery."

✧ *Evaluating the Text*

1. What can you infer about Armand's character and his past behavior from the fact that he has not punished one slave since his baby was born? How does his behavior toward Désirée change after the baby is three months old? What causes this change in his behavior?

2. What did you assume Désirée would do when she realizes Armand values his social standing more than he does her? In retrospect, what clues would have pointed you toward the truth disclosed at the end of the story?

---

[2]*corbeille*: a basket of linens, clothing, and accessories collected in anticipation of a baby's birth.

✧ *Exploring Different Perspectives*

1. How does race serve the same function in Chopin's story as caste does in India (see Viramma," "A Pariah's Life")?

2. Compare the role that race plays in Chopin's story and the one it plays in Gordon Parks's "Flavio's Home."

✧ *Extending Viewpoints through Writing and Research*

1. In a short essay, discuss the picture you formed of the society in which Chopin's story took place (late 1800s in Louisiana) and the extent to which race and class determined people's behavior.

2. At the end of the story we discover that Armand is of mixed racial parentage and assume that Désireée is white. How would the impact of the story change if we also knew that Désirée was of a mixed racial background as well as Armand?

3. For an analysis of Kate Chopin's life and works consult http://www.empirezine.com/spotlight/chopin/chopin1.htm.

Connecting Cultures

Mary Crow Dog and Richard Erdoes, "Civilize Them with a Stick"

How do Mary Crow Dog and Richard Erdoes, and Judith Ortiz Cofer in "The Myth of the Latin Woman" in Chapter 3 have to contend with limiting stereotypes?

Viramma, "A Pariah's Life"

Compare the superstitions and cultural beliefs in Viramma's account with those descibed by Gino Del Guercio in "The Secrets of Voodoo in Haiti" in Chapter 6.

Immaculée Ilibagiza, "Left to Tell"

In what way do Ilibagiza and Latifa Ali (with Richard Shears) in "Betrayed" in Chapter 3 fear for their lives because of cultural, ethnic, and religious intolerance?

Jo Goodwin Parker, "What Is Poverty?"

Discuss the deprivations caused by poverty in Parker's account with those caused by racial discrimination in Frederick Douglass's "My Bondage and My Freedom" in Chapter 7.

Gordon Parks, "Flavio's Home"

Compare the very different social environments and aspirations in Brazil in Parks's account with Don Kulick's and Thaïs Machado-Borges's in "Leaky" in Chapter 3.

Kate Chopin, "Désirée's Baby"

In what way does the color of one's skin overwhelmingly determine social status in Chopin's story and in Don Kulick's and Thaïs Machado-Borges's in "Leaky" in Chapter 3?

6

Experiencing a Different Culture

One's destination is never a place, but rather a new way of looking at things.

—Henry Miller (1891–1980), U.S. author; from *Big Sur and the Oranges of Hieronymus Bosch,* "The Oranges of the Millennium" (1957)

In some ways, our age—the age of the displaced person, and those whom society considers deviant, abnormal, or simply different—is defined by the condition of exile and otherness. Being brought up in one world and then emigrating to a different culture inevitably produces feelings of alienation. Moving to another country involves living among people who dress differently, eat unfamiliar foods, have puzzling customs, and speak another language. Without insight into the norms that govern behavior in a new environment, it is often difficult for immigrants to interpret the actions of others—to know what particular facial expressions and gestures might mean, what assumptions govern physical contact, how people express and resolve conflicts, or what topics of conversation are deemed appropriate.

The works in this chapter offer insights into how various groups define themselves and are perceived by others. Ralph Linton in "One Hundred Percent American" reveals how thoroughly international Americans are despite their occasional xenophobia. Poranee Natadecha-Sponsel in "Individualism as an American Cultural Value" describes the often perplexing cultural differences that she experienced after moving to America from Thailand. David R. Counts in "Too Many Bananas" reveals the many lessons about reciprocity he learned while doing field work in New Guinea. In "Doing Fieldwork among the Yąnomamö," Napoleon A. Chagnon describes the culture shock he experienced while living among a contentious tribe in Brazil. Gino Del Guercio in "The Secrets of Voodoo in Haiti" reveals that, in contrast to its stereotyped image, voodoo is part of a cohesive system of social control in Haiti. In "Of Ice and Men," Cameron M. Smith explains why the people who live in the Arctic do not want the polar bear to be declared a threatened species. The editors of the *Herald Sun*, a Melbourne newspaper, focus on the role that polar bears have come to play as a symbol of a species endangered by global warming. Fareed Zakaria in "The Challenger" provides startling evidence for China's emergence as a world power.

Taken together, these selections explore the way the assumptions we bring when visiting other cultures often need to be rethought.

To help you understand how the works in this chapter relate to each other, you might use one or several of the following guidelines before writing about experiencing a different culture.

1. What insight does the author provide into the values of other cultures?
2. In what way does the experience of encountering a different culture challenge the writer's assumptions and/or enhance his or her understanding?
3. What expertise or training does the author bring to his or her analysis?
4. Does the author approach the subject as a participant or as a reporter?
5. How was your view of the place visited by the author changed after reading the work?
6. Which of the different cultures discussed in this chapter would you wish to visit?

Recommended Films on This Theme

- *Z* (Algeria, 1969) A political thriller about the chaotic aftermath of the assassination of a popular liberal senator in Greece in the 1960s;
- *Prisoner of the Mountains* (Russia, 1996) A story of two Russian prisoners taken hostage in a remote Muslim village who bond with each other and their captors;
- *Hotel Rwanda* (Rwanda, 2004) The true story of a hotel manager who saves a thousand Tutsis during the civil war in Rwanda in 1994;
- *District 9* (New Zealand, 2009) A science fiction spectacular set in Johannesburg, South Africa, where a colony of exiled aliens who resemble prawns (who are forced to live in slums) try to return to their home;
- *Avatar* (United States, 2009) The blockbuster that puts an American marine into a spiritual, nativist culture on a distant planet.

Ralph Linton

One Hundred Percent American

Ralph Linton (1893–1953), one of the most prominent American anthropologists, was born in Philadelphia; graduated from Swarthmore College in 1915; and did graduate work at the University of Pennsylvania, Columbia University, and Harvard, where he received a Ph.D. in 1925. His many experiences include being a curator of Native American materials at the Field Museum of Chicago and doing extensive field work in Madagascar. He also taught at the University of Wisconsin, at Columbia University, and at Yale University. His best known works include The Study of Man *(1936), from which the following essay is drawn, and* The Tree of Culture, *published posthumously in 1955.*

Before You Read

How many of the materials you use in everyday life have been invented or manufactured elsewhere?

1 There can be no question about the average American's Americanism or his desire to preserve this precious heritage at all costs. Nevertheless, some insidious foreign ideas have already wormed their way into his civilization without his realizing what was going on. Thus dawn finds the unsuspecting patriot garbed in pajamas, a garment of East Indian origin; and lying in a bed built on a pattern which originated in either Persia or Asia Minor.[1] He is muffled to the ears in un-American materials: cotton, first domesticated in India; linen, domesticated in the Near East; wool from an animal native to Asia Minor; or silk whose uses were first discovered by the Chinese. All these substances have been transformed into cloth by methods invented in Southwestern Asia. If the weather is cold enough he may even be sleeping under an eiderdown quilt invented in Scandinavia.

2 On awakening he glances at the clock, a medieval European invention, uses one potent Latin word in abbreviated form, rises in haste, and goes to the bathroom. Here, if he stops to think about it, he must feel himself in the presence of a great American institution; he will have heard stories of both the quality and frequency of foreign plumbing and will know that in no other country does the average man perform his ablutions in the midst of such splendor. But the insidious foreign influence pursues him even here. Glass was invented by the

ancient Egyptians, the use of glazed tiles for floors and walls in the Near East, porcelain in China, and the art of enameling on metal by Mediterranean artisans of the Bronze Age. Even his bathtub and toilet are but slightly modified copies of Roman originals. The only purely American contribution to the ensemble is the steam radiator, against which our patriot very briefly and unintentionally places his posterior.

3 In this bathroom the American washes with soap invented by the ancient Gauls. Next he cleans his teeth, a subversive European practice which did not invade America until the latter part of the eighteenth century. He then shaves, a masochistic rite first developed by the heathen priests of ancient Egypt and Sumer. The process is made less of a penance by the fact that his razor is of steel, an iron-carbon alloy discovered in either India or Turkestan. Lastly, he dries himself on a Turkish towel.

4 Returning to the bedroom, the unconscious victim of un-American practices removes his clothes from a chair, invented in the Near East, and proceeds to dress. He puts on close-fitting tailored garments whose form derives from the skin clothing of the ancient nomads of the Asiatic steppes and fastens them with buttons whose prototypes appeared in Europe at the close of the Stone Age. This costume is appropriate enough for outdoor exercise in a cold climate, but is quite unsuited to American summers, steam-heated houses, and Pullmans.[2] Nevertheless, foreign ideas and habits hold the unfortunate man in thrall even when common sense tells him that the authentically American costume of gee string and moccasins would be far more comfortable. He puts on his feet stiff coverings made from hide prepared by a process invented in ancient Egypt and cut to a pattern which can be traced back to ancient Greece, and makes sure that they are properly polished, also a Greek idea. Lastly, he ties about his neck a strip of bright-colored cloth which is a vestigial survival of the shoulder shawls worn by seventeenth century Greeks. He gives himself a final appraisal in the mirror, an old Mediterranean invention, and goes downstairs to breakfast.

5 Here a whole new series of foreign things confronts him. His food and drink are placed before him in pottery vessels, the proper name of which—china—is sufficient evidence of their origin. His fork is a medieval Italian invention and his spoon a copy of a Roman original. He will usually begin the meal with coffee, an Abyssinian[3] plant first discovered by the Arabs. The American is quite likely to need it to dispel the morning-after effects of overindulgence in fermented drinks, invented in the Near East; or distilled ones, invented by the alchemists of medieval Europe. Whereas the Arabs took their coffee straight, he will probably sweeten it with sugar, discovered in India; and dilute it with cream, both the domestication of cattle and the technique of milking having originated in Asia Minor.

6 If our patriot is old-fashioned enough to adhere to the so-called American breakfast, his coffee will be accompanied by an orange, domesticated in the Mediterranean region, a cantaloupe domesticated in Persia, or grapes domesticated in Asia Minor. He will follow this with a bowl of cereal made from grain domesticated in the Near East and prepared by methods also invented there. From this he will go on to waffles, a Scandinavian invention with plenty of butter, originally a Near Eastern cosmetic. As a side dish he may have the egg of a bird domesticated in Southeastern Asia or strips of the flesh of an animal domesticated in the same region, which has been salted and smoked by a process invented in Northern Europe.

7 Breakfast over, he places upon his head a molded piece of felt, invented by the nomads of Eastern Asia, and, if it looks like rain, puts on outer shoes of rubber, discovered by the ancient Mexicans, and takes an umbrella, invented in India. He then sprints for his train—the train, not sprinting, being an English invention. At the station he pauses for a moment to buy a newspaper, paying for it with coins invented in ancient Lydia.[4] Once on board he settles back to inhale the fumes of a cigarette invented in Mexico, or a cigar invented in Brazil.[5] Meanwhile, he reads the news of the day, imprinted in characters invented by the ancient Semites by a process invented in Germany upon a material invented in China. As he scans the latest editorial pointing out the dire results to our institutions of accepting foreign ideas, he will not fail to thank a Hebrew God in an Indo-European language that he is a one hundred percent (decimal system invented by the Greeks) American (from Americus Vespucci, Italian geographer).

NOTES

1. A peninsula in West Asia between the Black and Mediterranean seas, including most of Asiatic Turkey.
2. A railroad sleeping car or parlor car invented by U.S. inventor and railroad car designer George Mortimer Pullman (1831–1897).
3. The former name of Ethiopia, a nation in East Africa.
4. An ancient kingdom in West Asia Minor.
5. A product prepared from the leaves of a plant indigenous to the New World.

✧ *Evaluating the Text*

1. How do the contributions from other cultures that Linton describes alter presumptions of an archetypal American identity?
2. How is Linton's analysis structured as a chronological account of a typical day in an American's life?
3. How would you characterize Linton's tone and his purpose in writing this analysis?

✧ *Exploring Different Perspectives*

1. How do both Linton and Fareed Zakaria in "The Challenger" deconstruct the concept of being American and the nature of China as a world power?
2. How do both Linton and Poranee Natadecha-Sponsel in "Individualism as an American Cultural Value" illustrate the benefits of looking at American culture from an external perspective?

✧ *Extending Viewpoints through Writing and Research*

1. Linton ends his essay when his average American boards a train, smokes, and reads the news. If you were to extend this average American's day, what additional contributions of other cultures would you be able to identify?
2. Keep a diary of a typical day or two in your life and research the origins of common objects and foods, other than those identified by Linton.
3. Deconstruct the foreign contributions to a supposedly American product such as a car. In what country were the components made, where was it assembled, and who paid for the advertising and marketing?

Poranee Natadecha-Sponsel

Individualism as an American Cultural Value

Poranee Natadecha-Sponsel was born and raised in a multiethnic Thai and Malay region in the southern part of Thailand. She received her B.A. with honors in English and philosophy from Chulalongkorn University in Bangkok, Thailand, in 1969. She has lived in the United States for more than thirty-five years, earning her M.A. in philosophy at Ohio University, in Athens, in 1973 and her Ed.D. in 1991 from the University of Hawaii at Manoa. She taught interdisciplinary courses in women's studies and coordinated the mentoring program for new women faculty at the University of Hawaii at Manoa. She is currently an assistant professor of Philosophy, Sociology, and Religion at Chaminade University in Honolulu.

Before You Read

Consider the different cultural assumptions that govern what Thai people consider appropriate to ask strangers.

1 "Hi, how are you?" "Fine, thank you, and you?" These are greetings that everybody in America hears and says every day—salutations that come ready-made and packaged just like a hamburger and fries. There is no real expectation for any special information in response to these greetings. Do not, under any circumstances, take up anyone's time by responding in depth to the programmed query. What or how you may feel at the moment is of little, if any, importance. Thai people would immediately perceive that our concerned American friends are truly interested in our welfare, and this concern would require polite reciprocation by spelling out the details of our current condition. We become very disappointed when we have had enough experience in the United States to learn that we have bored, amused, or even frightened many of our American acquaintances by taking the greeting "How are you?" so literally. We were reacting like Thai, but in the American context where salutations have a different meaning, our detailed reactions were inappropriate. In Thai society, a greeting among acquaintances usually requests specific information about the other person's condition, such as "Where are you going?" or "Have you eaten?"

2 One of the American contexts in which this greeting is most confusing and ambiguous is at the hospital or clinic. In these sterile and ritualistic settings, I have always been uncertain exactly how to answer when the doctor or nurse asks "How are you?" If I deliver a packaged answer of "Fine," I wonder if I am telling a lie. After all, I am there in the first place precisely because I am not so fine. Finally, after debating for some time, I asked one nurse how she expected a patient to answer the query "How are you?" But after asking this question, I then wondered if it was rude to do so. However, she looked relieved after I explained to her that people from different cultures have different ways to greet other people and that for me to be asked how I am in the hospital results in awkwardness. Do I simply answer, "Fine, thank you," or do I reveal in accurate detail how I really feel at the moment? My suspicion was verified when the nurse declared that "How are you?" was really no more than a polite greeting and that she didn't expect any answer more elaborate than simply "Fine." However, she told me that some patients do answer her by describing every last ache and pain from which they are suffering.

3 A significant question that comes to mind is whether the verbal pattern of greetings reflects any social relationship in American culture. The apparently warm and sincere greeting may initially suggest interest in the person, yet the intention and expectations are, to me, quite superficial. For example, most often the person greets you quickly and then walks by to attend to other business without even waiting for your response! This type of greeting is just like a package of American fast food! The person eats the food quickly without enjoying the taste. The convenience is like many other American accoutrements of living such as cars, household appliances, efficient telephones, or simple, systematic, and predictable arrangements of groceries in the supermarket. However, usually when this greeting is delivered, it seems to lack a personal touch and genuine feeling. It is little more than ritualized behavior.

4 I have noticed that most Americans keep to themselves even at social gatherings. Conversation may revolve around many topics, but little, if anything, is revealed about oneself. Without talking much about oneself and not knowing much about others, social relations seem to remain at an abbreviated superficial level. How could one know a person without knowing something about him or her? How much does one need to know about a person to really know that person?

5 After living in this culture for more than a decade, I have learned that there are many topics that should not be mentioned in conversations with American acquaintances or even close friends. One's personal life and one's income are considered to be very private and even taboo topics. Unlike my Thai culture, Americans do not show interest or curiosity by asking such personal questions, especially when one

just meets the individual for the first time. Many times I have been embarrassed by my Thai acquaintances who recently arrived at the University of Hawaii and the East-West Center. For instance, one day I was walking on campus with an American friend when we met another Thai woman to whom I had been introduced a few days earlier. The Thai woman came to write her doctoral dissertation at the East-West Center where the American woman worked, so I introduced them to each other. The American woman greeted my Thai companion in Thai language, which so impressed her that she felt immediately at ease. At once, she asked the American woman numerous personal questions such as, How long did you live in Thailand? Why were you there? How long were you married to the Thai man? Why did you divorce him? How long have you been divorced? Are you going to marry a Thai again or an American? How long have you been working here? How much do you earn? The American was stunned. However, she was very patient and more or less answered all those questions as succinctly as she could. I was so uncomfortable that I had to interrupt whenever I could to get her out of the awkward situation in which she had been forced into talking about things she considered personal. For people in Thai society, such questions would be appropriate and not considered too personal let alone taboo.

6 The way Americans value their individual privacy continues to impress me. Americans seem to be open and yet there is a contradiction because they are also aloof and secretive. This is reflected in many of their behavior patterns. By Thai standards, the relationship between friends in American society seems to be somewhat superficial. Many Thai students, as well as other Asians, have felt that they could not find genuine friendship with Americans. For example, I met many American classmates who were very helpful and friendly while we were in the same class. We went out, exchanged phone calls, and did the same things as would good friends in Thailand. But those activities stopped suddenly when the semester ended.

7 Privacy as a component of the American cultural value of individualism is nurtured in the home as children grow up. From birth they are given their own individual, private space, a bedroom separate from that of their parents. American children are taught to become progressively independent, both emotionally and economically, from their family. They learn to help themselves at an early age. In comparison, in Thailand, when parents bring a new baby home from the hospital, it shares the parents' bedroom for two to three years and then shares another bedroom with older siblings of the same sex. Most Thai children do not have their own private room until they finish high school, and some do not have their own room until another sibling moves out, usually when the sibling gets married. In Thailand, there are strong bonds within the extended family. Older siblings regularly help their

parents to care for younger ones. In this and other ways, the Thai family emphasizes the interdependence of its members.

8 I was accustomed to helping Thai babies who fell down to stand up again. Thus, in America when I saw babies fall, it was natural for me to try to help them back on their feet. Once at a summer camp for East-West Center participants, one of the supervisors brought his wife and their ten-month-old son with them. The baby was so cute that many students were playing with him. At one point he was trying to walk and fell, so all the Asian students, males and females, rushed to help him up. Although the father and mother were nearby, they paid no attention to their fallen and crying baby. However, as the students were trying to help and comfort him, the parents told them to leave him alone; he would be all right on his own. The baby did get up and stopped crying without any assistance. Independence is yet another component of the American value of individualism.

9 Individualism is even reflected in the way Americans prepare, serve, and consume food. In a typical American meal, each person has a separate plate and is not supposed to share or taste food from other people's plates. My Thai friends and I are used to eating Thai style, in which you share food from a big serving dish in the middle of the table. Each person dishes a small amount from the serving dish onto his or her plate and finishes this portion before going on with the next portion of the same or a different serving dish. With the Thai pattern of eating, you regularly reach out to the serving dishes throughout the meal. But this way of eating is not considered appropriate in comparison to the common American practice where each person eats separately from his or her individual plate.

10 One time my American host, a divorcée who lives alone, invited a Thai girlfriend and myself to an American dinner at her home. When we were reaching out and eating a small portion of one thing at a time in Thai style, we were told to dish everything we wanted onto our plates at one time and that it was not considered polite to reach across the table. The proper American way was to have each kind of food piled up on your plate at once. If we were to eat in the same manner in Thailand, eyebrows would have been raised at the way we piled up food on our plates, and we would have been considered to be eating like pigs, greedy and inconsiderate of others who shared the meal at the table.

11 Individualism as a pivotal value in American culture is reflected in many other ways. Material wealth is not only a prime status marker in American society but also a guarantee and celebration of individualism—wealth allows the freedom to do almost anything, although usually within the limits of law. The pursuit of material wealth through individual achievement is instilled in Americans from the youngest age. For example, I was surprised to see an affluent American couple, who

own a large ranch house and two BMW cars, send their nine-year-old son to deliver newspapers. He has to get up very early each morning to deliver the papers, even on Sunday! During summer vacation, the boy earns additional money by helping in his parents' gift shop from 10 A.M. to 5 P.M. His thirteen-year-old sister often earns money by babysitting, even at night.

12 In Thailand, only children from poorer families work to earn money to help the household. Middle- and high-income parents do not encourage their children to work until after they have finished their education. They provide economic support in order to free their children to concentrate on and excel in their studies. Beyond the regular schooling, families who can afford it pay for special tutoring as well as training in music, dance, or sports. However, children in low- and middle-income families help their parents with household chores and the care of younger children.

13 Many American children have been encouraged to get paid for their help around the house. They rarely get any gifts free of obligations. They even have to be good to get Santa's gifts at Christmas! As they grow up, they are conditioned to earn things they want; they learn that "there is no such thing as a free lunch." From an early age, children are taught to become progressively independent economically from their parents. Also, most young people are encouraged to leave home at college age to be on their own. From my viewpoint as a Thai, it seems that American family ties and closeness are not as strong as in Asian families whose children depend on family financial support until joining the work force after college age. Thereafter, it is the children's turn to help support their parents financially.

14 Modern American society and economy emphasize individualism in other ways. The nuclear family is more common than the extended family, and newlyweds usually establish their own independent household rather than initially living with either the husband's or the wife's parents. Parents and children appear to be close only when the children are very young. Most American parents seem to "lose" their children by the teenage years. They don't seem to belong to each other as closely as do Thai families. Even though I have seen more explicit affectionate expression among American family members than among Asian ones, the close interpersonal spirit seems to be lacking. Grandparents have relatively little to do with the grandchildren on any regular basis, in contrast to the extended family, which is more common in Thailand. The family and society seem to be graded by age to the point that grandparents, parents, and children are separated by generational subcultures that are evidently alienated from one another. Each group "does its own thing." Help and support are usually limited to whatever does not interfere with one's own life. In America, the locus of responsibility is more on the individual than on the family.

15 In one case I know of, a financially affluent grandmother with Alzheimer's disease is taken care of twenty-four hours a day by hired help in her own home. Her daughter visits and relieves the helper occasionally. The mature granddaughter, who has her own family, rarely visits. Yet they all live in the same neighborhood. However, each lives in a different house, and each is very independent. Although the mother worries about the grandmother, she cannot do much. Her husband also needs her, and she divides her time between him, her daughters and their children, and the grandmother. When the mother needs to go on a trip with her husband, a second hired attendant is required to care for the grandmother temporarily. When I asked why the granddaughter doesn't temporarily care for the grandmother, the reply was that she has her own life, and it would not be fair for the granddaughter to take care of the grandmother, even for a short period of time. Yet I wonder if it is fair for the grandmother to be left out. It seems to me that the value of individualism and its associated independence account for these apparent gaps in family ties and support.

16 In contrast to American society, in Thailand older parents with a long-term illness are asked to move in with their children and grandchildren if they are not already living with them. The children and grandchildren take turns attending to the grandparent, sometimes with help from live-in maids. Living together in the same house reinforces moral support among the generations within an extended family. The older generation is respected because of the previous economic, social, and moral support for their children and grandchildren. Family relations provide one of the most important contexts for being a "morally good person," which is traditionally the principal concern in the Buddhist society of Thailand.

17 In America, being young, rich, and/or famous allows one greater freedom and independence and thus promotes the American value of individualism. This is reflected in the mass appeal of major annual television events like the Super Bowl and the Academy Awards. The goal of superachievement is also seen in more mundane ways. For example, many parents encourage their children to take special courses and to work hard to excel in sports as a shortcut to becoming rich and famous. I know one mother who has taken her two sons to tennis classes and tournaments since the boys were six years old, hoping that at least one of them will be a future tennis star like Ivan Lendl. Other parents focus their children on acting, dancing, or musical talent. The children have to devote much time and hard work as well as sacrifice the ordinary activities of youth in order to develop and perform their natural talents and skills in prestigious programs. But those who excel in the sports and entertainment industries can become rich and famous, even at an early age, as for example Madonna, Tom Cruise, and Michael Jackson. Television and other media publicize these celebrities and thereby

reinforce the American value of individualism, including personal achievement and financial success.

18 Although the American cultural values of individualism and the aspiration to become rich and famous have had some influence in Thailand, there is also cultural and religious resistance to these values. Strong social bonds, particularly within the extended family, and the hierarchical structure of the kingdom run counter to individualism. Also, youth gain social recognition through their academic achievement. From the perspective of Theravada Buddhism, which strongly influences Thai culture, aspiring to be rich and famous would be an illustration of greed, and those who have achieved wealth and fame do not celebrate it publicly as much as in American society. Being a good, moral person is paramount, and ideally Buddhists emphasize restraint and moderation.

19 Beyond talent and skill in the sports and entertainment industries, there are many other ways that young Americans can pursue wealth. Investment is one route. One American friend who is only a sophomore in college has already invested heavily in the stock market to start accumulating wealth. She is just one example of the 1980s trend for youth to be more concerned with their individual finances than with social, political, and environmental issues. With less attention paid to public issues, the expression of individualism seems to be magnified through emphasis on lucrative careers, financial investment, and material consumption—the "Yuppie" phenomenon. This includes new trends in dress, eating, housing (condominiums), and cars (expensive European imports). Likewise, there appears to be less of a long-term commitment to marriage. More young couples are living together without either marriage or plans for future marriage. When such couples decide to get married, prenuptial agreements are made to protect their assets. Traditional values of marriage, family, and sharing appear to be on the decline.

20 Individualism as one of the dominant values in American culture is expressed in many ways. This value probably stems from the history of the society as a frontier colony of immigrants in search of a better life with independence, freedom, and the opportunity for advancement through personal achievement. However, in the beliefs and customs of any culture there are some disadvantages as well as advantages. Although Thais may admire the achievements and material wealth of American society, there are costs, especially in the value of individualism and associated social phenomena.

✧ *Evaluating the Text*

1. For the Thais, what are the kinds of private topics about which it would be rude to inquire? How do these differ from the topics that are taboo among Americans?
2. How do concepts of friendship and privacy differ in Natadecha-Sponsel's experience with the Thai and American cultures?
3. How do the examples involving the child who has fallen, the way food is served and eaten, and the newspaper route provide the author with significant insights into American cultural values? Do you agree with her interpretations?

✧ *Exploring Different Perspectives*

1. Contrast the lessons learned about a new culture by Natadecha-Sponsel and David R. Counts in "Too Many Bananas."
2. Contrast the different perspectives on what being an American means according to Natadecha-Sponsel and Ralph Linton in "One Hundred Percent American."

✧ *Extending Viewpoints through Writing and Research*

1. How do concepts of the care of the elderly and Buddhist philosophy provide strikingly different models for behavior in Thailand and in the United States?
2. What incidents in your own experience illustrate the value placed on individualism in American culture, a value that those from other cultures might find strange?

David R. Counts

Too Many Bananas

David R. Counts is a professor emeritus in the anthropology department at McMaster University in Ontario, Canada. Together with his wife, Dorothy A. Counts, he has edited a number of works, including Coping with the Final Tragedy: Dying and Grieving in Cross-Cultural Perspective *(1991) and* Aging and Its Transformations: Moving Toward Death in Pacific Societies *(1992). This selection is drawn from the book* The Humbled Anthropologist: Tales from the Pacific *(1990)* edited by Philip R. DeVita. *A recent work by David and Dorothy is the second edition of* Over the Next Hill: An Ethnography of RVing Seniors in North America *(2001).*

New Guinea, the world's second-largest island after Greenland, is located in the southwestern Pacific Ocean north of Australia. The western half of the island consists of two provinces administered by Indonesia. Papua, which occupies the eastern half of New Guinea, was formerly a territory of Australia. It became the independent nation of Papua New Guinea in 1975. As one might gather from David R. Counts's article, the chief food crops are bananas, taro roots, and yams. The economy of New Guinea is one of the least developed of any area in the world. Most of the people farm land and grow their own food.

Before You Read

Counts's essay is divided into three sections. Take a moment after reading each section to write a brief summary of the new information in that part about the role of food in a barter society.

No Watermelon at All

1 The woman came all the way through the village, walking between the two rows of houses facing each other between the beach and the bush, to the very last house standing on a little spit of land at the mouth of the Kaini River. She was carrying a watermelon on her head, and the house she came to was the government "rest house," maintained by the villagers for the occasional use of visiting officials. Though my wife and I were graduate students, not officials, and had asked for permission to stay in the village for the coming year, we were living in the rest house while the debate went on about where a house

would be built for us. When the woman offered to sell us the watermelon for two shillings, we happily agreed, and the kids were delighted at the prospect of watermelon after yet another meal of rice and bully beef. The money changed hands and the seller left to return to her village, a couple of miles along the coast to the east.

2 It seemed only seconds later that the woman was back, reluctantly accompanying Kolia, the man who had already made it clear to us that he was the leader of the village. Kolia had no English, and at that time, three or four days into our first stay in Kandoka Village on the island of New Britain in Papua New Guinea, we had very little Tok Pisin. Language difficulties notwithstanding, Kolia managed to make his message clear: The woman had been outrageously wrong to sell us the watermelon for two shillings and we were to return it to her and reclaim our money immediately. When we tried to explain that we thought the price to be fair and were happy with the bargain, Kolia explained again and finally made it clear that we had missed the point. The problem wasn't that we had paid too much; it was that we had paid at all. Here he was, a leader, responsible for us while we were living in his village, and we had shamed him. How would it look if he let guests in his village *buy* food? If we wanted watermelons, or bananas, or anything else, all that was necessary was to let him know. He told us that it would be all right for us to give little gifts to people who brought food to us (and they surely would), but *no one* was to sell food to us. If anyone were to try—like this woman from Lauvore—then we should refuse. There would be plenty of watermelons without us buying them.

3 The woman left with her watermelon, disgruntled, and we were left with our two shillings. But we had learned the first lesson of many about living in Kandoka. We didn't pay money for food again that whole year, and we did get lots of food brought to us . . . but we never got another watermelon. That one was the last of the season.

LESSON 1: In a society where food is shared or gifted as part of social life, you may not buy it with money.

Too Many Bananas

4 In the couple of months that followed the watermelon incident, we managed to become at least marginally competent in Tok Pisin, to negotiate the construction of a house on what we hoped was neutral ground, and to settle into the routine of our fieldwork. As our village leader had predicted, plenty of food was brought to us. Indeed, seldom did a day pass without something coming in—some sweet potatoes, a few taro, a papaya, the occasional pineapple, or some bananas—lots of bananas.

5 We had learned our lesson about the money, though, so we never even offered to buy the things that were brought, but instead made gifts, usually of tobacco to the adults or chewing gum to the children. Nor were we so gauche as to haggle with a giver over how much of a return gift was appropriate, though the two of us sometimes conferred as to whether what had been brought was a "two-stick" or a "three-stick" stalk, bundle, or whatever. A "stick" of tobacco was a single large leaf, soaked in rum and then twisted into a ropelike form. This, wrapped in half a sheet of newsprint (torn for use as cigarette paper), sold in the local trade stores for a shilling. Nearly all of the adults in the village smoked a great deal, and they seldom had much cash, so our stocks of twist tobacco and stacks of the Sydney *Morning Herald* (all, unfortunately, the same day's issue) were seen as a real boon to those who preferred "stick" to the locally grown product.

6 We had established a pattern with respect to the gifts of food. When a donor appeared at our veranda we would offer our thanks and talk with them for a few minutes (usually about our children, who seemed to hold a real fascination for the villagers and for whom most of the gifts were intended) and then we would inquire whether they could use some tobacco. It was almost never refused, though occasionally a small bottle of kerosene, a box of matches, some laundry soap, a cup of rice, or a tin of meat would be requested instead of (or even in addition to) the tobacco. Everyone, even Kolia, seemed to think this arrangement had worked out well.

7 Now, what must be kept in mind is that while we were following their rules—or seemed to be—we were *really still buying food.* In fact we kept a running account of what came in and what we "paid" for it. Tobacco as currency got a little complicated, but since the exchange rate was one stick to one shilling, it was not too much trouble as long as everyone was happy, and meanwhile we could account for the expenditure of "informant fees" and "household expenses." Another thing to keep in mind is that not only did we continue to think in terms of our buying the food that was brought, we thought of them as *selling it.* While it was true they never quoted us a price, they also never asked us if we needed or wanted whatever they had brought. It seemed clear to us that when an adult needed a stick of tobacco, or a child wanted some chewing gum (we had enormous quantities of small packets of Wrigley's for just such eventualities) they would find something surplus to their own needs and bring it along to our "store" and get what they wanted.

8 By late November 1966, just before the rainy season set in, the bananas were coming into flush, and whereas earlier we had received banana gifts by the "hand" (six or eight bananas in a cluster cut from the stalk), donors now began to bring bananas, "for the children," by the *stalk!* The Kaliai among whom we were living are not exactly

specialists in banana cultivation—they only recognize about thirty varieties, while some of their neighbors have more than twice that many—but the kinds they produce differ considerably from each other in size, shape, and taste, so we were not dismayed when we had more than one stalk hanging on our veranda. The stalks ripen a bit at the time, and having some variety was nice. Still, by the time our accumulation had reached *four* complete stalks, the delights of variety had begun to pale a bit. The fruits were ripening progressively and it was clear that even if we and the kids ate nothing but bananas for the next week, some would still fall from the stalk onto the floor in a state of gross overripeness. This was the situation as, late one afternoon, a woman came bringing yet another stalk of bananas up the steps of the house.

9 Several factors determined our reaction to her approach: one was that there was literally no way we could possibly use the bananas. We hadn't quite reached the point of being crowded off our veranda by the stalks of fruit, but it was close. Another factor was that we were tired of playing the gift game. We had acquiesced in playing it—no one was permitted to sell us anything, and in turn we only gave things away, refusing under any circumstances to sell tobacco (or anything else) for money. But there had to be a limit. From our perspective what was at issue was that the woman wanted something and she had come to trade for it. Further, what she had brought to trade was something we neither wanted nor could use, and it should have been obvious to her. So we decided to bite the bullet.

10 The woman, Rogi, climbed the stairs to the veranda, took the stalk from where it was balanced on top of her head, and laid it on the floor with the words, "Here are some bananas for the children." Dorothy and I sat near her on the floor and thanked her for her thought but explained, "You know, we really have too many bananas—we can't use these; maybe you ought to give them to someone else. . . ." The woman looked mystified, then brightened and explained that she didn't want anything for them, she wasn't short of tobacco or anything. They were just a gift for the kids. Then she just sat there, and we sat there, and the bananas sat there, and we tried again. "Look," I said, pointing up to them and counting, "we've got four stalks already hanging here on the veranda—there are too many for us to eat now. Some are rotting already. Even if we eat only bananas, we can't keep up with what's here!"

11 Rogi's only response was to insist that these were a gift, and that she didn't want anything for them, so we tried yet another tack: "Don't *your* children like bananas?" When she admitted that they did, and that she had none at her house, we suggested that she should take them there. Finally, still puzzled, but convinced we weren't going to keep the bananas, she replaced them on her head, went down the stairs, and made her way back through the village toward her house.

12 As before, it seemed only moments before Kolia was making his way up the stairs, but this time he hadn't brought the woman in tow. "What was wrong with those bananas? Were they no good?" he demanded. We explained that there was nothing wrong with the bananas at all, but that we simply couldn't use them and it seemed foolish to take them when we had so many and Rogi's own children had none. We obviously didn't make ourselves clear because Kolia then took up the same refrain that Rogi had—he insisted that we shouldn't be worried about taking the bananas, because they were a gift for the children and Rogi hadn't wanted anything for them. There was no reason, he added, to send her away with them—she would be ashamed. I'm afraid we must have seemed as if we were hard of hearing or thought he was, for our only response was to repeat our reasons. We went through it again—there they hung, one, two, three, *four* stalks of bananas, rapidly ripening and already far beyond our capacity to eat—we just weren't ready to accept any more and let them rot (and, we added to ourselves, pay for them with tobacco, to boot).

13 Kolia finally realized that we were neither hard of hearing nor intentionally offensive, but merely ignorant. He stared at us for a few minutes, thinking, and then asked: "Don't you frequently have visitors during the day and evening?" We nodded. Then he asked, "Don't you usually offer them cigarettes and coffee or milo?" Again, we nodded. "Did it ever occur to you to suppose," he said, "that your visitors might be hungry?" It was at this point in the conversation, as we recall, that we began to see the depth of the pit we had dug for ourselves. We nodded, hesitantly. His last words to us before he went down the stairs and stalked away were just what we were by that time afraid they might be. "When your guests are hungry, *feed them bananas!*"

LESSON 2: Never refuse a gift, and never fail to return a gift. If you cannot use it, you can always give it away to someone else—there is no such thing as too much—there are never too many bananas.

Not Enough Pineapples

14 During the fifteen years between that first visit in 1966 and our residence there in 1981 we had returned to live in Kandoka village twice during the 1970s, and though there were a great many changes in the village, and indeed for all of Papua New Guinea during that time, we continued to live according to the lessons of reciprocity learned during those first months in the field. We bought no food for money and refused no gifts, but shared our surplus. As our family grew, we continued to be accompanied by our younger children. Our place in the village came to be something like that of educated Kaliai who worked far away in New Guinea. Our friends expected us to come "home"

when we had leave, but knew that our work kept us away for long periods of time. They also credited us with knowing much more about the rules of their way of life than was our due. And we sometimes shared the delusion that we understood life in the village, but even fifteen years was not long enough to relieve the need for lessons in learning to live within the rules of gift exchange.

15 In the last paragraph I used the word *friends* to describe the villagers intentionally, but of course they were not all our friends. Over the years some really had become friends, others were acquaintances, others remained consultants or informants to whom we turned when we needed information. Still others, unfortunately, we did not like at all. We tried never to make an issue of these distinctions, of course, and to be evenhanded and generous to all, as they were to us. Although we almost never actually refused requests that were made of us, over the long term our reciprocity in the village was balanced. More was given to those who helped us the most, while we gave assistance or donations of small items even to those who were not close or helpful.

16 One elderly woman in particular was a trial for us. Sara was the eldest of a group of siblings and her younger brother and sister were both generous, informative, and delightful persons. Her younger sister, Makila, was a particularly close friend and consultant, and in deference to that friendship we felt awkward in dealing with the elder sister.

17 Sara was neither a friend nor an informant, but she had been, since she returned to live in the village at the time of our second trip in 1971, a constant (if minor) drain on our resources. She never asked for much at a time. A bar of soap, a box of matches, a bottle of kerosene, a cup of rice, some onions, a stick or two of tobacco, or some other small item was usually all that was at issue, but whenever she came around it was always to ask for something—or to let us know that when we left, we should give her some of the furnishings from the house. Too, unlike almost everyone else in the village, when she came, she was always empty-handed. We ate no taro from her gardens, and the kids chewed none of her sugarcane. In short, she was, as far as we could tell, a really grasping, selfish old woman—and we were not the only victims of her greed.

18 Having long before learned the lesson of the bananas, one day we had a stalk that was ripening so fast we couldn't keep up with it, so I pulled a few for our own use (we only had one stalk at the time) and walked down through the village to Ben's house, where his five children were playing. I sat down on his steps to talk, telling him that I intended to give the fruit to his kids. They never got them. Sara saw us from across the open plaza of the village and came rushing over, shouting, "My bananas!" Then she grabbed the stalk and went off gorging herself with them. Ben and I just looked at each other.

19 Finally it got to the point where it seemed to us that we had to do something. Ten years of being used was long enough. So there came the afternoon when Sara showed up to get some tobacco—again. But this time, when we gave her the two sticks she had demanded, we confronted her.

20 First, we noted the many times she had come to get things. We didn't mind sharing things, we explained. After all, we had plenty of tobacco and soap and rice and such, and most of it was there so that we could help our friends as they helped us, with folktales, information, or even gifts of food. The problem was that she kept coming to get things, but never came to talk, or to tell stories, or to bring some little something that the kids might like. Sara didn't argue—she agreed. "Look," we suggested, "it doesn't have to be much, and we don't mind giving you things—but you can help us. The kids like pineapples, and we don't have any—the next time you need something, bring something—like maybe a pineapple." Obviously somewhat embarrassed, she took her tobacco and left, saying that she would bring something soon. We were really pleased with ourselves. It had been a very difficult thing to do, but it was done, and we were convinced that either she would start bringing things or not come. It was as if a burden had lifted from our shoulders.

21 It worked. Only a couple of days passed before Sara was back, bringing her bottle to get it filled with kerosene. But this time, she came carrying the biggest, most beautiful pineapple we had seen the entire time we had been there. We had a friendly talk, filled her kerosene container, and hung the pineapple up on the veranda to ripen just a little further. A few days later we cut and ate it, and whether the satisfaction it gave came from the fruit or from its source would be hard to say, but it was delicious. That, we assumed, was the end of that irritant.

22 We were wrong, of course. The next afternoon, Mary, one of our best friends for years (and no relation to Sara), dropped by for a visit. As we talked, her eyes scanned the veranda. Finally she asked whether we hadn't had a pineapple there yesterday. We said we had, but that we had already eaten it. She commented that it had been a really nice-looking one, and we told her that it had been the best we had eaten in months. Then, after a pause, she asked, "Who brought it to you?" We smiled as we said, "Sara!" because Mary would appreciate our coup—she had commented many times in the past on the fact that Sara only *got* from us and never gave. She was silent for a moment, and then she said, "Well, I'm glad you enjoyed it—my father was waiting until it was fully ripe to harvest it for you, but when it went missing I thought maybe it was the one you had here. I'm glad to see you got it. I thought maybe a thief had eaten it in the bush."

LESSON 3: Where reciprocity is the rule and gifts are the idiom, you cannot demand a gift, just as you cannot refuse a request.

23 It says a great deal about the kindness and patience of the Kaliai people that they have been willing to be our hosts for all these years despite our blunders and lack of good manners. They have taught us a lot, and these three lessons are certainly not the least important things we learned.

✧ *Evaluating the Text*

1. How does Counts's initial experience of offering money for a watermelon teach him his first important lesson about the culture of New Guinea?
2. How does the idea of "too many bananas" sum up the important principle of reciprocity that Counts learns? In your own words, describe the principle involved.
3. How does the experience Counts has with Sara lead to his ironic realization of the third lesson about the culture of New Guinea?

✧ *Exploring Different Perspectives*

1. Compare the lessons Counts learns about reciprocity in New Guinea with what Poranee Natadecha-Sponsel learns about individualism in America, as told in "Individualism as an American Cultural Value."
2. How did Counts's experiences as an anthropologist resemble those of Wade Davis in Haiti, as reported by Gino Del Guercio in "The Secrets of Voodoo in Haiti" in terms of changing perspectives on native cultures?

✧ *Extending Viewpoints through Writing and Research*

1. What experiences have you had that involved the principle of reciprocity in your relationship with another? Discuss one incident and the lesson you learned.
2. If you were a "stranger in a strange land," would you feel more comfortable if you had many of your material possessions with you? Why or why not?

Napoleon A. Chagnon

Doing Fieldwork among the Yąnomamö

Napoleon Chagnon was born in Port Austin, Michigan, in 1938. In the 1960s he spent almost two years living with and studying the Yąnomamö, a tribe of roughly 10,000 Indians living on the border between Venezuela and Brazil. Chagnon's research into the genealogies of village members and the social aspects of tribal warfare resulted in his classic study Yąnomamö: The Fierce People *(1968), in which the following first appeared, and* Studying the Yąnomamö *(1974). Chagnon was professor of anthropology at the University of California at Santa Barbara and (with Tim Asch) created many award-winning documentary films on various aspects of Yąnomamö life. In 2000, Chagnon (with Lee Cronk and William Irons) edited* Adaptation and Human Behavior: An Anthropological Perspective.

Before You Read

What does the phrase *culture shock* suggest to you?

1 The Yąnomamö[1] Indians live in southern Venezuela and the adjacent portions of northern Brazil. Some 125 widely scattered villages have populations ranging from 40 to 250 inhabitants, with 75 to 80 people the most usual number. In total numbers their population approaches 10,000 people, but this is merely a guess. Many of the villages have not yet been contacted by outsiders, and nobody knows for sure exactly how many uncontacted villages there are, or how many people live in them. By comparison to African or Melanesian tribes, the Yąnomamö population is small. Still, they are one of the largest unacculturated tribes left in all of South America.

[1]The word *Yąnomamö* is nasalized through its entire length, indicated by the diacritical mark [ą]. When this mark appears on a word, the entire word is nasalized. The terminal vowel [-ö] represents a sound that does not occur in the English language. It corresponds to the phone [ɨ] of linguistic orthography. In normal conversation, Yąnomamö is pronounced like "Yah-no-mama," except that it is nasalized. Finally, the words having the [-ä] vowel are pronounced as that vowel with the "uh" sound of "duck." Thus the name Kąobawä would be pronounced "cow-ba-wuh," again nasalized.

2 But they have a significance apart from tribal size and cultural purity: the Yąnomamö are still actively conducting warfare. It is in the nature of man to fight, according to one of their myths, because the blood of "Moon" spilled on this layer of the cosmos, causing men to become fierce. I describe the Yąnomamö as "the fierce people" because that is the most accurate single phrase that describes them. That is how they conceive themselves to be, and that is how they would like others to think of them.

3 I spent nineteen months with the Yąnomamö,[2] during which time I acquired some proficiency in their language and, up to a point, submerged myself in their culture and way of life. The thing that impressed me most was the importance of aggression in their culture. I had the opportunity to witness a good many incidents that expressed individual vindictiveness on the one hand and collective bellicosity on the other. These ranged in seriousness from the ordinary incidents of wife beating and chest pounding to dueling and organized raiding by parties that set out with the intention of ambushing and killing men from enemy villages. One of the villages . . . was raided approximately twenty-five times while I conducted the fieldwork, six times by the group I lived among.

4 The fact that the Yąnomamö live in a state of chronic warfare is reflected in their mythology, values, settlement pattern, political behavior, and marriage practices. Accordingly, I have organized this case study in such a way that students can appreciate the effects of warfare on Yąnomamö culture in general and on their social organization and politics in particular.

5 I collected the data under somewhat trying circumstances, some of which I will describe in order to give the student a rough idea of what is generally meant when anthropologists speak of "culture shock" and "fieldwork." It should be borne in mind, however, that each field situation is in many respects unique, so that the problems I encountered do not necessarily exhaust the range of possible problems other anthropologists have confronted in other areas. There are a few problems, however, that seem to be nearly universal among anthropological fieldworkers, particularly those having to do with eating, bathing, sleeping, lack of privacy and loneliness, or discovering that primitive man is not always as noble as you originally thought.

---

[2]I spent a total of twenty-three months in South America of which nineteen were spent among the Yąnomamö on three separate field trips. The first trip, November 1964 through February 1966, was to Venezuela. During this time I spent thirteen months in direct contact with the Yąnomamö, using my periodic trips back to Caracas to visit my family and to collate the genealogical data I had collected upp to that point. On my second trip, January through March 1967, I spent two months among Brazilian Yąnomamö and one more month with the Venezuelan Yąnomamö. Finally, I returned to Venezuela for three more months among the Yąnomamö, January through April 1968.

6 This is not to state that primitive man everywhere is unpleasant. By way of contrast, I have also done limited fieldwork among the Yąnomamö's northern neighbors, the Carib-speaking Makiritare Indians. This group was very pleasant and charming, all of them anxious to help me and honor bound to show any visitor the numerous courtesies of their system of etiquette. In short, they approached the image of primitive man that I had conjured up, and it was sheer pleasure to work with them. The recent work by Colin Turnbull (1966) brings out dramatically the contrast in personal characteristics of two African peoples he has studied.

7 Hence, what I say about some of my experiences is probably equally true of the experiences of many other fieldworkers. I write about my own experiences because there is a conspicuous lack of fieldwork descriptions available to potential fieldworkers. I think I could have profited by reading about the private misfortunes of my own teachers; at least I might have been able to avoid some of the more stupid errors I made. In this regard there are a number of recent contributions by fieldworkers describing some of the discomforts and misfortunes they themselves sustained.[3] Students planning to conduct fieldwork are urged to consult them.

8 My first day in the field illustrated to me what my teachers meant when they spoke of "culture shock." I had traveled in a small, aluminum rowboat propelled by a large outboard motor for two and a half days. This took me from the Territorial capital, a small town on the Orinoco River, deep into Yąnomamö country. On the morning of the third day we reached a small mission settlement, the field "headquarters" of a group of Americans who were working in two Yąnomamö villages. The missionaries had come out of these villages to hold their annual conference on the progress of their mission work, and were conducting their meetings when I arrived. We picked up a passenger at the mission station, James P. Barker, the first non-Yąnomamö to make a sustained, permanent contact with the tribe (in 1950). He had just returned from a year's furlough in the United States, where I had earlier visited him before leaving for Venezuela. He agreed to accompany me to the village I had selected for my base of operations to introduce me to the Indians. This village was also his own home base, but he had not been there for over a year and did not plan to join me for another three months. Mr. Barker had been living with this particular group about five years.

---

[3]Maybury-Lewis 1967, "Introduction," and 1965*b*; Turnbull, 1966; L. Bohannan, 1964. Perhaps the most intimate account of the tribulations of a fieldworker is found in the posthumous diary of Bronislaw Malinowski (1967). Since the diary was not written for publication, it contains many intimate, very personal details about the writer's anxieties and hardships.

9 We arrived at the village, Bisaasi-teri, about 2:00 PM and docked the boat along the muddy bank at the terminus of the path used by the Indians to fetch their drinking water. It was hot and muggy, and my clothing was soaked with perspiration. It clung uncomfortably to my body, as it did thereafter for the remainder of the work. The small, biting gnats were out in astronomical numbers, for it was the beginning of the dry season. My face and hands were swollen from the venom of their numerous stings. In just a few moments I was to meet my first Yąnomamö, my first primitive man. What would it be like? I had visions of entering the village and seeing 125 social facts running about calling each other kinship terms and sharing food, each waiting and anxious to have me collect his genealogy. I would wear them out in turn. Would they like me? This was important to me; I wanted them to be so fond of me that they would adopt me into their kinship system and way of life, because I had heard that, successful anthropologists always get adopted by their people. I had learned during my seven years of anthropological training at the University of Michigan that kinship was equivalent to society in primitive tribes and that it was a moral way of life, "moral" being something "good" and "desirable." I was determined to work my way into their moral system of kinship and become a member of their society.

10 My heart began to pound as we approached the village and heard the buzz of activity within the circular compound. Mr. Barker commented that he was anxious to see if any changes had taken place while he was away and wondered how many of them had died during his absence. I felt into my back pocket to make sure that my notebook was still there and felt personally more secure when I touched it. Otherwise, I would not have known what to do with my hands.

11 The entrance to the village was covered over with brush and dry palm leaves. We pushed them aside to expose the low opening to the village. The excitement of meeting my first Indians was almost unbearable as I duck-waddled through the low passage into the village clearing.

12 I looked up and gasped when I saw a dozen burly, naked, filthy, hideous men staring at us down the shafts of their drawn arrows! Immense wads of green tobacco were stuck between their lower teeth and lips making them look even more hideous, and strands of dark-green slime dripped or hung from their noses. We arrived at the village while the men were blowing a hallucinogenic drug up their noses. One of the side effects of the drug is a runny nose. The mucus is always saturated with the green powder and the Indians usually let it run freely from their nostrils. My next discovery was that there were a dozen or so vicious, underfed dogs snapping at my legs, circling me as if I were going to be their next meal. I just stood there holding my notebook, helpless and pathetic. Then the stench of the decaying vegetation and filth struck me and I almost got sick. I was horrified. What sort of a

welcome was this for the person who came here to live with you and learn your way of life, to become friends with you? They put their weapons down when they recognized Barker and returned to their chanting, keeping a nervous eye on the village entrances.

13 We had arrived just after a serious fight. Seven women had been abducted the day before by a neighboring group, and the local men and their guests had just that morning recovered five of them in a brutal club fight that nearly ended in a shooting war. The abductors, angry because they lost five of the seven captives, vowed to raid the Bisaasiteri. When we arrived and entered the village unexpectedly, the Indians feared that we were the raiders. On several occasions during the next two hours the men in the village jumped to their feet, armed themselves, and waited nervously for the noise outside the village to be identified. My enthusiasm for collecting ethnographic curiosities diminished in proportion to the number of times such an alarm was raised. In fact, I was relieved when Mr. Barker suggested that we sleep across the river for the evening. It would be safer over there.

14 As we walked down the path to the boat, I pondered the wisdom of having decided to spend a year and a half with this tribe before I had even seen what they were like. I am not ashamed to admit, either, that had there been a diplomatic way out, I would have ended my fieldwork then and there. I did not look forward to the next day when I would be left alone with the Indians; I did not speak a word of their language, and they were decidedly different from what I had imagined them to be. The whole situation was depressing, and I wondered why I ever decided to switch from civil engineering to anthropology in the first place. I had not eaten all day, I was soaking wet from perspiration, the gnats were biting me, and I was covered with red pigment, the result of a dozen or so complete examinations I had been given by as many burly Indians. These examinations capped an otherwise grim day. The Indians would blow their noses into their hands, flick as much of the mucus off that would separate in a snap of the wrist, wipe the residue into their hair, and then carefully examine my face, arms, legs, hair, and the contents of my pockets. I asked Mr. Barker how to say "Your hands are dirty"; my comments were met by the Indians in the following way: They would "clean" their hands by spitting a quantity of slimy tobacco juice into them, rub them together, and then proceed with the examination.

15 Mr. Barker and I crossed the river and slung our hammocks. When he pulled his hammock out of a rubber bag, a heavy, disagreeable odor of mildewed cotton came with it. "Even the missionaries are filthy," I thought to myself. Within two weeks, everything I owned smelled the same way, and I lived with that odor for the remainder of the fieldwork. My own habits of personal cleanliness reached such levels that I didn't even mind being examined by the Indians, as I was not much cleaner than they were after I had adjusted to the circumstances.

16 So much for my discovery that primitive man is not the picture of nobility and sanitation I had conceived him to be. I soon discovered that it was an enormously time-consuming task to maintain my own body in the manner to which it had grown accustomed in the relatively antiseptic environment of the northern United States. Either I could be relatively well fed and relatively comfortable in a fresh change of clothes and do very little fieldwork, or, I could do considerably more fieldwork and be less well fed and less comfortable.

17 It is appalling how complicated it can be to make oatmeal in the jungle. First, I had to make two trips to the river to haul the water. Next, I had to prime my kerosene stove with alcohol and get it burning, a tricky procedure when you are trying to mix powdered milk and fill a coffee pot at the same time: the alcohol prime always burned out before I could turn the kerosene on, and I would have to start all over. Or, I would turn the kerosene on, hoping that the element was still hot enough to vaporize the fuel, and start a small fire in my palm-thatched hut as the liquid kerosene squirted all over the table and walls and ignited. It was safer to start over with the alcohol. Then I had to boil the oatmeal and pick the bugs out of it. All my supplies, of course, were carefully stored in Indian-proof, rat-proof, moisture-proof, and insect-proof containers, not one of which ever served its purpose adequately. Just taking things out of the multiplicity of containers and repacking them afterward was a minor project in itself. By the time I had hauled the water to cook with, unpacked my food, prepared the oatmeal, milk, and coffee, heated water for dishes, washed and dried the dishes, repacked the food in the containers, stored the containers in locked trunks and cleaned up my mess, the ceremony of preparing breakfast had brought me almost up to lunch time!

18 Eating three meals a day was out of the question. I solved the problem by eating a single meal that could be prepared in a single container, or, at most, in two containers, washed my dishes only when there were no clean ones left, using cold river water, and wore each change of clothing at least a week to cut down on my laundry problem, a courageous undertaking in the tropics. I was also less concerned about sharing my provisions with the rats, insects, Indians, and the elements, thereby eliminating the need for my complicated storage process. I was able to last most of the day on *café con leche,* heavily sugared espresso coffee diluted about five to one with hot milk. I would prepare this in the evening and store it in a thermos. Frequently, my single meal was no more complicated than a can of sardines and a package of crackers. But at least two or three times a week I would do something sophisticated, like make oatmeal or boil rice and add a can of tuna fish or tomato paste to it. I even saved time by devising a water system that obviated the trips to the river. I had a few sheets of zinc roofing brought in and made a rain-water trap; I caught the water on

the zinc surface, funneled it into an empty gasoline drum, and then ran a plastic hose from the drum to my hut. When the drum was exhausted in the dry season, I hired the Indians to fill it with water from the river.

19 I ate much less when I traveled with the Indians to visit other villages. Most of the time my travel diet consisted of roasted or boiled green plantains . . . that I obtained from the Indians, but I always carried a few cans of sardines with me in case I got lost or stayed away longer than I had planned. I found peanut butter and crackers a very nourishing food, and a simple one to prepare on trips. It was nutritious and portable, and only one tool was required to prepare the meal, a hunting knife that could be cleaned by wiping the blade on a leaf. More importantly, it was one of the few foods the Indians would let me eat in relative peace. It looked too much like animal feces to them to excite their appetites.

20 I once referred to the peanut butter as the dung of cattle. They found this quite repugnant. They did not know what "cattle" were, but were generally aware that I ate several canned products of such an animal. I perpetrated this myth, if for no other reason than to have some peace of mind while I ate. Fieldworkers develop strange defense mechanisms, and this was one of my own forms of adaptation. On another occasion I was eating a can of frankfurters and growing very weary of the demands of one of my guests for a share in my meal. When he asked me what I was eating, I replied: "Beef." He then asked, "What part of the animal are you eating?" to which I replied, "Guess!" He stopped asking for a share.

21 Meals were a problem in another way. Food sharing is important to the Yąnomamö in the context of displaying friendship. "I am hungry," is almost a form of greeting with them. I could not possibly have brought enough food with me to feed the entire village, yet they seemed not to understand this. All they could see was that I did not share my food with them at each and every meal. Nor could I enter into their system of reciprocities with respect to food; every time one of them gave me something "freely," he would dog me for months to pay him back, not with food, but with steel tools. Thus, if I accepted a plantain from someone in a different village while I was on a visit, he would most likely visit me in the future and demand a machete as payment for the time that he "fed" me. I usually reacted to these kinds of demands by giving a banana, the customary reciprocity in their culture—food for food—but this would be a disappointment for the individual who had visions of that single plantain growing into a machete over time.

22 Despite the fact that most of them knew I would not share my food with them at their request, some of them always showed up at my hut during mealtime. I gradually became accustomed to this and learned to ignore their persistent demands while I ate. Some of them would get

angry because I failed to give in, but most of them accepted it as just a peculiarity of the subhuman foreigner. When I did give in, my hut quickly filled with Indians, each demanding a sample of the food that I had given one of them. If I did not give all a share, I was that much more despicable in their eyes.

23 A few of them went out of their way to make my meals unpleasant, to spite me for not sharing; for example, one man arrived and watched me eat a cracker with honey on it. He immediately recognized the honey, a particularly esteemed Yąnomamö food. He knew that I would not share my tiny bottle and that it would be futile to ask. Instead, he glared at me and queried icily, "Shaki![4] What kind of animal semen are you eating on that cracker?" His question had the desired effect, and my meal ended.

24 Finally, there was the problem of being lonely and separated from your own kind, especially your family. I tried to overcome this by seeking personal friendships among the Indians. This only complicated the matter because all my friends simply used my confidence to gain privileged access to my cache of steel tools and trade goods, and looted me. I would be bitterly disappointed that my "friend" thought no more of me than to finesse our relationship exclusively with the intention of getting at my locked up possessions, and my depression would hit new lows every time I discovered this. The loss of the possession bothered me much less than the shock that I was, as far as most of them were concerned, nothing more than a source of desirable items; no holds were barred in relieving me of these, since I was considered something subhuman, a non-Yąnomamö.

25 The thing that bothered me most was the incessant, passioned, and aggressive demands the Indians made. It would become so unbearable that I would have to lock myself in my mud hut every once in a while just to escape from it: Privacy is one of Western culture's greatest achievements. But I did not want privacy for its own sake; rather, I simply had to get away from the begging. Day and night for the entire time I lived with the Yąnomamö I was plagued by such demands as: "Give me a knife, I am poor!"; "If you don't take me with you on your next trip to Widokaiya-teri I'll chop a hole in your canoe!"; "Don't point your camera at me or I'll hit you!"; "Share your food with me!"; "Take me across the river in your canoe and be quick about it!"; "Give me a cooking pot!"; "Loan me your flashlight so I can go hunting

[4]"Shaki," or, rather, "Shakiwä," is the name they gave me because they could not pronounce "Chagnon." They like to name people for some distinctive feature when possible. *Shaki* is the name of a species of noisome bee; they accumulate in large numbers around ripening bananas and make pests of themselves by eating into the fruit, showering the people below with the debris. They probably adopted this name for me because I was also a nuisance, continuously prying into their business, taking pictures of them, and, in general, being where they did not want me.

tonight!"; "Give me medicine . . . I itch all over!"; "Take us on a week-long hunting trip with your shot-gun!"; and "Give me an axe or I'll break into your hut when you are away visiting and steal one!" And so I was bombarded by such demands day after day, months on end, until I could not bear to see an Indian.

26 It was not as difficult to become calloused to the incessant begging as it was to ignore the sense of urgency, the impassioned tone of voice, or the intimidation and aggression with which the demands were made. It was likewise difficult to adjust to the fact that the Yąnomamö refused to accept "no" for an answer until or unless it seethed with passion and intimidation—which it did after six months. Giving in to a demand always established a new threshold; the next demand would be for a bigger item or favor, and the anger of the Indians even greater if the demand was not met. I soon learned that I had to become very much like the Yąnomamö to be able to get along with them on their terms: sly, aggressive, and intimidating.

27 Had I failed to adjust in this fashion I would have lost six months of supplies to them in a single day or would have spent most of my time ferrying them around in my canoe or hunting for them. As it was, I did spend a considerable amount of time doing these things and did succumb to their outrageous demands for axes and machetes, at least at first. More importantly, had I failed to demonstrate that I could not be pushed around beyond a certain point, I would have been the subject of far more ridicule, theft, and practical jokes than was the actual case. In short, I had to acquire a certain proficiency in their kind of interpersonal politics and to learn how to imply subtly that certain potentially undesirable consequences might follow if they did such and such to me. They do this to each other in order to establish precisely the point at which they cannot goad an individual any further without precipitating retaliation. As soon as I caught on to this and realized that much of their aggression was stimulated by their desire to discover my flash point, I got along much better with them and regained some lost ground. It was sort of like a political game that everyone played, but one in which each individual sooner or later had to display some sign that his bluffs and implied threats could be backed up. I suspect that the frequency of wife beating is a component of this syndrome, since men can display their ferocity and show others that they are capable of violence. Beating a wife with a club is considered to be an acceptable way of displaying ferocity and one that does not expose the male to much danger. The important thing is that the man has displayed his potential for violence and the implication is that other men better treat him with respect and caution.

28 After six months, the level of demand was tolerable in the village I used for my headquarters. The Indians and I adjusted to each other and knew what to expect with regard to demands on their part for goods, favors, and services. Had I confined my fieldwork to just that

village alone, the field experience would have been far more enjoyable. But, as I was interested in the demographic pattern and social organization of a much larger area, I made regular trips to some dozen different villages in order to collect genealogies or to recheck those I already had. Hence, the intensity of begging and intimidation was fairly constant for the duration of the fieldwork. I had to establish my position in some sort of pecking order of ferocity at each and every village.

29 For the most part, my own "fierceness" took the form of shouting back at the Yąnomamö as loudly and as passionately as they shouted at me, especially at first, when I did not know much of their language. As I became more proficient in their language and learned more about their political tactics, I became more sophisticated in the art of bluffing. For example, I paid one young man a machete to cut palm trees and make boards from the wood. I used these to fashion a platform in the bottom of my dugout canoe to keep my possessions dry when I traveled by river. That afternoon I was doing informant work in the village; the long-awaited mission supply boat arrived, and most of the Indians ran out of the village to beg goods from the crew. I continued to work in the village for another hour or so and went down to the river to say "hello" to the men on the supply boat. I was angry when I discovered that the Indians had chopped up all my palm boards and used them to paddle their own canoes[5] across the river. I knew that if I overlooked this incident I would have invited them to take even greater liberties with my goods in the future. I crossed the river, docked amidst their dugouts, and shouted for the Indians to come out and see me. A few of the culprits appeared, mischievous grins on their faces. I gave a spirited lecture about how hard I had worked to put those boards in my canoe, how I had paid a machete for the wood, and how angry I was that they destroyed my work in their haste to cross the river. I then pulled out my hunting knife and, while their grins disappeared, cut each of their canoes loose, set it into the current, and let it float away. I left without further ado and without looking back.

30 They managed to borrow another canoe and, after some effort, re-covered their dugouts. The headman of the village later told me with an approving chuckle that I had done the correct thing. Everyone in the village, except, of course, the culprits, supported and defended my action. This raised my status.

31 Whenever I took such action and defended my rights, I got along much better with the Yąnomamö. A good deal of their behavior toward me was directed with the forethought of establishing the point at which I would react defensively. Many of them later reminisced about the early days of my work when I was "timid" and a little afraid of them, and they could bully me into giving goods away.

[5]The canoes were obtained from missionaries, who, in turn, got them from a different tribe.

32 Theft was the most persistent situation that required me to take some sort of defensive action. I simply could not keep everything I owned locked in trunks, and the Indians came into my hut and left at will. I developed a very effective means for recovering almost all the stolen items. I would simply ask a child who took the item and then take that person's hammock when he was not around, giving a spirited lecture to the others as I marched away in a faked rage with the thief's hammock. Nobody ever attempted to stop me from doing this, and almost all of them told me that my technique for recovering my possessions was admirable. By nightfall the thief would either appear with the stolen object or send it along with someone else to make an exchange. The others would heckle him for getting caught and being forced to return the item.

33 With respect to collecting the data I sought, there was a very frustrating problem. Primitive social organization is kinship organization, and to understand the Yąnomamö way of life I had to collect extensive genealogies. I could not have deliberately picked a more difficult group to work with in this regard: They have very stringent name taboos. They attempt to name people in such a way that when the person dies and they can no longer use his name, the loss of the word in the language is not inconvenient. Hence, they name people for specific and minute parts of things, such as "toenail of some rodent," thereby being able to retain the words "toenail" and "(specific) rodent," but not being able to refer directly to the toenail of that rodent. The taboo is maintained even for the living: One mark of prestige is the courtesy others show you by not using your name. The sanctions behind the taboo seem to be an unusual combination of fear and respect.

34 I tried to use kinship terms to collect genealogies at first, but the kinship terms were so ambiguous that I ultimately had to resort to names. They were quick to grasp that I was bound to learn everybody's name and reacted, without my knowing it, by inventing false names for everybody in the village. After having spent several months collecting names and learning them, this came as a disappointment to me: I could not cross-check genealogies with other informants from distant villages.

35 They enjoyed watching me learn these names. I assumed, wrongly, that I would get the truth to each question and that I would get the best information by working in public. This set the stage for converting a serious project into a farce. Each informant tried to outdo his peers by inventing a name even more ridiculous than what I had been given earlier, or by asserting that the individual about whom I inquired was married to his mother or daughter, and the like. I would have the informant whisper the name of the individual in my ear, noting that he was the father of such and such a child. Everybody would then insist that I repeat the name aloud, roaring in hysterics as I clumsily pronounced the name. I assumed that the laughter was in response to the violation of the name taboo or to my pronunciation. This was a reasonable

interpretation, since the individual whose name I said aloud invariably became angry. After I learned what some of the names meant, I began to understand what the laughter was all about. A few of the more colorful examples are: "hairy vagina," "long penis," "feces of the harpy eagle," and "dirty rectum." No wonder the victims were angry.

36 I was forced to do my genealogy work in private because of the horseplay and nonsense. Once I did so, my informants began to agree with each other and I managed to learn a few new names, real names. I could then test any new informant by collecting a genealogy from him that I knew to be accurate. I was able to weed out the more mischievous informants this way. Little by little I extended the genealogies and learned the real names. Still, I was unable to get the names of the dead and extend the genealogies back in time, and even my best informants continued to deceive me about their own close relatives. Most of them gave me the name of a living man as the father of some individual in order to avoid mentioning that the actual father was dead.

37 The quality of a genealogy depends in part on the number of generations it embraces, and the name taboo prevented me from getting any substantial information about deceased ancestors. Without this information, I could not detect marriage patterns through time. I had to rely on older informants for this information, but these were the most reluctant of all. As I became more proficient in the language and more skilled at detecting lies, my informants became better at lying. One of them in particular was so cunning and persuasive that I was shocked to discover that he had been inventing his information. He specialized in making a ceremony out of telling me false names. He would look around to make sure nobody was listening outside my hut, enjoin me to never mention the name again, act very nervous and spooky, and then grab me by the head to whisper the name very softly into my ear. I was always elated after an informant session with him, because I had several generations of dead ancestors for the living people. The others refused to give me this information. To show my gratitude, I paid him quadruple the rate I had given the others. When word got around that I had increased the pay, volunteers began pouring in to give me genealogies.

38 I discovered that the old man was lying quite by accident. A club fight broke out in the village one day, the result of a dispute over the possession of a woman. She had been promised to Rerebawä, a particularly aggressive young man who had married into the village. Rerebawä had already been given her older sister and was enraged when the younger girl began having an affair with another man in the village, making no attempt to conceal it from him. He challenged the young man to a club fight, but was so abusive in his challenge that the opponent's father took offense and entered the village circle with his son, wielding a long club. Rerebawä swaggered out to the duel and hurled insults at

both of them, trying to goad them into striking him on the head with their clubs. This would have given him the opportunity to strike them on the head. His opponents refused to hit him, and the fight ended. Rerebawä had won a moral victory because his opponents were afraid to hit him. Thereafter, he swaggered around and insulted the two men behind their backs. He was genuinely angry with them, to the point of calling the older man by the name of his dead father. I quickly seized on this as an opportunity to collect an accurate genealogy and pumped him about his adversary's ancestors. Rerebawä had been particularly nasty to me up to this point, but we became staunch allies: We were both outsiders in the local village. I then asked about other dead ancestors and got immediate replies. He was angry with the whole group and not afraid to tell me the names of the dead. When I compared his version of the genealogies to that of the old man, it was obvious that one of them was lying. I challenged his information, and he explained that everybody knew that the old man was deceiving me and bragging about it in the village. The names the old man had given me were the dead ancestors of the members of a village so far away that he thought I would never have occasion to inquire about them. As it turned out, Rerebawä knew most of the people in that village and recognized the names.

39 I then went over the complete genealogical records with Rerebawä, genealogies I had presumed to be in final form. I had to revise them all because of the numerous lies and falsifications they contained. Thus, after five months of almost constant work on the genealogies of just one group, I had to begin almost from scratch!

40 Discouraging as it was to start over, it was still the first real turning point in my fieldwork. Thereafter, I began taking advantage of local arguments and animosities in selecting my informants, and used more extensively individuals who had married into the group. I began traveling to other villages to check the genealogies, picking villages that were on strained terms with the people about whom I wanted information. I would then return to my base camp and check with local informants the accuracy of the new information. If the informants became angry when I mentioned the new names I acquired from the unfriendly group, I was almost certain that the information was accurate. For this kind of checking I had to use informants whose genealogies I knew rather well: they had to be distantly enough related to the dead person that they would not go into a rage when I mentioned the name, but not so remotely related that they would be uncertain of the accuracy of the information. Thus, I had to make a list of names that I dared not use in the presence of each and every informant. Despite the precautions, I occasionally hit a name that put the informant into a rage, such as that of a dead brother or sister that other informants had not reported. This always terminated the day's work with that informant, for he would be too touchy to continue any further, and

I would be reluctant to take a chance on accidentally discovering another dead kinsman so soon after the first.

41 These were always unpleasant experiences, and occasionally dangerous ones, depending on the temperament of the informant. On one occasion I was planning to visit a village that had been raided about a week earlier. A woman whose name I had on my list had been killed by the raiders. I planned to check each individual on the list one by one to estimate ages, and I wanted to remove her name so that I would not say it aloud in the village. I knew that I would be in considerable difficulty if I said this name aloud so soon after her death. I called on my original informant and asked him to tell me the name of the woman who had been killed. He refused, explaining that she was a close relative of his. I then asked him if he would become angry if I read off all the names on the list. This way he did not have to say her name and could merely nod when I mentioned the right one. He was a fairly good friend of mine, and I thought I could predict his reaction. He assured me that this would be a good way of doing it. We were alone in my hut so that nobody could overhear us. I read the names softly, continuing to the next when he gave a negative reply. When I finally spoke the name of the dead woman he flew out of his chair, raised his arm to strike me, and shouted: "You son-of-a-bitch! If you ever say that name again, I'll kill you!" He was shaking with rage, but left my hut quickly. I shudder to think what might have happened if I had said the name unknowingly in the woman's village. I had other, similar experiences in different villages, but luckily the dead person had been dead for some time and was not closely related to the individual into whose ear I whispered the name. I was merely cautioned to desist from saying any more names, lest I get people angry with me. . . .

REFERENCES

Bohannan, Laura, 1964, *Return to Laughter*. New York: Doubleday & Co., Inc.

Malinowski, Bronislaw, 1967, *A Diary in the Strict Sense of the Term*. New York: Harcourt, Brace & World, Inc.

Maybury-Lewis, David, 1965, *The Savage and the Innocent*. London: Evans Bros.

———, 1967, *Akwẽ-Shavante Society*. Oxford: Clarendon Press.

Turnbull, Colin M., 1966, "Report from Africa: A People Apart." *Natural History*, Vol. 75, pp. 8–14.

✧ *Evaluating the Text*

1. What role does aggression play in the Yąnomamö culture?
2. What details best illustrate the sense of culture shock that Chagnon experienced?

3. How did Chagnon cope with the taboo against revealing tribal names that impeded his research on genealogy?

✧ *Exploring Different Perspectives*

1. Compare the Yąnomamös' attitude toward drugs with the mind-altering concoction in Haiti as described by Gino Del Guercio in "The Secrets of Voodoo in Haiti."
2. Compare the predicament of anthropologists struggling to understand unfamiliar cultures in the accounts by Chagnon and David R. Counts in "Too Many Bananas."

✧ *Extending Viewpoints through Writing and Research*

1. Try to construct a family tree. To what extent did your experiences with interviewing family members correspond to those of Chagnon?
2. Have you ever experienced culture shock in ways that challenged your expectations and assumptions? Describe your experiences.
3. Compare the way reciprocal gift giving operates in American society with the experiences Chagnon describes.

How does this image of a Yąnomamö man preparing hallucinogenic snuff reinforce Chagnon's descriptions?

Gino Del Guercio

The Secrets of Voodoo in Haiti

Gino Del Guercio is a national science writer for United Press International and was a MACY fellow at Boston's television station WGBH. He is currently a documentary filmmaker, specializing in scientific and medical subjects, for Boston Science Communications, Inc. "The Secrets of Haiti's Living Dead" was first published in Harvard Magazine *(January/February 1986). In 1982, Wade Davis, a Harvard-trained ethnobotanist whose exploits formed the basis for this article, traveled into the Haitian countryside to investigate accounts of zombies—the infamous living dead of Haitian folklore. Davis's research led him to obtain the poison associated with the process. His findings were first presented in* The Serpent and the Rainbow *(1986), a work that served as the basis for the movie of the same name, directed by Wes Craven, and later in* Passage of Darkness *(1988). Del Guercio's report reveals the extent to which Haitian life is controlled by voodoo, a religious belief, West African in origin, that is characterized by induced trances and magical rituals. Until the twentieth century, voodoo (also known as vodoun) was the state religion and continues to flourish despite opposition from Roman Catholicism, the other major religion in Haiti. In 2009, Del Guercio completed a two-hour feature film titled* Greeley *about an expedition in the high Arctic.*

Before You Read

Consider the extent to which your concept of zombies is influenced by films and television.

1 Five years ago, a man walked into l'Estére, a village in central Haiti, approached a peasant woman named Angelina Narcisse, and identified himself as her brother Clairvius. If he had not introduced himself using a boyhood nickname and mentioned facts only intimate family members knew, she would not have believed him. Because, eighteen years earlier, Angelina had stood in a small cemetery north of her village and watched as her brother Clairvius was buried.

2 The man told Angelina he remembered that night well. He knew when he was lowered into his grave, because he was fully conscious, although he could not speak or move. As the earth was thrown over his coffin, he felt as if he were floating over the grave. The scar on his right cheek, he said, was caused by a nail driven through his casket.

3 The night he was buried, he told Angelina, a voodoo priest raised him from the grave. He was beaten with a sisal whip and carried off to a sugar plantation in northern Haiti where, with other zombies, he was forced to work as a slave. Only with the death of the zombie master were they able to escape, and Narcisse eventually returned home.

4 Legend has it that zombies are the living dead, raised from their graves and animated by malevolent voodoo sorcerers, usually for some evil purpose. Most Haitians believe in zombies, and Narcisse's claim is not unique. At about the time he reappeared, in 1980, two women turned up in other villages saying they were zombies. In the same year, in northern Haiti, the local peasants claimed to have found a group of zombies wandering aimlessly in the fields.

5 But Narcisse's case was different in one crucial respect; it was documented. His death had been recorded by doctors at the American-directed Schweitzer Hospital in Deschapelles. On April 30, 1962, hospital records show, Narcisse walked into the hospital's emergency room spitting up blood. He was feverish and full of aches. His doctors could not diagnose his illness, and his symptoms grew steadily worse. Three days after he entered the hospital, according to the records, he died. The attending physicians, an American among them, signed his death certificate. His body was placed in cold storage for twenty hours, and then he was buried. He said he remembered hearing his doctors pronounce him dead while his sister wept at his bedside.

6 At the Centre de Psychiatrie et Neurologie in Port-au-Prince, Dr. Lamarque Douyon, a Haitian-born, Canadian-trained psychiatrist, has been systematically investigating all reports of zombies since 1961. Though convinced zombies were real, he had been unable to find a scientific explanation for the phenomenon. He did not believe zombies were people raised from the dead, but that did not make them any less interesting. He speculated that victims were only made to *look* dead, probably by means of a drug that dramatically slowed metabolism. The victim was buried, dug up within a few hours, and somehow reawakened.

7 The Narcisse case provided Douyon with evidence strong enough to warrant a request for assistance from colleagues in New York. Douyon wanted to find an ethnobotanist, a traditional-medicines expert, who could track down the zombie potion he was sure existed. Aware of the medical potential of a drug that could dramatically lower metabolism, a group organized by the late Dr. Nathan Kline—a New York psychiatrist and pioneer in the field of psychopharmacology—raised the funds necessary to send someone to investigate.

8 The search for that someone led to the Harvard Botanical Museum, one of the world's foremost institutes of ethnobiology. Its director, Richard Evans Schultes, Jeffrey professor of biology, had spent thirteen years in the tropics studying native medicines. Some of his best-known work is the investigation of curare, the substance used by the nomadic

people of the Amazon to poison their darts. Refined into a powerful muscle relaxant called D-tubocurarine, it is now an essential component of the anesthesia used during almost all surgery.

9 Schultes would have been a natural for the Haitian investigation, but he was too busy. He recommended another Harvard ethnobotanist for the assignment, Wade Davis, a 28-year-old Canadian pursuing a doctorate in biology.

10 Davis grew up in the tall pine forests of British Columbia and entered Harvard in 1971, influenced by a *Life* magazine story on the student strike of 1969. Before Harvard, the only Americans he had known were draft dodgers, who seemed very exotic. "I used to fight forest fires with them," Davis says. "Like everybody else, I thought America was where it was at. And I wanted to go to Harvard because of that *Life* article. When I got there, I realized it wasn't quite what I had in mind."

11 Davis took a course from Schultes, and when he decided to go to South America to study plants, he approached his professor for guidance. "He was an extraordinary figure," Davis remembers. "He was a man who had done it all. He had lived alone for years in the Amazon." Schultes sent Davis to the rain forest with two letters of introduction and two pieces of advice: wear a pith helmet and try ayahuasca, a powerful hallucinogenic vine. During that expedition and others, Davis proved himself an "outstanding field man," says his mentor. Now, in early 1982, Schultes called him into his office and asked if he had plans for spring break.

12 "I always took to Schultes's assignments like a plant takes to water," says Davis, tall and blond, with inquisitive blue eyes. "Whatever Schultes told me to do, I did. His letters of introduction opened up a whole world." This time the world was Haiti.

13 Davis knew nothing about the Caribbean island—and nothing about African traditions, which serve as Haiti's cultural basis. He certainly did not believe in zombies. "I thought it was a lark," he says now.

14 Davis landed in Haiti a week after his conversation with Schultes, armed with a hypothesis about how the zombie drug—if it existed—might be made. Setting out to explore, he discovered a country materially impoverished, but rich in culture and mystery. He was impressed by the cohesion of Haitian society; he found none of the crime, social disorder, and rampant drug and alcohol abuse so common in many of the other Caribbean islands. The cultural wealth and cohesion, he believes, spring from the country's turbulent history.

15 During the French occupation of the late eighteenth century, 370,000 African-born slaves were imported to Haiti between 1780 and 1790. In 1791, the black population launched one of the few successful slave revolts in history, forming secret societies and overcoming first the French plantation owners and then a detachment of troops from

Napoleon's army, sent to quell the revolt. For the next hundred years Haiti was the only independent black republic in the Caribbean, populated by people who did not forget their African heritage. "You can almost argue that Haiti is more African than Africa," Davis says. "When the west coast of Africa was being disrupted by colonialism and the slave trade, Haiti was essentially left alone. The amalgam of beliefs in Haiti is unique, but it's very, very African."

16 Davis discovered that the vast majority of Haitian peasants practice voodoo, a sophisticated religion with African roots. Says Davis, "It was immediately obvious that the stereotypes of voodoo weren't true. Going around the countryside, I found clues to a whole complex social world." Vodounists believe they communicate directly with, indeed are often possessed by, the many spirits who populate the everyday world. Vodoun society is a system of education, law, and medicine; it embodies a code of ethics that regulates social behavior. In rural areas, secret vodoun societies, much like those found on the west coast of Africa, are as much or more in control of everyday life as the Haitian government.

17 Although most outsiders dismissed the zombie phenomenon as folklore, some early investigators, convinced of its reality, tried to find a scientific explanation. The few who sought a zombie drug failed. Nathan Kline, who helped finance Davis's expedition, had searched unsuccessfully, as had Lamarque Douyon, the Haitian psychiatrist. Zora Neale Hurston, an American black woman, may have come closest. An anthropological pioneer, she went to Haiti in the Thirties, studied vodoun society, and wrote a book on the subject, *Tell My Horse,* first published in 1938. She knew about the secret societies and was convinced zombies were real, but if a powder existed, she too failed to obtain it.

18 Davis obtained a sample in a few weeks.

19 He arrived in Haiti with the names of several contacts. A BBC reporter familiar with the Narcisse case had suggested he talk with Marcel Pierre. Pierre owned the Eagle Bar, a bordello in the city of Saint Marc. He was also a voodoo sorcerer and had supplied the BBC with a physiologically active powder of unknown ingredients. Davis found him willing to negotiate. He told Pierre he was a representative of "powerful but anonymous interests in New York," willing to pay generously for the priest's services, provided no questions were asked. Pierre agreed to be helpful for what Davis will only say was a "sizable sum." Davis spent a day watching Pierre gather the ingredients—including human bones—and grind them together with mortar and pestle. However, from his knowledge of poison, Davis knew immediately that nothing in the formula could produce the powerful effects of zombification.

20 Three weeks later, Davis went back to the Eagle Bar, where he found Pierre sitting with three associates. Davis challenged him. He called him a charlatan. Enraged, the priest gave him a second vial, claiming that this was the real poison. Davis pretended to pour the

powder into his palm and rub it into his skin. "You're a dead man," Pierre told him, and he might have been, because this powder proved to be genuine. But, as the substance had not actually touched him, Davis was able to maintain his bravado, and Pierre was impressed. He agreed to make the poison and show Davis how it was done.

21 The powder, which Davis keeps in a small vial, looks like dry black dirt. It contains parts of toads, sea worms, lizards, tarantulas, and human bones. (To obtain the last ingredient, he and Pierre unearthed a child's grave on a nocturnal trip to the cemetery.) The poison is rubbed into the victim's skin. Within hours he begins to feel nauseated and has difficulty breathing. A pins-and-needles sensation afflicts his arms and legs, then progresses to the whole body. The subject becomes paralyzed; his lips turn blue for lack of oxygen. Quickly—sometimes within six hours—his metabolism is lowered to a level almost indistinguishable from death.

22 As Davis discovered, making the poison is an inexact science. Ingredients varied in the five samples he eventually acquired, although the active agents were always the same. And the poison came with no guarantee. Davis speculates that sometimes instead of merely paralyzing the victim, the compound kills him. Sometimes the victim suffocates in the coffin before he can be resurrected. But clearly the potion works well enough often enough to make zombies more than a figment of Haitian imagination.

23 Analysis of the powder produced another surprise. "When I went down to Haiti originally," says Davis, "my hypothesis was that the formula would contain *cončombre zombi*, the 'zombie's cucumber,' which is a *Datura* plant. I thought somehow *Datura* was used in putting people down." *Datura* is a powerful psychoactive plant, found in West Africa as well as other tropical areas and used there in ritual as well as criminal activities. Davis had found *Datura* growing in Haiti. Its popular name suggested the plant was used in creating zombies.

24 But, says Davis, "there were a lot of problems with the *Datura* hypothesis. Partly it was a question of how the drug was administered. *Datura* would create a stupor in huge doses, but it just wouldn't produce the kind of immobility that was key. These people had to appear dead, and there aren't many drugs that will do that."

25 One of the ingredients Pierre included in the second formula was a dried fish, a species of puffer or blowfish, common to most parts of the world. It gets its name from its ability to fill itself with water and swell to several times its normal size when threatened by predators. Many of these fish contain a powerful poison known as tetrodotoxin. One of the most powerful nonprotein poisons known to man, tetrodotoxin turned up in every sample of zombie powder that Davis acquired.

26 Numerous well-documented accounts of puffer fish poisoning exist, but the most famous accounts come from the Orient, where *fugu*

fish, a species of puffer, is considered a delicacy. In Japan, special chefs are licensed to prepare *fugu*. The chef removes enough poison to make the fish nonlethal, yet enough remains to create exhilarating physiological effects—tingles up and down the spine, mild prickling of the tongue and lips, euphoria. Several dozen Japanese die each year, having bitten off more than they should have.

27 "When I got hold of the formula and saw it was the *fugu* fish, that suddenly threw open the whole Japanese literature," says Davis. Case histories of *fugu* poisoning read like accounts of zombification. Victims remain conscious but unable to speak or move. A man who had "died" after eating *fugu* recovered seven days later in the morgue. Several summers ago, another Japanese poisoned by *fugu* revived after he was nailed into his coffin. "Almost all of Narcisse's symptoms correlated. Even strange things such as the fact that he said he was conscious and could hear himself pronounced dead. Stuff that I thought had to be magic, that seemed crazy. But, in fact, that is what people who get *fugu*-fish poisoning experience."

28 Davis was certain he had solved the mystery. But far from being the end of his investigation, identifying the poison was, in fact, its starting point. "The drug alone didn't make zombies," he explains. "Japanese victims of puffer-fish poisoning don't become zombies, they become poison victims. All the drug could do was set someone up for a whole series of psychological pressures that would be rooted in the culture. I wanted to know why zombification was going on," he says.

29 He sought a cultural answer, an explanation rooted in the structure and beliefs of Haitian society. Was zombification simply a random criminal activity? He thought not. He had discovered that Clairvius Narcisse and "Ti Femme," a second victim he interviewed, were village pariahs. Ti Femme was regarded as a thief. Narcisse had abandoned his children and deprived his brother of land that was rightfully his. Equally suggestive, Narcisse claimed that his aggrieved brother had sold him to a *bokor,* a voodoo priest who dealt in black magic; he made cryptic reference to having been tried and found guilty by the "masters of the land."

30 Gathering poisons from various parts of the country, Davis had come into direct contact with the vodoun secret societies. Returning to the anthropological literature on Haiti and pursuing his contacts with informants, Davis came to understand the social matrix within which zombies were created.

31 Davis's investigations uncovered the importance of the secret societies. These groups trace their origins to the bands of escaped slaves that organized the revolt against the French in the late eighteenth century. Open to both men and women, the societies control specific territories of the country. Their meetings take place at night, and in many rural parts of Haiti the drums and wild celebrations that characterize the gatherings can be heard for miles.

32 Davis believes the secret societies are responsible for policing their communities, and the threat of zombification is one way they maintain order. Says Davis, "Zombification has a material basis, but it also has a societal logic." To the uninitiated, the practice may appear a random criminal activity, but in rural vodoun society, it is exactly the opposite—a sanction imposed by recognized authorities, a form of capital punishment. For rural Haitians, zombification is an even more severe punishment than death, because it deprives the subject of his most valued possessions: his free will and independence.

33 The vodounists believe that when a person dies, his spirit splits into several different parts. If a priest is powerful enough, the spiritual aspect that controls a person's character and individuality, known as *ti bon ange,* the "good little angel," can be captured and the corporeal aspect, deprived of its will, held as a slave.

34 From studying the medical literature on tetrodotoxin poisoning, Davis discovered that if a victim survives the first few hours of the poisoning, he is likely to recover fully from the ordeal. The subject simply revives spontaneously. But zombies remain without will, in a trance like state, a condition vodounists attribute to the power of the priest. Davis thinks it possible that the psychological trauma of zombification may be augmented by *Datura* or some other drug; he thinks zombies may be fed a *Datura* paste that accentuates their disorientation. Still, he puts the material basis of zombification in perspective: "Tetrodotoxin and *Datura* are only templates on which cultural forces and beliefs may be amplified a thousand times."

35 Davis has not been able to discover how prevalent zombification is in Haiti. "How many zombies there are is not the question," he says. He compares it to capital punishment in the United States: "It doesn't really matter how many people are electrocuted, as long as it's a possibility." As a sanction in Haiti, the fear is not of zombies, it's of becoming one.

36 Davis attributes his success in solving the zombie mystery to his approach. He went to Haiti with an open mind and immersed himself in the culture. "*My intuition unhindered by biases served me well,*" he says. "I didn't make any judgments." He combined this attitude with what he had learned earlier from his experiences in the Amazon. "Schultes's lesson is to go and live with the Indians as an Indian." Davis was able to participate in the vodoun society to a surprising degree, eventually even penetrating one of the Bizango societies and dancing in their nocturnal rituals. His appreciation of Haitian culture is apparent. "Everybody asks me how did a white person get this information? To ask the question means you don't understand Haitians—they don't judge you by the color of your skin."

37 As a result of the exotic nature of his discoveries, Davis has gained a certain notoriety. He plans to complete his dissertation soon, but he has already finished writing a popular account of his adventures. To be

published in January by Simon and Schuster, it is called *The Serpent and the Rainbow,* after the serpent that vodounists believe created the earth and the rainbow spirit it married. Film rights have already been optioned; in October Davis went back to Haiti with a screenwriter. But Davis takes the notoriety in stride. "All this attention is funny," he says. "For years, not just me, but all Schultes's students have had extraordinary adventures in the line of work. The adventure is not the end point, it's just along the way of getting the data. At the Botanical Museum, Schultes created a world unto itself. We didn't think we were doing anything above the ordinary. I still don't think we do. And you know," he adds, "the Haiti episode does not begin to compare to what others have accomplished—particularly Schultes himself."

✧ *Evaluating the Text*

1. To what extent does Del Guercio's account gain credibility because he begins with the mysterious case of Clairvius Narcisse? How is Narcisse's identification by his sister intended to put the case beyond all doubt and leave the process of zombification as the only possible explanation for his otherwise inexplicable "death"?
2. Why is it important to Del Guercio's account that he mentions physicians from the United States as well as Haitian doctors who certified the "death" of Clairvius Narcisse? What is Del Guercio's attitude toward this phenomenon? How is this attitude revealed in the way he constructs his report?
3. How does the threat of zombification serve as a preventive measure that ensures social control in deterring crimes against the community? How did it operate in the cases of Clairvius Narcisse and "Ti Femme"? In what way is the reality of the social mechanism of zombification quite different from how it has been presented in movies and popular culture?
4. What kind of independent confirmation of the effects of tetrodotoxin, a potent neurotoxin that drastically reduces metabolism and produces paralysis, did Davis discover in his research on the effects of Japanese victims of *fugu* fish poisoning?

✧ *Exploring Different Perspectives*

1. Compare the discoveries made by Wade Davis and by David R. Counts, in "Too Many Bananas," as they venture into the unfamiliar territories of Haiti and New Guinea respectively.
2. Compare the different cultural viewpoints that Del Guercio and Cameron M. Smith in "Of Ice and Men" needed to understand in order to pursue their research in Haiti and the Arctic.

✧ *Extending Viewpoints through Writing and Research*

1. If you are familiar with or interested in the processes by which various religious cults enlist and program their members, you might compare their methods to those of the vodoun priests in terms of positive and negative reinforcement of psychological, sociological, and physiological conditioning.
2. If you have had the opportunity to see the movie *The Serpent and the Rainbow* (1988), directed by Wes Craven, you might wish to compare its representation of the events described in this article with Wade Davis's book *The Serpent and the Rainbow*. For further research on this subject, you might consult Wade Davis, *Passage of Darkness: The Ethnobiology of the Haitian Zombie*, an in-depth study of the political, social, and botanical mechanisms of zombification.
3. The African origins of voodoo are described in depth at http://www.swagga.com/voodoo.htm.

How does this image illustrate the way rituals enhance the belief system of voodoo?

Cameron M. Smith

Of Ice and Men

Cameron M. Smith is an archeologist at Portland State University who has written articles for Scientic American, MIND, Archeology, Spaceflight, Playboy, *and other magazines. The following essay first appeared in* Cultural Survival Quarterly, *Summer 2008. In it, Smith provides evidence that the Iñupiat, a native people living in the Arctic, are opposed to declaring polar bears an endangered species. A recent book of his is* The Top Ten Myths About Evolution *(2006).*

Before You Read

Would people who have lived their entire lives in the habitat of the polar bear in the Arctic be able to offer an accurate assessment about whether these bears were endangered?

1 As the thin end of the global warming wedge begins prying apart the foundations of traditional life in the Alaskan Arctic, you might think that the native people there would welcome the federal listing of the polar bear as a threatened species. After all, everyone loves polar bears (Knud, the Berlin Zoo's über-cute furball, appeared on the cover of the May 2007 *Vanity Fair,* photographed by none other than Annie Leibovitz), and they bring tourism dollars to the Arctic, raising awareness of global warming at the same time. But the Iñupiat—the indigenous people around Barrow, for whom the bears are a cornerstone of their traditional hunting culture, along with whales, seals and caribou—argue that listing the polar bear as threatened won't save it. And as I explored the polar bear's frozen-sea habitat on the north coast of Alaska in the winter of 2007, I came to understand their point of view.

2 Dragging my supply sled toward my base in Barrow one frigid morning—it had been 30 below the night before, and I didn't dare to check the temperature before I crawled out of my sleeping bag—I recalled the simple wonders of the past week. I'd heard the Arctic described as a wasteland, but nobody who'd taken the time to walk here could call it anything less than a thriving ecosystem. Cold, yes, but without question thriving, electric with life. I wanted to learn what native people thought about what was being done to protect this priceless wilderness in the face of increasing oil and gas exploration, and I thought the proposed listing of the polar bear as a threatened species might help smooth the way.

3 But Billy Leavitt, an Iñupiat hunter who picked me up on the outskirts of Barrow, blew that idea to pieces with a few words. As we tore down an ice road in his battered pickup truck, and a 60-below windchill blew through an open window—just about killing me but cooling him nicely—Billy gestured at the landscape, speaking in long, flat vowels and drawn-out consonants.

4 "It's too warm for this time of year," he said. "That global warming is really happening."

5 "Yeah, I hear the polar bear is in trouble," I replied, trying to sympathize. Billy tensed up.

6 "No," he said, "That's your Greenpeace people sayin' that. That's your conservationists"—he spat the last word—"people who watch that Discovery Channel and then come up here to tell us how to hunt." I considered myself a conservationist, but I had no reply to that conversation-stopper. I sat there wondering what else I might be wrong about.

7 Still, Billy cordially shook my hand when he dropped me off in Barrow, inviting me to come to his cabin out on the land. "You'll learn a lot," he said. Although I didn't have a chance to visit him, I did take another trek, and learned a little more about his point of view. On March 7th, the residents of Barrow (over 60 percent Iñupiat) met with representatives of the U.S. Fish and Wildlife Service, the federal agency then considering listing the polar bear as threatened.

8 The Iñupiat Heritage Center, where the meeting was held, is a modern, multi-million-dollar facility at once a museum displaying relics of pre-contact life, a meeting hall, and a work area where walrushide boats are sewn together in preparation for whale-hunts. Once everyone's snowmobiles had been parked it was quiet in the meeting hall, but the atmosphere was tense. A handful of Fish and Wildlife presenters sat at a table in the front of the hall, looking out at a hundred mostly native Barrow residents, who awaited the government's presentation with patience, but no smiles.

9 The meeting began with the government representatives presenting their case for listing the polar bear, supported by two main points. First, the polar bear's sea ice habitat has been steadily reduced in the past 30 years, a finding of 5 independent studies that nobody can deny: today, satellite imagery shows us an Alaska-sized hole in the summer sea ice cover, where 30 years ago it was a solid sheet, and the prediction is that by 2050, most of the Arctic Ocean will be ice-free in the summer, driving polar bears either to adapt to land in that season, or go extinct. The Iñupiat agreed with this, saying in fact that they'd been trying to raise the alarm over global warming for years. Still, they let this point slide.

10 Second, Fish and Wildlife argued that polar bear populations are already in decline, as seen in a study of the western Hudson Bay polar

bear population, which they claimed has decreased by over 20 percent in the last 20 years. The Iñupiat weren't so sure of this; like their Canadian counterparts, the Inuit, they believed that polar bear numbers were actually up, but that the bears had migrated out of the scientists' survey areas. Still, Fish and Wildlife concluded that while overhunting, disease, and other factors do not threaten the polar bear throughout its natural range, it should be listed as threatened because of the well documented decline of sea ice.

11 Then the Iñupiat took the podium. For two hours they presented their own testimony, questioning Fish and Wildlife's assumptions and facts, and making a strong case for entrusting the survival of the polar bear not to regulations dictated from Washington, D.C., but to the Iñupiat and other native polar people.

12 It's not surprising that the Iñupiat's discussion of polar bear biology, behavior, ecology, habitat, and population was more sophisticated than that of the Fish and Wildlife representatives; after all, the federal representatives had flown in from Washington or Anchorage, and would fly out in a day or two, while the Iñupiat lived their entire lives in the polar bear's habitat. They were not new to the polar bear, and they weren't impressed by 30-year studies that Fish and Wildlife called "long-term." The Iñupiat had cultural knowledge about polar bears—and the rest of their ecosystem—that went back far longer. "As the ice retreats," one hunter said, "some bears will follow it, and others will get stranded on land, like some of them are now, when the ice retreats in the summer. Those that follow the ice will survive, and those that live on the land will have to adapt, just like their ancestors did." Glenn Sheehan, executive director of the Barrow Arctic Science Consortium, pointed out that the polar bear had been living with climate changes for more than 200,000 years, and that it had survived at least one other warming episode, the Medieval Warm period. "Have you considered that at all?" he asked the Fish and Wildlife representatives. "Do you even have data going back more than 50 years?"

13 The Iñupiat speakers included common citizens, native hunters, several whaling captains, and North Slope Borough mayor Edward S. Itta, all of whom looked hard into the eyes of the Fish and Wildlife representatives. After all, in this modest meeting they were doing nothing less than fighting to prevent yet another important part of their traditional life from being wrested away from them by a distant federal agency.

14 The Iñupiat based their opposition to polar bear listing on three main facts. First, in their experience polar bear numbers were not declining, an observation also noted by native Canadians on Hudson Bay, who say the decline there has been misunderstood by scientists who drop in from time to time, but fail to understand polar bear migration behavior. One resident pointed out that scientists were fond of

saying they needed "holistic, long-term studies" of the polar bear, but were—insultingly and stupidly—ignoring exactly that kind of knowledge by relying on studies that "only went back a generation or two." Mayor Itta sharply pointed out that the Fish and Wildlife study did not actually have empirical data for the population increase or decrease of polar bears in northern Alaska, only projections and estimates based on the Hudson Bay population, 4,000 miles away. If the tables were turned, Itta noted, Washington wouldn't respond to hypotheses or hearsay; they'd want real, empirical data, and the Iñupiat deserved the same. In short, Fish and Wildlife's data on the polar bear population was largely theoretical (they had admitted this in their own presentation), and based on no more empirical facts or observations than the Iñupiats' own. The implication was clear to all: who would you rather trust about these numbers—the people who live in the area and observe the polar bear population day by day, or federal government monitors?

15 The Iñupiats' second point was that they simply don't take enough bears to threaten the species, only about 20 a year. Indeed, Fish and Wildlife's own study concluded that over-hunting was not a threat in Canada (because of sound management policies there) or Alaska (because of the 30-year-old Marine Mammal Protection Act). Barrow Arctic Science Consortium president and native hunter Richard Glenn told Fish and Wildlife, "If you want to address over-hunting, go to Russia, where they poach 200 polar bears a year!"

16 The third point, mentioned time and again, was summarized by Mayor Itta: "Listing the polar bear does not address the problem!" Whaling captain Charlie Brower said, "The problem—pointed out in your own study—is shrinking sea ice, which is caused by carbon dioxide emissions!" The Iñupiat said that listing the polar bear as threatened does nothing to address sea ice retreat; it's just a measure meant to make people of the Lower 48 feel as though they're "saving the polar bear" when in fact they're doing nothing at all.

17 Listing a species as threatened or endangered is meant to force federally backed action to preserve that species' critical habitat. If that habitat isn't delineated, however, the listing has little value. In this case, the Fish and Wildlife Department found that the bears' habitat needs were "undeterminable." The proposed listing did not mention greenhouse gas or carbon emissions at all, an omission that was made overt when Secretary of the Interior Dirk Kempthorne announced the official threatened listing for polar bears on May 18, 2008. "The most significant part of today's decision," he said, "is what President Bush observed about climate change policy last month. President Bush noted that 'The Clean Air Act, the Endangered Species Act and the National Environmental Policy Act were never meant to regulate global climate change.'"

18 If the polar bear's critical sea ice habitat isn't defined, the Iñupiat argued, and its reduction isn't linked to human-induced warming brought about by greenhouse gas emissions, then listing the polar bear will not work as a lever to force action on climate change.

19 In short, the science brought by the Fish and Wildlife representatives to justify listing the polar bear as threatened looked great on paper, but was incomplete—even to other scientists—and ignored Iñupiat traditional knowledge. And putting the polar bear on the endangered list wouldn't stop illegal poaching in Russia, or the sea ice from retreating, or anything else that was actually affecting polar bear populations. In fact it would mask the real issue of climate change.

20 The Iñupiat solution was for Washington to address climate change head-on by legislating global warming preventatives, and leave the polar bears to the native peoples of the Arctic. After all, they are subsistence hunters who manage animal populations so that they will be there in the future. The word "sustainable" has been in the American consciousness for about a generation, while it has been the cornerstone of Iñupiat life for millennia. Not taking their lead in this issue would be a terrible loss of opportunity, especially considering that they are living on the front line of global warming, where change is felt first and foremost.

✧ *Evaluating the Text*

1. How has the seeming decline in the polar bear population not accounted for their migration behavior?
2. Why don't the Iñupiat trust the Fish and Wildlife data on polar bear population numbers?
3. Why have the Iñupiat argued that listing the polar bear as an endangered species will have no effect on those attempting to force action on climate change?

✧ *Exploring Different Perspectives*

1. What assumptions underlying the *Herald Sun* (Melbourne) report (see "Bears Feel Global Heat; Polor Icon Faces Wipeout") do the Iñupiat challenge?
2. How do both Gino Del Guercio in "The Secrets of Voodoo in Haiti" and Smith in the Arctic bring in an entirely new perspective on long-held stereotypes (as in voodoo and global warming, respectively)?

✧ *Extending Viewpoints through Writing and Research*

1. Are there other instances of well-meaning conservationists who are seeking to change public policy to make people feel better, but the facts don't warrant such change?

2. Research current policies and theories about climate change. For example, have recent discoveries based on sunspot activity suggested that a global cooling rather than a global warming cycle is on its way? You might wish to read Robert W. Felix's *Not by Fire but by Ice* (2005) and *Magnetic Reversals and Evolutionary Leaps* (2009).

Herald Sun (Melbourne)

Bears Feel Global Heat; Polar Icon Faces Wipeout

In contrast to the previous selection by Cameron M. Smith, the news release covered in an Australian newspaper article highlights the conclusions drawn by the U.S. Fish and Wildlife Service about the status of polar bears in northern Alaska. Their projections and estimates were largely theoretical and were disputed by the empirical experiences of the Iñupiat native peoples who live and hunt in the Arctic. This study was conducted over a period of thirty years, and its conclusion marked a change in the George W. Bush administration's position on the effects of global warming.

Before You Read

How have newspapers, magazines, and television ads used the polar bear to promote acceptance of global warming?

1 WASHINGTON—Polar bears should be listed as an endangered species because of warming temperatures, the Bush White House has proposed.

2 It was the first time the administration had identified climate change as the driving force behind the potential end of a species, the *Washington Post* reported.

3 "We've reviewed all the available data that leads us to believe the sea ice the polar bear depends on has been receding," an Interior Department official said. "Obviously, the sea ice is melting because the temperatures are warmer."

4 The official said US Fish and Wildlife Service officials had concluded that polar bears could be endangered within 45 years.

5 The Bush administration has consistently rejected scientific theses that human activity contributed to global warming and has resisted capping greenhouse gas emissions as bad for business and US workers.

6 Greenhouse gases like carbon dioxide, produced by burning fossil fuels, trap heat in the atmosphere. Scientists say rising temperatures could raise sea levels and cause more droughts, floods and heatwaves.

7 An Interior Department official said the decision to propose polar bears as threatened with extinction "wasn't easy for us" because "there is still some significant uncertainty" about what could happen to bear populations in the future.

8 The proposal was being submitted yesterday for publication in the Federal Register, meeting a deadline under a legal settlement with environmental advocacy groups that argue the government had failed to respond quickly enough to the polar bear's plight.

9 One of the lawyers who filed suit against the administration, Andrew Wetzler of the Natural Resources Defence Council, welcomed the proposal. "It's such a loud recognition that global warming is real," he said.

10 "It is rapidly threatening the polar bear and, in fact, an entire ecosystem with utter destruction."

✧ *Evaluating the Text*

1. Why has the U.S. Fish and Wildlife Service urged the step of declaring the polar bear an endangered species?
2. What reasons and evidence does the service cite in reaching this decision?
3. How would you characterize the tone of this announcement—well reasoned, alarmist, politically motivated, or neutral?
4. Why was this decision a first for the then-governing Bush administration?

✧ *Exploring Different Perspectives*

1. What reasons cited by Cameron M. Smith in "Of Ice and Men" go against the assumptions in this announcement reported in the *Herald Sun*?
2. To what extent is the proposed legislation reported by the *Herald Sun* a reflection of how Americans view themselves, as described by Poranee Natadecha-Sponsel in "Individualism as an American Cultural Value"?

✧ *Extending Viewpoints through Writing and Research*

1. Look through current magazines and describe how the polar bear has been used as an icon for the acceptance of global warming.
2. To what extent have films used climate change (either warming or cooling) as a backdrop? See, for example, *The Ice Age* series, including the original *Ice Age* (2002), *Ice Age: The Meltdown* (2006), and *Ice Age: Dawn of the Dinosaurs* (2009).

How does this photograph of a polar bear on an ice floe illustrate why it has become an icon for endangered species?

Fareed Zakaria

The Challenger

Fareed Zakaria was born in 1964 in Mumbai, India. He was educated at Yale and Harvard and since 2000 has served as an editor of Newsweek International. *In the following essay from his book* The Post-American World *(2008), he outlines the unique and awesome position of power that China has come to occupy.*

Before You Read

What is the current relationship between the United States and China? How has it been influenced by factors such as trade, the value of their respective currencies, and human rights?

1 Americans may admire beauty, but they are truly dazzled by bigness. Think of the Grand Canyon, the California redwoods, Grand Central Terminal, Disney World, SUVs, the American armed forces, General Electric, the Double Quarter Pounder (with Cheese), and the Venti Latte. Europeans prefer complexity, the Japanese revere minimalism. But Americans like size, preferably supersize.

2 That's why China hits the American mind so hard. It is a country whose scale dwarfs the United States. With 1.3 billion people, it has four times America's population. For more than a hundred years, American missionaries and businessmen dreamed of the possibilities—1 billion souls to save, 2 billion armpits to deodorize—but never went beyond dreams. China was very big, but very poor. Pearl Buck's bestselling book (and play and movie), *The Good Earth,* introduced a lasting portrait of China: an agrarian society with struggling peasants, greedy landowners, famines and floods, plagues, and poverty.

3 Napoleon famously, and probably apocryphally, said, "Let China sleep, for when China wakes, she will shake the world." And for almost two hundred years, China seemed to follow his instruction, staying dormant and serving as little more than an arena in which the other great powers acted out their ambitions. In the twentieth century, Japan, once China's imitator, bested it in war and peace. During World War II, the United States allied with it and gave it aid and, in 1945, a seat on the UN Security Council. When Washington and Beijing became foes after the Communist takeover of 1949, China slipped further behind. Mao Zedong dragged the country through a series of

catastrophic convulsions that destroyed its economic, technological, and intellectual capital. Then, in 1979, things began shaking.

4 China's awakening is reshaping the economic and political landscape, but it is also being shaped by the world into which it is rising. Beijing is negotiating the same two forces that are defining the post-American world more broadly—globalization and nationalism. On the one hand, economic and technological pressures are pushing Beijing toward a cooperative integration into the world. But these same forces produce disruption and social upheaval in the country, and the regime seeks new ways to unify an increasingly diverse society. Meanwhile, growth also means that China becomes more assertive, casting a larger shadow on the region and the world. The stability and peace of the post-American world will depend, in large measure, on the balance that China strikes between these forces of integration and disintegration.

5 When historians look back at the last decades of the twentieth century, they might well point to 1979 as a watershed. That year, the Soviet Union invaded Afghanistan, digging its grave as a superpower. And that year, China launched its economic reforms. The signal for the latter event came in December 1978 at an unlikely gathering: the Third Plenum of the Eleventh Central Committee of the Communist Party of China, typically an occasion for empty rhetoric and stale ideology. Before the formal meeting, at a working-group session, the newly empowered party boss, Deng Xiaoping, gave a speech that turned out to be the most important in modern Chinese history. He urged that the regime focus on economic development and let facts—not ideology—guide its path. "It doesn't matter if it is a black cat or a white cat," Deng said. "As long as it can catch mice, it's a good cat." Since then, China has done just that, pursuing a path of modernization that is ruthlessly pragmatic.

6 The results have been astonishing. China has grown over 9 percent a year for almost thirty years, the fastest rate for a major economy in recorded history. In that same period, it has moved around 400 million people out of poverty, the largest reduction that has taken place anywhere, anytime. The average Chinese person's income has increased nearly sevenfold. China, despite drawbacks and downsides, has achieved, on a massive scale, the dream of every Third World country—a decisive break with poverty. The economist Jeffrey Sachs puts it simply: "China is the most successful development story in world history."

7 The magnitude of change in China is almost unimaginable. The size of the economy has *doubled* every eight years for three decades. In 1978, the country made 200 air conditioners a year; in 2005, it made 48 million. China today exports in a single day more than it exported in all of 1978. For anyone who has been visiting the country during this period, there are more examples and images of change than one can recount. Fifteen years ago, when I first went to Shanghai, Pudong, in

the east of the city, was undeveloped countryside. Today, it is the city's financial district, densely studded with towers of glass and steel and lit like a Christmas tree every night. It is eight times the size of London's new financial district, Canary Wharf, and only slightly smaller than the entire city of Chicago. The city of Chongqing, meanwhile, actually patterns itself after Chicago, which was the world's fastest-growing city a hundred years ago. Chongqing, which is expanding every year by 300,000 people, would probably get that designation today. And Chongqing is just the head of a pack; the twenty fastest-growing cities in the world are all in China.

8 Despite Shanghai's appeal to Westerners, Beijing remains the seat of Chinese politics, culture, and art, and even its economy. The city is being remade to an extent unprecedented in history. (The closest comparison is Haussmann's makeover of Paris in the nineteenth century.) Largely in preparation for the 2008 Olympics, Beijing is building six new subway lines, a 43-kilometer light-rail system, a new airport terminal (the world's largest, of course), 25 million square kilometers of new property, a 125-kilometer "green belt," and a 12-square-kilometer Olympic Park. When looking at the models of a new Beijing, one inevitably thinks of Albert Speer's grandiose plans for postwar Berlin, drawn up in the 1940s; in fact, Albert Speer Jr., the son, also an architect, designed the 8-kilometer boulevard that will run from the Forbidden Palace to the Olympic Park. He sees no real comparison between the transformation of Beijing and his father's designs for Hitler. This is "bigger," he says. "Much bigger."

9 Every businessman these days has a dazzling statistic about China, meant to stun the listener into silence. And they are impressive numbers—most of which will be obsolete by the time you read them. China is the world's largest producer of coal, steel, and cement. It is the largest cell phone market in the world. It had 28 billion square feet of space under construction in 2005, more than five times as much as in America. Its exports to the United States have grown by 1,600 percent over the past fifteen years. At the height of the industrial revolution, Britain was called "the workshop of the world." That title belongs to China today. It manufactures two-thirds of the world's photocopiers, microwave ovens, DVD players, and shoes.

10 To get a sense of how completely China dominates low-cost manufacturing, take a look at Wal-Mart. Wal-Mart is one of the world's largest corporations. Its revenues are eight times those of Microsoft and account for 2 percent of America's GDP [gross domestic product]. It employs 1.4 million people, more than GM, Ford, GE, and IBM put together. It is legendary for its efficient—some would say ruthless—efforts to get the lowest price possible for its customers. To that end, it has adeptly used technology, managerial innovation, and, perhaps most significantly, low-cost manufacturers. Wal-Mart imports about

$18 billion worth of goods from China each year. The vast majority of its foreign suppliers are there. Wal-Mart's global supply chain is really a China supply chain.

11 China has also pursued a distinctly open trade and investment policy. For this among many reasons, it is not the new Japan. Beijing has not adopted the Japanese (or South Korean) path of development, which was an export-led strategy that kept the domestic market and society closed. Instead, China opened itself up to the world. (It did this partly because it had no choice, since it lacked the domestic savings of Japan or South Korea.) Now China's trade-to-GDP ratio is 70 percent, which makes it one of the most open economies in the world. Over the last fifteen years, imports from the United States have increased more than sevenfold. Procter & Gamble now earns $2.5 billion a year in China, and familiar products like Head & Shoulders shampoo and Pampers diapers are extradinarily popular with consumers there. Starbucks predicts that by 2010 it will have more cafés in China than in the United States. China is also very open to international brand names, whether of goods or people. Foreign architects have built most of the gleaming towers and grand developments that define the new China. And when looking for the man to direct China's debut on the world stage, the Olympic opening festivities, Beijing chose an American, Steven Spielberg. It is inconceivable that Japan or India would have given a foreigner such a role.

12 China is also the world's largest holder of money. Its foreign-exchange reserves are $1.5 trillion, 50 percent more than those of the next country (Japan) and three times the holdings of the entire European Union. Holding such massive reserves may or may not be a wise policy, but it is certainly an indication of China's formidable resilience in the face of any shocks or crises. At the end of the day, it is this combination of factors that makes China unique. It is the world's largest country, fastest-growing major economy, largest manufacturer, second-largest consumer, largest saver, and (almost certainly) second-largest military spender.[1] China will not replace the United States as the world's superpower. It is unlikely to surpass it on any dimension—military, political, or economic—for decades, let alone have dominance in all areas. But on issue after issue, it has become the second-most-important country in the world, adding a wholly new element to the international system.

[1]China's official military budget would put it third in the world, after the United States and the United Kingdom. But most analysts agree that many large expenditures are not placed on the official budget, and that, properly accounted for, China's military spending is second—though a very distant second—to that of the United States.

✧ *Evaluating the Text*

1. Why are Americans impressed by the scale of everything connected with China?
2. What new information does Zakaria provide that supports his assessment of China as a challenger to the United States? How has it reached this status?
3. Why has China's trade policy taken it in a different direction from that of Japan or South Korea?

✧ *Exploring Different Perspectives*

1. Compare how wealth and possessions are defined in Counts's essay (see "Too Many Bananas") and in China as described by Zakaria.
2. To what extent has China adopted and improved upon American character traits of self-reliance as described by Poranee Natadecha-Sponsel in "Individualism as an American Cultural Value"?

✧ *Extending Viewpoints through Writing and Research*

1. Discuss the implications of this chapter appearing in Zakaria's book titled *The Post-American World* (2009).
2. Examine your personal possessions, such as your clothes, shoes, films, and appliances, to discover what percentage of them are made in China.

Connecting Cultures

Ralph Linton, "One Hundred Percent American"

Compare the perspectives of Linton with those of Harold Miner in "Body Ritual among the Nacirema" in Chapter 8.

Poranee Natadecha-Sponsel, "Individualism as an American Cultural Value"

To what extent do American parents' expectations for their children as viewed by Natadecha-Sponsel contrast with those of Chinese parents as described by the editors of *Psychology Today* in "Plight of the Little Emperors" in Chapter 1.

David R. Counts, "Too Many Bananas"

How does Counts provide additional insight into traditional societies before consumerism took over, as discussed by Helena Norberg-Hodge in "Learning from Ladakh" in Chapter 4?

Napoleon A. Chagnon, "Doing Fieldwork among the Yąnomamö"

Compare the Yanomamös' attitude toward drugs with those described by Philip Slater in "Want-Creation Fuels Americans' Addictiveness" in Chapter 8.

Gino Del Guercio, "The Secrets of Voodoo in Haiti"

Compare the cultural viewpoints that Del Guercio described in Haiti and Robert Levine and Ellen Wolff (in "Social Time: The Heartbeat of Culture" in Chapter 8) needed to understand in order to pursue their research in Brazil.

Cameron M. Smith, "Of Ice and Men"

In what ways do both Smith and Douchan Gersi in "Initiated into an Iban Tribe of Headhunters" in Chapter 2 have to rethink their personal assumptions?

Herald Sun *(Melbourne), "Bears Feel Global Heat; Polar Icon Faces Wipeout"*

In your opinion, are family dinners as endangered as the polar bear? See Patricia Hampl's "Grandmother's Sunday Dinner" in Chapter 1.

Fareed Zakaria, "The Challenger"

How do both the accounts by Zakaria and the editors of *Psychology Today* in "Plight of the Little Emperors" in Chapter 1 provide complementary perspectives on life in China today?

7

The Role of Food in Different Cultures

There is no love sincerer than the love of food.
—George Bernard Shaw (1856–1950), *Anglo-Irish playwright and critic. Spoken by Tanner in* Man and Superman, *Act I.*

People around the world have evolved unique food preferences in ways that reflect the values of their particular culture. Sharing food creates a social bond and, in many cultures, offering food to guests is a central value. At certain times of the year, during festivals, holidays, and special occasions, sharing food as a part of ritual celebrations plays a key role. The food practices of many societies can reflect religious and cultural taboos. For example, Islamic dietary laws prohibit pork and alcohol; Hindus and Buddhists are mainly vegetarians; and Mormons prohibit stimulants such as alcohol, coffee, and tea.

In the twenty-first century, genetically modified foods have become the subject of much debate. In the first essay, "Genetically Modified Food Is Safe," Mark I. Schwartz argues that genetically engineered foods are present in over seventy-five percent of the foods we find in supermarkets and in fact are safer than conventional foods. The opposite view is presented by Jeffrey M. Smith in "Genetically Engineered Foods May Cause Rising Food Allergies." Smith claims that genetically modified foods have been shown to produce a host of allergic reactions. Amy Tan in "Fish Cheeks" relates the ambivalence she experienced when her mother prepared an authentic Chinese feast for their minister and his family at Christmas. Frederick Douglass in "My Bondage and My Freedom" offers an unusual window into the past when he tells about the differences between the lavish feasts consumed by slaveowners and the meager rations allotted to the slaves. Ethel G. Hofman in "An Island Passover" relates how her mother, on their isolated Scottish island, would prepare an authentic holiday meal for her family and hundreds of soldiers stationed there during World War II. In "Grinding It Out: The Making of McDonald's," the founder, Ray Kroc, describes the approach he took in order to get new items on the menus of this popular franchise. Chris Maynard and Bill Scheller in "Manifold Destiny" offer guidance to those who wish to cook meals on their engines while traveling. Andrew X. Pham in "Foreign-Asians" describes the dramatic events when he ordered a meal at a local inn on his way to his hometown in Vietnam. Saira Shah in "The Storyteller's Daughter" evokes the splendors of her father's native country, Afghanistan, through the aromatic and imaginative dishes he prepares and the stories he tells.

To help you understand how the works in this chapter relate to each other, you might use one or several of the following guidelines before writing about the role food plays in different cultures.

1. What specific problem, issue, or conflict is at the center of the author's account?
2. Which of these writers changed the way you think about the issue?
3. What is the expressed or implied argument and what form of evidence does the writer use to make the case?
4. Does the writer imply that people change events or that events change people?
5. How does the author adapt the technical nature of the subject for the readers?
6. If the writer offers a solution, does it seem realistic and feasible?

Recommended Films on this Theme

- *Tampopo* (Japan, 1985) A widowed noodle chef, encouraged by a truck driver and his friends, becomes a first-class chef;
- *Babette's Feast* (Denmark, 1987) A delightful story of a widowed French woman who prepares a lavish meal for her father's hundredth birthday and invites the very conservative villagers of his town;
- *Big Night* (United States, 1996) Two brothers whose Italian restaurant faces bankruptcy stake everything on a grand evening with Louis Prima as a guest;
- *Ratatouille* (United States, 2007) A delightful animated film about a provincial rat who wishes to become a great French chef.

Mark I. Schwartz

Genetically Modified Food Is Safe

Mark I. Schwartz is an attorney who practices food and drug law in Washington, D.C. He argues that genetically modified food crops are safe and have produced minimal health problems in the United States, where seventy-five percent of supermarket items are already genetically modified. He concludes that genetically modified (GM) foods are actually safer than those from conventional crops.

Before You Read
What benefits might genetically modified foods offer?

1 Last week [the first week in February 2008], France filed a request with the European Union [EU] to formally ban the commercial use of "MON 810," a variety of corn developed by Monsanto, the U.S. biotech firm. This corn variety was the only genetically modified [GM] crop grown in the French nation, and one of only two approved for cultivation in the EU. The Union and its member states have long raised concerns about the safety of biotech foods, despite substantial scientific evidence contradicting these concerns, and have effectively precluded the cultivation or sale of biotech crops or foods anywhere on the continent.

2 Several years ago, Canada, the United States and Argentina formally lodged a complaint with the World Trade Organization [WTO], arguing that there was no scientific evidence to justify the EU's effective ban on biotech foods, and that it was an unfair barrier to companies that wanted to export to Europe. In 2006, the WTO agreed, and deemed the restrictions imposed on biotech foods by European countries to be illegal. The EU has yet to comply with the global trade body's ruling.

3 On the other hand, in North America, dozens of new crops and foods resulting from recombinant DNA technology have been marketed over the past decade, and they have been an overwhelming success. Indeed, fully 90% of the soybeans currently planted in the U.S. are of a biotech variety, and close to 80% of cotton and 60% of corn are of a biotech variety. Furthermore, fully three-quarters of the processed

foods in our supermarkets contain ingredients from recombinant DNA modified plants.

Genetically Modified Foods Have Many Benefits

4 The seamless integration of biotech foods into our food supply has its origin in the Co-ordinated Framework for Regulation of Biotechnology, a document that laid the groundwork for establishing that the characteristics of the end-product determine the risk level, and hence the level of regulation, rather than the characteristics of the process by which the end-product is developed. This conclusion is based on the fact that the genes of virtually all organisms consist of DNA and, scientifically speaking, it's what the DNA produces, not where it comes from, that matters. The result is that biotech foods here are effectively regulated no differently than conventional foods. Furthermore, because the end product, not the process, determines the level of risk, biotech foods are generally not labelled any differently than conventional foods.

5 The relative importance of regulating the process (as in the EU) instead of the end product is referred to as the "process-product paradigm." With 10 years of hindsight to guide us, which is the better regulatory framework? Whether we compare these products on the basis of their production costs, diversity of new varietals, or safety, the clear winner is end-product regulation of biotech crops and foods.

6 For instance, farmers who have used crops containing genes enhancing resistance to pests have significantly reduced their reliance on pesticides, and simultaneously increased their yields. For cotton plants alone, the net financial gain to American farmers has been in the hundreds of millions of dollars. Also, one of the most promising areas of new crop development involves the marketing of genetically engineered plant varieties carrying traits to improve basic nutrition, particularly in the Third World, by increasing the crops' content of essential minerals and vitamins.

Conventional Crops Can Be Less Safe than GM Crops

7 As for safety, by the end of 2007, the U.S. Food and Drug Administration had evaluated approximately 70 biotech food products and found them all to be as safe as their conventional counterparts. Furthermore, a large body of independent scientific evidence confirms that there is nothing about biotech foods that causes them to be inherently more dangerous than foods made from conventional crops. For instance, a large study by the National Academy of Sciences evaluated the likelihood of unintended health effects as a result of various methods of developing new strains, and concluded that mutagen breeding, a century-old "conventional" means of altering crops, was more likely to

be genetically disruptive than any form of genetic engineering. Mutagen breeding also produced the widest range of unintended effects.

8 What many opponents of bioengineering refuse to acknowledge is that many traditional plant breeding techniques are simply imprecise forms of the very genetic engineering that they claim to reject. For instance, mutagen-breeding techniques involve bombarding plants with X-rays, gamma rays, fast neutrons, or one of a variety of toxic chemicals, in an attempt to induce favourable chromosomal changes and genetic mutations. These techniques are so imprecise that researchers never know which chromosomes they are disrupting, let alone the genes on these chromosomes that they are mutating.

9 Examples of products developed using these conventional methods include some of the most common varieties of grapefruit, watermelon, wheat, barley, rice, peanuts and lettuce, as well as hundreds of other fruits, vegetables, grains and legumes that are in supermarkets around the world. Indeed, not one of the foods produced through the use of mutagen breeding is labelled "mutagen bred" or "engineered using ionizing radiation or toxic chemicals."

GM Crops Can Have Fewer Toxins Than Traditional Crops

10 Ironically, an increasing number of studies have concluded that biotech foods are actually healthier and safer in many respects than their conventional counterparts. Examples include some of the very products that France and the EU have banned, namely, varieties of biotech corn. Minute quantities of the fungal toxin Fumonisin have been linked to cancer, liver toxicity and neural tube defects in newborns. The principal way these toxins enter the food supply is via insect-damaged plants. Certain biotech crops, such as MON 810 (sold under the tradename of YieldGard), are engineered to produce a protein that is toxic to many boring insects, but perfectly safe to mammals, thereby substantially reducing damage to crops, which are the vehicle by which fungal toxins enter our food supply. These crops have been shown to contain 900% fewer fungal toxins than the non-GM corn varieties grown by organic and traditional farmers.

11 Indeed, these scientific conclusions have led to suggestions that health claims be allowed on these biotech varieties or that warning labels be mandated on certain conventional products, turning on its head the argument that bioengineered foods be labelled as "genetically engineered" in order to enable consumers to seek out the "safer" conventional products.

12 There is now abundant scientific evidence, from countless independent studies, that biotech crops and foods are safe, can lower production costs, reduce reliance on pesticides, and improve basic nutrition. If France and the other EU countries do not comply with the

WTO's ruling deeming Europe's trade restrictions to be illegal, Canada and the United States will just leave the Europeans to toil on their own in what will eventually come to be known there as the dark ages of European science.

✧ *Evaluating the Text*

1. How much of America's crops of soybeans, cotton, and corn have already been genetically modified?
2. According to Schwartz, in what ways might genetically modified food actually be safer than conventional crops?
3. Why are recent reports by the U.S. Department of Agriculture (USDA), Environmental Protection Agency (EPA), and the Food and Drug Administration (FDA) significant?

✧ *Exploring Different Perspectives*

1. In what respects does Schwartz's viewpoint differ from that of Jeffrey M. Smith in "Genetically Engineered Foods May Cause Rising Food Allergies"?
2. What do both this article and Ray Kroc's account in "Grinding It Out: The Making of McDonald's" suggest about Americans' eating habits?

✧ *Extending Viewpoints through Writing and Research*

1. To what extent has the rift between the European Union (EU) and the United States, Canada, and Argentina been narrowed? If the situation is the same as Schwartz describes, why do you think this is the case?
2. Would knowing that a certain food you liked was genetically modified change your mind about it? Why or why not? In your opinion, should these foods be labeled as such?

Jeffrey M. Smith

Genetically Engineered Foods May Cause Rising Food Allergies

Jeffrey M. Smith is the author of Seeds of Deception: Exposing Industry and Government Lies About the Safety of Genetically Engineered Foods *(2003). He argues that the toxin known as Bt, which is genetically engineered directly into foods and acts as a pesticide, has been shown to produce severe allergic reactions.*

Before You Read

Would knowing that some crops have their own built-in pesticides change your mind about eating or wearing products made from them?

1 The biotech industry is fond of saying they offer genetically modified (GM) crops that resist pests. This might conjure up the image of insects staying away from GM crop fields. But "resisting pests" is just a euphemism for contains its own built-in pesticide. When bugs take a bite of the GM plant, the toxins split open their stomach and kill them.

2 The idea that we consume that same toxic pesticide in every bite is hardly appetizing. But the biotech companies and the Environmental Protection Agency—which regulates plant produced pesticides—tell us not to worry. They contend that the pesticide called Bt *(Bacillus thuringiensis)* is produced naturally from a soil bacterium and has a history of safe use. Organic farmers, for example, have used solutions containing the natural bacteria for years as a method of insect control. Genetic engineers simply remove the gene that produces the Bt in bacteria and then insert it into the DNA of corn and cotton plants, so that the plant does the work, not the farmer. Moreover, they say that Bt-toxin is quickly destroyed in our stomach; and even if it survived, since humans and other mammals have no receptors for the toxin, it would not interact with us in any case.

3 These arguments, however, are just that—unsupported assumptions. Research tells a different story.

Bt Spray Is Dangerous to Humans

4 When natural Bt was sprayed over areas around Vancouver [Canada] and Washington State to fight gypsy moths, about 500 people reported reactions—mostly allergy or flu-like symptoms. Six people had to go to the emergency room for allergies or asthma. Workers who applied Bt sprays reported eye, nose, throat, and respiratory irritation, and some showed an antibody immune response linked to Bt. Farmers exposed to liquid Bt formulations had reactions including infection, an ulcer on the cornea, skin irritation, burning, swelling, and redness. One woman who was accidentally sprayed with Bt also developed fever, altered consciousness, and seizures.

5 In fact, authorities have long acknowledged that "people with compromised immune systems or preexisting allergies may be particularly susceptible to the effects of Bt." The Oregon Health Division advises that "individuals with . . . physician-diagnosed causes of severe immune disorders may consider leaving the area during the actual spraying." A spray manufacturer warns, "repeated exposure via inhalation can result in sensitization and allergic response in hypersensitive individuals." So much for the contention that Bt does not interact with humans.

6 As for being thoroughly destroyed in the digestive system, mouse studies disproved this as well. Mice fed Bt-toxin showed significant immune responses—as potent as cholera toxin. In addition, the Bt caused their immune system to become sensitive to formerly harmless compounds. This suggests that exposure might make a person allergic to a wide range of substances. *The EPA's own expert advisors said that the mouse and farm worker studies above "suggest that Bt proteins could act as antigenic and allergenic sources."*

The Toxin in GM Plants Is More Dangerous Than Natural Sprays

7 The Bt-toxin produced in GM crops is "vastly different from the bacterial [Bt-toxins] used in organic and traditional farming and forestry." First of all, GM plants produce about 3,000–5,000 times the amount of toxin as the sprays. And the spray form is broken down within a few days to two weeks by sunlight, high temperatures, or substances on the leaves of plants; and it can be "washed from leaves into the soil by rainfall," or rinsed by consumers. A Bt producing GM plant, on the other hand, continuously produces the toxin in every cell where it does not dissipate by weather and cannot be washed off.

8 The natural toxin produced in bacteria is inactive until it gets inside the alkaline digestive tract of an insect. Once inside, a "safety

catch" is removed and the Bt becomes toxic. But scientists change the sequence of the Bt gene before inserting it into GM plants. The Bt toxin it produces usually comes without the safety catch. The plant-produced Bt toxin is always active and more likely to trigger an immune response than the natural variety.

Bt-Toxin Fails Safety Studies

9 Tests cannot verify that a GM protein introduced into the food supply for the first time will not cause allergies in some people. The World Health Organization (WHO) and UN Food and Agriculture Organization (FAO) offer criteria designed to reduce the likelihood that allergenic GM crops are approved. They suggest examining a protein for 1) similarity of its amino acid sequence to known allergens, 2) digestive stability and 3) heat stability. These properties aren't predictive of allergenicity, but their presence, according to experts, should be sufficient to reject the GM crop or at least require more testing. The Bt-toxin produced in GM corn fails all three criteria.

10 For example, the specific Bt-toxin found in Monsanto's Yield Guard and Syngenta's Bt 11 corn varieties is called Cry1Ab. In 1998, an FDA researcher discovered that Cry1Ab shared a sequence of 9–12 amino acids with vitellogenin, an egg yolk allergen. The study concluded that "the similarity . . . might be sufficient to warrant additional evaluation." No additional evaluation took place.

11 Cry1Ab is also very resistant to digestion and heat. It is nearly as stable as the type of Bt-toxin produced by StarLink corn. StarLink was a GM variety not approved for human consumption because experts believed that its highly stable protein might trigger allergies. Although it was grown for use in animal feed, it contaminated the U.S. food supply in 2000. Thousands of consumers complained to food manufacturers about possible reactions and over 300 items were subject to recall. After the StarLink incident, expert advisors to the EPA had called for "surveillance and clinical assessment of 'exposed individuals' to confirm the allergenicity of Bt products." Again, no such monitoring has taken place.

Bt Cotton Triggers Allergic Reactions

12 A 2005 report by medical investigators in India describes an ominous finding. Hundreds of agricultural workers are developing moderate or severe allergic reactions when exposed to Bt cotton. This includes those picking cotton, loading it, cleaning it, or even leaning against it. Some at a ginning factory must take antihistamines daily, in order to go to work. Reactions are only triggered with the Bt varieties. Furthermore, the symptoms are virtually identical to those described by the 500 people in Vancouver and Washington who were sprayed with

Bt. Only "exacerbations of asthma" were in one list and not the other. (We are unaware of similar reports in the U.S., where 83 percent of the cotton is Bt. But in the U.S., cotton is harvested by machine, not by hand.)

13 The experience of the Indian workers begs the question, "How long does the Bt-toxin stay active in the cotton?" Is there any risk using cotton diapers, tampons, or bandages? In the latter case, if the Bt-toxin interfered with healing it could be a disaster. With diabetics, for example, unhealed wounds may be cause for amputation.

14 Cottonseed is also used for cottonseed oil—used in many processed foods in the U.S. The normal methods used to extract oil likely destroy the toxin, although cold pressed oil may still retain some of it. Other parts of the cotton plant, however, are routinely used as animal feed. . . .

Bt Corn Pollen May Cause Allergies

15 Bt-toxin is produced in GM corn and can be eaten intact. It is also in pollen, which can be breathed in. In 2003, during the time when an adjacent Bt cornfield was pollinating, virtually an entire Filipino village of about 100 people were stricken by a disease. The symptoms included headaches, dizziness, extreme stomach pain, vomiting, chest pains, fever and allergies, as well as respiratory, intestinal, and skin reactions. The symptoms appeared first in those living closest to the field, and then progressed to others by proximity. Blood samples from 39 individuals showed antibodies in response to Bt-toxin; this supports, but does not prove a link to the symptoms. When the same corn was planted in four other villages the following year, however, the symptoms returned in all four areas—only during the time of pollination. . . .

16 Allergic reactions are a defensive, often harmful immune system response to an external irritant. The body interprets something as foreign, different and offensive, and reacts accordingly. All GM foods, by definition, have something foreign and different. According to GM food safety expert Arpad Pusztai, "a consistent feature of all the studies done, published or unpublished . . . indicates major problems with changes in the immune status of animals fed on various GM crops/foods."

17 In addition to immune responses, several studies and reports from the field provide evidence that GM foods are toxic.

✧ *Evaluating the Text*

1. What is Bt? Why is Smith alarmed about its incorporation into common crops such as corn and cotton?
2. What kinds of health effects have been shown to be the result of genetically modified plants that contain Bt?
3. What are the main pieces of evidence that Smith cites to support his argument?

✧ *Exploring Different Perspectives*

1. In what respects does Smith come to very different conclusions than Mark I. Schwartz in "Genetically Modified Food Is Safe" regarding the safety of genetically modified crops?
2. In what ways are the allergies exacerbated by genetically modified crops analogous to the unhealthy effects of the foods the slave-owners consumed as described by Frederick Douglass in "My Bondage and My Freedom"?

✧ *Extending Viewpoints through Writing and Research*

1. If you are prone to allergies, would you be more careful about what you ate and wore after reading Smith's article?
2. Research whether there are current instances anywhere in the world akin to those reported in India (in 2005) and the Philippines (in 2003) caused by Bt toxins.

Amy Tan

Fish Cheeks

Amy Tan was born in 1952 in Oakland, California, and received a B.A. in 1973 and an M.A. in 1974 from San Jose State University. Her acclaimed novels include The Joy Luck Club *(1989),* The Kitchen God's Wife *(1991),* The Hundred Secret Senses *(1995), and* The Bonesetter's Daughter *(2001). The following short essay first appeared in* Seventeen *(1987).*

Before You Read

Take a few minutes to write about what it would be like to make dinner for people from another culture.

1 I fell in love with the minister's son the winter I turned fourteen. He was not Chinese, but as white as Mary in the manger. For Christmas I prayed for this blond-haired boy, Robert, and a slim new American nose.

2 When I found out that my parents had invited the minister's family over for Christmas Eve dinner, I cried. What would Robert think of our shabby Chinese Christmas? What would he think of our noisy Chinese relatives who lacked proper American manners? What terrible disappointment would he feel upon seeing not a roasted turkey and sweet potatoes but Chinese food?

3 On Christmas Eve I saw that my mother had outdone herself in creating a strange menu. She was pulling black veins out of the backs of fleshy prawns. The kitchen was littered with appalling mounds of raw food: A slimy rock cod with bulging eyes that pleaded not to be thrown into a pan of hot oil. Tofu, which looked like stacked wedges of rubbery white sponges. A bowl soaking dried fungus back to life. A plate of squid, their backs crisscrossed with knife markings so they resembled bicycle tires.

4 And then they arrived—the minister's family and all my relatives in a clamor of doorbells and rumpled Christmas packages. Robert grunted hello, and I pretended he was not worthy of existence.

5 Dinner threw me deeper into despair. My relatives licked the ends of their chopsticks and reached across the table, dipping them into the dozen or so plates of food. Robert and his family waited patiently for platters to be passed to them. My relatives murmured with pleasure

when my mother brought out the whole steamed fish. Robert grimaced. Then my father poked his chopsticks just below the fish eye and plucked out the soft meat. "Amy, your favorite," he said, offering me the tender fish cheek. I wanted to disappear.

6 At the end of the meal my father leaned back and belched loudly, thanking my mother for her fine cooking. "It's a polite Chinese custom to show you are satisfied," explained my father to our astonished guests. Robert was looking down at his plate with a reddened face. The minister managed to muster up a quiet burp. I was stunned into silence for the rest of the night.

7 After everyone had gone, my mother said to me, "You want to be the same as American girls on the outside." She handed me an early gift. It was a miniskirt in beige tweed. "But inside you must always be Chinese. You must be proud you are different. Your only shame is to have shame."

8 And even though I didn't agree with her then, I knew that she understood how much I had suffered during the evening's dinner. It wasn't until many years later—long after I had gotten over my crush on Robert—that I was able to fully appreciate her lesson and the true purpose behind our particular menu. For Christmas Eve that year, she had chosen all my favorite foods.

✧ *Evaluating the Text*

1. Why is Tan apprehensive when she finds out that a boy she has a crush on will be coming to Christmas dinner at her house?
2. What does Tan's mother try to show her by cooking an authentic Chinese dinner, including Amy's favorite dishes, for the non-Chinese minister and his family? To what does the title refer?
3. What did Tan learn from this experience?

✧ *Exploring Different Perspectives*

1. What similarities and differences can you discover in Tan's account and that of Ethel G. Hofman's in "An Island Passover"?
2. How do the accounts by Tan and Andrew X. Pham in "Foreign-Asians" illustrate the concept of culture shock?

✧ *Extending Viewpoints through Writing and Research*

1. What experiences have you had that required you to adjust to a different culture at a dinner, celebration, or holiday?

2. What are some of your favorite holiday foods and how would they appear to someone from a different culture?
3. Research a specific ethnic food (such as hagis, baccala, gefilte fish) and describe what you learned in terms of what it adds to Tan's narrative.

Frederick Douglass

My Bondage and My Freedom

Frederick Douglass (1817–1895) was born into slavery in Maryland, where he worked as a field hand and servant. In 1838, after previous failed attempts to escape, for which he was beaten and tortured, he successfully made his way to New York using the identity papers of a freed black sailor. There he adopted the last name of Douglass (his given name was Bailey) and subsequently settled in New Bedford, Massachusetts. The first black American to rise to prominence as a national figure, Douglass gained renown as a speaker for the Massachusetts Anti-Slavery League and was an editor for the the North Star, *an abolitionist newspaper, from 1847 to 1860. He was a friend to John Brown, helped convince President Lincoln to issue the Emancipation Proclamation, and became ambassador to several foreign countries. The following selection is drawn from the second of his three autobiographies,* My Bondage and My Freedom *(1855) and emphasizes how hunger made Douglass observant when it came to the social inequities that motivated him to seek freedom.*

Before You Read

What contrast do you think existed between the food plantation slaves were given and what their masters and their guests ate?

1 As a general rule, slaves do not come to the quarters for either breakfast or dinner, but take their "ash cake" with them, and eat it in the field. This was so on the home plantation; probably, because the distance from the quarter to the field, was sometimes two, and even three miles.

2 The dinner of the slaves consisted of a huge piece of ash cake, and a small piece of pork, or two salt herrings. Not having ovens, nor any suitable cooking utensils, the slaves mixed their meal with a little water, to such thickness that a spoon would stand erect in it; and, after the wood had burned away to coals and ashes, they would place the dough between oak leaves and lay it carefully in the ashes, completely covering it; hence, the bread is called ash cake. The surface of this peculiar bread is covered with ashes, to the depth of a sixteenth part of an inch, and the ashes, certainly, do not make it very grateful to the teeth, nor render it very palatable. The bran, or coarse part of the meal, is baked with the fine, and bright scales run through the bread. This bread, with

its ashes and bran, would disgust and choke a northern man, but it is quite liked by the slaves. They eat it with avidity, and are more concerned about the quantity than about the quality. They are far too scantily provided for, and are worked too steadily, to be much concerned for the quality of their food. The few minutes allowed them at dinner time, after partaking of their coarse repast, are variously spent. Some lie down on the "turning row," and go to sleep; others draw together, and talk; and others are at work with needle and thread, mending their tattered garments. Sometimes you may hear a wild, hoarse laugh arise from a circle, and often a song. Soon, however, the overseer comes dashing through the field. "*Tumble up! Tumble up,* and to *work, work,*" is the cry; and, now, from twelve o'clock (midday) till dark, the human cattle are in motion, wielding their clumsy hoes; hurried on by no hope of reward, no sense of gratitude, no love of children, no prospect of bettering their condition; nothing, save the dread and terror of the slave-driver's lash. So goes one day, and so comes and goes another.

3 The close-fisted stinginess that fed the poor slave on coarse cornmeal and tainted meat; that clothed him in crashy tow-linen, and hurried him on to toil through the field, in all weathers, with wind and rain beating through his tattered garments; that scarcely gave even the young slave-mother time to nurse her hungry infant in the fence corner; wholly vanishes on approaching the sacred precincts of the great house, the home of the Lloyds. There the scriptural phrase finds an exact illustration; the highly favored inmates of this mansion are literally arrayed "in purple and fine linen," and fare sumptuously every day! The table groans under the heavy and blood-bought luxuries gathered with pains-taking care, at home and abroad. Fields, forests, rivers and seas, are made tributary here. Immense wealth, and its lavish expenditure, fill the great house with all that can please the eye, or tempt the taste. Here, appetite, not food, is the great *desideratum*. Fish, flesh and fowl, are here in profusion. Chickens, of all breeds; ducks, of all kinds, wild and tame, the common, and the huge Muscovite; Guinea fowls, turkeys, geese, and pea fowls, are in their several pens, fat and fatting for the destined vortex. The graceful swan, the mongrels, the black-necked wild goose; partridges, quails, pheasants and pigeons; choice water fowl, with all their strange varieties, are caught in this huge family net. Beef, veal, mutton and venison, of the most select kinds and quality, roll bounteously to this grand consumer. The teeming riches of the Chesapeake bay, its rock, perch, drums, crocus, trout, oysters, crabs, and terrapin, are drawn hither to adorn the glittering table of the great house. The dairy, too, probably the finest on the Eastern Shore of Maryland—supplied by cattle of the best English stock, imported for the purpose, pours its rich donations of fragrant cheese, golden butter, and delicious cream, to heighten the attraction of the gorgeous, unending round of

feasting. Nor are the fruits of the earth forgotten or neglected. The fertile garden, many acres in size, constituting a separate establishment, distinct from the common farm—with its scientific gardener, imported from Scotland, (a Mr. McDermott,) with four men under his direction, was not behind, either in the abundance or in the delicacy of its contributions to the same full board. The tender asparagus, the succulent celery, and the delicate cauliflower; egg plants, beets, lettuce, parsnips, peas, and French beans, early and late; radishes, cantelopes, melons of all kinds; the fruits and flowers of all climes and of all descriptions, from the hardy apple of the north, to the lemon and orange of the south, culminated at this point. Baltimore gathered figs, raisins, almonds and juicy grapes from Spain. Wines and brandies from France; teas of various flavor, from China; and rich, aromatic coffee from Java, all conspired to swell the tide of high life, where pride and indolence rolled and lounged in magnificence and satiety.

4 Behind the tall-backed and elaborately wrought chairs, stand the servants, men and maidens—fifteen in number—discriminately selected, not only with a view to their industry and faithfulness, but with special regard to their personal appearance, their graceful agility and captivating address. Some of these are armed with fans, and are fanning reviving breezes toward the over-heated brows of the alabaster ladies; others watch with eager eye, and with fawn-like step anticipate and supply, wants before they are sufficiently formed to be announced by word or sign.

5 These servants constituted a sort of black aristocracy on Col. Lloyd's plantation. They resembled the field hands in nothing, except in color, and in this they held the advantage of a velvet-like glossiness, rich and beautiful. The hair, too, showed the same advantage. The delicate colored maid rustled in the scarcely worn silk of her young mistress, while the servant men were equally well attired from the overflowing wardrobe of their young masters; so that, in dress, as well as in form and feature, in manner and speech, in tastes and habits, the distance between these favored few, and the sorrow and hunger-smitten multitudes of the quarter in the field, was immense; and this is seldom passed over.

6 Let us now glance at the stables and carriage house, and we shall find the same evidences of pride and luxurious extravagance. Here are three splendid coaches, soft within and lustrous without. Here, too, are gigs, phætons, barouches, sulkeys and sleighs. Here are saddles and harnesses—beautifully wrought and silver mounted—kept with every care. In the stable you will find, kept only for pleasure, full thirty-five horses, or the most approved blood for speed and beauty. There are two men here constantly employed in taking care of these horses. One of these men must be always in the stable, to answer every call from the great house. Over the way from the stable, is a house built expressly

for the hounds—a pack of twenty-five or thirty—whose fare would have made glad the heart of a dozen slaves. Horses and hounds are not the only consumers of the slave's toil. There was practiced, at the Lloyd's, a hospitality which would have astonished and charmed any health-seeking northern divine or merchant, who might have chanced to share it. Viewed from his own table, and *not* from the field, the colonel was a model of generous hospitality. His house was, literally, a hotel, for weeks during the summer months. At these times, especially, the air was freighted with the rich fumes of baking, boiling, roasting and broiling. The odors I shared with the winds; but the meats were under a more stringent monopoly—except that, occasionally, I got a cake from Mas' Daniel. In Mas' Daniel I had a friend at court, from whom I learned many things which my eager curiosity was excited to know. I always knew when company was expected, and who they were, although I was an outsider, being the property, not of Col. Lloyd, but of a servant of the wealthy colonel. On these occasions, all that pride, taste and money could do, to dazzle and charm, was done.

7 Who could say that the servants of Col. Lloyd were not well clad and cared for, after witnessing one of his magnificent entertainments? Who could say that they did not seem to glory in being the slaves of such a master? Who, but a fanatic, could get up any sympathy for persons whose every movement was agile, easy and graceful, and who evinced a consciousness of high superiority? And who would ever venture to suspect that Col. Lloyd was subject to the troubles of ordinary mortals? Master and slave seem alike in their glory here? Can it all be seeming? Alas! it may only be a sham at last! This immense wealth; this gilded splendor; this profusion of luxury; this exemption from toil; this life of ease; this sea of plenty; aye, what of it all? Are the pearly gates of happiness and sweet content flung open to such suitors? *far from it!* The poor slave, on his hard, pine plank, but scantily covered with his thin blanket, sleeps more soundly than the feverish voluptuary who reclines upon his feather bed and downy pillow. Food, to the indolent lounger, is poison, not sustenance. Lurking beneath all their dishes, are invisible spirits of evil, ready to feed the self-deluded gormandizers with aches, pains, fierce temper, uncontrolled passions, dyspepsia, rheumatism, lumbago and gout; and of these the Lloyds got their full share.

✧ *Evaluating the Text*

1. What contrast did Douglass observe between the diet of the slaves (including Douglass himself) and the guests of Col. Lloyd?
2. What privileges were given to slaves who worked in the master's house as opposed to those working in the fields?

3. What advantage did the slaves' diet confer that Col. Lloyd and his family and guests did not enjoy?

✧ *Exploring Different Perspectives*

1. What aspects of the accounts by Douglass and Ethel G. Hofman in "An Island Passover" emphasize the homegrown as opposed to imported foods that were served during holidays?
2. How do both Douglass and Amy Tan in "Fish Cheeks" structure their accounts as a study of contrasts?

✧ *Extending Viewpoints through Writing and Research*

1. How does Douglass's account communicate the inequities produced by slavery?
2. What moments of hunger have you experienced and how did they change your perceptions?
3. Get the book *My Bondage and My Freedom,* from which this selection is taken, and discuss the role that hunger played in making Douglass plan his escape.

Ethel G. Hofman

An Island Passover

Ethel G. Hofman, a syndicated food journalist, cookbook author, and past president of the International Association of Culinary Professionals, grew up in the Shetland Islands, off the coast of northern Scotland. Her parents, originally from Russia, continued to maintain Jewish traditions, and this chapter from her memoir, Mackerel at Midnight: Growing Up Jewish on a Remote Scottish Island *(2005), describes the Passover seder her family made for the hundreds of Jewish men and women stationed there during World War II.*

Before You Read

How much do you know about the Passover celebration?

1 The countdown began exactly two months before Passover. Ma checked the dates on the *Jewish Echo* calendar, which hung on a rusty nail under the mantelpiece, where matchboxes, letters, and china ornaments were crammed together in no particular order.

2 The *Jewish Echo,* now defunct, was the weekly Jewish newspaper, published in Glasgow. The calendar was Ma's guide for Holiday dates as well as Sabbath candle-lighting times. By the time of the High Holidays in September, the pages were well thumbed and grease-stained. Since dusk in the north comes later in summer and earlier in winter, Ma adjusted candle-lighting times accordingly, rationalizing thus: "As long as I light candles, God doesn't mind what time it is."

3 The *Echo* was her only connection to the Glasgow Jewish community. As she scrutinized the births, marriages, and deaths published each week, she could be heard to exclaim, "Oh my, Annie Smith has passed away. We used to go together to the Locarno dances every Saturday night." Or, "Ettie Goldstone has had a baby. . . . That must be Ronnie Goldstone's daughter-in-law."

4 Planning ahead was essential. Deliveries were unreliable. The steamship *St. Magnus,* carrying supplies from the Scottish mainland, arrived in Shetland only twice a week, on Tuesdays and Fridays. And if the weather was stormy, deliveries could be delayed. Shetland sea captains were highly skilled, but none would risk the North Sea crossing from Aberdeen while fighting one-hundred-mile-an-hour gales. "That would be madness," to quote a feisty captain of the 1930s. Besides

dealing with this uncertainty over getting food on time, Ma divided her days between working in the shop and cooking for the family.

5 Two days before the Holidays, Ma had extra help. There were no freezers, so cooking could not be done very far ahead. Thankfully, in early spring, Shetland weather is cold, so food was stored outside in a meat safe, a wire-mesh box hung high off the ground, or in our unheated, enclosed back porch.

6 Putting together the Passover order was a family affair and the beginning of weeks of joyful anticipation. "Go fetch a writing pad and pencil," Ma instructed me. Jostling each other to be next to her, we dragged kitchen chairs across the linoleum floor. "I want to sit here."

7 "No, I was here first"—this from Roy as he was pushed off the chair.

8 This went on until Ma intervened. "Ethel, you sit on one side and Roy you can sit on the other side."

9 Pencil in hand, she began to compile the list. At first, it was not very detailed. In the 1940s the only Passover items available for the eight-day holiday were *matzo* meal, *matzos,* and wine. And from 1940 to 1945, food was rationed so that coupons in the ration books were saved for special occasions. Lerwick shops stocked sugar, butter, flour, jams, and other basic necessities. But Michael Morrison's delicatessen in Glasgow, still in existence, carried foods we tasted only on holidays: sharp and tangy, sweet and sour, exotic and exciting.

10 Ian Morrison remembers, as a teenager, packing the jars to go to Shetland. "Everything had to be wrapped in two or three sheets of newspaper; then each jar was placed in the box, separated by cardboard. That way, if one jar broke, the contents wouldn't mess up the remaining jars."

11 The list became longer as each of us added our favorite "Jewish foods." Ma yearned for pickles and sauerkraut, which she used to buy in Glasgow whenever she needed to, so half a dozen cans of each was the standard order. Dad insisted on two five-pound wursts (salami). As soon as they were unpacked, the long, fat, garlicky sausages were attached with wooden clothespins to a line strung across the back porch, which served as a natural refrigerator, the temperature in April rarely exceeding fifty degrees. For a Passover snack, Dad sprinted up the steep wooden stairs leading from the back shop, through the kitchen, to the porch. Pulling a silver penknife from his trouser pocket, he cut off a hunk of wurst and ran back to the shop again, savoring small bites on the way. Customers never complained if, at times, he reeked of garlic. And if our supply of olive oil was low, six one-gallon cans were also ordered, Ma never tiring of informing us once more, "I was cooking with olive oil long before it became fashionable."

12 Finally, there was the *matzo* order—fifteen boxes. "How much can one family eat?" came a call from Michael Morrison before mailing the first of many packages to "the Greenwalds in Shetland." Ma began to

explain, "I need a box for Granny Hunter, one for the Laurenson family in Hamnavoe, one for the Mullays who live at the top of the lane . . . ," before the exasperated deli owner finally hung up on Lerwick 269, one of his best customers. Most of the *matzos* were delivered to our Christian neighbors, who anxiously waited for the unleavened bread, symbolic of the exodus of the Jews from Egypt—and, in their eyes, we were indeed the Chosen People.

13 When I was eight years old, my birthday fell during Passover. Determined that I should not feel deprived, Ma placed a surprise order. Along with the enormous brown-paper-wrapped boxes containing the Passover order, there was a small package. "Open it," said my mother. I tore off the paper, Ma helping with scissors, and I gasped. Inside, framed in a froth of white tissue-paper, nestled a magnificent, layered, chocolate nut cake. It had been packed so carefully that the swirly rosettes of chocolate frosting, each crowned with a toasted hazelnut, had retained their shapes perfectly—miraculously surviving the fourteen-hour ocean journey in the ship's hold. Memory being enhanced by nostalgia, this remains the most glorious birthday cake I have ever had.

14 We ate fish every day, but meat only occasionally. Like every island household, we stored a barrel of salt herring to carry us over the winter, when the weather was too rough for the fishing boats to go out. We stored our herring in the garage, covering the barrel with a slatted, easily removable wooden lid. It was my job to brave the wind and rain, sprinting from the back door of our house to push open the rickety garage door to "get a *fry*." Of course, that didn't mean the herring would be fried. It is the Shetland expression meaning "enough to feed the family," in our case, a family of five. Ma rinsed and soaked a few herring, as needed, to make pickled herring, chopped herring, and, occasionally, when fresh herring was out of season, to make potted herring (rolled and baked in a vinegar–bay leaf mixture).

15 One month before Passover, she put up a ten-pound jar of pickled herring. First, the fish was soaked in cold water to leach out the salt. Then, in a single slash with a razor-edged knife, the head and backbone, with all the tiny bones attached, were removed, later to be tossed outside to delighted seagulls. The fillets were cut into bite-sized pieces, then packed into an empty ten-pound glass *sweetie* jar, layered with thick onion slices (after the *sweeties* were sold, there was no further use for the jars, except in our house). Finally, vinegary brine was poured over the fish to cover it completely. Bay leaves, peppercorns, and fronds of dill floating throughout helped give a piquant flavor, which mellowed over the weeks. The lid was tightly screwed on, and the jar set on a shelf high above the jams and jellies in the back porch. The pickled herring was perfectly marinated by Passover. To make chopped herring, Ma drained a couple of handfuls of pickled herring and hacked it on a

big wooden board with a broad-bladed *messer*. She mixed in chopped onion and hard cooked eggs before spooning the sharp, savory mixture into a bowl. Good plain food—no apples, sugar, mayonnaise, or preservatives added to mask the taste of homespun ingredients.

16 Two days before Passover, our kitchen was the scene of frenzied activity: Ma, Granny Hunter, and "the girl," darting around like hens vying for their daily grain feed. Ma directed culinary operations while she mixed and whisked—never measuring. "Keep that stove stoked . . . bring in more buckets of peat . . . top up the kettle; we need more boiling water." Her cohort cooks followed directions explicitly. The Raeburn stove devoured huge quantities of coal and peat to keep up the oven heat. To boil water, needed to scrub all the pots and cooking utensils, they carried water from the cold-water sink to a stout aluminum kettle on the hob.

17 Before the chicken soup could be started, chickens were plucked of feathers, then singed over a gas flame, to be sure not a scrap of feathers remained. Nothing was wasted, Ma insisting, "Chicken feet have all the flavor." Accordingly, the scaly feet were thoroughly scraped and scalded in boiling water before they were added to the pot, along with an assortment of root vegetables.

18 Fresh beets—boiled, cooled, and peeled—were grated on the coarse side of a grater to make sweet and sour borscht. Ladled over a chunky potato from a Dunrossness *croft* (where the soil was said to help produce the mealy texture) the ruby-red soup, flecked with soured heavy cream, was my father's favorite meal. He would sit back in his chair, licking his lips, pronouncing it the best—a *meichle*.

19 Ma's favorite combination for gefilte fish was halibut and hake, delivered to the door by a neighbor fisherman. He had usually gutted them, but Ma had to skin and bone them. "Pull away the oilcloth," she ordered whoever was around, usually me. "Now hold the grinder steady while I clamp it onto the kitchen table." The grinder was ancient, made of heavy cast iron, but Ma handled it with enviable ease as she pressed the fish through the funnel and into the blade.

20 We always served two varieties of gefilte fish. One big pot contained oval-shaped balls of the chopped-fish mixture, simmered with onion skins; the rest of the mixture was formed into patties and fried in hot olive oil in an enormous black iron skillet. Not just for Passover, fried gefilte fish topped with a dollop of salad cream (Scottish mayonnaise) and eaten at room temperature was a weekly Sabbath dinner.

21 Instead of the rich buttery cakes usually baked each Friday morning, Passover cakes were feathery sponge cakes, each made with a dozen new-laid eggs, beaten to a foam with a hand whisk. Baked and cooled, the cakes were sprinkled with sugar, then snugly wrapped in greaseproof wax paper; wine biscuits, coconut pyramids, and cinnamon balls were stored in tight-lidded, round, five-pound tins, recycled from Quality

Sweet chocolates, another item making up the conglomeration of goods sold in Greenwald's shop. The last of the bottled plums and gooseberries were transformed into sweet compotes and *matzo* fruit puddings.

22 Everything was stored on shelves in the back porch. Food poisoning was unheard of. In April, the temperature in the unheated porch was rarely more than fifty degrees. The "girl from the country," the maid, did the menial jobs like scrubbing the floor, then laying down newspapers, "to prevent the floor from getting dirty," as Ma ordered. As for eight days of *matzos,* it was no hardship. We slathered each sheet with fresh, salty Shetland butter, then covered it with a thick layer of Ma's homemade, heather-scented, blackcurrant jam.

23 Although we usually ate all our meals in the kitchen in front of the peat fire, at Passover we dined in the "front room," the parlor, where lace-curtained bay windows overlooked the fields across the one-lane road. The room was large enough to seat family and guests comfortably. The drop-leaf oak table was set with a white lace tablecloth and the best china and glassware (we didn't possess crystal). Our close friends dressed up in their Sunday-best church clothes. Rebe, a few years older than I, arrived in a new black and yellow tartan kilt, her white satin blouse with a frilly collar peeping out under a black velvet jacket. I was insanely jealous and pestered my parents until, the following year, I was given a similar outfit—not quite the same, but I was happy. Children and adults were silent as my father, in his heavy Russian-accented Shetland dialect, recited parts of the *Haggadah,* first in Hebrew, then in English. I repeated the four questions, and my mother explained the symbolism of the foods on the *Seder* plate. Each year, discussions became more animated, as our devout Christian guests added their comments and views, always in a respectful manner.

24 Our Passover *Seders* continued, even though the peaceful existence of the Shetland community was shattered by the onset of World War II. My parents had an added fear. Norway, only two hundred miles east of the Shetland Islands, was under German occupation. It was obvious from the bold signage above the shop, announcing the name Greenwald, that Jews owned the store. A German invasion would have meant certain death for our family. Fortunately, the islands being well protected, that never happened. With Lerwick's natural harbor a strategic base for naval operations from 1939 until 1945, thousands of troops, including more than three hundred Jewish men and women, were based throughout the islands. They far outnumbered the local community.

25 In 1941, Ma decided to organize a Passover *Seder* for the Jewish soldiers, knowing our flat could not hold all those who would have come to celebrate with us. "These poor souls must have a *Seder*. If there are too many for our house, then we'll hold it at the camp." This became her annual mission. It took an enormous amount of dedicated planning. She called the Commanding Officer (CO) in Lerwick to explain.

26 "Could we have a hut for the evening?"

27 The head of the forces stationed in Shetland knew Ma from coming into the shop, where he was given preferential treatment and often bought items not available in the PX (the soldiers' commissary). He listened to her plans.

28 "What else can we do to help?"

29 "Well, for a start, can we use part of your kitchens?" and, she wheedled, "maybe a couple of helpers. You know, we'll be cooking for about three hundred people."

30 "You just go in and tell the cooks to give you whatever you need. I'll make sure that they work with you."

31 Ma gave a sigh of relief. "That's one hurdle taken care of. I wasn't sure if he would agree." The military's Nissen hut was at the north end of Commercial Road, on the edge of town, but Ma had an army truck with a driver at her disposal. "Just call when you need it," assured the CO. "He'll be there in five minutes."

32 Ma spent days on the telephone, calling Glasgow and London for donations.

33 "Just send it to Jean Greenwald, in care of the Commanding Officer, Shetland Naval Air Station. It'll find me," she said—adding scornfully, after she had hung up, "Ignoramuses. They have no idea where Shetland is."

34 Boxes of *matzos, matzo* meal, pickles, and olive oil arrived. A kosher wine merchant in London agreed to send wine. When the cases were finally unloaded in the camp kitchen, Ma poured a fingerful to taste. She knew good wine. Describing it as "putrid," she ran to the sink, spitting it out. Furious, she immediately called the liquor store. She screamed into the telephone, with Dad shushing her in the background.

35 "Don't think that because we're in Shetland you can send us inferior wine. This wine is sour . . . it's undrinkable. I will not serve this to the men and women who are fighting for you and your family . . . you should be ashamed!"

36 A fresh shipment arrived on the next boat, along with a letter of profuse apology.

37 "I had *chutzpah,*" she later told us. "But I wasn't asking for myself. These soldiers were away from their homes and giving up their lives to protect us. The least these shopkeepers could do was to donate the Passover wine."

38 A team of army cooks and women friends worked together to prepare a complete *Seder* meal, with Ma supervising. They cooked up enormous amounts of chicken soup and *Knaidlach,* chopped herring and gefilte fish (even in wartime, fish was plentiful), roast chicken and potato *kugels,* sponge cake and dried fruit compotes. These dishes were

reminiscent of the *Seder* meal they would have had if they had been able to celebrate with their families.

39 But most thrilling for the soldiers and for our family was the arrival of Great Britain's Chief Rabbi, Israel Brodie, the day before the first *Seder*. Ma had arranged for him to come to Shetland to conduct Passover services. The rabbi presented her with two leather-bound Holiday prayer books, signed by him, in appreciation of her tireless work on behalf of the Jewish troops stationed in Shetland in World War II. Now newly bound, the books are a family heirloom. For many of the Holidays, rabbis from England and Scotland made the journey to conduct services in the most northerly point of the British Isles. This continued under my mother's direction until 1945, when the war officially ended and troops were demobbed (demobilized). But the friendships lasted for years, many of the men and women returning with their families to see the Greenwalds, who had given them a Jewish home away from home, and to say thank you.

40 Three thousand miles across the Atlantic in Philadelphia, my Passover table is set with fine china and crystal. An Israeli *Seder* plate, of hand-wrought silver, contains the symbolic foods, and my husband Walter conducts our *Seder* with warmth, compassion, and humor. But the *Seders* that instilled a lasting pride in my heritage and laid the firm foundation for my Jewish identity were held in Lerwick, on the remote Shetland Islands, where the Greenwald family, in the midst of Christian culture, held fast to their faith.

✧ *Evaluating the Text*

1. What obstacles did Hofman's mother have to overcome to create a Passover celebration?

2. What were some of the different steps Hofman's mother took to stage this event for her family and the hundreds of soldiers she also invited?

3. How did this seder dinner come to represent a way of connecting to important Jewish traditions and cultural values?

✧ *Exploring Different Perspectives*

1. How do both Hofman and Chris Maynard and Bill Scheller in "Manifold Destiny" enhance their accounts by providing culinary details for the foods they discuss?

2. How do both Hofman and Amy Tan in "Fish Cheeks" blend different religious and cultural elements connected with food when they describe Passover and Christmas, respectively?

✧ *Extending Viewpoints through Writing and Research*

1. What ethnic foods are particularly important in your holiday celebrations? How does the preparation of these foods create a sense of community?
2. How did Hofman's account change your perception of what it would be like to be a member of a minority on an isolated island off the coast of Scotland?
3. For a research project, investigate the significance of Passover or any other religious holiday connected with certain foods.

Ray Kroc

Grinding It Out: The Making of McDonald's

Ray Kroc (1902–1984), the entrepreneur responsible for the success of the McDonald's fast-food franchise, wrote Grinding It Out: The Making of McDonald's *(1977) in which the following essay first appeared. In this essay, Kroc describes how many of the now familiar food items came to be included on the menu.*

Before You Read

What percentage of your meals are from McDonald's or other fast–food franchises?

1 Some of my detractors, and I've acquired a few over the years, say that my penchant for experimenting with new menu items is a foolish indulgence. They contend that it stems from my never having outgrown my drummer's desire to have something new to sell. "McDonald's is in the hamburger business," they say. "How can Kroc even consider serving chicken?" Or, "Why change a winning combination?"

2 Of course, it's not difficult to demonstrate how much our menu has changed over the years, and nobody could argue with the success of additions such as the Filet-O-Fish, the Big Mac, Hot Apple Pie, and Egg McMuffin. The most interesting thing to me about these items is that each evolved from an idea of one of our operators. So the company has benefited from the ingenuity of its small businessmen while they were being helped by the system's image and our cooperative advertising muscle. This, to my way of thinking, is the perfect example of capitalism in action. Competition was the catalyst for each of the new items. Lou Groen came up with Filet-O-Fish to help him in his battle against the Big Boy chain in the Catholic parishes of Cincinnati. The Big Mac resulted from our need for a larger sandwich to compete against Burger King and a variety of specialty shop concoctions. The idea for Big Mac was originated by Jim Delligatti in Pittsburgh.

3 Harold Rosen, our operator in Enfield, Connecticut, invented our special St. Patrick's Day drink, The Shamrock Shake. "It takes a guy with a name like *Rosen* to think up an Irish drink," Harold told me. He wasn't kidding. "You may be right," I said. "It takes a guy with a name like Kroc to come up with a Hawaiian sandwich . . . Hulaburger." He

didn't say anything. He didn't know whether I was kidding or not. Operators aren't the only ones who come up with creative ideas for our menu. My old friend Dave Wallerstein, who was head of the Balaban & Katz movie chain and has a great flair for merchandising—he's the man who put the original snack bars in Disneyland for Walt Disney—is an outside director of McDonald's, and he's the one who came up with the idea for our large size order of french fries. He said he loved the fries, but the small bag wasn't enough and he didn't want to buy two. So we kicked it around and he finally talked us into testing the larger size in a store near his home in Chicago. They have a window in that store that they now call "The Wallerstein Window," because every time the manager or a crew person would look up, there would be Dave peering in to see how the large size fries were selling. He needn't have worried. The large order took off like a rocket, and it's now one of our best-selling items. Dave really puts his heart into his job as a director, now that he's retired and has plenty of time. There's nothing he likes more than traveling with me to check out stores.

4 Our Hot Apple Pie came after a long search for a McDonald's kind of dessert. I felt we had to have a dessert to round out our menu. But finding a dessert item that would fit readily into our production system and gain wide acceptance was a problem. I thought I had the answer in a strawberry shortcake. But it sold well for only a short time and then slowed to nothing. I had high hopes for pound cake, too, but it lacked glamor. We needed something we could romance in advertising. I was ready to give up when Litton Cochran suggested we try fried pie, which he said is an old southern favorite. The rest, of course, is fast-food history. Hot Apple Pie, and later Hot Cherry Pie, has that special quality, that classiness in a finger food, that made it perfect for McDonald's. The pies added significantly to our sales and revenues. They also created a whole new industry for producing the filled, frozen shells and supplying them to our stores.

5 During the Christmas holidays in 1972, I happened to be visiting in Santa Barbara, and I got a call from Herb Peterson, our operator there, who said he had something to show me. He wouldn't give me a clue as to what it was. He didn't want me to reject it out of hand, which I might have done, because it was a crazy idea—a breakfast sandwich. It consisted of an egg that had been formed in a Teflon circle, with the yolk broken, and was dressed with a slice of cheese and a slice of grilled Canadian bacon. This was served open-face on a toasted and buttered English muffin. I boggled a bit at the presentation. But then I tasted it, and I was sold. Wow! I wanted to put this item into all of our stores immediately. Realistically, of course, that was impossible. It took us nearly three years to get the egg sandwich fully integrated into our system. Fred Turner's wife, Patty, came up with the name that helped make it an immediate hit—Egg McMuffin.

6 The advent of Egg McMuffin opened up a whole new area of potential business for McDonald's, the breakfast trade. We went after it like the Sixth Fleet going into action. It was exhilarating to see the combined forces of our research and development people, our marketing and advertising experts, and our operations and supply specialists all concentrating on creating a program for catering to the breakfast trade. There were a great many problems to overcome. Some of them were new to us, because we were dealing with new kinds of products. Pancakes, for example, have to be offered if you intend to promote a complete breakfast menu. But they have an extremely short holding time, and this forced us to devise a procedure for "cooking to order" during periods of low customer count. Our food assembly lines, so swift and efficient for turning out hamburgers and french fries, had to be geared down and realigned to produce items for the breakfast trade. Then, after all the planning and all the working out of supply and production problems, it remained for the individual operator to figure out whether to adopt breakfast in his store. It meant longer hours for him, of course, and he'd probably have to hire more crew members and give the ones he had additional training. Consequently, the breakfast program is growing at a very moderate rate. But I can see it catching on across the country, and I can visualize extensions for a lot of stores, such as brunch on Sunday.

7 I keep a number of experimental menu additions in the works all the time. Some of them now being tested in selected stores may find their way into general use. Others, for a variety of reasons, will never make it. We have a complete test kitchen and experimental lab on my ranch, where all of our products are tested; this is in addition to the creative facility in Oak Brook. Fred Turner has a tendency to look askance at any new menu ideas. He'll usually try to put them down with some wisecrack such as, "That may be all right, but when are we going to start serving grilled bananas? We could put a little container of maple syrup on the side, and maybe for dinner we could serve them flaming." Such sarcasm doesn't bother me. I know Fred's thinking, and I respect it. He doesn't want us going hog wild with new items. We aren't going to, but we are going to stay flexible and change as the market demands it. There are some things we can do and maintain our identity, and there are others we could never do. For example, it's entirely possible that one day we might have pizza. On the other hand, there's damned good reason we should never have hot dogs. There's no telling what's inside a hot dog's skin, and our standard of quality just wouldn't permit that kind of item.

✧ *Evaluating the Text*

1. How did the need to originate new items evolve from the need to be competitive with other fast-food franchises?

How does this image in Manila convey McDonald's worldwide success?

2. What kind of research and development process goes in to bringing out a new item at McDonald's? For example, what chain of events was responsible for the Egg McMuffin?
3. McDonald's must produce food efficiently in a standardized manner that can be easily duplicated in thousands of McDonald's all over the world. How is this standardization a key element in their success?

✧ *Exploring Different Perspectives*

1. How does Amy Tan's account in "Fish Cheeks" differ from Ray Kroc's in terms of knowing or not knowing what you'll be served?
2. How do the accounts by Kroc and Maynard and Scheller in "Manifold Destiny" communicate the American cultural trait of efficiency?

✧ *Extending Viewpoints through Writing and Research*

1. How has McDonald's adapted to meet the challenge of the consumer's desire to have healthier meals? Have you ever had, for example, a salad instead of a hamburger at McDonald's?
2. If you have already seen or can rent the documentary *Supersize Me* (2004) by Morgan Spurlock, discuss the validity of his conclusions.

3. Discuss the unique appeal of any of your favorite fast-food franchises in terms of architecture, advertising, menu items, and the ritual aspects of having a meal there; for example, selections must always be called by their exact names. How is the predictability and familiarity of the experience part of their success?

Chris Maynard and Bill Scheller

Manifold Destiny

Chris Maynard, a photographer, traveled across the country with writer Bill Scheller. The following essay describes how they used their car engine to cook wholesome meals along the way. This essay first appeared in Manifold Destiny *(1989).*

Before You Read

What is the most unlikely impromptu meal you ever made or had while traveling?

1 Neither of us can leave Montreal without stopping first at Schwartz's, on Boulevard St.-Laurent.

2 Schwartz's is a little storefront deli that cures and smokes its own beef briskets, which it heaps high in the front window partly for display and partly so the countermen can quickly spear and slice them. "Smoked meat" is what Montreal prosaically calls this apotheosis of pastrami, and Schwartz's makes the best. You can eat it in the store. You can take it out and eat it at home. Or you may have to eat it on the sidewalk half a block away when the aroma coming through the butcher paper drives you nuts. What we had in mind, one summer's day in 1985, was to pack some in the car for a rest-stop picnic on our way back to Boston.

3 We were barely out of the city when we started to talk about what a shame it was that our pound of Schwartz's wouldn't be so alluringly hot when we pulled over for lunch. When you order this stuff the way Montreal insiders do—"easy on the lean"—room temperature just doesn't do it justice.

4 It was then that the idea hit. One of us remembered those stories we used to hear thirty years ago, about lonely truckers cooking hot dogs and beans on their engines. Why not Schwartz's smoked meat? It wouldn't even be cooking it—Schwartz had already done that—but just borrowing a little heat from the engine to warm it up. So we decided what the hell; if it worked for Teamsters, why not us?

5 We pulled off the interstate in Burlington, Vermont, bought a roll of aluminum foil, and triple-wrapped the sliced brisket. Opening the hood, we spied a nice little spot under the air filter of the '84 VW Rabbit, which seemed the perfect place to tuck in the package, and off we went.

An hour later we arrived at a standard-issue Vermont highway rest stop, the kind that looks like they wash the trees, and *voilà!*—in minutes, we were putting away hot smoked-meat sandwiches that actually had steam rising off them. Best of all, we nearly made two women at the next picnic table choke on their sprouts when they saw that instead of a busted fan belt, we had actually just dragged our lunch from the Rabbit's greasy maw.

6 Necessity, to rewrite the old chestnut, is the mother of necessary inventions—like ways to heat smoked meat when you don't have a steam table handy. But since inspired foolishness is the *real* hallmark of civilization, it wasn't long before we were inventing necessities. For instance, a dire need to roast a pork tenderloin on I-95 between Philadelphia and Providence. Car engines, we discovered, are good for a lot more than simply heating things up.

7 Soon we were calling each other (not on car phones, thank God) with news of our latest accomplishments:

8 "I poached a fillet of sole."

9 "I roasted a stuffed eggplant."

10 "I figured out how to do game hens."

11 "I made baked apples."

12 Before long, those rest-stop stares of disbelief had been replaced by reactions infinitely more delightful to savor—like that of the toll collector who swore he smelled chicken and tarragon, but couldn't figure out where the hell it was coming from.

13 What we didn't realize, during those early years of random experimentation, was that our burgeoning skills as car-engine cooks were going to serve us splendidly as we competed in one of the most grueling sporting events on the planet: the Cannonball One Lap of America Rally. The One Lap is an eight-thousand-mile-plus highway marathon, seven days of nonstop driving in which participants must adhere to strict rules while reeking of spilled coffee and unchanged underwear. It might be the most exhausting and disorienting event anyone would pay money to enter, but of course it makes you feel like a kid with nothing to do except ride his bike in the park for a week—with no grown-ups around.

14 Trouble is, it's damned difficult to stick to the rally routes and get anything decent to eat. Most people who run the One Lap follow a regimen of truck-stop breakfasts (not necessarily eaten at breakfast time) and assorted pack-along calories drawn from the canned and bottled food groups. Our wonderful epiphany, shared by none of the fifty-seven other teams in the 1988 event, was that if we cooked on the big V-8 under the hood of our sponsor's stretch Lincoln Town Car, we could eat like epicures without screwing up our time and distance factors.

15 Here's what we did. Two days before the rally started in Detroit, we worked out a menu and did our shopping. Then we commandeered

the kitchen of our friend Marty Kohn, a feature writer for the *Detroit Free Press,* and put together enough uncooked entrées to last us at least all the way to our midway layover in Los Angeles. Boneless chicken breasts with prosciutto and provolone, fillet of flounder, a whole pork tenderloin, a ham steak (a reversion to our simple heat-through days)—everything was seasoned, stuffed, and splashed according to our own recipes, sealed up tightly in three layers of aluminum foil, and promptly frozen. We felt like we were turning Marty's kitchen into a tiny suburban version of those factories where they make airplane food, with one big difference—our stuff was good.

16 The next day we transferred our frosty little aluminum packages to the kitchen freezer at the Westin Hotel in the Renaissance Center (try pulling a request like *that* on the next concierge you meet) and had them brought up with our coffee and croissants on the morning of the rally. The food went into a cooler, the cooler went into our Lincoln, and off we went. Every afternoon between Detroit and the West Coast we'd haul out another dinner, throw it on the engine, and cook it as we lopped a few hundred more miles off the route. Let our competitors use the drive-thrus at McDonald's. We ate well, very well indeed.

17 We would have done the same thing in L.A. for the return trip, but we didn't have the time. Anyway, it occurred to us somewhere around Albuquerque that we *couldn't* have done it, since none of the people we know in L.A have freezers. Everyone there eats out all the time, subsisting entirely on a diet of langoustine ravioli on a coulis of roasted red peppers.

18 By the time the rally ended, we'd gained more fame for our means of sustenance than for our position in the final standings: Everybody, it seemed, had something to say about car-engine cooking. Half the comments were expressions of pure disbelief (and this book is an attempt to convert the disbelievers), while the rest amounted to variations on "Truck drivers have been doing that for years." *Please*. All the truck drivers we've ever heard of who cook on their diesels are still punching vent holes in cans of Dinty Moore stew.

19 This is not to say we refuse to acknowledge the pioneers. We are by no means the first people to cook food on car engines. The idea dates back so far, in fact, that it predates cars altogether.

20 The Huns of the fourth and fifth centuries lived on horseback, and subsisted to a great extent on meat. When a Hun wanted to enjoy a hunk of unsmoked brisket—say, when he was tearing around in the One Lap of the Western Roman Empire (with points for pillage)—he would take the meat and put it under his saddle cloth, and the friction between Hun and horse would have a tenderizing and warming effect. (We think they used saddle cloths. If not, well, just don't think about it.) Since this was a situation in which a "cooking" effect was achieved by the application of excess heat generated by the means of propulsion, it

is clearly part of the line of descent that leads to hot lunch buckets in the cab of a steam locomotive, and to stuffed chicken breasts à la Lincoln Town Car. We can't say for sure, but it may also have been the origin of steak tartare.

21 But let's get back to that important qualification—*excess heat generated by the means of propulsion*. This disqualifies a lot of other attempts at mobile cookery, or at least relegates them to a different branch of evolution. We read recently, for instance, that the big, handsomely outfitted carriage Napoleon Bonaparte used during his military campaigns was equipped with an oil lantern mounted above and behind the rear seat that could be used for cooking as well as lighting. But whether or not the little corporal used his lantern to heat up leftover veal Marengo, the fact is that lanterns don't make carriages go. What Napoleon was really on to here was the ancestor of the latest yuppie doodad, the dashboard microwave. Don't laugh—these are hard upon us, touted as just the thing for people too important to waste time revving up the molecules of frozen Danish in their kitchens. The traffic accident of the future will involve some boob who, peeling a memo off his on-board fax machine, doesn't see the lady in the next lane taking a Pop-Tart out of her micro.

22 No such risk with car-engine cooking. Since you can't check to see if your dinner is done without getting out of the vehicle and looking under the hood, it's no more dangerous than pulling over to change a tire—a lot less dangerous, in fact, since you don't get to pick the location for a flat tire. As engine cooking spreads in popularity—which it will—interstate rest areas will take on a new, homey character. People will ask each other what smells so good, and lend each other oven mitts; those two rich farts in the Grey Poupon ad who are always borrowing each other's mustard will be joined by plenty of ordinary folks. Like most slow, low-tech enterprises, car-engine cooking will bring people together. Don't take this lightly; the only other way to promote sociability on the road is to smile at strangers in the Howard Johnson's, and God knows where that could get you.

23 But ultimately, gastronomy overrides sociability. The best reason to cook on your car engine is the same desire to avoid indigestion that motivated us during the rally. Unless you're carrying with you the collected works of Calvin Trillin or Jane and Michael Stern and have the time to detour to all the wonderful diners and rib joints they have chronicled, a long car trip is likely to bring you up short in the eats department. And it's not like the good old days were any better. We recently came across Henry Miller's *The Air-Conditioned Nightmare,* based on a six-month cross-country trip he took in a '32 Buick back in 1941. Miller finished the trip in Los Angeles, not only dyspeptic over the philistines and materialists he claimed to have encountered all over

the republic, but with his innards devastated from eating in one greasy spoon after another. Poor devil—that '32 Buick probably had a lovely flathead six, as choice a cooking device as any six-burner restaurant range. If only he'd known. And being Henry Miller, he'd probably have felt better about America if only he'd known that in little more than a decade the philistines and materialists at Rambler were going to produce a car with a backseat that folded into a bed.

24 But we digress. The point is that you can make better meals for yourself, on your engine, than the vast majority of the roadside stands can make for you. Not to mention that engine cooking is a great way to sample regional foods. Think about crayfish in Louisiana. Lake perch in Wisconsin. Abalone in Northern California. . . . And think of the fun you could have on vacation, with endless, monotonous rides made bearable by salivating over that dinner cooking right under your own hood. Instead of "When are we going to get there?" the kids will ask, "When will the chicken be done?" Finally, the car-engine chef is using one of the tastiest and most healthful cooking methods, simmering foods in their own juices in a sealed package—*en papillote,* as they say when they cook on their Renaults in France.

25 We could go on, maybe even mentioning the conservation benefits of cooking with heat that otherwise would be wasted—at the risk, of course, of sounding like refugees from the 1970s gas shortage Moral Equivalent of War. But who knows? If there's another energy crisis, we might be hailed as the heralds of a kinder, gentler way to cook dinner.

✧ *Evaluating the Text*

1. What ingenious idea did the authors think of to assure themselves of having a cooked meal while traveling long distances in their car?

2. How did their new cooking method keep them well supplied with food during a cross-country car marathon?

3. How did the authors incorporate historical figures and popular writers in their narrative? What was the effect?

✧ *Exploring Different Perspectives*

1. Why do the authors believe their method produces better food than does McDonald's? (See Ray Kroc, "Grinding It Out: The Making of McDonald's.")

2. In what sense are the accounts by Maynard and Scheller and Andrew X. Pham (see "Foreign-Asians") travel narratives in which food plays an important part?

✧ *Extending Viewpoints through Writing and Research*

1. Discuss both the advantages and disadvantages of the method of cooking devised by Maynard and Scheller.
2. Would the authors' cooking method appeal to you? Why or why not?
3. Describe a trip you took by car—for example, to the beach, mountains, desert, or other destination—where you needed to prepare and pack food for an extended period of time. Which foods survived best?

Andrew X. Pham

Foreign-Asians

Andrew X. Pham was born in 1967 in Vietnam and came to the United States with his family in 1977. His adventure of bicycling through parts of Asia, including Vietnam, led to his book Catfish and Mandala: A Two-Wheeled Voyage through the Landscape and Memory of Vietnam *(1999), from which the following essay is drawn. In 2008, he wrote* The Eaves of Heaven: A Life in Three Wars, *which tells the story of his father's experiences during the Vietnam War. In 2009, he received a Guggenheim Fellowship and is currently writing* Twilight Territory *about Vietnam.*

Before You Read

What is the longest bicycle trip you or a friend ever took? How did it work out?

1 The morning following my return to Vung Tau from Mekong Delta, I aim myself north toward Hanoi and start pedaling. After Minh Luong Prison, I took a day ride down the Mekong River on a banana boat, caught an all-night bus back to Saigon, then shuttled back to Vung Tau. Yesterday evening was spent tuning my rickety bike for what will probably be its last journey.

2 As usual, I leave early, quietly fading into the dawn. Today I am going to Phan Thiet, the place of my birth. Out on the road, I feel vulnerable, especially when passing through villages. Vietnam seems full of villages, squalid gatherings of dwellings and shops every two miles along any road. The road is busy with peasants commuting up to ten miles daily on the saddest-looking bicycles on the planet. I slip into an easy rhythm, conversing with other riders. On the recommendation of a stranger, I take a fork in the road, opting for the more scenic coastal route to Phan Thiet.

3 Around noon, a white sun broils the land. Even the road dust feels baking hot. I fry inside my helmet. The sun-block cream is inadequate, milking down my face with my sweat. By one in the afternoon, the red-brown skin on my arms is covered with tiny blisters like fine sprays of sweat. They pop watery when I scratch them. The sun burns my arms raw. I don't have any long-sleeve shirt except my sweatshirt and my rain jacket. I spot women sitting at sewing machines in thatched huts. They

graciously cut up one of my T-shirts to make sleeves for the one I am wearing. Within minutes, I am handsomely outfitted with sleeves. They refuse payment, saying it is a gift. I thank them and get back on the road in better spirits, still thinking I can make Phan Thiet by nightfall.

4 The countryside opens up with an endless patchwork of four- or five-acre farms, the houses hidden among the willowy trees and banana palms. In the lightly wooded areas, herders, rangy men with broad-brimmed hats, dusty clothes, and long bamboo staves, move quietly, watching their cattle grazing. The land is rich, green shooting up everywhere—out of the paddies, along the river, between the cracks in the road. The asphalt ends abruptly without road signs, and I find myself struggling on a red dirt road, sandy and full of children trudging home from school. Every five or six miles, there is an abandoned guardhouse with a boom-gate which is no longer levered across the road but raised like a flagpole. These are relics from the dark decade following the War, when the new Communist government kept a firm lid on civilian movement. People had to apply for inter provincial travel. Now children play in these guard stations and people pass through the gates without glancing at them. It seems as though, here in the back-country, the government simply got bored and went back to the big cities. The only souls making a big racket out here are batches of twelve-year-olds riding two or three to a bicycle, going here and there, racing each other. I catch up with one large group. They are going to the local hot spring. They say they make the six-mile round-trip every other day. The way they twitter and yip, it sounds like the best way to bathe.

5 Although there are people everywhere, I am hesitant to ask for directions because everyone wants me to come in for tea. I manage to take several wrong turns. The hungry, curious way people gawk at me makes me feel spoiled, self-indulgent. I am also embarrassed to be "adventuring" through their homes, bedecked in outlandish gear they could never afford. At last, I summon enough courage to talk to a few poor peasants whose villages have only a handful of motorbikes each. Many villagers haven't ventured farther than a day's bike distance from the place of their birth. No one seems to have a solid concept of the distance to the next town, Ham Tan. Dusk is falling and I know my shaky legs won't make it to Phan Thiet. My touring instinct urges me to look for a suitable place to strike camp, but as far as I can see in the weakening light, the land has been cut up into bite-sized lots, each one devoid of trees and surrounded by pigsties, gardens, and rice plots. The air is coarse with smoke from cooking fires.

6 Two hours after dark, I creak and bump to a commoner's inn in Ham Tan village. It is a clean but run-down place that houses merchants and traveling peasants. Bolted to the concrete floor, plywood partitions, three feet short of the ceiling, section the dormitory into

individual cubicles. I pay my three-dollar fee and turn my travel papers over to the owner for processing with the local constable. Both natives and foreigners must register every night. Bureaucrats still keep a record of travelers.

7 Across from the inn is a corner diner, a corrugated-tin-and-plywood-scrap place, its concrete floor an inch higher than the mud. It has the looks of the shoddiest establishments in the old gold-rush towns, where streets eternally switched between whipped mud and dust fog. Dinner conversations die the moment I step inside, and the only things blaring are the TV and my sixth sense. Raw-faced men crowd four of the six tables, facing the television until I arrive. On the tables are nests of empty beer bottles.

8 A woman looks out from the kitchen. She approaches guardedly, twisting a rag in her hands. She eyes the men and asks me, *"What do you want?"*

9 *"Hello, Sister. Are you still serving dinner?"* I nod toward the inn across the street. *"I'm staying over there. The owner recommended your place."*

10 She hesitates, then flicks the rag at the back table near the kitchen. I sit obediently, wondering yet again why Vietnamese prefer kindergarten furniture. I haven't acquired the penchant to sit with my butt lower than my knees. With the tabletop so low, whenever I eat I feel as though I am licking myself like a dog. A string of black ants marches crumbs off the table. Houseflies buzz around my head. People stare openly at me, so I try to keep myself from batting the flies and squashing the ants. I play stoic and take immense interest in the Vietnamese soap opera playing on television.

11 "Oy! You," a man slurs in English. He sits up front and is obviously drunk and talking to me. I groan, pretending not to hear.

12 "OY! YOU!"

13 Oh, Lord. I show him my friendliest smile and nod, fingering my pocket for the tiny canister of pepper spray.

14 The speaker switches to Vietnamese, his English apparently at its limit. *"Brother, I want to ask you a question."*

15 *"Please do."*

16 *"How is it you speak Viet so well?"*

17 I grin. This is easy. *"I'm Vietnamese."*

18 He hitches up one corner of his mouth and blows out a note of disgust. His liquored eyes flicker over to his drinking partner, a shifty man with a knifish look—a perfect killer right out of some bad Chinese mafia movie. He mutters privately to Killer, who smirks in agreement. Pointing a grubby finger in my direction, my antagonist raises his voice: *"You're not Vietnamese. Where's your birth-roots?"*

19 *"Phan Thiet."*

20 *"Say it again."*

21 *"Phan Thiet."*

22 *"Liar. You're not from Phan Thiet. You didn't pronounce it like a man from Phan Thiet."*

23 *"I've been in America a long time. My Viet isn't perfect."*

24 *"Liar. You're Korean, aren't you?"*

25 *"Chinese,"* offers Killer.

26 *"Japanese,"* counters another.

27 I am the tallest one present, my skin the palest. My wire-rimmed eyeglasses make me look foreign. Worse, I have a closely cropped crew cut. My hair is straight and spiky. Vietnamese call it "nail hair," a style commonly seen on Korean expatriates working in Vietnam.

28 I should know better, but I insist, *"Really, I'm Vietnamese."*

29 The drunk bolts up in his seat, pounds the table, then points at his own nose with his index finger. He slur-screeches, *"Brother, you call me stupid?"*

30 *"Oh, no, Brother. No,"* I blurt, thinking, Oh, shit. Oh, shit.

31 He starts spieling his body of knowledge on the matter: *"I've been to the City* [Saigon]. *I know what's going on in the world. All you foreigners come into the country to work. You go to the university, learning about . . . about mathematics, history, books . . . all that. You live in the City for a couple of years and you think you can pass as a Vietnamese. I know all about you foreign Asians. My brother-in-law lives in the City. I'm a poor villager, but I'm not dumb."* He encompasses the room with a sweep of his hand. *"We're not stupid!"*

32 Magically, his insult becomes theirs, and the whole rooms falls in behind him. A hostile grumble rises, amplified by the noisy television. Someone growls, *Motherfucker*. Another mumbles, *Bastard thinks he can come into our place and lie to our faces*. The whole affair has taken all of thirty seconds, and I realize with horrible dismay this is not how I want things to turn out at all. I'm here to learn about them, about my roots, about me—and they look like they want to cut me up. My pepper spray isn't going to handle this crowd. Damn! I haven't even eaten yet.

33 I raise an appeasing hand, smiling, making chuckling sounds. *"You're all right! I was just joking. Sorry. I am Korean. You're very sharp. Most people can't pick me out. I've been in the country three years. Studied Viet at the University. Pretty good, eh? So sorry. Beg your pardon."*

34 My tormentor seems happy at my concession to his intellect, but his friends appear even more riled. They cuss. I palm the canister beneath the table. A couple of mean-looking guys give me the eye as they mutter among themselves. This is definitely out of hand. I have seen three fights break out in Vietnamese bars over smaller issues than this. The last time, one drunk with a hatchet amputated a few fingers and hospitalized four men before he was subdued. I must get out quickly, but the exit is blocked by this hostile crowd.

35 BAM! I jump in my seat. The waitress is next to me, slamming down plates and bowls of food on my table so hard the whole room

fixates on her. A huge plate of rice covered with stir-fried cabbage. A bowl of stewed pork and eggs. A bowl of squash soup. A saucer of pickled radish. A mug of hot tea. She glowers at them as she rearranges my meal.

36 I gape at the food I hadn't ordered.

37 She turns on the men, challenging them with her hot eyes. She speaks slowly, as though reprimanding boys who should know better: *"Let a man eat. Remember your manners."*

38 My foe says something under his breath. She whirls on him, fists cocked on hips, yelling: *"What, Lang?"*

39 He turns to the television. She pans the room for dissenters. When no one says a word, she marches back into the kitchen without looking in my direction. I lower my eyes to the food and dig into it cyclo style—chopsticks in one hand for picking up morsels, tablespoon in the other for shoveling rice. I eat *binh dan*—like a commoner—fast and hungry, sipping soup with the spoon once every three mouthfuls. I am shocked that they actually leave me to my rice. This is the last place I expect the observance of that old custom my father had taught me when I was a boy.

40 Father stocked bamboo canes around the house so that whenever I was due for a whacking, he could lay his hand on a wand-of-discipline quicker than I could flee the room. My sister Chi and I must have been rotten kids because he caned us regularly. The only time he didn't was during mealtimes. If the food had been put on the table, he would postpone the punishment till well after the meal. My mother said that hitting a person when he is eating was the cruelest, most uncivilized thing anyone could do. And that if you caused a person to cry into his rice—*souping rice with tears,* she said—you would be cursed with the bitterness he swallowed.

41 I figure I'm safe until the last bite. Lang and Killer are watching me, plotting something between themselves. The others argue over the pros and cons of Vietnam opening its market. Wondering if and when the waitress will return and bail me out again, I glance at the kitchen and notice a back door near where she washes dishes.

42 Halfway through my food—I am still hungry—the TV program switches over to news and everyone turns to the anchorman announcing the headline stories. In a blink, I breeze out of my chair, making for the kitchen. My mouth full, I hand the waitress a large bill and bolt through the back door, across the street.

43 The inn owner is sitting at the front door, smoking and chatting with a neighbor. He sees me running and asks if anything is wrong. Abruptly, the waitress is at my elbow. I jump, startled. She hands me the change, unfamiliar with the custom of tipping. She briefs the old man on my dilemma. I stand by looking helpless. He cusses and hollers for his sons and the servants.

44 *"Go inside. I'll take care of those dog-spawned. I'm sorry they bothered you. Go, go."* His beatific face now thunderous with anger.

45 He doesn't need to tell me twice. Killer, Lang, and four men are coming toward the inn. By the time they cross the street, I am out of sight. Five of the inn's men run to the front with machetes. A shouting match ensues. Someone is dispatched to get the police. The bullies back off. I go back to my cubicle, lock the toy door, and crawl inside my mosquito netting.

46 Too jazzed with adrenaline to sleep, I count the geckos scrawling across the ceiling. I am inexplicably happy, thrilled not by my escape but by the goodness of my hosts. This is Vietnam. These are my people. Phan Thiet, the village of my childhood, and Mui Ne, the gateway of our family's flight from the fatherland, await me down the road, merely a day away.

✧ *Evaluating the Text*

1. Why did Pham feel out of place as an American of Vietnamese origin taking a bicycle trip to his hometown?

2. What led the people in the small corner diner to become so hostile toward Pham? Why did he agree to confirm their untrue suspicions?

3. Despite his feelings of discomfort and danger, why did Pham feel a sense of happiness at the end of this episode?

✧ *Exploring Different Perspectives*

1. How do the accounts by Pham and Amy Tan in "Fish Cheeks" focus on questions of identity and ethnicity?

2. How do the accounts by Pham and Ray Kroc in "Grinding It Out: The Making of McDonald's" emphasize the importance of maintaining a psychological feeling of security while eating?

✧ *Extending Viewpoints through Writing and Research*

1. Just as Pham is mistaken for a non-Vietnamese, have you ever been mistaken for or tried to pass as someone from a different ethnic, racial, or social group? What happened?

2. Pham mentions that he dug into his food with chopsticks. How does using them produce a unique relationship with the food you are eating?

Saira Shah

The Storyteller's Daughter

Saira Shah was born in Britain of an Afghan family in 1964. At age twenty-one, she became a correspondent covering the guerrilla war between the Soviets and the Afghan resistance. Under the concealment of a burka, she filmed Beneath the Veil, *a CNN documentary on women's lives under the Taliban (2001). The following selection is a chapter drawn from her book* The Storyteller's Daughter *(2003). In this chapter, she describes how her father's cooking transported his family back to Afghanistan.*

Before You Read

What exotic landscapes do some foods evoke?

1 I am three years old. I am sitting on my father's knee. He is telling me of a magical place: the fairytale landscape you enter in dreams. Fountains fling diamond droplets into mosaic pools. Coloured birds sing in the fruit-laden orchards. The pomegranates burst and their insides are rubies. Fruit is so abundant that even the goats are fed on melons. The water has magical properties: you can fill to bursting with fragrant *pilau,*[1] then step to the brook and drink—and you will be ready to eat another meal.

2 On three sides of the plateau majestic mountains tower, capped with snow. The fourth side overlooks a sunny valley where, gleaming far below, sprawls a city of villas and minarets. And here is the best part of the story: it is true.

3 The garden is in Paghman, where my family had its seat for nine hundred years. The jewel-like city it overlooks is the Afghan capital, Kabul. The people of Paghman call the capital Kabul *jan:* beloved Kabul. We call it that too, for this is where we belong.

4 "Whatever outside appearances may be, no matter who tells you otherwise, this garden, this country, these are your origin. This is where you are truly from. Keep it in your heart, Saira *jan.* Never forget."

5 Any Western adult might have told me that this was an exile's tale of a lost Eden: the place you dream about, to which you can never

[1]*pilau*: Also known as pilaf, a dish made of rice, boiled in a seasoned liquid that may contain meat or fish.

return. But even then, I wasn't going to accept that. Even then, I had absorbed enough of the East to feel I belonged there. And too much of the West not to try to nail down dreams.

6 My father understood the value of stories: he was a writer. My parents had picked Kent as an idyllic place to bring up their children, but we were never allowed to forget our Afghan background.

7 Periodically during my childhood, my father would come upon the kitchen like a storm. Western systematic method quickly melted before the inspiration of the East. Spice jars tumbled down from their neat beechwood rack and disgorged heaps of coloured powder on to the melamine sideboard. Every pan was pressed into service and extra ones were borrowed from friends and neighbours. The staid old Aga wheezed exotic vapours—*saffran, zeera, gashneesh;* their scents to this day are as familiar to me as my own breath.

8 In the midst of this mayhem presided my father, the alchemist. Like so many expatriates, when it came to maintaining the traditions, customs and food of his own country he was *plus royaliste que le roi*. Rather than converting lead into gold, my father's alchemical art transported our English country kitchen to the furthest reaches of the Hindu Kush.

9 We children were the sorcerer's apprentices: we chopped onions and split cardamom pods, nibbling the fragrant black seeds as we worked. We crushed garlic and we peeled tomatoes. He showed us how to steep saffron, to strain yoghurt and to cook the rice until it was *danadar,* possessing grains—that is, to the point where it crumbles into three or four perfect round seeds if you rub it between your fingers.

10 In the kitchen, my father's essential *Afghaniyat,* Afghanness, was most apparent. The Afghan love of *pilau* is as fundamental to the national character as the Italian fondness for spaghetti. The Amir Habibullah, a former ruler of Afghanistan, would demolish a vast meal of *pilau,* meatballs and sauce for lunch, then turn to his courtiers and ask: "Now, noblemen and friends, what shall we cook tonight?"

11 We knew to produce at least three times more *pilau* than anyone could ever be expected to eat. Less would have been an insult to our name and contrary to the Afghan character. As my great-great-great-grandfather famously roared: "How dare you ask me for a *small* favour?"

12 If, at any point, my father found himself with an unexpected disaster—rice that went soggy or an overboiling pan that turned the Aga's hotplate into a sticky mess—he would exclaim: "Back in Afghanistan, we had cooks to do this work!"

13 He would tell us, with Afghan hyperbole: "We are making a *Shahi pilau,* a *pilau* fit for kings. This recipe has been handed down through our family since it was prepared for up to four thousand guests at the court of your ancestors. It is far better than the *pilau* you will find when you visit homes in Afghanistan today."

14 On one notable occasion, my father discovered the artificial food colouring, tartrazine. A *pilau*-making session was instantly convened. Like a conjurer pulling off a particularly effective trick, he showed us how just one tiny teaspoon could transform a gigantic cauldron of *pilau* to a virulent shade of yellow. We were suitably impressed. From that moment on, traditional saffron was discarded for this intoxicating substance.

15 Years later, I learned that all of the Afghan dishes my father had taught me diverged subtly from their originals. His method of finishing off the parboiled rice in the oven, for example, was an innovation of his own. Straining yoghurt through cheesecloth turned out to be merely the first stage in an elaborate process. In Kent, rancid sheep's fat was hard to come by, so he substituted butter. Cumin was an Indian contamination. And so it went on.

16 Yet although his methods and even his ingredients were different, my father's finished dishes tasted indistinguishable from the originals. He had conveyed their essential quality; the minutiae had been swept away.

17 During these cookery sessions, we played a wonderful game. We planned the family trip to Afghanistan that always seemed to be just round the corner. How we would go back to Paghman, stroll in the gardens, visit our old family home and greet the relatives we had never met. When we arrived in the Paghman mountains, the men would fire their guns in the air—we shouldn't worry, that was the Afghan way of welcome and celebration. They would carry us on their shoulders, whooping and cheering, and in the evening we would eat a *pilau* that eclipsed even the great feasts of the court of our ancestors.

18 My mother's family background, which is Parsee from India, rarely got a look in. As far as my father was concerned, his offspring were pure Afghan. For years, the mere mention of the Return was enough to stoke us children into fits of excitement. It was so much more alluring than our mundane Kentish lives, which revolved round the family's decrepit Land Rover and our pet Labrador, Honey.

19 "Can we take the Land Rover?" asked my brother Tahir.

20 "We shall take a fleet of Land Rovers," said my father grandly.

21 My sister Safia piped up: "Can we take Honey?"

22 There was an uncomfortable pause. Even my father's flight of fantasy balked at introducing to Afghans as a beloved member of our family that unclean animal, the dog.

23 When I was fifteen, the Soviet Union invaded and occupied Afghanistan. During a *pilau*-making session quite soon after that, I voiced an anxiety that had been growing for some time now. How could my father expect us to be truly Afghan when we had grown up outside an Afghan community? When we went back home, wouldn't we children be strangers, foreigners in our own land? I expected, and possibly

hoped for, the soothing account of our triumphant and imminent return to Paghman. It didn't come. My father looked tired and sad. His answer startled me: "I've given you stories to replace a community. They are your community."

24 "But surely stories can't replace experience."

25 He picked up a packet of dehydrated onion. "Stories are like these onions—like dried experience. They aren't the original experience but they are more than nothing at all. You think about a story, you turn it over in your mind, and it becomes something else." He added hot water to the onion. "It's not fresh onion—fresh experience—but it is something that can help you to recognize experience when you come across it. Experiences follow patterns, which repeat themselves again and again. In our tradition, stories can help you recognize the shape of an experience, to make sense of and to deal with it. So, you see, what you may take for mere snippets of myth and legend encapsulate what you need to know to guide you on your way anywhere among Afghans."

26 "Well, as soon as I'm eighteen I'm going to go to see for myself," I said, adding craftily: "Then perhaps I'll have fresh experiences that will help me grow up."

27 My father had been swept along on the tide of his analogy. Now, he suddenly became a parent whose daughter was at an impressionable age and whose country was embroiled in a murderous war.

28 "If you would only grow up a little in the first place," he snapped, "then you would realize that you don't need to go at all."

✧ *Evaluating the Text*

1. How does Shah conjure up the fantasy of an idyllic Afghanistan when describing her father's methods of preparing the unique foods of that country?

2. How was Shah's father a magician when it came to using the local foods available where she grew up in Kent, England, to cook authentic Afghani meals?

3. How did her father's meals become a springboard for Shah's desire to travel to Afghanistan? Why is her father worried when he realizes she really wants to go there?

✧ *Exploring Different Perspectives*

1. In what way do both Shah's narrative and Andrew X. Pham's account in "Foreign-Asians" illustrate the conflict between the authors' naive beliefs and what is really taking place in Afghanistan and Vietnam?

2. How do both Shah and Ethel G. Hofman in "An Island Passover" reveal how ethnic feasts can invoke a distant culture?

✧ *Extending Viewpoints through Writing and Research*

1. Discuss the idea put forward by Shah's father that good stories "can help you recognize the shape of an experience."
2. In your opinion, how can a certain meal evoke another time and place, either real or imagined?

Connecting Cultures

Mark I. Schwartz, "Genetically Modified Food Is Safe"

In what light do Schwartz and Kulick and Machado-Borges in "Leaky" in Chapter 3 present innovative technologies concerning diet?

Jeffrey M. Smith, "Genetically Engineered Foods May Cause Rising Food Allergies"

What evidence leads Jeffrey M. Smith and Cameron M. Smith in "Of Ice and Men" in Chapter 6 to go against popular views regarding genetically engineered food and the extinction of polar bears, respectively?

Amy Tan, "Fish Cheeks"

In what way do the dinners described by Tan and Patricia Hampl in "Grandmother's Sunday Dinner" in Chapter 1 serve as a kind of drama to express important cultural values?

Frederick Douglass, "My Bondage and My Freedom"

How does Douglass's narrative reveal the same discriminatory social system as portrayed by Kate Chopin in "Désirée's Baby" in Chapter 5?

Ethel G. Hofman, "An Island Passover"

In what way do the dinners described by Hofman and Patricia Hampl in "Grandmother's Sunday Dinner" in Chapter 1 serve as important cultural rituals?

Ray Kroc, "Grinding It Out: The Making of McDonald's"

How do Kroc and Firoozeh Dumas in "Save Me, Mickey" in Chapter 1 portray revered American commercial icons, that is, McDonald's and Disneyland?

Chris Maynard and Bill Scheller, "Manifold Destiny"

What insights do Maynard and Scheller and Jack Owens in "Don't Shoot! We're Republicans!" in Chapter 4 offer into the culture of cars in America?

Andrew X. Pham, "Foreign-Asians"

How do Pham and Sucheng Chan in "You're Short, Besides!" in Chapter 2 contend with prejudices directed toward them by other Asians based on their personal appearance?

Saira Shah, "The Storyteller's Daughter"

Discuss the differences between Shah's father from Afghanistan and Latifa Ali's father in "Betrayed," in Kurdistan/Iraq?

8

Customs, Rituals, and Values

The world is a beautiful book, but of little use to him who cannot read it.

—Carlo Goldoni (1707–1793), Italian dramatist;
Lord Arthur, in *Pamela,* act 1, sc. 14 (1746)

In the customs, rituals, and values that a society embraces, we can see most clearly the hidden cultural logic and unconscious assumptions people in that society rely on to interpret everything that goes on in their world. Customs and rituals that may seem bizarre or strange to an outsider appear entirely normal and natural to those within the culture. Unfortunately, the potential for conflict exists as soon as people from different cultures whose "natural" ways do not coincide make contact with each other.

As communications, immigration, and travel make the world smaller, the potential for cross-cultural misunderstanding accelerates. Correspondingly, the need to become aware of the extent to which our own and other people's conclusions about the world are guided by different cultural presuppositions grows. Analysis of the customs of cultures other than our own allows us to temporarily put aside our taken-for-granted ways of seeing the world, even if we are normally unaware of the extent to which we rely on these implicit premises—to understand that the meanings we give to events, actions, and statements are not their only possible meanings. The range and diversity of the selections in this chapter will allow you to temporarily replace your own way of perceiving the world and become aware, perhaps for the first time, of the cultural assumptions that govern your interpretations of the world.

Philip Slater in "Want-Creation Fuels Americans' Addictiveness" investigates whether the national preference for quick fixes is the cause of a rising trend in drug use. Harold Miner in "Body Ritual among the

Nacirema" describes the strange obsessions of a little known North American tribe. Robert Levine and Ellen Wolff in "Social Time: The Heartbeat of Culture" broadens our perceptions about something seemingly as indisputable as clock time by disclosing how the concept of being early, on time, or late varies from culture to culture. Based on his field work in the Republic of the Congo, Colin Turnbull in "The Mbuti Pygmies" describes the importance of rituals in shaping the behavior of children in Mbuti society. Valerie Steele and John S. Major in "China Chic: East Meets West" analyze the hidden political and social meanings of the custom of foot binding in ancient China. Serena Nanda in "Arranging a Marriage in India" describes her participation in the lengthy process of getting her friend's son married.

To help you understand how the works in this chapter relate to each other, you might use one or several of the following guidelines before writing about customs, rituals, and values.

1. How do your reactions to the subject coincide with or differ from those of the authors?
2. What idea or concept does the author wish to communicate to his or her readers?
3. How did the writer enhance your understanding of the unique values of that culture?
4. Is the author enthusiastic or doubtful about the values of the culture he or she writes about?
5. What does the writer discover about the culture he or she investigates?
6. Does the author mainly value the connotations rather than denotations of terms?

Recommended Films on This Theme

- *Ran* (Japan, 1985) This film is a masterful adaptation of Shakespeare's *King Lear* by the renowned director, Ikira Kurosawa, about an aging warlord in medieval Japan and the ambition and greed of his family;
- *Cinema Paradisio* (Italy, 1988) A captivating tale of a young boy's experience working in a movie theater in a small town in Italy just after World War II;
- *Spring, Summer, Fall, Winter, and Spring* (Korea, 2003) A beautiful study of a boy being trained as a Buddhist monk in a small floating temple;
- *Harry Potter and the Half-Blood Prince* (England, 2009) The last in the series of Harry Potter delves into the mysterious forces that threaten the school of Hogwarts.

Philip Slater

Want-Creation Fuels Americans' Addictiveness

Philip Slater (b. 1927) was a professor of sociology at Harvard and is author of The Pursuit of Loneliness *(1970) and* Wealth-Addiction *(1980). Slater argues that the premium Americans put on success causes many people to resort to drugs to feel better about themselves and to cope with feelings of inadequacy. Slater cites a broad range of examples from everyday life to demonstrate that advertisers exploit societal pressures in order to sell products. The following article first appeared in the* St. Paul Pioneer Press Dispatch *(September 6, 1984). In 2009, Slater wrote* Chrysalis Effect: The Metamorphosis of Global Culture.

Before You Read

Consider the extent to which a quick fix mentality could be responsible for the prevalence of addictions in America.

1 Imagine what life in America would be like today if the surgeon general convinced Congress that cigarettes, as America's most lethal drug, should be made illegal.

2 The cost of tobacco would increase 5,000 percent. Law enforcement budgets would quadruple but still be hopelessly inadequate to the task. The tobacco industry would become mob-controlled, and large quantities of Turkish tobacco would be smuggled into the country through New York and Miami.

3 Politicians would get themselves elected by inveighing against tobacco abuse. Some would argue shrewdly that the best enforcement strategy was to go after the growers and advertisers—making it a capital offense to raise or sell tobacco. And a great many Americans would try smoking for the first time.

4 Americans are individualists. We like to express our opinions much more than we like to work together. Passing laws is one of the most popular pastimes, and enforcing them one of the least. We make laws like we make New Year's resolutions—the impulse often exhausted by giving voice to it. Who but Americans would have their food grown and harvested by people who were legally forbidden to be in the country?

5 We are a restless, inventive, dissatisfied people. We like novelty. We like to try new things. We may not want to change in any basic sense, any more than other people, but we like the illusion of movement.

6 We like anything that looks like a quick fix—a new law, a new road, a new pill. We like immediate solutions. We want the pain to stop, the dull mood to pass, the problem to go away. The quicker the action, the better we like it. We like confrontation better than negotiation, antibiotics better than slow healing, majority rule better than community consensus, demolition better than renovation.

7 When we want something we want it fast and we want it cheap. Obstacles and complications annoy us. We don't want to stop to think about side effects, the Big Picture, or how it's going to make things worse in the long run. We aren't too interested in the long run, as long as something brings more money, a promotion or a new status symbol in the short.

8 Our model for problem-solving is the 30-second TV commercial, in which change is produced instantaneously and there is always a happy ending. The side effects, the pollution, the wasting diseases, the slow poisoning—all these unhappy complications fall into the great void outside that 30-second frame.

9 Nothing fits this scenario better than drugs—legal and illegal. The same impatience that sees an environmental impact report as an annoying bit of red tape makes us highly susceptible to any substance that can make us feel better within minutes after ingesting it—whose immediate effects are more or less predictable and whose negative aspects are generally much slower to appear.

10 People take drugs everywhere, of course, and there is no sure way of knowing if the United States has more drug abusers than other countries. The term "abuse" itself is socially defined.

11 The typical suburban alcoholic of the '40s and '50s and the wealthy drunks glamorized in Hollywood movies of that period were not considered "drug abusers." Nor is the ex-heroin addict who has been weaned to a lifetime addiction to Methadone.

12 In the 19th century, morphine addicts (who were largely middle-aged, middle-class women) maintained their genteel but often heavy addictions quite legally, with the aid of the family doctor and local druggist. Morphine only became illegal when its use spread to young, poor, black males. (This transition created some embarrassment for political and medical commentators, who argued that a distinction had to be made between "drug addicts" and "dope fiends.")

13 Yet addiction can be defined in a way that overrides these biases. Anyone who cannot or will not let a day pass without ingesting a substance should be considered addicted to it, and by this definition Americans are certainly addiction-prone.

14 It would be hard to find a society in which so great a variety of different substances have been "abused" by so many different kinds of people. There are drugs for every group, philosophy and social class: marijuana and psychedelics for the '60s counter-culture, heroin for the hopeless of all periods, PCP for the angry and desperate, and cocaine for modern Yuppies and Yumpies.[1]

15 Drugs do, after all, have different effects, and people select the effects they want. At the lower end of the social scale people want a peaceful escape from a hopeless and depressing existence, and for this heroin is the drug of choice. Cocaine, on the other hand, with its energized euphoria and illusion of competence is particularly appealing to affluent achievers—those both obsessed and acquainted with success.

16 Addiction among the affluent seems paradoxical to outsiders. From the viewpoint of most people in the world an American man or woman making over $50,000 a year has everything a human being could dream of. Yet very few such people—even those with hundreds of millions of dollars—feel this way themselves. While they may not suffer the despair of the very poor, there seems to be a kind of frustration and hopelessness that seeps into all social strata in our society. The affluent may have acquired a great deal, but they seem not to have acquired what they wanted.

17 Most drugs—heroin, alcohol, cocaine, speed, tranquilizers, barbiturates—virtually all of them except the psychedelics and to some extent marijuana—have a numbing effect. We might then ask: Why do so many Americans need to numb themselves?

18 Life in modern society is admittedly harsh and confusing considering the pace for which our bodies were designed. Noise pollution alone might justify turning down our sensory volume: It's hard today even in a quiet suburb or rural setting to find respite from the harsh sound of "labor-saving" machines.

19 But it would be absurd to blame noise pollution for drug addiction. This rasping clamor that grates daily on our ears is only a symptom—one tangible consequence of our peculiar lifestyle. For each of us wants to be able to exert his or her will and control without having to negotiate with anyone else.

20 "I have a right to run my machine and do my work" even if it makes your rest impossible. "I have a right to hear my music" even if this makes it impossible to hear your music, or better yet, enjoy that most rare and precious of modern commodities: silence. "I have a right to make a profit" even if it means poisoning you, your children and your children's children. "I have a right to have a drink when I want to and drive my car when I want to" even if it means totaling your car and crippling your life.

---

[1]Yumpies: young, upper-middle-class professionals.

21 This intolerance of any constraint or obstacle makes our lives rich in conflict and aggravation. Each day we encounter the noise, distress and lethal fallout of the dilemmas we brushed aside so impatiently the day before. Each day the postponed problems multiply, proliferate, metastasize—but this only makes us more aggravated and impatient than we were before. And since we're unwilling to change our ways it becomes more and more necessary to anesthetize ourselves to the havoc we've wrought.

22 We don't like the thought of attuning ourselves to nature or to a group or community. We like to fantasize having control over our lives, and drugs seem to make this possible. With drugs you are not only master of your fate and captain of your soul, you are dictator of your body as well.

23 Unwilling to respond to its own needs and wants, you goad it into activity with caffeine in the morning and slow it down with alcohol at night. If the day goes poorly, a little cocaine will set it right, and if quiet relaxation and sensual enjoyment is called for, marijuana.

24 Cocaine or alcohol makes a party or a performance go well. Nothing is left to chance. The quality of experience is measured by how many drugs or drinks were consumed rather than by the experience itself. Most of us are unwilling to accept the fact that life has good days and bad days. We attempt—unsuccessfully but valiantly—to postpone all the bad days until that fateful moment when the body presents us with all our IOUs, tied up in a neat bundle called cancer, heart disease, cirrhosis or whatever.

25 Every great sage and spiritual leader throughout history has emphasized that happiness comes not from getting more but from learning to want less. Clearly this is a hard lesson for humans, since so few have learned it.

26 But in our society we spend billions each year creating want. Covetousness, discontent and greed are taught to our children, drummed into them—they are bombarded with it. Not only through advertising, but in the feverish emphasis on success, on winning at all costs, on being the center of attention through one kind of performance or another, on being the first at something—no matter how silly or stupid (*The Guinness Book of Records*). We are an addictive society.

27 Addiction is a state of wanting. It is a condition in which the individual feels he or she is incomplete, inadequate, lacking, not whole, and can only be made whole by the addition of something external.

28 This need not be a drug. It can be money, food, fame, sex, responsibility, power, good deeds, possessions, cleaning—the addictive impulse can attach itself to anything, real or symbolic. You're addicted to something whenever you feel it completes you—that you wouldn't

be a whole person without it. When you try to make sure it's always there, that there's always a good supply on hand.

29 Most of us are a little proud of the supposed personality defects that make addiction "necessary"—the "I can't . . . ," "I have to . . . ," "I always . . . ," "I never . . ." But such "lacks" are all delusional. It's fun to brag about not being able to live without something but it's just pomposity. We are all human, and given water, a little food, and a little warmth, we'll survive.

30 But it's very hard to hang onto this humanity when we're told every day that we're ignorant, misguided, inadequate, incompetent and undesirable and that we will emerge from this terrible condition only if we eat or drink or buy something, at which point we'll magically and instantly feel better.

31 We may be smart enough not to believe the silly claims of the individual ad, but can we escape the underlying message on which all of them agree? That you can only be made whole and healthy by buying or ingesting something? Can we reasonably complain about the amount of addiction in our society when we teach it every day?

32 A Caribbean worker once said, apropos of the increasing role of Western products in the economy of his country: "Your corporations are like mosquitoes. I don't so much mind their taking a little of my blood, but why do they have to leave that nasty itch in its place?"

33 It seems futile to spend hundreds of billions of dollars trying to intercept the flow of drugs—arresting and imprisoning those who meet the demand for them, when we activate and nourish that demand every day. Until we get tired of encouraging the pursuit of illusory fixes and begin to celebrate and refine what we already are and have, addictive substances will always proliferate faster than we can control them.

✧ *Evaluating the Text*

1. In Slater's view, how is the quick fix mentality responsible for rampant drug use and addiction in the United States?

2. Consider the definition of addiction that Slater presents. Do you agree or disagree with the way he frames the debate? Why or why not?

✧ *Exploring Different Perspectives*

1. Compare the methods that Americans use to relieve tension with those described by Colin Turnbull in "The Mbuti Pygmies."

2. What similarities can you discover between Slater's portrait of American culture and Harold Miner's discussion of the Nacirema?

✧ *Extending Viewpoints through Writing and Research*

1. What current ads set up hypothetically stressful situations and then push products as a quick and easy way to relieve the stress? Analyze a few of these ads.
2. To what extent have performance-enhancing drugs or steroids become an important component of sports? In your opinion, are athletes coerced into taking these drugs in order to remain competitive? Why or why not?
3. The author's home page is available at http://www.philipslater.com/bio.htm

Harold Miner

Body Ritual among the Nacirema

Horace Mitchell (Harold) Miner (1912–1993) studied at the University of Chicago and taught at the University of Michigan (1946–1985). An early work is St. Denis: A French Canadian Parish (1939). This classic essay (written as a spoof) was originally published in the American Anthropologist, *in June 1956 and has become a defining work in an ever-expanding field devoted to research on this little known North American tribe.*

Before You Read

Consider how an everyday ritual of yours might be viewed as an anthropological curiosity.

1 The anthropologist has become so familiar with the diversity of ways in which different peoples behave in similar situations that he is not apt to be surprised by even the most exotic customs. In fact, if all of the logically possible combinations of behavior have not been found somewhere in the world, he is apt to suspect that they must be present in some yet undescribed tribe. This point has, in fact, been expressed with respect to clan organization by Murdock (1949: 71). In this light, the magical beliefs and practices of the Nacirema present such unusual aspects that it seems desirable to describe them as an example of the extremes to which human behavior can go.

2 Professor Linton first brought the ritual of the Nacirema to the attention of anthropologists twenty years ago (1936: 326), but the culture of this people is still very poorly understood. They are a North American group living in the territory between the Canadian Cree, the Yaqui and Tarahumare of Mexico, and the Carib and Arawak of the Antilles. Little is known of their origin, though tradition states that they came from the east. According to Nacirema mythology, their nation was originated by a culture hero, Notgnishaw, who is otherwise known for two great feats of strength—the throwing of a piece of wampum across the river Pa-To-Mac and the chopping down of a cherry tree in which the Spirit of Truth resided.

3 Nacirema culture is characterized by a highly developed market economy which has evolved in a rich natural habitat. While much of

the people's time is devoted to economic pursuits, a large part of the fruits of these labors and a considerable portion of the day are spent in ritual activity. The focus of this activity is the human body, the appearance and health of which loom as a dominant concern in the ethos of the people. While such a concern is certainly not unusual, its ceremonial aspects and associated philosophy are unique.

4 The fundamental belief underlying the whole system appears to be that the human body is ugly and that its natural tendency is to debility and disease. Incarcerated in such a body, man's only hope is to avert these characteristics through the use of the powerful influences of ritual and ceremony. Every household has one or more shrines devoted to this purpose. The more powerful individuals in the society have several shrines in their houses and, in fact, the opulence of a house is often referred to in terms of the number of such ritual centers it possesses. Most houses are of wattle and daub construction, but the shrine rooms of the more wealthy are walled with stone. Poorer families imitate the rich by applying pottery plaques to their shrine walls.

5 While each family has at least one such shrine, the rituals associated with it are not family ceremonies but are private and secret. The rites are normally only discussed with children, and then only during the period when they are being initiated into these mysteries. I was able, however, to establish sufficient rapport with the natives to examine these shrines and to have the rituals described to me.

6 The focal point of the shrine is a box or chest which is built into the wall. In this chest are kept the many charms and magical potions without which no native believes he could live. These preparations are secured from a variety of specialized practitioners. The most powerful of these are the medicine men, whose assistance must be rewarded with substantial gifts. However, the medicine men do not provide the curative potions for their clients, but decide what the ingredients should be and then write them down in an ancient and secret language. This writing is understood only by the medicine men and by the herbalists who, for another gift, provide the required charm.

7 The charm is not disposed of after it has served its purpose, but is placed in the charm-box of the household shrine. As these magical materials are specific for certain ills, and the real or imagined maladies of the people are many, the charm-box is usually full to overflowing. The magical packets are so numerous that people forget what their purposes were and fear to use them again. While the natives are very vague on this point, we can only assume that the idea in retaining all the old magical materials is that their presence in the charm-box, before which the body rituals are conducted, will in some way protect the worshipper.

8 Beneath the charm-box is a small font. Each day every member of the family, in succession, enters the shrine room, bows his head before

the charm-box, mingles different sorts of holy water in the font, and proceeds with a brief rite of ablution. The holy waters are secured from the Water Temple of the community, where the priests conduct elaborate ceremonies to make the liquid ritually pure.

9 In the hierarchy of magical practitioners, and below the medicine men in prestige, are specialists whose designation is best translated "holy-mouth-men." The Nacirema have an almost pathological horror and fascination with the mouth, the condition of which is believed to have a supernatural influence on all social relationships. Were it not for the rituals of the mouth, they believe that their teeth would fall out, their gums bleed, their jaws shrink, their friends desert them, and their lovers reject them. (They also believe that a strong relationship exists between oral and moral characteristics. For example, there is a ritual ablution of the mouth for children which is supposed to improve their moral fiber.)

10 The daily body ritual performed by everyone includes a mouth-rite. Despite the fact that these people are so punctilious about care of the mouth, this rite involves a practice which strikes the uninitiated stranger as revolting. It was reported to me that the ritual consists of inserting a small bundle of hog hairs into the mouth, along with certain magical powders, and then moving the bundle in a highly formalized series of gestures.

11 In addition to the private mouth-rite, the people seek out a holy-mouth-man once or twice a year. These practitioners have an impressive set of paraphernalia, consisting of a variety of augers, awls, probes, and prods. The use of these objects in the exorcism of the evils of the mouth involves almost unbelievable ritual torture of the client. The holy-mouth-man opens the client's mouth and, using the above mentioned tools, enlarges any holes which decay may have created in the teeth. Magical materials are put into these holes. If there are no naturally occurring holes in the teeth, large sections of one or more teeth are gouged out so that the supernatural substance can be applied. In the client's view, the purpose of these ministrations is to arrest decay and to draw friends. The extremely sacred and traditional character of the rite is evident in the fact that the natives return to the holy-mouth-men year after year, despite the fact that their teeth continue to decay.

12 It is to be hoped that, when a thorough study of the Nacirema is made, there will be a careful inquiry into the personality structure of these people. One has but to watch the gleam in the eye of a holy-mouth-man, as he jabs an awl into an exposed nerve, to suspect that a certain amount of sadism is involved. If this can be established, a very interesting pattern emerges, for most of the population shows definite masochistic tendencies. It was to these that Professor Linton referred in discussing a distinctive part of the daily body ritual which is performed only by men. This part of the rite involves scraping and

lacerating the surface of the face with a sharp instrument. Special women's rites are performed only four times during each lunar month, but what they lack in frequency is made up in barbarity. As part of this ceremony, women bake their heads in small ovens for about an hour. The theoretically interesting point is that what seems to be a preponderantly masochistic people have developed sadistic specialists.

13 The medicine men have an imposing temple, or *latipso,* in every community of any size. The more elaborate ceremonies required to treat very sick patients can only be performed at this temple. These ceremonies involve not only the thaumaturge but a permanent group of vestal maidens who move sedately about the temple chambers in distinctive costume and headdress.

14 The *latipso* ceremonies are so harsh that it is phenomenal that a fair proportion of the really sick natives who enter the temple ever recover. Small children whose indoctrination is still incomplete have been known to resist attempts to take them to the temple because "that is where you go to die." Despite this fact, sick adults are not only willing but eager to undergo the protracted ritual purification, if they can afford to do so. No matter how ill the supplicant or how grave the emergency, the guardians of many temples will not admit a client if he cannot give a rich gift to the custodian. Even after one has gained admission and survived the ceremonies, the guardians will not permit the neophyte to leave until he makes still another gift.

15 The supplicant entering the temple is first stripped of all his or her clothes. In every-day life the Nacirema avoids exposure of his body and its natural functions. Bathing and excretory acts are performed only in the secrecy of the household shrine, where they are ritualized as part of the body-rites. Psychological shock results from the fact that body secrecy is suddenly lost upon entry into the *latipso.* A man, whose own wife has never seen him in an excretory act, suddenly finds himself naked and assisted by a vestal maiden while he performs his natural functions into a sacred vessel. This sort of ceremonial treatment is necessitated by the fact that the excreta are used by a diviner to ascertain the course and nature of the client's sickness. Female clients, on the other hand, find their naked bodies are subjected to the scrutiny, manipulation, and prodding of the medicine men.

16 Few supplicants in the temple are well enough to do anything but lie on their hard beds. The daily ceremonies, like the rites of the holy-mouth-men, involve discomfort and torture. With ritual precision, the vestals awaken their miserable charges each dawn and roll them about on their beds of pain while performing ablutions, in the formal movements of which the maidens are highly trained. At other times they insert magic wands in the supplicant's mouth or force him to eat substances which are supposed to be healing. From time to time the medicine men come to their clients and jab magically treated needles

into their flesh. The fact that these temple ceremonies may not cure, and may even kill the neophyte, in no way decreases the people's faith in the medicine men.

17 There remains one other kind of practitioner, known as a "listener." This witch-doctor has the power to exorcise the devils that lodge in the heads of people who have been bewitched. The Nacirema believe that parents bewitch their own children. Mothers are particularly suspected of putting a curse on children while teaching them the secret body rituals. The counter-magic of the witch-doctor is unusual in its lack of ritual. The patient simply tells the "listener" all his troubles and fears, beginning with the earliest difficulties he can remember. The memory displayed by the Nacirema in these exorcism sessions is truly remarkable. It is not uncommon for the patient to bemoan the rejection he felt upon being weaned as a babe, and a few individuals even see their troubles going back to the traumatic effects of their own birth.

18 In conclusion, mention must be made of certain practices which have their base in native esthetics but which depend upon the pervasive aversion to the natural body and its functions. There are ritual fasts to make fat people thin and ceremonial feasts to make thin people fat. Still other rites are used to make women's breasts large if they are small, and smaller if they are large. General dissatisfaction with breast shape is symbolized in the fact that the ideal form is virtually outside the range of human variation. A few women afflicted with almost inhuman hyper-mammary development are so idolized that they make a handsome living by simply going from village to village and permitting the natives to stare at them for a fee.

19 Reference has already been made to the fact that excretory functions are ritualized, routinized, and relegated to secrecy. Natural reproductive functions are similarly distorted. Intercourse is taboo as a topic and scheduled as an act. Efforts are made to avoid pregnancy by the use of magical materials or by limiting intercourse to certain phases of the moon. Conception is actually very infrequent. When pregnant, women dress so as to hide their condition. Parturition takes place in secret, without friends or relatives to assist, and the majority of women do not nurse their infants.

20 Our review of the ritual life of the Nacirema has certainly shown them to be a magic-ridden people. It is hard to understand how they have managed to exist so long under the burdens which they have imposed upon themselves. But even such exotic customs as these take on real meaning when they are viewed with the insight provided by Malinowski when he wrote (1948: 70):

> Looking from far and above, from our high places of safety in the developed civilization, it is easy to see all the crudity and irrelevance

of magic. But without its power and guidance early man could not have mastered his practical difficulties as he has done, nor could man have advanced to the higher stages of civilization.

REFERENCES

Linton, Ralph. 1936. *The Study of Man.* New York, D. Appleton-Century Co.

Malinowski, Bronislaw. 1948. *Magic, Science, and Religion.* Glencoe, The Free Press.

Murdock, George P. 1949. *Social Structure.* New York, The Macmillan Co.

✧ *Evaluating the Text*

1. What bizarre attitude do the Nacirema have toward the human body?
2. What different kinds of body rituals, shrines, and practioners do the Nacirema resort to based on their obsession with the human body?

✧ *Exploring Different Perspectives*

1. What rituals, when viewed objectively, are as bizarre among the Nacirema as foot binding was for the Chinese as described by Valerie Steele and John S. Major in "China Chic: East Meets West"?
2. What obsessions and rituals characterize the Nacirema? How are they similar to those described by Slater in "Want-Creation Fuels Americans' Addictiveness"?

✧ *Extending Viewpoints through Writing and Research*

1. Have you ever heard of the Nacirema or their hero Notgnishaw? Which of their rituals might well be commonplace in our culture?
2. How would an objective observer describe any commonplace obsessive ritual in our culture other than those described by Miner—for example, fitness clubs, yoga, pilates, teeth whitening?
3. Resources on the Nacirema people are available at http://www.beadsland.com/nacirema/.

Robert Levine and Ellen Wolff

Social Time: The Heartbeat of Culture

Robert Levine's research as a social psychologist sought to measure the importance of being on time in a variety of cultures around the world. His findings, correlated with the help of Ellen Wolff, were published in Psychology Today *(March 1985), where the following essay first appeared. He currently teaches at California State University at Fresno. He has also written* Power of Persuasion: How We're Bought and Sold *(2003).*

Before You Read

Are you more likely to be early, on time, or late for appointments?

1 *"If a man does not keep pace with his companions, perhaps it is because he hears a different drummer."* This thought by Thoreau strikes a chord in so many people that it has become part of our language. We use the phrase "the beat of a different drummer" to explain any pace of life unlike our own. Such colorful vagueness reveals how informal our rules of time really are. The world over, children simply "pick up" their society's time concepts as they mature. No dictionary clearly defines the meaning of "early" or "late" for them or for strangers who stumble over the maddening incongruities between the time sense they bring with them and the one they face in a new land.

2 I learned this firsthand, a few years ago, and the resulting culture shock led me halfway around the world to find answers. It seemed clear that time "talks." But what is it telling us?

3 My journey started shortly after I accepted an appointment as visiting professor of psychology at the federal university in Niterói, Brazil, a midsized city across the bay from Rio de Janeiro. As I left home for my first day of class, I asked someone the time. It was 9:05 a.m., which allowed me time to relax and look around the campus before my 10 o'clock lecture. After what I judged to be half an hour, I glanced at a clock I was passing. It said 10:20! In panic, I broke for the classroom, followed by gentle calls of "Hola, professor" and "Tudo bem, professor?" from unhurried students, many of whom, I later realized, were my own. I arrived breathless to find an empty room.

4 Frantically, I asked a passerby the time. "Nine forty-five" was the answer. No that couldn't be. I asked someone else. "Nine fifty-five." Another said: "Exactly 9:43." The clock in a nearby office read 3:15. I had learned my first lesson about Brazilians: Their timepieces are consistently inaccurate. And nobody minds.

5 My class was scheduled from 10 until noon. Many students came late, some very late. Several arrived after 10:30. A few showed up closer to 11. Two came after that. All of the latecomers wore the relaxed smiles that I came, later, to enjoy. Each one said hello, and although a few apologized briefly, none seemed terribly concerned about lateness. They assumed that I understood.

6 The idea of Brazilians arriving late was not a great shock. I had heard about "mãnha," the Portuguese equivalent of "mañana" in Spanish. This term, meaning "tomorrow" or "the morning," stereotypes the Brazilian who puts off the business of today until tomorrow. The real surprise came at noon that first day, when the end of class arrived.

7 Back home in California, I never need to look at a clock to know when the class hour is ending. The shuffling of books is accompanied by strained expressions that say plaintively, "I'm starving. . . . I've got to go to the bathroom. . . . I'm going to suffocate if you keep us one more second." (The pain usually becomes unbearable at two minutes to the hour in undergraduate classes and five minutes before the close of graduate classes.)

8 When noon arrived in my first Brazilian class, only a few students left immediately. Others slowly drifted out during the next 15 minutes, and some continued asking me questions long after that. When several remaining students kicked off their shoes at 12:30, I went into my own "starving/bathroom/suffocation" routine.

9 I could not, in all honesty, attribute their lingering to my superb teaching style. I had just spent two hours lecturing on statistics in halting Portuguese. Apparently, for many of my students, staying late was simply of no more importance than arriving late in the first place. As I observed this casual approach in infinite variations during the year, I learned that the "mãnha" stereotype oversimplified the real Anglo/Brazilian differences in conceptions of time. Research revealed a more complex picture.

10 With the assistance of colleagues Laurie West and Harry Reis, I compared the time sense of 91 male and female students in Niterói with that of 107 similar students at California State University in Fresno. The universities are similar in academic quality and size, and the cities are both secondary metropolitan centers with populations of about 350,000.

11 We asked students about their perceptions of time in several situations, such as what they would consider late or early for a hypothetical lunch appointment with a friend. The average Brazilian student defined

lateness for lunch as 33½ minutes after the scheduled time, compared to only 19 minutes for the Fresno students. But Brazilians also allowed an average of about 54 minutes before they'd consider someone early, while the Fresno students drew the line at 24.

12 Are Brazilians simply more flexible in their concepts of time and punctuality? And how does this relate to the stereotype of the apathetic, fatalistic and irresponsible Latin temperament? When we asked students to give typical reasons for lateness, the Brazilians were less likely to attribute it to a lack of caring than the North Americans were. Instead, they pointed to unforeseen circumstances that the person couldn't control. Because they seemed less inclined to feel personally responsible for being late, they also expressed less regret for their own lateness and blamed others less when they were late.

13 We found similar differences in how students from the two countries characterized people who were late for appointments. Unlike their North American counterparts, the Brazilian students believed that a person who is consistently late is probably more successful than one who is consistently on time. They seemed to accept the idea that someone of status is expected to arrive late. Lack of punctuality is a badge of success.

14 Even within our own country, of course, ideas of time and punctuality vary considerably from place to place. Different regions and even cities have their own distinct rhythms and rules. Seemingly simple words like "now," snapped out by an impatient New Yorker, and "later," said by a relaxed Californian, suggest a world of difference. Despite our familiarity with these homegrown differences in tempo, problems with time present a major stumbling block to Americans abroad. Peace Corps volunteers told researchers James Spradley of Macalester College and Mark Phillips of the University of Washington that their greatest difficulties with other people, after language problems, were the general pace of life and the punctuality of others. Formal "clock time" may be a standard on which the world agrees, but "social time," the heartbeat of society, is something else again.

15 How a country paces its social life is a mystery to most outsiders, one that we're just beginning to unravel. Twenty-six years ago, anthropologist Edward Hall noted in *The Silent Language* that informal patterns of time "are seldom, if ever, made explicit. They exist in the air around us. They are either familiar and comfortable, or unfamiliar and wrong." When we realize we are out of step, we often blame the people around us to make ourselves feel better.

16 Appreciating cultural differences in time sense becomes increasingly important as modern communications put more and more people in daily contact. If we are to avoid misreading issues that involve time perceptions, we need to understand better our own cultural biases and those of others.

17 When people of different cultures interact, the potential for misunderstanding exists on many levels. For example, members of Arab and Latin cultures usually stand much closer when they are speaking to people than we usually do in the United States, a fact we frequently misinterpret as aggression or disrespect. Similarly, we assign personality traits to groups with a pace of life that is markedly faster or slower than our own. We build ideas of national character, for example, around the traditional Swiss and German ability to "make the trains run on time." Westerners like ourselves define punctuality using precise measures of time: 5 minutes, 15 minutes, an hour. But according to Hall, in many Mediterranean Arab cultures there are only three sets of time: no time at all, now (which is of varying duration) and forever (too long). Because of this, Americans often find difficulty in getting Arabs to distinguish between waiting a long time and a very long time.

18 According to historian Will Durant, "No man in a hurry is quite civilized." What do our time judgments say about our attitude toward life? How can a North American, coming from a land of digital precision, relate to a North African who may consider a clock "the devil's mill"?

19 Each language has a vocabulary of time that does not always survive translation. When we translated our questionnaires into Portuguese for my Brazilian students, we found that English distinctions of time were not readily articulated in their language. Several of our questions concerned how long the respondent would wait for someone to arrive, as compared with when they hoped for arrival or actually expected the person would come. In Portuguese, the verbs "to wait for," "to hope for" and "to expect" are all translated as "esperar." We had to add further words of explanation to make the distinction clear to the Brazilian students.

20 To avoid these language problems, my Fresno colleague Kathy Bartlett and I decided to clock the pace of life in other countries by using as little language as possible. We looked directly at three basic indicators of time: the accuracy of a country's bank clocks, the speed at which pedestrians walked and the average time it took a postal clerk to sell us a single stamp. In six countries on three continents, we made observations in both the nation's largest urban area and a medium-sized city: Japan (Tokyo and Sendai), Taiwan (Taipei and Tainan), Indonesia (Jakarta and Solo), Italy (Rome and Florence), England (London and Bristol) and the United States (New York City and Rochester).

21 What we wanted to know was: Can we speak of a unitary concept called "pace of life"? What we've learned suggests that we can. There appears to be a very strong relationship between the accuracy of clock time, walking speed and postal efficiency across the countries we studied.

22 We checked 15 clocks in each city, selecting them at random in downtown banks and comparing the time they showed with that

reported by the local telephone company. In Japan, which leads the way in accuracy, the clocks averaged just over half a minute early or late. Indonesian clocks, the least accurate, were more than three minutes off the mark.

23 I will be interested to see how the digital-information age will affect our perceptions of time. In the United States today, we are reminded of the exact hour of the day more than ever, through little symphonies of beeps emanating from people's digital watches. As they become the norm, I fear our sense of precision may take an absurd twist. The other day, when I asked for the time, a student looked at his watch and replied, "Three twelve and eighteen seconds."

> "'Will you walk a little faster?' said a whiting to a snail. 'There's a porpoise close behind us, and he's treading on my tail.'"

24 So goes the rhyme from *Alice in Wonderland,* which also gave us that famous symbol of haste, the White Rabbit. He came to mind often as we measured the walking speeds in our experimental cities. We clocked how long it took pedestrians to walk 100 feet along a main downtown street during business hours on clear days. To eliminate the effects of socializing, we observed only people walking alone, timing at least 100 in each city. We found, once again, that the Japanese led the way, averaging just 20.7 seconds to cover the distance. The English nosed out the Americans for second place—21.6 to 22.5 seconds—and the Indonesians again trailed the pack, sauntering along at 27.2 seconds. As you might guess, speed was greater in the larger city of each nation than its smaller one.

25 Our final measurement, the average time it took postal clerks to sell one stamp, turned out to be less straightforward than we expected. In each city, including those in the United States, we presented clerks with a note in the native language requesting a common-priced stamp—a 20-center in the United States, for example. They were also handed paper money, the equivalent of a $5 bill. In Indonesia, this procedure led to more than we bargained for.

26 At the large central post office in Jakarta, I asked for the line to buy stamps and was directed to a group of private vendors sitting outside. Each of them hustled for my business: "Hey, good stamps, mister!" "Best stamps here!" In the smaller city of Solo, I found a volleyball game in progress when I arrived at the main post office on Friday afternoon. Business hours, I was told, were over. When I finally did get there during business hours, the clerk was more interested in discussing relatives in America. Would I like to meet his uncle in Cincinnati? Which did I like better: California or the United States? Five people behind me in line waited patiently. Instead of complaining, they began paying attention to our conversation.

27 When it came to efficiency of service, however, the Indonesians were not the slowest, although they did place far behind the Japanese postal clerks, who averaged 25 seconds. That distinction went to the Italians, whose infamous postal service took 47 seconds on the average.

"A man who wastes one hour of time has not discovered the meaning of life. . . ."

28 That was Charles Darwin's belief, and many share it, perhaps at the cost of their health. My colleagues and I have recently begun studying the relationship between pace of life and well-being. Other researchers have demonstrated that a chronic sense of urgency is a basic component of the Type A, coronary-prone personality. We expect that future research will demonstrate that pace of life is related to rate of heart disease, hypertension, ulcers, suicide, alcoholism, divorce and other indicators of general psychological and physical well-being.

29 As you envision tomorrow's international society, do you wonder who will set the pace? Americans eye Japan carefully, because the Japanese are obviously "ahead of us" in measurable ways. In both countries, speed is frequently confused with progress. Perhaps looking carefully at the different paces of life around the world will help us distinguish more accurately between the two qualities. Clues are everywhere but sometimes hard to distinguish. You have to listen carefully to hear the beat of even your own drummer.

✧ *Evaluating the Text*

1. How does Robert Levine's sense of time differ from those of his Brazilian students?
2. How does social time differ from clock time?
3. What general correlations between pace of life and nationality did Levine and his colleagues discover? What three measures did they use to gain a country's sense of time?

✧ *Exploring Different Perspectives*

1. Compare the cultural assumptions about time between what Levine and his colleagues found in Brazil and what Colin Turnbull discovered in "The Mbuti Pygmies."
2. What is the attitude of the Nacirema toward the use of time as compared with people in Brazil as discussed by Levine and Wolff?

✧ *Extending Viewpoints through Writing and Research*

1. How do your expectations about when classes are scheduled to begin and end differ from those of Brazilian students?
2. If you perform some of the same experiments as Levine and his colleagues did in your town or on your campus, what would you discover and what conclusions would you draw?

Colin Turnbull

The Mbuti Pygmies

Colin Turnbull (1924–1994) was educated at Oxford University and did anthropological research on the Ik of northern Uganda and the pygmies of the Ituri forest in the Republic of the Congo (where he observed them for four years). His works include In a Pygmy Camp *(1969) and* The Mbuti Pygmies: Change and Adaptation *(1983), from which the following essay is drawn. Turnbull admired the way the Mbuti people evolved nonviolent games and rituals for resolving conflicts.*

Before You Read

How do children's games express important cultural values such as competition or cooperation?

The Educational Process

1 . . . In the first three years of life every Mbuti alive experiences almost total security. The infant is breast-fed for those three years, and is allowed almost every freedom. Regardless of gender, the infant learns to have absolute trust in both male and female parent. If anything, the father is just another kind of mother, for in the second year the father formally introduces the child to its first solid food. There used to be a beautiful ritual in which the mother presented the child to the father in the middle of the camp, where all important statements are made (anyone speaking from the middle of the camp must be listened to). The father took the child and held it to his breast, and the child would try to suckle, crying *"ema, ema,"* or "mother." The father would shake his head, and say "no, father . . . eba," but like a mother (the Mbuti said), then give the child its first solid food.

2 At three the child ventures out into the world on its own and enters the *bopi,* what we might call a playground, a tiny camp perhaps a hundred yards from the main camp, often on the edge of a stream. The *bopi* were indeed playgrounds, and often very noisy ones, full of fun and high spirits. But they were also rigorous training grounds for eventual economic responsibility. On entry to the *bopi,* for one thing, the child discovers the importance of age as a structural principle, and the relative unimportance of gender and biological kinship. The *bopi* is the private world of the children. Younger youths may occasionally

venture in, but if adults or elders try, as they sometimes do when angry at having their afternoon snooze interrupted, they invariably get driven out, taunted, and ridiculed. Children, among the Mbuti, have rights, but they also learn that they have responsibilities. Before the hunt sets out each day it is the children, sometimes the younger youths, who light the hunting fire.

3 Ritual amoung the Mbuti is often so informal and apparently casual that it may pass unnoticed at first. Yet insofar as ritual involves symbolic acts that represent unspoken, perhaps even unthought, concepts or ideals, or invoke other states of being, alternative frames of mind and reference, then Mbuti life is full of ritual. The hunting fire is one of the more obvious of such rituals. Early in the morning children would take firebrands from the *bopi,* where they always lit their own fire with embers from their family hearths, and set off on the trail by which the hunt was to leave that day (the direction of each day's hunt was always settled by discussion the night before). Just a short distance from the camp they lit a fire at the base of a large tree, and covered it with special leaves that made it give off a column of dense smoke. Hunters leaving the camp, both men and women, and such youths and children as were going with them, had to pass by this fire. Some did so casually, without stopping or looking, but passing through the smoke. Others reached into the smoke with their hands as they passed, rubbing the smoke into their bodies. A few always stopped, for a moment, and let the smoke envelop them, only then almost dreamily moving off.

4 And indeed it *was* a form of intoxication, for the smoke invoked the spirit of the forest, and by passing through it the hunters sought to fill themselves with that spirit, not so much to make the hunt successful as to minimize the sacrilege of killing. Yet they, the hunters, could not light the fire themselves. After all, they were already contaminated by death. Even youths, who daily joined the hunt at the edges, catching any game that escaped the nets, by hand, if they could, were not pure enough to invoke the spirits of forestness. But young children were uncontaminated, as yet untainted by contact with the original sin of the Mbuti. It was their responsibility to light the fire, and if it was not lit then the hunt would not take place, or, as the Mbuti put it, the hunt *could* not take place.

5 In this way even the children in Mbuti society, at the first of the four age levels that dominate Mbuti social structure, are given very real social responsibility and see themselves as a part of that structure, by virtue of their purity. After all, they have just been born from the source of all purity, the forest itself. By the same reasoning, the elders, who are about to return to that ultimate source of all being, through death, are at least closer to purity than the adults, who are daily contaminated by killing. Elders no longer go on the hunt. So, like the

children, the elders have important sacred ritual responsibilities in the Mbuti division of labor by age.

6 In the *bopi* the children play, but they have no "game" in the strict sense of the word. Levi-Strauss has perceptively compared games with ritual,s suggesting that whereas in a game the players start theoretically equal but end up unequal, in a ritual just the reverse takes place. All are equalized. Mbuti children could be seen every day playing in the *bopi,* but not once did I see a game, not one activity that smacked of any kind of competition, except perhaps that competition that it is necessary for us all to feel from time to time, competition with our own private and personal inadequacies. One such pastime (rather than game) was tree climbing. A dozen or so children would climb up a young sapling. Reaching the top, their weight brought the sapling bending down until it almost touched the ground. Then all the children leapt off together, shrieking as the young tree sprang upright again with a rush. Sometimes one child, male or female, might stay on a little too long, either out of fear, or out of bravado, or from sheer carelessness or bad timing. Whatever the reason, it was a lesson most children only needed to be taught once, for the result was that you got flung upward with the tree, and were lucky to escape with no more than a few bruises and a very bad fright.

7 Other pastimes taught the children the rules of hunting and gathering. Frequently elders, who stayed in camp when the hunt went off, called the children into the main camp and enacted a mock hunt with them there. Stretching a discarded piece of net across the camp, they pretended to be animals, showing the children how to drive them into the nets. And, of course, the children played house, learning the patterns of cooperation that would be necessary for them later in life. They also learned the prime lesson of egality, other than for purposes of division of labor making no distinction between male and female, this nuclear family or that. All in the *bopi* were *apua'i* to each other, and so they would remain throughout their lives. At every age level—childhood, youth, adulthood, or old age—everyone of that level is *apua'i* to all the others. Only adults sometimes (but so rarely that I think it was only done as a kind of joke, or possibly insult) made the distinction that the Bira do, using *apua'i* for male and *amua'i* for female. Male or female, for the Mbuti, if you are the same age you are *apua'i,* and that means that you share everything equally, regardless of kinship or gender.

Youth and Politics

8 Sometimes before the age of puberty boys or girls, whenever they feel ready, move back into the main camp from the *bopi* and join the youths. This is when they must assume new responsibilities, which for

the youths are primarily political. Already, in the *bopi,* the children become involved in disputes, and are sometimes instrumental in settling them by ridicule, for nothing hurts an adult more than being ridiculed by children. The art of reason, however, is something they learn from the youths, and it is the youths who apply the art of reason to the settlement of disputes.

9 When puberty comes it separates them, for the first time in their experience, from each other as *apua'i.* Very plainly girls are different from boys. When a girl has her first menstrual period the whole camp celebrates with the wild *elima* festival, in which the girl, and some of her chosen girl friends, are the center of all attention, living together in a special *elima* house. Male youths sit outside the *elima* house and wait for the girls to come out, usually in the afternoon, for the *elima* singing. They sing in antiphony, the girls leading, the boys responding. Boys come from neighboring territories all around, for this is a time of courtship. But there are always eligible youths within the camp as well, and the *elima* girl may well choose girls from other territories to come and join her, so there is more than enough excuse for every youth to carry on several flirtations, legitimate or illegitimate. I have known even first cousins to flirt with each other, but learned to be prudent enough not to pull out my kinship charts and point this out—well, not in public anyway.

10 The *elima* is more than a premarital festival, more than a joint initiation of youth into adulthood, and more than a rite of passage through puberty, though it is all those things. It is a public recognition of the opposition of male and female, and every *elima* is used to highlight the *potential* for conflict that lies in that opposition. As at other times of crisis, at puberty, a time of change and uncertainty, the Mbuti bring all the major forms of conflict out into the open. And the one that evidently most concerns them is the male/female opposition.

11 The adults begin to play a special form of "tug of war" that is clearly a ritual rather than a game. All the men are on one side, the women on the other. At first it looks like a game, but quickly it becomes clear that the objective is for *neither* side to win. As soon as the women begin to win, one of them will leave the end of the line and run around to join the men, assuming a deep male voice and in other ways ridiculing manhood. Then, as the men begin to win, a male will similarly join the women, making fun of womanhood as he does so. Each adult on changing sides attempts to outdo all the others in ridiculing the opposite sex. Finally, when nearly all have switched sides, and sexes, the ritual battle between the genders simply collapses into hysterical laughter, the contestants letting go of the rope, falling onto the ground, and rolling over with mirth. Neither side wins, both are equalized very nicely, and each learns the essential lesson, that there should be *no* contest. . . .

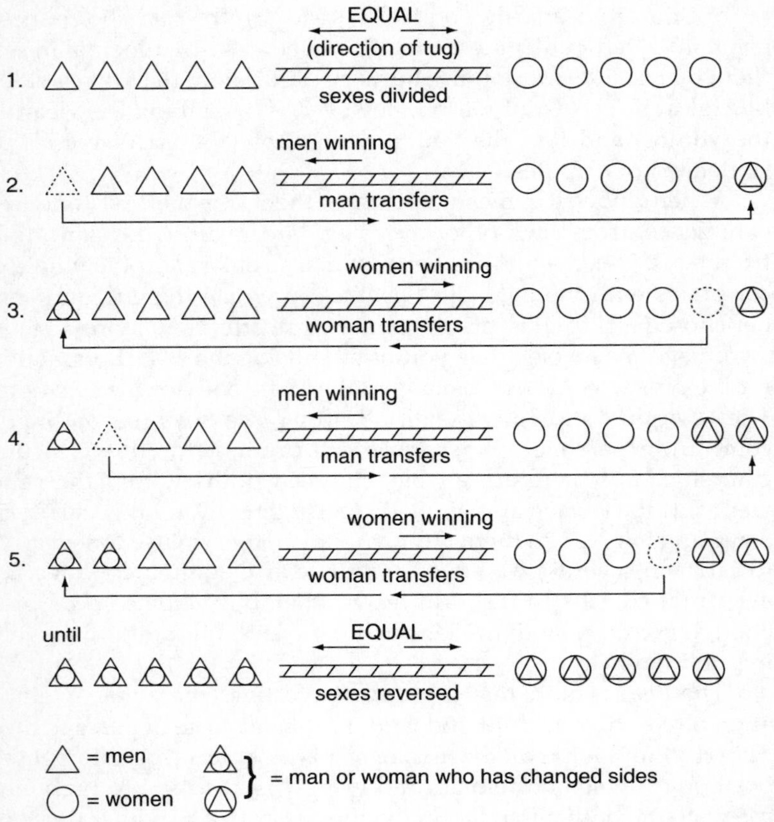

Tug of War. This is one of the Mbuti's many techniques of conflict resolution, involving role reversal and the principle of opposition without hostility.

✧ *Evaluating the Text*

1. In what way is the age of the child's peer group important in determining his or her identity among the Mbuti?
2. What are some of the rituals in which children take part?
3. What values are communicated by the tug of war game the Mbuti play?

✧ *Exploring Different Perspectives*

1. Compare the rituals practiced by the Mbuti with those of the Nacirema as described by Harold Miner to discover what values are important to these different societies.

What insight do you get into the relationship between parents and children among the Mbuti from this picture of a mother painting her daughter's face?

2. Which of the societies studied by Levine and his colleagues in "Social Time: The Heartbeat of Culture" do the Mbutis most resemble?

✧ *Extending Viewpoints through Writing and Research*

1. Were the games you played as a child competitive, noncompetive, or a combination?
2. Research the important values of the Mbuti and compare them with those of other African tribes such as the Maasai in Kenya and Tanzania or the !Kung in Botswana.

Valerie Steele and John S. Major

China Chic: East Meets West

Valerie Steele is director of the Museum at the Fashion Institute of Technology (FIT). Steele organized a major exhibition at FIT to coincide with the 1999 publication of China Chic: East Meets West. *She is the editor of* Fashion Theory: The Journal of Dress, Body, and Culture. *John S. Major is director of the China Council of the Asia Society. He is the author of* The Silk Route: 7,000 Miles of History *(1996). More recently, Steele has written* Gothic: Dark Glamour *(2008), with Jennifer Park, and* Isabel Toledo: Fashion from the Inside Out *(2009), with Patricia Mears. John S. Major has also written* Huguenot on the Hackensack *(2008) and translated and edited* Huainanzi: A Guide to the Theory and Practice of Government in Early Han China *(2010). The following essay, from China Chic, examines foot binding in the context of China's political, economic, and cultural history and its correspondence to fashions in the West.*

Before You Read

Consider how foot binding in China (accomplished through deforming the foot by dislocating its bones) was a symbol of fashion just as high-heeled shoes are in the West today.

1 Foot binding lasted for a thousand years. It apparently began in the declining years of the Tang dynasty and it persisted in remote areas of China until the middle of the twentieth century. Yet despite its manifest significance within Chinese history, foot binding has been the subject of surprisingly little scholarly research. Recently, however, scholars such as Dorothy Ko have begun to explore the subject—with surprising results. As Ko points out, "It is natural for modern-day reformers to consider footbinding a men's conspiracy to keep women crippled and submissive, but this is an anachronistic view that finds no support in the historical records."[1]

2 Many of the sources on which our understanding of foot binding are based are themselves highly problematic. Western missionaries attacked the "barbaric" practice of foot binding, but they did so within the context of a prejudiced and ignorant denunciation of many other aspects of Chinese civilization. Most of the Chinese literature on the subject was written by men, who often emphasized the erotic appeal of foot binding. For a better understanding of foot binding, it is necessary to search for evidence

of what Chinese women themselves thought to search for evidence of what Chinese women themselves thought about the practice. It is also necessary to place foot binding within its (changing) historical context. As Ko puts it, "Foot binding is not one monolithic, unchanging experience that all unfortunate women in each succeeding dynasty went through, but is rather an amorphous practice that meant different things to different people . . . It is, in other words, a situated practice."[2]

3 What did foot binding signify to the Chinese, and why did they maintain the practice for so long? Although historians do not know exactly how or why foot binding began, it was apparently initially associated with dancers at the imperial court and professional female entertainers in the capital. During the Song dynasty (960–1279) the practice spread from the palace and entertainment quarters into the homes of the elite. "By the thirteenth century, archeological evidence shows clearly that foot-binding was practiced among the daughters and wives of officials," reports Patricia Buckley Ebrey, whose study of Song women reproduces photographs of shoes from that period. The Fujian tomb of Miss Huang Sheng (1227–43), for example, contained shoes measuring between 13.3 and 14 cm. (5¼ to 5½ inches), while the Jiangxi tomb of Miss Zhou (1240–74) contained shoes that were 18 to 22 cm. (7 to 8⅝ inches) long.[3] Over the course of the next few centuries foot binding became increasingly common among gentry families, and the practice eventually penetrated the mass of the Chinese people.

4 Foot binding generally began between the ages of five and seven, although many poorer families delayed beginning for several years, sometimes even until the girl was an adolescent, so they could continue to benefit from her labor and mobility. First-person accounts of foot binding testify that the procedure was extremely painful. The girl's feet were tightly bound with bandages, which forced the small toes inward and under the sole of the foot, leaving only the big toe to protrude. Then the heel and toe were drawn forcefully together, breaking the arch of the foot.

5 This was the most extreme type of foot binding. However, many girls apparently had their feet "bound in less painful styles that 'merely' kept the toes compressed or limited the growth of the foot, but did not break any bones."[4] Nevertheless, there is no doubt that foot binding was a radical form of body modification. As early as the Song dynasty, Che Ruoshui made perhaps the first protest against foot binding. He wrote: "Little children not yet four or five *sui* [i.e. five to seven years old], who have done nothing wrong, nevertheless are made to suffer unlimited pain to bind [their feet] small. I do not know what use this is."[5]

6 In fact, foot binding served a number of uses. To begin with, as Ebrey suggests, by making the feet of Chinese women so much smaller than those of Chinese men, it emphasized that men and women were different. Then, too, since only Chinese women bound their feet, the

practice also served to distinguish between Chinese and non-Chinese. An investigation of the political situation suggests why this might have been thought desirable. At the time when foot binding began (in the late Tang) and spread (in the Song), China was in bad shape. Various foreign people who lived along the frontiers repeatedly raided and invaded China, sometimes conquering sizeable portions of Chinese territory and establishing their own dynasties on land that the Chinese regarded as properly theirs—as the Khitans did in the northeast when they defeated the Tang and established the Liao dynasty (907–1125), as the Tanguts did in the west when they established the XiXia Kingdom, and again as the Jürchens did in the north when they established the Jin dynasty (1115–1260) to succeed the Khitan Liao.

7 Although the Chinese managed to establish the Song dynasty in 960, after the turmoil that accompanied the fall of the Tang, it occupied only a portion of what had been Chinese territory, and even that portion decreased dramatically. Chinese men must often have been reminded of their military inferiority in the face of the aggressive "barbarians" encroaching from the north. Did they, perhaps, feel reassured about their strength and masculinity when they compared themselves to their crippled female counterparts? It may be possible to infer something of the sort when we analyze Song erotic poetry, devoted to the charms of tiny feet and a hesitant gait.

8 The suggestion that the spread of foot binding in the Song may have been related to the perceived need on the part of the Chinese gentry to emphasize the distinctions between men and women, Chinese and non-Chinese is strongly supported by Ebrey's analysis. "Because the ideal upper-class man was by Sung times a relatively subdued and refined figure, he might seem effeminate unless women could be made even more delicate, reticent, and stationary," she writes. In other words, anxieties about masculinity and national identity, rather than the desire to oppress women, *per se,* contributed to the spread of foot binding. "But," Ebrey adds, "we must also come to grips with women's apparently eager participation." A crucial element here, she argues, was the competition between wives and concubines. Chinese mothers may have become enthusiastic proponents of foot binding because small feet were regarded as sexually attractive, yet unlike the other tricks used by courtesans and concubines, there was nothing "forward" or "immodest" about having bound feet.[6]

9 The spread of foot binding during the Song dynasty also coincided with a philosophical movement known as Neo-Confucianism, which placed a pronounced ideological emphasis on female inferiority. (In Neo-Confucian metaphysics, the *yang* male principle was seen as superior to the *yin* female principle in both a cosmological and a moral sense.) Moreover, as already seen, political developments in the Song contributed to the demise of the great aristocratic families and the

corresponding proliferation of gentry families, whose social and economic position was much more insecure, and whose predominant social function was to serve as bureaucrats. Members of this new class may have been especially receptive to foot binding, because the practice simultaneously provided reassurance about their social status, proper gender relations, and Chinese identity.

10 Foot binding may have been reassuring to the Chinese, but it did not prevent the Mongols from becoming the first foreigners to conquer all of China. Genghiz Khan unified the Mongols, and Kublai Khan established the Yuan dynasty (1279–1368). Similar anxieties about sexual and racial boundaries appeared again several centuries later toward the end of the Ming dynasty, when the Chinese began to be threatened by the Manchus. Moreover, when the Manchus succeeded in conquering China and establishing the Qing dynasty in the mid-seventeenth century, they passed edicts ordering Chinese men to shave their foreheads and Chinese women to cease foot binding.

11 The resulting "hysterical atmosphere" was "full of sexual overtones," since both cutting men's hair and unbinding women's feet were perceived by Chinese males almost as a symbolic mutilation or castration, which might even be worse than death. As Ko points out, "Although no one openly advocated footbinding, the very establishment of the Manchu dynasty created a need to reemphasize the differences between 'we' and 'they' and between 'he' and 'she.' The ban on footbinding, thus doomed from the start, was rescinded in 1668, four years after its promulgation."[7]

12 Contrary to popular belief, it was not only the wealthy who bound their daughters' feet. By the Qing dynasty, the majority of Chinese women had bound feet—peasants included—although there did exist variations in the degree and type of foot binding. According to one Qing observer, "The practice of footbinding is more widespread in Yangzhou than in other places. Even coolies, servants, seamstresses, the poor, the old, and the weak have tiny feet and cramped toes."[8] Manchu women, however, did not bind their feet, nor did members of other ethnic minority groups. Indeed, under the Qing, Manchu women were specifically forbidden to bind their feet, which is intriguing, since it implies a desire to do so.

13 Because foot binding is usually interpreted today as a gruesome example of women's oppression, it is important to stress that women who experienced the practice rarely perceived it in those terms. Indeed, Ko has unearthed considerable evidence that many Chinese women felt proud of their bound feet, which they regarded as beautiful and prestigious. Foot binding was a central part of the women's world. The rituals surrounding foot binding were female-exclusive rituals, presided over by the women of the family, especially the girl's mother, who prayed to deities such as the Tiny Foot Maiden and the

goddess Guanyin. According to Ko, these rituals "and the beliefs behind them help explain the longevity and spread of the custom."

> For all its erotic appeal to men, without the cooperation of the women concerned, footbinding could not have been perpetuated for a millennium. In defining the mother–daughter tie in a private space barred to men, in venerating the fruits of women's handiwork, and in the centrality of female-exclusive religious rituals, footbinding embodied the essential features of a woman's culture documented by the writings of the women themselves.[9]

Women wrote poems about lotus shoes and they exchanged them with friends. Proverbs emphasized women's control over foot binding: "A plain face is given by heaven, but poorly bound feet are a sign of laziness."[10]

14 Good mothers were supposed to bind their daughters' feet tightly so they could make advantageous marriages, just as they made their sons study hard so they could pass their examinations. The Victorian traveler Isabella Bird visited China and reported that "The butler's little daughter, aged seven, is having her feet 'bandaged' for the first time, and is in torture, but bears it bravely in the hope of 'getting a rich husband' . . . The mother of this suffering infant says, with a quiet air of truth and triumph, that Chinese women suffer less in the process of being crippled than foreign women do from wearing corsets!"[11]

15 Indeed, Chinese and westerners alike not infrequently compared foot binding with corsetry, debating their relative injuriousness and irrationality. Yet measurements of existing corsets and lotus shoes indicate that both the sixteen-inch waist and the three-inch golden lotus were only achieved by a minority of women. Writing at the turn of the century, the sociologist Thorstein Veblen used foot binding (as well as such western fashions as corsets and long skirts) as examples of what he called "conspicuous leisure," because they supposedly indicated that the wearer could not perform productive labor. Yet, contrary to popular belief, neither bound feet nor corsets prevented women from working and walking; most Chinese women worked very hard, albeit usually at home. Moreover, although foot binding was believed to ensure female chastity by, literally, preventing women from straying, in fact women were far more restricted by social and legal constraints.

16 Although for many centuries most Chinese men and women approved of foot binding, the practice eventually ceased to be valorized as a way of emphasizing the beauty and virtue of Chinese women and/or the virility and civility of Chinese men. Writing in the early nineteenth century, the novelist Li Ruzhun attacked foot binding on the grounds that it oppressed women. His novel *Flowers in the Mirror* included a satirical sequence about a country where women ruled and men had their feet bound.

17 Missionary efforts undoubtedly played a role in the demise of foot binding, as the Chinese were made aware that Westerners thought the practice was "barbaric," unhealthy, and oppressive to women. The Chinese girls who attended mission schools were taught that foot binding was bad. More significantly, however, growing numbers of young Chinese men (and a few educated Chinese women) began to reinterpret foot binding as a "backward" practice that hindered national efforts to resist western imperialism.

18 Chinese reformers began to discuss whether China could be strengthened *vis-à-vis* the West, if only Chinese women became stronger physically. This, in turn, seemed to depend on the elimination of what was increasingly regarded by progressive Chinese as the "feudal" practice of foot binding. Organizations such as the Natural Foot Society were founded, and struggled to change the idea that unbound female feet were "big" and ugly. Indeed, it was apparently difficult to convince the Chinese that foot binding was any more "unnatural" than other kinds of bodily adornment, such as clothing, jewelry, hairstyles, or cosmetics.[12]

19 There is even some evidence that the introduction of western high-heeled shoes, which give the visual illusion of smaller feet and produce a swaying walk, may have eased the transition away from the bound foot ideal. Manchu shoes were another alternative to lotus shoes in the early years of the anti-foot-binding movement, although with the rise of anti-Manchu nationalism at the time of the 1911 Revolution, this style disappeared.

20 Foot binding had never been mandated by any Chinese government. Indeed, various Qing rulers had sporadically attempted to abolish foot binding, without success. After the Qing dynasty was overthrown and a republic was declared, foot binding was outlawed. Laws alone would not have sufficed to end the practice, however, had it not already ceased to claim the allegiance of significant segments of the Chinese population, but once foot binding began to be regarded as "backward," modern-thinking Chinese increasingly attacked the practice.

21 Older brothers argued that their sisters should not have their feet bound, or should try to let their feet out—a process that was itself painful and only partly feasible. Sometimes husbands even abandoned wives who had bound feet, and looked for new, suitably modern brides. Obviously, these developments took place within the context of broader social change. The new generation of educated, urban Chinese increasingly argued that many aspects of traditional Chinese culture should be analyzed and improved. Women, as well as men, should be educated and should participate in athletic activities. Arranged marriages should be replaced by love matches. The Chinese nation should modernize and strengthen itself.

NOTES

1. Dorothy Ko, *Teachers of the Inner Chambers: Women and Culture in Seventeenth-Century China* (Stanford: Stanford University Press, 1994), p. 148.
2. Dorothy Ko, "The Body as Attire: The Shifting Meanings of Footbinding in Seventeenth Century China," *Journal of Women's History* 8.4 (1997), p. 15.
3. Patricia Buckley Ebrey, *The Inner Quarters: Marriage and the Lives of Chinese Women in the Sung Period* (Berkeley: University of California Press, 1993), pp. 38–39.
4. Feng Jicai, *The Three-Inch Golden Lotus,* trans. David Wakefield (Honolulu: University of Hawaii Press, 1994), p. 236.
5. Cited in Ebrey, *The Inner Quarters,* p. 40.
6. Ebrey, *The Inner Quarters,* pp. 42–43.
7. Ko, *Teachers of the Inner Chambers,* p. 149.
8. Ibid., p. 263.
9. Ibid., p. 150.
10. Ibid., p. 171.
11. Isabella Bird, *The Golden Chersonese and the Way Thither* (first published London, 1883; reprinted, Singapore: Oxford University Press, 1990), p. 66.
12. Ko, "The Body as Attire," pp. 17–19.

✧ *Evaluating the Text*

1. What is the practice of foot binding? What political and social meanings did it communicate within the context of Chinese culture at the time it was practiced?

2. Why do Steele and Major draw a distinction between Western condemnation of foot binding and what the practice meant to Chinese women at the time?

✧ *Exploring Different Perspectives*

1. How can the analyses of Steele and Major and Serena Nanda in "Arranging a Marriage in India" be understood as attempts to explain practices that define cultural identity?

2. How do the rituals described by Harold Miner in "Body Ritual among the Nacirema" define sought-after cultural values as bound feet did in ancient China?

✧ *Extending Viewpoints through Writing and Research*

1. What do the kind of shoes you wear say about you? What are your favorite styles, heel heights, and colors? Given the choice between a pair of fashionable or comfortable shoes, which would you buy? Alternatively, compare the meanings communicated by various traditional shoe types—including moccasins, sandals, mules, boots, and clogs—and their modern variants.

2. The so-called lotus foot (named because the walk of a woman whose foot was bound was thought to resemble the swaying of the lotus plant in the wind) captivated the Chinese imagination such that the foot took on the role of a sexual object. In what way do "shoes that have no relationship to the natural foot shape" (high heels) communicate the same psychological meaning in the West?
3. An illustrated Web site on foot binding is available at http://www.ccds.charlotte.nc.us/History/China/04/hutchins/hutchins.htm.

Why is this modern photo of a young woman wearing high-heeled boots ironic in light of Steele and Major's analysis?

Serena Nanda

Arranging a Marriage in India

Serena Nanda is Professor Emerita of anthropology at John Jay College of Criminal Justice, City University of New York. She has carried out field studies in India, in tribal development, and on the social lives of women in urban India. Her published works include Neither Man nor Woman: The Hijras of India *(1990), which won the Ruth Benedict Prize. The following selection first appeared in* The Naked Anthropologist: Tales from Around the World, *edited by Philip R. DeVita (1992). A recent work (with Richard L. Warms) is* Cultural Anthropology, *ninth edition (2006). In 2009, Nanda and Joan Gregg wrote* Gift of a Bride: A Tale of Anthropology, Matrimony, and Murder. *Nanda looks at the cultural forces that have resulted in the practice of arranged marriages in Indian society.*

Before You Read

Note the considerations that are important in arranging a marriage in India and how these reflect important cultural values.

> *Sister and doctor brother-in-law invite correspondence from North Indian professionals only, for a beautiful, talented, sophisticated, intelligent sister, 5′3″, slim, M.A. in textile design, father a senior civil officer. Would prefer immigrant doctors, between 26–29 years. Reply with full details and returnable photo.*
>
> *A well-settled uncle invites matrimonial correspondence from slim, fair, educated South Indian girl, for his nephew, 25 years, smart, M.B.A., green card holder, 5′6″. Full particulars with returnable photo appreciated.*
>
> —Matrimonial Advertisements, *India Abroad*

1 In India, almost all marriages are arranged. Even among the educated middle classes in modern, urban India, marriage is as much a concern of the families as it is of the individuals. So customary is the practice of arranged marriage that there is a special name for a marriage which is not arranged: It is called a "love match."

2 On my first field trip to India, I met many young men and women whose parents were in the process of "getting them married." In many cases, the bride and groom would not meet each other before the

marriage. At most they might meet for a brief conversation, and this meeting would take place only after their parents had decided that the match was suitable. Parents do not compel their children to marry a person who either marriage partner finds objectionable. But only after one match is refused will another be sought.

3 As a young American woman in India for the first time, I found this custom of arranged marriage oppressive. How could any intelligent young person agree to such a marriage without great reluctance? It was contrary to everything I believed about the importance of romantic love as the only basis of a happy marriage. It also clashed with my strongly held notions that the choice of such an intimate and permanent relationship could be made only by the individuals involved. Had anyone tried to arrange my marriage, I would have been defiant and rebellious!

4 At the first opportunity, I began, with more curiosity than tact, to question the young people I met on how they felt about this practice. Sita, one of my young informants, was a college graduate with a degree in political science. She had been waiting for over a year while her parents were arranging a match for her. I found it difficult to accept the docile manner in which this well-educated young woman awaited the outcome of a process that would result in her spending the rest of her life with a man she hardly knew, a virtual stranger, picked out by her parents.

5 "How can you go along with this?" I asked her, in frustration and distress. "Don't you care who you marry?"

6 "Of course I care," she answered. "This is why I must let my parents choose a boy for me. My marriage is too important to be arranged by such an inexperienced person as myself. In such matters, it is better to have my parents' guidance."

7 I had learned that young men and women in India do not date and have very little social life involving members of the opposite sex. Although I could not disagree with Sita's reasoning, I continued to pursue the subject.

8 "But how can you marry the first man you have ever met? Not only have you missed the fun of meeting a lot of different people, but you have not given yourself the chance to know who is the right man for you."

9 "Meeting with a lot of different people doesn't sound like any fun at all," Sita answered. "One hears that in America the girls are spending more time worrying about whether they will meet a man and get married. Here we have the chance to enjoy our life and let our parents do this work and worrying for us."

10 She had me there. The high anxiety of the competition to "be popular" with the opposite sex certainly was the most prominent feature of life as an American teenager in the late fifties. The endless worrying about the rules that governed our behavior and about our popularity ratings sapped both our self-esteem and our enjoyment of adolescence.

I reflected that absence of this competition in India most certainly may have contributed to the self-confidence and natural charm of so many of the young women I met.

11 And yet, the idea of marrying a perfect stranger, whom one did not know and did not "love," so offended my American ideas of individualism and romanticism, that I persisted with my objections.

12 "I still can't imagine it," I said. "How can you agree to marry a man you hardly know?"

13 "But of course he will be known. My parents would never arrange a marriage for me without knowing all about the boy's family background. Naturally we will not rely only on what the family tells us. We will check the particulars out ourselves. No one will want their daughter to marry into a family that is not good. All these things we will know beforehand."

14 Impatiently, I responded, "Sita, I don't mean know the family, I mean, know the man. How can you marry someone you don't know personally and don't love? How can you think of spending your life with someone you may not even like?"

15 "If he is a good man, why should I not like him?" she said. "With you people, you know the boy so well before you marry, where will be the fun to get married? There will be no mystery and no romance. Here we have the whole of our married life to get to know and love our husband. This way is better, is it not?"

16 Her response made further sense, and I began to have second thoughts on the matter. Indeed, during months of meeting many intelligent young Indian people, both male and female, who had the same ideas as Sita, I saw arranged marriages in a different light. I also saw the importance of the family in Indian life and realized that a couple who took their marriage into their own hands was taking a big risk, particularly if their families were irreconcilably opposed to the match. In a country where every important resource in life—a job, a house, a social circle—is gained through family connections, it seemed foolhardy to cut oneself off from a supportive social network and depend solely on one person for happiness and success.

17 Six years later I returned to India to again do fieldwork, this time among the middle class in Bombay, a modern, sophisticated city. From the experience of my earlier visit, I decided to include a study of arranged marriages in my project. By this time I had met many Indian couples whose marriages had been arranged and who seemed very happy. Particularly in contrast to the fate of many of my married friends in the United States who were already in the process of divorce, the positive aspects of arranged marriages appeared to me to outweigh the negatives. In fact, I thought I might even participate in arranging a marriage myself. I had been fairly successful in the United States in

"fixing up" many of my friends, and I was confident that my matchmaking skills could be easily applied to this new situation, once I learned the basic rules. "After all," I thought, "how complicated can it be? People want pretty much the same things in a marriage whether it is in India or America."

18 An opportunity presented itself almost immediately. A friend from my previous Indian trip was in the process of arranging for the marriage of her eldest son. In India there is a perceived shortage of "good boys," and since my friend's family was eminently respectable and the boy himself personable, well educated, and nice looking, I was sure that by the end of my year's fieldwork, we would have found a match.

19 The basic rule seems to be that a family's reputation is most important. It is understood that matches would be arranged only within the same caste and general social class, although some crossing of subcastes is permissible if the class positions of the bride's and groom's families are similar. Although dowry is now prohibited by law in India, extensive gift exchanges took place with every marriage. Even when the boy's family do not "make demands," every girl's family nevertheless feels the obligation to give the traditional gifts, to the girl, to the boy, and to the boy's family. Particularly when the couple would be living in the joint family—that is, with the boy's parents and his married brothers and their families, as well as with unmarried siblings—which is still very common even among the urban, upper-middle class in India, the girl's parents are anxious to establish smooth relations between their family and that of the boy. Offering the proper gifts, even when not called "dowry," is often an important factor in influencing the relationship between the bride's and groom's families and perhaps, also, the treatment of the bride in her new home.

20 In a society where divorce is still a scandal and where, in fact, the divorce rate is exceedingly low, an arranged marriage is the beginning of a lifetime relationship not just between the bride and groom but between their families as well. Thus, while a girl's looks are important, her character is even more so, for she is being judged as a prospective daughter-in-law as much as a prospective bride. Where she would be living in a joint family, as was the case with my friend, the girl's ability to get along harmoniously in a family is perhaps the single most important quality in assessing her suitability.

21 My friend is a highly esteemed wife, mother, and daughter-in-law. She is religious, soft-spoken, modest, and deferential. She rarely gossips and never quarrels, two qualities highly desirable in a woman. A family that has the reputation for gossip and conflict among its womenfolk will not find it easy to get good wives for their sons. Parents will not want to send their daughter to a house in which there is conflict.

22 My friend's family were originally from North India. They had lived in Bombay, where her husband owned a business, for forty years.

The family had delayed in seeking a match for their eldest son because he had been an Air Force pilot for several years, stationed in such remote places that it had seemed fruitless to try to find a girl who would be willing to accompany him. In their social class, a military career, despite its economic security, has little prestige and is considered a drawback in finding a suitable bride. Many families would not allow their daughters to marry a man in an occupation so potentially dangerous and which requires so much moving around.

23 The son had recently left the military and joined his father's business. Since he was a college graduate, modern, and well traveled, from such a good family, and, I thought, quite handsome, it seemed to me that he, or rather his family, was in a position to pick and choose. I said as much to my friend.

24 While she agreed that there were many advantages on their side, she also said, "We must keep in mind that my son is both short and dark; these are drawbacks in finding the right match." While the boy's height had not escaped my notice, "dark" seemed to me inaccurate; I would have called him "wheat" colored perhaps, and in any case, I did not realize that color would be a consideration. I discovered, however, that while a boy's skin color is a less important consideration than a girl's, it is still a factor.

25 An important source of contacts in trying to arrange her son's marriage was my friend's social club in Bombay. Many of the women had daughters of the right age, and some had already expressed an interest in my friend's son. I was most enthusiastic about the possibilities of one particular family who had five daughters, all of whom were pretty, demure, and well educated. Their mother had told my friend, "You can have your pick for your son, whichever one of my daughters appeals to you most."

26 I saw a match in sight. "Surely," I said to my friend, "we will find one there. Let's go visit and make our choice." But my friend held back; she did not seem to share my enthusiasm, for reasons I could not then fathom.

27 When I kept pressing for an explanation of her reluctance, she admitted, "See, Serena, here is the problem. The family has so many daughters, how will they be able to provide nicely for any of them? We are not making any demands, but still, with so many daughters to marry off, one wonders whether she will even be able to make a proper wedding. Since this is our eldest son, it's best if we marry him to a girl who is the only daughter, then the wedding will truly be a gala affair." I argued that surely the quality of the girls themselves made up for any deficiency in the elaborateness of the wedding. My friend admitted this point but still seemed reluctant to proceed.

28 "Is there something else," I asked her, "some factor I have missed?" "Well," she finally said, "there is one other thing. They have

one daughter already married and living in Bombay. The mother is always complaining to me that the girl's in-laws don't let her visit her own family often enough. So it makes me wonder, will she be that kind of mother who always wants her daughter at her own home? This will prevent the girl from adjusting to our house. It is not a good thing." And so, this family of five daughters was dropped as a possibility.

29 Somewhat disappointed, I nevertheless respected my friend's reasoning and geared up for the next prospect. This was also the daughter of a woman in my friend's social club. There was clear interest in this family and I could see why. The family's reputation was excellent; in fact, they came from a subcaste slightly higher than my friend's own. The girl, who was an only daughter, was pretty and well educated and had a brother studying in the United States. Yet, after expressing an interest to me in this family, all talk of them suddenly died down and the search began elsewhere.

30 "What happened to that girl as a prospect?" I asked one day. "You never mention her any more. She is so pretty and so educated, what did you find wrong?"

31 "She is too educated. We've decided against it. My husband's father saw the girl on the bus the other day and thought her forward. A girl who 'roams about' the city by herself is not the girl for our family." My disappointment this time was even greater, as I thought the son would have liked the girl very much. But then I thought, my friend is right, a girl who is going to live in a joint family cannot be too independent or she will make life miserable for everyone. I also learned that if the family of the girl has even a slightly higher social status than the family of the boy, the bride may think herself too good for them, and this too will cause problems. Later my friend admitted to me that this had been an important factor in her decision not to pursue the match.

32 The next candidate was the daughter of a client of my friend's husband. When the client learned that the family was looking for a match for their son, he said, "Look no further, we have a daughter." This man then invited my friends to dinner to see the girl. He had already seen their son at the office and decided that "he liked the boy." We all went together for tea, rather than dinner—it was less of a commitment—and while we were there, the girl's mother showed us around the house. The girl was studying for her exams and was briefly introduced to us.

33 After we left, I was anxious to hear my friend's opinion. While her husband liked the family very much and was impressed with his client's business accomplishments and reputation, the wife didn't like the girl's looks. "She is short, no doubt, which is an important plus point, but she is also fat and wears glasses." My friend obviously thought she could do better for her son and asked her husband to make his excuses to his client by saying that they had decided to postpone the boy's marriage indefinitely.

34 By this time almost six months had passed and I was becoming impatient. What I had thought would be an easy matter to arrange was turning out to be quite complicated. I began to believe that between my friend's desire for a girl who was modest enough to fit into her joint family, yet attractive and educated enough to be an acceptable partner for her son, she would not find anyone suitable. My friend laughed at my impatience: "Don't be so much in a hurry," she said. "You Americans want everything done so quickly. You get married quickly and then just as quickly get divorced. Here we take marriage more seriously. We must take all the factors into account. It is not enough for us to learn by our mistakes. This is too serious a business. If a mistake is made we have not only ruined the life of our son or daughter, but we have spoiled the reputation of our family as well. And that will make it much harder for their brothers and sisters to get married. So we must be very careful."

35 What she said was true and I promised myself to be more patient, though it was not easy. I had really hoped and expected that the match would be made before my year in India was up. But it was not to be. When I left India my friend seemed no further along in finding a suitable match for her son than when I had arrived.

36 Two years later, I returned to India and still my friend had not found a girl for her son. By this time, he was close to thirty, and I think she was a little worried. Since she knew I had friends all over India, and I was going to be there for a year, she asked me to "help her in this work" and keep an eye out for someone suitable. I was flattered that my judgment was respected, but knowing now how complicated the process was, I had lost my earlier confidence as a matchmaker. Nevertheless, I promised that I would try.

37 It was almost at the end of my year's stay in India that I met a family with a marriageable daughter whom I felt might be a good possibility for my friend's son. The girl's father was related to a good friend of mine and by coincidence came from the same village as my friend's husband. This new family had a successful business in a medium-sized city in central India and were from the same subcaste as my friend. The daughter was pretty and chic; in fact, she had studied fashion design in college. Her parents would not allow her to go off by herself to any of the major cities in India where she could make a career, but they had compromised with her wish to work by allowing her to run a small dressmaking boutique from their home. In spite of her desire to have a career, the daughter was both modest and home-loving and had had a traditional, sheltered upbringing. She had only one other sister, already married, and a brother who was in his father's business.

38 I mentioned the possibility of a match with my friend's son. The girl's parents were most interested. Although their daughter was not eager to marry just yet, the idea of living in Bombay—a sophisticated,

extremely fashion-conscious city where she could continue her education in clothing design—was a great inducement. I gave the girl's father my friend's address and suggested that when they went to Bombay on some business or whatever, they look up the boy's family.

39 Returning to Bombay on my way to New York, I told my friend of this newly discovered possibility. She seemed to feel there was potential but, in spite of my urging, would not make any moves herself. She rather preferred to wait for the girl's family to call upon them. I hoped something would come of this introduction, though by now I had learned to rein in my optimism.

40 A year later I received a letter from my friend. The family had indeed come to visit Bombay, and their daughter and my friend's daughter, who were near in age, had become very good friends. During that year, the two girls had frequently visited each other. I thought things looked promising.

41 Last week I received an invitation to a wedding: My friend's son and the girl were getting married. Since I had found the match, my presence was particularly requested at the wedding. I was thrilled. Success at last! As I prepared to leave for India, I began thinking, "Now, my friend's younger son, who do I know who has a nice girl for him . . . ?"

Epilogue

42 *This essay was written from the point of view of a family seeking a daughter-in-law. Arranged marriage looks somewhat different from the point of view of the bride and her family. Arranged marriage continues to be preferred, even among the more educated, westernized sections of the Indian population. Many young women from these families still go along, more or less willingly, with the practice and also with the specific choices of their families. Young women do get excited about the prospects of their marriage, but there is also ambivalence and increasing uncertainty as the bride contemplates leaving the comfort and familiarity of her own home where, as a "temporary guest," she had often been indulged, to live among strangers. Even in the best situation she will now come under the close scrutiny of her husband's family. How she dresses, how she behaves, how she gets along with others, where she goes, how she spends her time, her domestic abilities—all this and much more—will be observed and commented on by a whole new set of relations. Her interaction with her family of birth will be monitored and curtailed considerably. Not only will she leave their home, but with increasing geographic mobility she may also live very far from them, perhaps even on another continent. Too much expression of her fondness for her own family or her desire to visit them may be interpreted as an inability to adjust to her new family and may become a source of conflict. In an arranged marriage the burden of adjustment is clearly heavier for a woman than for a man. And this is in the best of situations.*

43 *In less happy circumstances, the bride may be a target of resentment and hostility from her husband's family, particularly her mother-in-law or her husband's unmarried sisters, for whom she is now a source of competition for the affection, loyalty, and economic resources of their son or brother. If she is psychologically or even physically abused, her options are limited, because returning to her parents' home or divorce is still very stigmatized. For most Indians, marriage and motherhood are still considered the only suitable roles for a woman, even for those who have careers, and few women can comfortably contemplate remaining unmarried. Most families still consider "marrying off" their daughter as a compelling religious duty and social necessity. This increases a bride's sense of obligation to make the marriage a success, at whatever cost to her own personal happiness.*

44 *The vulnerability of a new bride may also be intensified by the issue of dowry, which, although illegal, has become a more pressing issue in the consumer-conscious society of contemporary urban India. In many cases, if a groom's family is not satisfied with the amount of dowry that a bride brings to her marriage, the young bride will be constantly harassed to get her parents to give more. In extreme cases, the bride may even be murdered, and the murder disguised as an accident or suicide. This also offers the husband's family an opportunity to arrange another match for him, thus bringing in another dowry. This phenomenon, called dowry death, calls attention not just to the evils of dowry, but also to larger issues of the powerlessness of women.*

✧ *Evaluating the Text*

1. From an Indian perspective, what are the advantages of an arranged marriage?
2. What considerations are taken into account in arranging a marriage in India?
3. What role does Nanda play in helping to find a suitable bride for her friend's son? How would you characterize Nanda's attitude toward arranged marriage and in what way does it change over the course of events?

✧ *Exploring Different Perspectives*

1. Discuss the expectations regarding the role of women by their families in India and in ancient China as described by Valerie Steele and John S. Major in "China Chic: East Meets West."
2. What are the differences and similarities between customs in India as described by Nanda and those of the Nacirema as discussed by Harold Miner in "Body Ritual among the Nacirema"?

✧ *Extending Viewpoints through Writing and Research*

1. Would you ever consider allowing your parents to arrange a marriage for you? If so, why would this be more advantageous or disadvantageous than finding someone for yourself?
2. What circumstances led your parents to get married? What considerations, in your opinion, played the most important role?
3. What did this essay add to your understanding of the pressures couples experience when getting married in India? To what extent are these pressures similar to or different from those experienced by couples in the United States?
4. For research on arranged marriages throughout the world, consult http://marriage.about.com/od/arrangedmarriages/Arranged_Marriages.htm.

Connecting Culture

Philip Slater, "Want-Creation Fuels Americans' Addictiveness"

How analogous do you find Slater's explanation for addictive behavior in America with that of the endorsement of surgery and extreme diets in Brazil as discussed by Kulick and Machado-Borges in "Leaky" in Chapter 3?

Harold Miner, "Body Ritual among the Nacirema"

Are the rituals that Enid Schildkrout discusses in "Body Art as Visual Language" in Chapter 2 really so different from those discussed by Miner? If so, why?

Robert Levine and Ellen Wolff, "Social Time: The Heartbeat of Culture"

In light of the discussion by Levine and Wolff, how did Anwar F. Accawi's account in "The Telephone" in Chapter 2 offer insights into a shift in tempo in his village in Lebanon?

Colin Turnbull, "The Mbuti Pygmies"

What social pressures caused the Ladakh to become competitive (see Helena Norberg-Hodge's "Learning from Ladakh" in Chapter 4), while cooperation remained the hallmark of the Mbuti as described by Turnbull?

Valerie Steele and John S. Major, "China Chic: East Meets West"

In what way did foot binding symbolize sought-after attributes much as extreme thinness and cosmetic surgery do in Brazil according to Kulick and Machado-Borges in "Leaky" in Chapter 3?

Serena Nanda, "Arranging a Marriage in India"

Compare the protocol involved with marriage in India as discussed by Nanda with that of the Vietnamese in America as described by K. Oanh Ha in "American Dream Boat" in Chapter 1.

Pronunciation Key

The pronunciation of each of the following names is shown in parentheses according to the following pronunciation key.

1. A heavy accent′ is placed after a syllable with the primary accent.
2. The letters and symbols used to represent given sounds are pronounced as in the examples below.

a	bat, nap	j	jam, fudge	s	see, miss
ā	way, cape	k	keep, kind	sh	show, push
â	dare, air				
ä	art, far	l	love, all	t	tell, ten
		m	my, am	th	thin, path
b	cabin, back	n	in, now	th̸	that, smooth
ch	beach, child	ng	sing, long		
d	do, red			u	up, butter
e	bet, merry	o	box, hot	u̇	put, burn
ē	equal, beet	ō	boat, go	ü	rule, ooze
ė	learn, fern	ô	ought, order		
f	fit, puff	oi	voice, joy	v	river, save
		oo	ooze, rule	w	west, will
g	give, go	ou	loud, out	y	yes, yet
h	how, him			z	zeal, lazy
i	pin, big	p	pot, paper	zh	vision, measure
ī	deny, ice	r	read, run		

ə occurs only in unaccented syllables and indicates the sound of

a	in alone	i	in pencil	u	in circus
e	in taken	o	in gallop		

FOREIGN SOUNDS

a	as in French *ami*
Y	as in French *do*; or as in German *über*
œ	as in French *feu*; or as in German *schön*
N	as in French *bon*
H	as in German *ach*; or as in Scottish *loch*
R	as in Spanish *pero*; or as in German *mare*

EXAMPLES

Firoozeh Dumas	(fi ro͞o′ zhə do͞o mäs)
Immaculée Ilibagiza	(im mak′ yo͞o lē il lä bä gē′ zə)
Tomoyuki Iwashita	(tō mō yü′ kē i wä shē′ tä)
Meeta Kaur	(mē′ tə kôr)
Tepilit Ole Saitoti	(te′ pə lit ō′ le sī tō′ tē)
Fareed Zakaria	(fə rēd′ zə kär′ ēə)

Credits

Anwar F. Accawi, "The Telephone," permission from the author. First published in *The Sun*, Knoxville, TN.

Latifa Ali, Chapter 18 from *Betrayed*. Edited by Richard Shears. Copyright © 2009. Reprinted by permission of New Holland Publishers.

Joe Bageant, "Valley of the Gun." From *Deer Hunting with Jesus: Dispatches from America's Class War* by Joe Bageant, copyright © 2007 by Joseph L. Bageant. Used by permission of Crown Publishers, a division of Random House, Inc.

Christy Brown, "The Letter 'A'" from *My Left Foot*. Copyright © 1955 by Christy Brown. Reprinted by permission of Martin Secker & Warburg, Ltd.

Jose Antonio Burciaga, "My Ecumenical Father," from *Drink Cultura*. Copyright © 1993. Reprinted by permission.

Napoleon A. Chagnon, "Doing Fieldwork Among the Yąnomamö" from *Yąnomamö: The Fierce People*, 1st ed. © 1968 Wadsworth, a part of Cengage Learning, Inc. Reproduced by permission. www.cengage.com/permissions.

Sucheng Chan, "You're Short, Besides!" from *Making Waves: An Anthology of Writings By and About Asian American Women* (Boston: Beacon Press, 1989). Copyright © 1989 by Asian Women United of California. Reprinted by permission.

Taylor Clark, "Plight of the Little Emperors," from *Psychology Today* Online, July 1, 2008. Reprinted with permission from Psychology Today Magazine (Copyright © 2008 Sussex Publishers, LLC).

Judith Ortiz Cofer, "The Myth of the Latin Woman: I Just Met a Girl Named Maria" from *The Latin Deli: Prose and Poetry*. © 1993 by Judith Ortiz Cofer. Reprinted by permission of The University of Georgia Press.

David R. Counts, "Too Many Bananas, Not Enough Pineapples, and No Watermelon at All: Three Object Lessons in Living with Reciprocity," from *The Humbled Anthropologist: Tales from the Pacific*, edited by Philip R. DeVita. Belmont, CA: Wadsworth, 1990. Reprinted by permission of the author.

Mary Crow Dog with Richard Erdoes, from "Civilize Them with a Stick" from *Lakota Woman* by Mary Crow Dog with Richard Erdoes. Copyright © 1990 by Mary Crow Dog and Richard Erdoes. Used by permission of Grove/Atlantic, Inc.

Waris Dirie, "The Tragedy of Female Circumcision," *Marie Claire*, March 1996. Permission of the author.

Firoozeh Dumas, "Save Me, Mickey," from *Funny In Farsi*, copyright © 2003 by Firoozeh Dumas. Used by permission of Villard Books, a division of Random House, Inc.

Bill Geist, From *Way Off the Road: Discovering the Peculiar Charms of Small-Town America*. Copyright © 2007 by Bill Geist. Used by permission of Broadway Books, a division of Random House, Inc.

Douchan Gersi, "Initiated into an Iban Tribe of Headhunters" from *Explorer*. Los Angeles: Jeremy P. Tarcher, 1987, pp. 272–276. Copyright © 1987 by Douchan Gersi. Reprinted by permission of the author.

Gino Del Guercio, "The Secrets of Haiti's Living Dead," *Harvard Magazine* (January/February 1986). Copyright © 1986 by Gino Del Guercio. Reprinted with the permission of the author.

K. Oanh Ha, "American Dreamboat," from *Modern Maturity*, May–June 2002. Reprinted by permission of the author.

Patricia Hampl, "Grandmother's Sunday Dinner" from *A Romantic Education*. Copyright © 1981 by Patricia Hampl. Used by permission of W. W. Norton

Herald Sun, "Bears Feel Global Heat; Polar Icon Faces Wipeout," *Herald Sun*, Melbourne, Dec. 28, 2006. Thomson-Reuters.

Ethel G. Hofman, "An Island Passover," from *Mackerel at Midnight: Growing Up Jewish on a Remote Scottish Island*. Reprinted with permission from Ethel G. Hofman. (Philadelphia: Camino Books, Inc., 2005.)

Kris Holloway, from *Monique and the Mango Rains: Two Years with a Midwife in Mali*. Reprinted by permission of Waveland Press, Inc. (Long Grove, IL: Waveland Press, 2007). All rights reserved.

Immaculée Ilibagiza, with Steve Erwin, from *Left to Tell: Discovering God Amidst the Rwandan Holocaust*, pp. 73–82. Copyright © 2006 by Immaculée Ilibagiza. Reprinted by permission of Hay House, Inc.

Tomoyuki Iwashita, "Why I Quit the Company," *New Internationalist*, May 1992, issue 231. Reprinted by kind permission of the *New Internationalist*. Copyright New Internationalist. www.newint.org

Meeta Kaur, "Journey by Inner Light" from *Homelands: Women's Journeys Across Race, Place, and Time*, edited by Patricia Justine Tumang and Jenesha de Rivera. Copyright © 2006 Patricia Justine Tumang and Jenesha de Rivera. Reprinted by permission of Seal Press, a member of Perseus Books Group.

Nicholas Kristof, "Striking the Brothels' Bottom Line," from *The New York Times*, January 11, 2009. Copyright © 2009. Reprinted by permission of The New York Times Co.

Ray Kroc, "Grinding It Out: The Making of McDonald's" from *Grinding It Out: The Making of McDonald's*. Chicago: Henry Regnery, 1977. © 1977 by Ray Kroc. Reprinted by arrangement with Contemporary Books, Inc.

Don Kulick and Thaïs Machado-Borges, "Leaky" from *Fat: The Anthropology of an Obsession*, edited by Don Kulick and Anne Meneley. New York: Jeremy P. Tarcher, 2005. Copyright © 2004 by Don Kulick and Thaïs Machado-Borges. Reprinted by permission of the authors.

Robert Levine and Ellen Wolff , "Social Time: The Hearbeat of Culture," from *Psychology Today*, March 1985. Reprinted with permission from *Psychology Today Magazine* (Copyright © 1985 Sussex Publishers, LLC).

Ralph Linton, "One Hundred Percent American," *The American Mercury* (April 1937). Reprinted by permission of the Estate of Ralph Linton.

Chris Maynard and Bill Scheller, reprinted with the permission of Simon & Schuster, Inc. from *Manifold Destiny: The One! The Only! Guide to Cooking on Your Car Engine!*, Revised, Updated Edition. Copyright © 1989, 1998, 2008 by Chris Maynard and Bill Scheller.

Lydia Minatoya, pages 31–36 from *Talking to High Monks in the Snow*. Copyright © 1992 by Lydia Minatoya. Reprinted by permission of HarperCollins Publishers.

Serena Nanda, "Arranging a Marriage in India" from *The Naked Anthropologist: Tales from Around the World*, edited by Philip R. DeVita (Belmont, CA: Wadsworth, 1992). Reprinted by permission of Serena Nanda.

Poranee Natadecha-Sponsel, "The Young, the Rich, and the Famous: Individualism as an American Cultural Value" from Philip R. DeVita and James D. Armstrong, eds., *Distant Mirrors: America as a Foreign Culture*. Belmont, CA: Wadsworth, 1993. Copyright © 1993 by Poranee Natadecha-Sponsel. Reprinted with the permission of the author.

Helena Norberg-Hodge, "Money Makes the World Go Round" from *Ancient Futures: Learning from Ladakh*, by Helena Norberg-Hodge. Copyright © 1991 by Helena Norberg-Hodge. Reprinted with permission by Sierra Club Books.

Jack Owens, "Don't Shoot! We're Republicans," from *Don't Shoot! We're Republicans: Memoirs of an FBI Agent Who Did Things His Own Way*. Copyright © 2009. Reprinted by permission of History Publishing Company, LLC.

Jo Goodwin Parker, "What is Poverty?" from *America's Other Children: Public Schools Outside the Suburbs* by George Henderson. Rerpinted by permission of University of Oklahoma Press.

Gordon Parks, "Flavio's Home," from *Voices in the Mirror*. Copyright © 1990 by Gordon Parks. Used by permission of Doubleday, a division of Random House, Inc.

Fritz Peters, "Boyhood with Gurdjieff" from *Gurdjieff Remembered*. First published in 1965. Reprinted by permission of Arete Communications, Fairfax, CA.

Andrew X. Pham, "Foreign-Asians" from *Catfish and Mandala: A Two-Wheeled Voyage through the Landscape and Memory of Vietnman*. Copyright © 1999 by Andrew X. Pham. Reprinted by permission of Farrar, Straus and Giroux, LLC.

Tepilit Ole Saitoti, from *The Worlds of a Maasai Warrior* by Tepilit Ole Saitoti, copyright © 1986 by Tepilit Ole Saitoti. Used by permission of Random House, Inc. (The title "The Initiation of a Maasai Warrior" is not original to Random House, Inc.'s book.)

Marjane Satrapi, "The Convocation," from *Persepolis 2: The Story of a Return*. Translated by Anjali Singh, translation copyright © 2004 by Anjali Singh. Used by permission of Pantheon Books, a division of Random House, Inc.

Enid Schildkrout, "Body Art as Visual Language," *AnthroNotes*, Winter 2001. Reprinted by permission of Anthropology Outreach Office, Smithsonian Institution, Washington, DC.

Mark I. Schwartz, "Genetically Safer; Europe Continues to Resist Genetically Modified Crops, Though They're Actually Safer than Conventional Ones," *National Post*, Feb. 13, 2008. Copyright © National Post Company.

Saira Shah, from *The Storyteller's Daughter*. Copyright © 2003 by Saira Shah. Used by permission of Alfred A. Knopf, a division of Random House, Inc.

Philip Slater, "Want-Creation Fuels Americans' Addictiveness," *Newsday* (September 2, 1984). Used by permission of the author.

Cameron W. Smith, "Of Ice and Men," from *Cultural Survival Quarterly*, Summer 2008. Reprinted by permission of Cultural Survival Quarterly, www.culturalsurvival.org.

Jeffrey M. Smith, "Genetically Engineered Foods May Cause Rising Food Allergies." Reprinted by permission of the author

Valerie Steele and John S. Major, from *China Chic: East Meets West*, 37–44. Copyright © 1999 by the authors. Reprinted by permission of Yale University Press.

Andrew Sullivan, "My Big Fat Straight Wedding," originally published in *The Atlantic*. Copyright © 2008 by Andrew Sullivan, used with permission of The Wylie Agency LLC.

Amy Tan, "Fish Cheeks". Copyright © 1987 by Amy Tan. First appeared in *Seventeen Magazine*. Reprinted by permission of the author and the Sandra Dijkstra Literary Agency.

Colin Turnbull, "The Mbuti Pygmies," Houghton Mifflin, Harcourt Publishing Company.

Viramma, "Pariah" Will Hobson, Verso Books.

Vivienne Walt and Amanda Bower, "Follow the Money," from *Time*, November 26, 2005. Reprinted by permission.

Fareed Zakaria, from *The Post-American World*. Copyright © 2008 by Fareed Zakaria. Used by permission of W. W. Norton

PHOTO CREDITS

Page 36: Daniel O.Todd/Corbis

Page 115: Peter M. Fisher/Corbis

Page 120: Corbis

Page 154: Reuters/Corbis

Page 174: istockphoto

Page 268: istockphoto

Page 312: Robin Hanbury-Tenison/Robert Harding World Imagery/Corbis

Page 321: Bradley Smith/Corbis

Page 330: Corbis

Page 368: Paul A. Soulders/Corbis

Page 415: Wendy Stone/Corbis

Page 423: Jeffrey Aronson/Network Aspen

Geograpical Index

Index of Authors and Titles